The Cherokees
and Their Chiefs

▼ ▼ ▼ ▼ ▼ ▼

The Cherokees

and Their Chiefs

In the Wake of Empire

▼ ▼ ▼ ▼ ▼ ▼ ▼

STANLEY W. HOIG

The University of Arkansas Press
Fayetteville   1998

02 01 00 99   5 4 3 2

Designed by Liz Lester

☉   The paper used in this publication meets the minimum requirements of the American National Standard for Permanence of Paper for Printed Library Materials Z39.48-1984.

Library of Congress Cataloging-in-Publication Data

Hoig, Stan.
        The Cherokees and their chiefs : in the wake of empire /
Stanley W. Hoig.
            p.   cm.
        Includes bibliographical references and index.
        ISBN 1-55728-527-6 (cloth : alk. paper). —ISBN 1-55728-528-4
(pbk. : alk. paper)
            1. Cherokee Indians—History.   2. Cherokee Indians—Kings and
rulers.   3. Cherokee Indians—Politics and government.   I. Title.
E99.C5H7   1998
973'.049755—dc21   98-28930
                                                    CIP

This book is dedicated to the memory of my mother
and father, Melvin Erwin and Kathleen Keever Hoig

Contents

Foreword

The Cherokee Nation has survived against many adversities in the last few centuries. This has been due to the resilience and the ability of the Cherokee people to adapt when necessary. While much of their culture was lost in these adaptations, other items were added that have become a part of current Cherokee culture. To the Cherokees, however, the survival of their identity as Cherokees is of paramount importance.

This book deals with the many adversities and changes in Cherokee culture that have occurred since the first contact with the "white man" in the early sixteenth century. One of the first and major changes was the Cherokees becoming dependent upon European trade goods. Not only did this greatly change their daily lifestyles, but it also changed their governmental structure. The Europeans were used to one monarch ruling the entire nation, while the Cherokees were ruled by town chiefs with no cohesive central government. In order to deal with the Europeans, the Cherokees had to adapt their government and select a principal ruler for the nation. These adaptations by the Cherokees over many years and involving many interesting events are dealt with in detail in this book.

The Cherokee people faced many other tragedies as the white settlers became greedy for the Cherokee lands. This finally resulted in the extinction of the title to all Cherokee lands east of the Mississippi and the splintering of the nation into various groups. Many of the little-known aspects of this splintering are given in this book. A major contribution is the section on the Arkansas Cherokees and the Texas Cherokees. The Arkansas Cherokees, especially, have had very little written about them.

Following the forced removal of the majority of the Cherokees to present Oklahoma, the Cherokee Nation was involved in a virtual civil war. This divisiveness has been written about in the past but not in the detail that is given in these pages. The personal feuding that resulted in a large number of murders is a story that has needed to be told.

An interesting bit of Cherokee history reminiscent of current times occurred in 1888. The election of August 1887 was not certified by the Cherokee National Council. Chief Dennis Bushyhead continued to maintain the office of chief and refused to turn the office over to the elected chief, Joel B. Mayes. The issue was not resolved until January 1888, when a group of Mayes supporters went into the Cherokee capitol building and broke into the locked executive offices, counted the votes, and installed Mayes as chief. The same building in 1997 housed the Cherokee Supreme Court offices. In June 1997 the justices and their clerks were locked out of their offices under orders of the principal chief and did not regain their offices until August 1997.

This book is a tribute to the survival of the Cherokee people. Be assured that the Cherokee Nation will also survive its current strife.

Jack D. Baker

Preface

Though more than a century has elapsed since the end of the Indian wars, today most Native American people remain largely apart from the mainstream U.S. culture. With quiet determination they attempt to hold to their own native identities and traditions against the influences of white society and incessant changes of the modern world.

The effects of these influences upon Indian people have been severe. Indians have endured not only governmental and societal limitations on their tribal and personal liberty, but have suffered an elimination of the native environment that was an essential part of their lives. Though it cannot be said that today they live in bondage, by the literal interpretation of the word, many Indian people still exist under great social restraint and intimidation. And they are intensely aware of the lost freedom of their past and the demise of their tribal being.

Today's Indians face the real danger of an eroding of their native selves. Of momentous concern to them is whether or not Indian identity and tribal culture will survive in the years beyond the twentieth century. Accordingly, the Cherokees and other tribes have undertaken programs to reawaken their tribal culture among their young and keep alive the memory and traditions of their past.

There is also another issue relative to the Indian presence in America. It comes from the tendency of the white majority to write national history in its own self-serving image. All too often we have attempted to erase from memory or wrongly view that which is negative and displeasing and exalt that which is favorable of our national existence. But interpreting history is not rightly the prerogative of any one segment of society.

Without question, there is a greater body of recorded lore concerning the Cherokees than of any other group of American Indians. They are particularly unique among native tribes in that they, having the special ability of written communication in their own language as well as English, have been able to share in recording their views and events in their great contest for survival against white society and culture.

The Cherokees are also among the most studied of American Indians. This book has drawn upon much of the abundant primary material of Cherokee history as well as secondary writing. Recognizing that volumes could be written about many of the individual leaders alone, this work attempts to present the Cherokee leaders in the setting of Cherokee historical events and to illuminate their personal contributions and failings without embellishment. Among them will be found men and women who measure shoulder to shoulder with, and at times well above, their white counterparts in history.

Readers of these pages are asked to accept the figurative rather than the literal meaning of certain words. Just as the word *heart* is commonly used to symbolize the center of the human spirit, the word *blood* has been applied in the metaphorical sense to indicate progeny inheritance, even though it is physiologically incorrect. "Half blood," "mixed blood," and other designators were popularly accepted for describing racial mixture; however, the science of today tells us that human traits are determined by DNA and social development rather than by blood mixture.

It is necessary to speak in terms of "full blood" and "half blood," however, because of the consideration these designations were given by past generations, both Indian and white. These terms were used to generalize the factors that separated and distinguished each race, and they still have value in communicating that figurative meaning.

The concept of "blood" and "racial mixture" was such a powerful and charged issue among the Cherokees that it is impossible to relate their internal tribal strife without using such commonly accepted terms. It must be noted, however, that the issue among the Cherokees was not primarily a matter of prejudice of race against race, but a social and political conflict that became focused upon homeland and cultural values. To ignore this critical contest between full bloods and those designated as half or mixed bloods is to distort Cherokee history.

A word or two should be said about the spelling of Cherokee and other Indian names. The Englishmen who first contacted Indian people were required to make individual judgments in translating Indian enunciations into English phonetics. Many different interpretations resulted, and it often would be difficult to make the case that any one English verbalism or any one spelling was *the* correct one. Some early translators, for instance, said "Telliquo," while others said "Tellico." Was it "Chote" or "Chota?" Both are used often in early records.

Further, many Cherokee leaders had at least two means by which they were identified: their Indian-pronounced name and their English-interpreted name; for example, Attakullakulla, or the Little Carpenter. At times, they were known by their title, such as Outacite, meaning man killer. Generally, this work has used the most commonly accepted title for Cherokee people and locations.

Full appreciation must be extended to the many Cherokee scholars whose research and writing prepared the way for this synthesis study of Cherokee history and leaders as well as to the dedicated librarians and archivists in the institutions where my own research was undertaken. On a personal level, I wish to extend my appreciation to Cherokee descendants Jack Baker, Marjorie Johnson Lowe, and Oleta Kite, and to my wife, Patricia Corbell Hoig, for their generous help and guidance.

The Cherokees
and Their Chiefs

▼　▼　▼　▼　▼　▼

PROLOGUE

Historical Overview

By the time the white man came upon them, the Cherokees were a homogenous tribal group. They spoke the same tongue, followed a common culture, knew common enemies, and considered themselves to be one people. They were divided only by clan affiliations and by their home village locations. Their native territory, that is the area in which they felt safe to live or hunt, included portions of present Virginia, North Carolina, Tennessee, Georgia, and Alabama. By virtue of their numbers, estimated at about twenty-two thousand, and the size of their territory, they became known as the Cherokee Nation.

They also possessed an organized society by which town groups functioned under leaders who met regularly in established council halls and debated the issues of the day. Oratory, the use of rational argument, and vigorous personality were the forces of persuasion. There were peace leaders and war leaders, both men and women, the power of each depending upon his or her standing among the tribe and the matter at hand.

The leadership of eighteenth-century full-blood chiefs such as Attakullakulla, Oconostota, and Corn Tassel are revealing of high ability in reasoning, eloquence, and diplomacy. These attributes were thus already well developed before the Cherokees began their assimilation through the extensive intermarriage with whites—principally English, Scottish, and Irish—that took place during the eighteenth and nineteenth centuries. With this commingling, however, came the power of formal education, written communication, and Western knowledge. An elite group of young half-blood intellectuals arose out of mission school education. Soon Cherokee leaders could stand before church assemblies, treaty councils, legislatures, and even presidents of the United States and effectively argue the causes of their people.

The influx of European goods and the practice of barter and exchange not only drew the Cherokee people farther and farther away from dependency upon their old habits of hunting and gathering, but also developed their skills in the arts of trade and enterprise. At the same time, the tribal culture was being modified by white influences. This, unfortunately, included the holding of slaves, though it was from the African worker and craftsman that the tribespeople learned much regarding agrarian operations. Nancy Ward, the famous Cherokee war woman, was a leading force in the Cherokee adaptation to the modern practices of stock raising and farming.

Many Cherokees had begun spinning and weaving. On occasion they manufactured products such as spinning wheels and plows. Some became successful and even wealthy plantation owners, traders, and businessmen. By an account of the highly regarded Cherokee leader George Lowrey, Sequoyah, the noted inventor of the Cherokee syllabary and a stout tribal traditionalist, was himself involved in the new trend of personal industry as a youth. In support of his mother and himself, Sequoyah tended a small number of dairy cows that he milked. He would wash the milk pails, strain the milk, and store it in a cool spring house that he had constructed. Later in life, Sequoyah engaged in the manufacture of silver ornaments of his own design.[1]

Uniquely, it was this man, not the educated elite, who produced the Cherokees' most striking advancement. Sequoyah, or by his English name of George Gist (Guess), was half white, but by life mode and loyalty of being he was a full blood. He had absolutely no formal education and could neither read nor write any language. Yet, it was he who in 1821 accomplished such a feat as can be laid to no other single person in the history of mankind—creation of a syllabary for an existing native language. With his invention, Sequoyah brought the power of literacy to his people and proved before a skeptical world that the tribal American was the intellectual equal of any race.

Early in the nineteenth century, the full-blood chiefs began ceding their political authority to those who could best communicate and negotiate with the white man.

"I cannot write as you and your beloved Men do," Skiagunsta had told Governor Glen of South Carolina even in 1751. "My tongue is my pen and mouth my paper. When I look upon writing I am as if I were blind and in the dark."[2]

Under the more progressive leaders, the tribal political structure was reorganized in the image of the U.S. government, with a legislative council, a court system, and an elected head of state. Also, through the work of missionaries, many Cherokees were being converted away from the old worshiping of tribal gods to Christianity.

From these many advancements, it would appear that the Cherokees could have existed effectively side by side with white Americans, administering their own affairs and determining their own destiny on their own homeland. But there were two enormous problems: the bias that whites held against tribal people and the incessant desire of whites to obtain their land. The latter issue was at the heart of Cherokee relations with England and the United States throughout the nineteenth century. Cherokee chief Corn Tassel had wryly and aptly stated the situation when he observed: "Truth is, if we had no land we should have fewer enemies."[3]

The white man's ravenous appetite for land, fueled by his drive for power and empire, was the one constant element in tribal conflict with Euro-Americans. The Spaniard had come to America in the main for metallic riches; the French largely for trade; the British to colonize. All of them sought to dominate the territory they occupied and to administer control over it. The Anglo-American wanted land. He also wanted the native occupants removed, not only for right of possession but also because he did not wish to live side by side with native people.

In part this intolerance by whites was caused by frontier conflict, in part by social discomfort, and in part by attitudes of racial superiority over a darker-skinned people whose cultural mores and habits were different. The cause was also partially religious, based on the notion that the God-given rights (the right of possessing land, in particular) of a people characterized as "pagan savages" were inferior to those of a Christian society. These attitudes were reflected by individual citizens on the frontier; but it was through the state and federal governments that they were collectively expressed on an imperial level.

The Cherokees were capable players in the great debate over territorial rights and tribal sovereignty. Their leaders were men who could intelligently cite the written law, argue their case with clear and compelling logic, and match the best of orators in quoting the Bible, Shakespeare, the Greeks, and other classical references. Seldom were they defeated in their contests with the government on the merits of their case but usually by the unwillingness of government officials to adhere to their own ethics and written laws.

There was great contradiction in the way the United States conducted its relations with native tribes. The government first signed peace, protection, and territorial recognition agreements with the tribes. The pacts were initiated essentially to protect the white man's trade and travel on the frontier. Time and constant expansion of the frontier would prove their promises to the tribes to be false in all respects. Frontier whites were often the ones who violated the treaty and broke the peace; the United States had neither the resources nor often the true desire to protect the tribes; and in the eyes of most Anglo-Americans, tribal rights to territory were fragile indeed.

At the time of the American Revolution, the Cherokees' territory had been reduced essentially to what is today eastern Tennessee, northern Georgia, and northern Alabama. Though the Revolution altered the ruling government in America, the Cherokee country was still being intruded upon by the same covetous whites with their insatiable hunger for more and more land. The demands of these citizens rang out loudly in the new state legislatures and upward into the halls of the federal government.

Efforts to satisfy the wants of white constituents resulted in other treaties, each succeeding pact further shrinking the Cherokee domain. Conditions proffered by the United States, in fact, meant little to frontier whites, who continued to violate Indian land until still another treaty was worked out to ratify their intrusion. In the end, however, the United States, under President Andrew Jackson, supported the Georgia claim that these pacts with the Cherokees and others were secondary to agreements with states. By this usurpation of contract all promises made to Indian people, legally issued in the name of the United States, were subject to nullification.

The Western Cherokee treaty of 1828 was typical of the explicit contractual promises and assurances in the name of the United States regarding tribal sovereignty and proprietorship: "to secure to the Cherokee nation of Indians . . . a *permanent* [emphasis made by treaty document] home, and which shall, under the most solemn guarantees of the United States, be and remain, theirs forever."[4]

Still another such pledge was made in 1835 at New Echota: "The United States hereby covenant and agree that the lands ceded to the Cherokee nation [in the Indian Territory, now essentially the state of Oklahoma] shall in no future time without their consent, be included within the territorial limits or jurisdiction of any State or Territory."[5]

In 1887, less than half a century after the Cherokees had been removed on their infamous Trail of Tears and resettled in the West, the U.S. Congress approved the Dawes Severalty Act. With it began the forced transfer of Indian lands in the Indian Territory from tribal to individual ownership and the stripping away of authority of tribal government. More capable than most at defending themselves in court, the Cherokees managed to stave off denationalization until Congress passed the Curtis Act of 1898. The measure essentially nullified Cherokee Nation ownership of the territory assigned to it by the Treaty of New Echota, and in 1907 the Cherokee Nation was made a part of the newly created state of Oklahoma.

Throughout their history, the Cherokees have fought battles from within as well as from without. In their early years, they were internally split between pro-English and pro-French alliances. The American period prior to 1800 found them divided between those looking to peace and conciliation and those favoring armed resistance and war against white intrusion. During the removal period, which lasted roughly from 1808 to 1838, and after, the Cherokees were caught in the bitter factionalism of those who deemed it wisest to give in and move west and those who, especially under Chief John Ross, resisted removal to the end. Having taken up new homes in the Indian Territory, they were again wrenched apart during the American Civil War by the bloody schism between those Cherokees favoring the South and those loyal to the North. After the war, the Cherokee Nation again became intensely divided over efforts to dissolve their sovereignty and destroy the tribal system altogether.

Inherent in much of this conflict was the cultural and economic divergence between the schooled, more affluent mixed bloods and the communal half bloods. This was no simple problem, but the Cherokees bear responsibility for not mitigating their intersocietal passions and reducing the enormous self-destructive violence and bloodshed that sprang from it. For certain, a unified tribal body would have been far more effective in fronting the demands made upon them by Anglo-Americans and their governments, though it is doubtful that even then they could have resisted the determined force of Andrew Jackson and Georgia.

Today the Cherokees exist in three main bodies: the Cherokee Nation of Oklahoma, the United Band of Keetoowahs, and the Cherokee Reservation of North Carolina. Though they have become extensively intermarried over the years, the Cherokees have survived as a distinct racial entity. Their history presents to us a compelling story of a native people whose social and political struggles have been deeply enmeshed in the expansion and evolution of an American nation.

CHAPTER 1

Out of a Mystic Past

On the morning of May 30, 1540, the Spanish army of Capt. Hernando de Soto arrived at an Indian village called Guasili (or Guaxule) in the far western tip of present North Carolina. The native residents were greatly alarmed at the sudden appearance of an alien body: a procession of five hundred bearded men dressed in glistening armor and brightly colored silks and velvets. Some of the strange men rode on the backs of large animals.

The villagers were disquieted not only by the guns and lances of de Soto's men but also by the sight of the enslaved Indian porters with them. Before marching north from Florida, de Soto had captured several hundred Tameme Indians. Men and women alike wore neck and leg irons and were heavily burdened with the food supplies and equipment of de Soto's army. The hapless captives were prevented from escape by vicious attack hounds trained to tear them apart if they tried.

The chiefs and leading men of the village wore their finest skin robes and feathered headdresses when they went out to meet the Spaniards. They greeted the visitors warmly and offered them gifts and assistance. But it was probably fear more than hospitality that caused them to provide corn and small dogs, which they raised, for the Spaniards to eat. And well they did. De Soto and his men, who were ruthless to the extreme elsewhere, created no disturbance at Guasili. Fortunately for the natives, they had no gold; and the Spaniards moved on quickly.[1]

Within half a century of the arrival of Columbus in America, Hernando Cortez had brutally conquered the Aztecs of Mexico. Just as cruelly, Francisco Pizarro had crushed the Incas of Peru and stolen their treasures. De Soto, who had won great wealth in his service with Pizarro in 1532, returned to the Americas in 1538. A year later he sailed from his base at Havana, Cuba, and landed on the west coast of Florida. While there the Spaniard had heard such tales of gold, and he was determined to find it. In making his long, futile trek across southern North America in search of treasures, de Soto would be the first European to contact the tribal group known today as the Cherokee Indians and introduce them into recorded history.

This first brief visit was scantily chronicled by four members of the expedition. They described the Cherokees as being peaceful, domestic, and hospitable, even though they had little food or possessions. However, the de Soto journals reveal little about the Cherokee people or their leaders. We learn only that their village consisted of some three hundred houses surrounded by a broad walkway. De Soto and his officers were given lodging in the chief's house, which stood on a high elevation at the village center.

Buried in the manuscripts and archives division of Spain's Escuela de Diplomática are records of mining operations and visitations conducted among the Cherokees by the Spanish during the sixteenth and seventeenth centuries. These, plus the recorded visit of Capt. Juan Pardo to the Cherokee town of Otari (believed to have been near present Charlotte, North Carolina) in 1567, give evidence of pre-English contacts. Much of this Spain kept secret, and little is revealed of the Cherokees of that time.[2]

It would be left to the British a century later to make a substantive introduction to Cherokee culture as it was at the onset of European influence. Through these first contacts, Cherokee life can be seen as it existed in its natural state prior to white influence. Further insight into early Cherokee society is provided through tribal legends, archeology, language, and other ethnological evidence. From these clues, speculation has been made on the origin, migratory trace, and governance of the Cherokees.

One tribal tradition has it that the Cherokees did not come to America from Asia but were placed in *Ah-ma-ye-li* (the midst of the waters) by Nel-ho-nu-hi when the earth was divided. This account says that their forefathers crossed no water, while others say that they came over a great bridge that later sank to the bottom of the ocean. The word *Cherokee*, it states, means *Esh-he-el-o-archie*, Keeper of the Sacred Fire.[3]

Another tradition recounts that the early Cherokees believed that their ancestors had come out of the ground, where they then resided long before the discovery of America. They said that they had not moved about from place to place like other tribes; yet they claimed that all the lands northward to the Great Lakes had once belonged to them.[4]

Modern scholars are divided on where the Cherokees may have

been located before coming to where they were first encountered in the North American southeast. One theory is that they were once at home in South and Central America, this based upon their employing a method of basket weaving identical to that of natives in the Orinoco and Amazon river valleys of Venezuela and Brazil. Design and production techniques of Cherokee pottery were also found to be similar to those of Caribbean tribes.[5]

These clues are believed by some to point to an association of the two Indian cultures and the migration of the Cherokees northward through Mexico. It is equally as logical to assume that the South and Central American Indians had at one time lived in North America in contact with the ancestors of the Cherokees—or stemming from a common ancestor—and that they were the ones who migrated, taking with them the shared cultural habits.

The concept that at some prehistoric time the Cherokees migrated into the American South from the Great Lakes region to the north is given much greater credence. The similarity of their physical appearance to the Iroquois and their Iroquoian-based language give clue of a relationship to that Canadian and northern U.S. Indian group.[6] Tribesman Elias C. Boudinot claimed that the Cherokees once had extensive settlements on the Appomattox River of Virginia and formed the principal tribe in the Powhatan Confederation, whose chief was a Cherokee.[7]

Cherokee tradition also supports the theory of migration from the north. Chief Charles Hicks, a noted and highly respected Cherokee intellectual, recounted an ancient oration as it was once recited annually at the Cherokee Green Corn festival. By it the Cherokee ancestral home was located to the northeast of their southern domain. The recitation speaks of the Cherokees migrating into the region of the southern Appalachian Mountains of western North and South Carolina, eastern Tennessee, and northern Georgia, where, as their numbers increased rapidly, they adapted to an agricultural as well as a hunter-gatherer livelihood.[8]

Eighteenth-century contact with the Cherokees found them located in small villages scattered across western North and South Carolina, northeastern Georgia, and eastern Tennessee. In 1730 the Cherokee Nation was seen to be organized into three identifiable town groups— the Lower Towns of far western South Carolina (featuring the towns of Keowee and Estatoe, among others); the Middle Towns along the Appalachian Mountains of western North Carolina and Georgia

(Etchoe, Stecoe); and the Overhill Towns clustered along the Little Tennessee, west of the Chilhowee Mountains (Settico, Tellico).[9]

It is theorized by some that when the Lower and Middle Cherokees arrived in the American South, they may have emulated the tradition of their Muskogee/Creek neighbors in building their towns on and around the burial mounds of their priestly chieftains. Other scholars feel they may have simply chosen the sites of already existing mounds for their settlements.

The still-shadowy mound-building culture of pre-Columbus North America extended from the East Coast to eastern Oklahoma. The Spiro Mounds near the Oklahoma-Arkansas border reveal artifacts that are Aztecan in design. This leads to the question of trade association of the early Cherokees with other tribes and their known propensity to wander and explore. There is still much to learn about the relationship of prehistoric tribes throughout the Americas and their migrations.

Hicks's account tells us of an early leadership structure based upon a priesthood cult known as the "Proud," not unlike those of ancient Muskogean and Aztecan cultures.[10] Eventually these Cherokee shamans came to wield great power over the people. They became so tyrannical that at night they would go through the villages and select women for themselves, all the while chanting that it was the will of the gods. But such arrogance was their downfall. A Cherokee hunter rebelled when his wife was demanded. He killed the offending priest, and with his brother led a bloody revolt against the Proud.

Still another factor may well have contributed to the demise of the priests. Arriving behind the Lower and Middle people was a group of Cherokees who now occupied an area west of the Appalachians along the Tennessee, Holston, and Little Tennessee Rivers. This more militant group, whose "Eldest Fire of All" was considered predominant over the "Mother Fire" of the Lower and Middle Cherokees, became known as the Overhills. Headed by a strong war leadership, the Overhills fought with the Muskogees (or Creeks) to the south as well as the "Northward" tribes. It is believed that their war leaders may have helped reduce the power of the Proud priesthood.[11]

In 1730 Sir Alexander Cuming found the Cherokee Nation governed by seven Mother Towns. Each Mother Town chose a reigning chief—Cuming termed them "kings." These chiefs were elected out of certain families, whose line of descent was purely matrilineal. There were other towns with lesser-ranked chiefs, whom Cuming called "princes." Each town had a head warrior, whose authority was at times greater than the civil authority of the chief. It was possible that one man could occupy both posts.[12]

When Lt. Henry Timberlake visited the Cherokee villages along the Little Tennessee thirty-one years after Cuming, a new town called Chota had become the Cherokee capital.[13] This had come about following a long power struggle between it and Tellico. Chota had won out by virtue of strong leaders such as Connecorte (or Cannacaughte, whom whites gave the inelegant name of "Old Hop" because of a limp caused by a youthful leg wound), Attakullakulla (the Little Carpenter), and Oconostota. Although the town faded from existence following the killing of Chief Corn Tassel and other chiefs in 1788, it was the principal Cherokee seat of government during the Cherokee conflicts with the English and Americans.[14]

Timberlake described the Cherokee government as he found it in 1761: "Their government, if I may call it government, which has neither law or power to support it, is a mixed aristocracy and democracy, the chiefs being chose according to their merit in war, or policy at home."[15] Another observer of the same period told of a king "whose power is rather persuasive than coercive, and he is reverenced as a father, more than a feared monarch. He has no guards, no prisons, no Officers of justice."[16]

It was evident then that the Cherokees by no means operated a consolidated government presided over by a single chieftain system. Nor did their chiefs rule through enforcement of enacted laws. But there was a formulated governance, accepted leaders, a format for decision making, and an established place where chiefs and other officials could meet and discuss matters. Cherokee towns were ruled separately by local chiefs. A local leader might become powerful enough to rule over more than one town or over a region. In addition to the local chiefs, there were Elder Councils in the various towns and Grand Elders who held forth at Mother Towns.

The Cherokee council house, in which all public business was transacted, was described by Timberlake as an earth-covered, loaf-shaped building with a single entrance. The council houses at both Tommatly and Settico could hold five hundred people in the raised-tier seating around a central fireplace. The head chiefs and warriors were positioned closest to the fire, where canes were burned for both heat and light. With no windows and poor ventilation, the room was dark and smoke filled.[17]

Cherokees gave their peace chiefs the honored title of "Beloved

Man." The royalty-minded English were prone to assigning Cherokee leading men exalted titles such as emperor, king, and prince in lieu of chief.

> The head chiefs and the war chiefs represented the top echelon of political dichotomy in the Cherokee Nation. They were, respectively, the White (Peace) and the Red (War) Groups—the person holding such a high office was variously known as the "Uku," "Ookah," or "Ugutuyr." Although each town had a White chief of its own, the White chief of the Echota (Chota) was regarded as the principal chief of the nation.[18]

In the Cherokee peace and war factions can be found the basis of a dual leadership that continued to exist during the seventeenth and eighteenth centuries—peace chiefs, who held the most authority in normal times, and war chiefs, who ruled in times of strife. The peace chiefs were represented by the color white, and the more belligerent war chiefs were represented by the color red.[19]

The Spanish scholar Manuel Serrano y Sanz wrote: "Far from being held down by a monarch, they governed themselves in matters of common interest by assemblies of chiefs and warriors from each village."[20] Peace chiefs are believed to have evolved from the Proud priesthood. Old Hop, one of the earliest known Cherokee headmen, was referred to as a "priest" by James Adair, a trader who lived among the Indians during the colonial period and wrote an initial history of the southern tribes. Indications are, however, that the civic aspect of the peace chief became more pronounced after the arrival of white people and that the Cherokee spiritual tradition was continued by lesser shamans.

The authority of the peace chief was based entirely upon the respect he commanded from the people. Adair noted that a chief could exert his wishes upon the people only by the "force of good-nature and clear reasoning, or coloring things, so as to suit their prevailing passions."[21] It was merit alone, Adair insisted, that gave the chief distinction above others. Capt. Raymond Demere, an English officer, similarly described the Cherokee chiefs as generally being older men who were capable of persuading their independent-minded tribesmen with their wisdom.[22]

The civic chiefs held a place of prominence at the head of town or regional councils. These councils functioned on a very orderly, democratic basis.

> Here it is that their orators employ, and display those talents which distinguish them for eloquence and knowledge of public business; in

both of which some of them are admirable . . . The chief skill of these orators in giving an artful turn to affairs, and in expressing their thoughts in a bold figurative manner, much stronger than we could bear in this part of the world, and with gestures equally violent, but often extremely natural and expressive.[23]

Each council member was given a chance to rise and give his views freely, speaking with great courtesy and uninterrupted by others.[24] Such a format based upon the power of reason, with emotional haranguing purposefully excluded, lent itself effectively to a high respect for rational wisdom and thus to the rise of leaders of quality.

It has been stated that the early Cherokees employed an inheritance system of chiefs. The offices were hereditary rather than elective and were handed down to the son of the oldest sister.[25] This method of choosing chiefs, however, did not carry into modern times. John Reid, in A Law of Blood, correctly pointed out: "Cherokee headmen were self-made, and to think of public office being handed down from generation to generation, or from brother to brother, is to distort the Cherokee political system."[26]

As with almost all other societies of people, there were those among the Cherokee towns who won laurels and high respect for their achievements in battle. For the most part, Cherokee war parties were groups of independent warriors who set out on forays after being recruited by a leader. There was no organized warring structure as such with a hierarchy of war leaders, though some men rose to prominence in the tribe as war chiefs and were known by title/names such as Great Warrior, Mankiller (or Outacite, pronounced "Outa-city"), Raven, or Slave-Catcher.

Though normally the war chief was inferior to the peace chief, in times of crisis he was listened to and followed in lieu of the civil chief. While the peace chiefs led the people with calm reasoning, the war chiefs used high passion to urge warriors into battle. The spiritual mystique of dream tales, recounting of battle feats, fasting and purification rituals, singing of war songs, and blood-stirring war dances were employed to excite the fighting fervor of the young men.

Timberlake observed that those who lead the warriors "chuse to go, for there is no laws or compulsion on those that refuse to follow, or punishment to those that forsake their chief: he strives, therefore, to inspire them with a sort of enthusiasm, by the war-song, as the ancient bards did once in Britain."[27]

William de Brahm, builder of Fort Loudoun, Tennessee, in 1757, noted that before a war expedition the warriors would fast until a fifteen- to sixteen-inch leather belt would fit around their waist. A conjuror would prepare the whole troop using medicinal decoctions from roots. The men would neither drink a handful of water nor eat a bite more than their leader, whose orders and example were followed in every detail. If, even accidentally, one member should fail in this, fatal consequences were believed to result.[28]

Timberlake was struck by the capacity of the early Cherokee leaders, even when in strong competition with one another, to live together harmoniously. He cited the case of Attakullakulla and Ostenaco, who were rivals of power and heads of opposing factions. Despite the strong differences of the two and dislike for one another, Ostenaco's own brother joined a war party under Attakullakulla. "Warm in opposing one another, as their interest continually clash," Timberlake observed, "yet these [two men] have no farther animosity, no family-quarrels or resentment."[29]

Commonly, it was men who ruled among the early tribes, but not always. There are notable exceptions to be found in the annals of Cherokee history. The existence of women leaders and "war women" among the Cherokees is well established. One account tells of an incident in which a chief's wife, Cuhtahlatah, witnessed the death of her husband in battle and the routing of the Cherokee warriors. Grabbing up her husband's tomahawk, she rushed at the enemy with such fury that the retreating Cherokees re-formed and won a victory.[30]

Another famous Cherokee "war woman" was Nancy Ward. Her exploits in battle and wisdom as a leader in council won her the title of "Ghighau," or "Beloved Woman."[31] Timberlake wrote of the war women:

> These chiefs, or headmen, likewise compose the assemblies of the nation, into which the war-women are admitted. The reader will not be a little surprised to find the story of *Amazons* not so great a fable as we imagined, many of the Indian women being as famous in war, as powerful in council . . .
>
> This is the only title females can enjoy; but it abundantly recompenses them, by the power they acquire by it, which is so great that they can, by the wave of a swan's wing, deliver a wretch condemned by the council, and already tied to the stake.[32]

Chief Attakullakulla once made the point during a meeting with the governor of South Carolina that, unlike the all-male bodies of the whites, Cherokee councils were participated in by women who played important roles in tribal affairs. Adair noted that the Cherokees "have been for a considerable while under petticoat government."[33]

The position of Cherokee women was undoubtedly influenced by the strong character of Nancy Ward. Because of her, increased respect was accorded Cherokee women; and in each clan they began choosing members for a woman's council, which at times had the power of overriding the authority of the chiefs.[34]

It appears, however, that this trend did not continue long past the time of Nancy Ward. The recent rise of Chief Wilma Mankiller to Cherokee leadership is more a reflection of her own personal ability and the belated acknowledgment of women's value by modern Western society in general than of Cherokee tradition. Still, the women enjoyed a strong role in Cherokee affairs. Timberlake, who arrived among the Cherokees not long after Fort Loudoun was abandoned in 1760, told of Cherokee women who were married to white soldiers at the fort. Despite the Cherokee siege of the post, they continued to bring food to their husbands and families, openly defying a war chief who threatened them.[35]

Historian John Phillip Reid views Cherokee leadership as being crisis oriented. He contends that historically the Cherokee Nation "responded to leadership only when in peril."[36] His arguments for this, however, are based upon the formative pre–Revolutionary War period of Cherokee government. Even then certain men rose to towering positions of respect. They set the stage for hierarchic oversight of political matters.

Yet despite the exalted position of Beloved Men such as Moytoy, Old Hop, Attakullakulla, Oconostota, Corn Tassel, and others, Cherokee national leadership remained dichotomized into peace and war factions through most of the eighteenth century. During the English period Chota and Tellico vied for supremacy; later the peace-minded full bloods of the northern towns were challenged by the half-blood-controlled Chickamaugans to the south. It was only after the Chickamaugan uprising of 1794 that the Cherokee Nation began to coalesce under a single head of government. At the same time, a new dimension was given to Cherokee leadership through the advent of the educated mixed blood.

In him there was intertwined the primal Indian character and the sophistication of European influence. The result was a combination that was more than capable of operating effectively within the structure of the white man's organized legal system. The Cherokees' loss of homeland during the nineteenth century did not result from a lack of competent leadership in dealing with whites on a legal basis. In the main,

Cherokee misfortunes stemmed from the white man's refusal to abide by his own enacted laws and treaty contracts.

The concept of one single head of the tribe was promoted by both the British and Americans, who needed a single, unifying government that could speak for the entirety of the Cherokee people. It was far easier to persuade—by whatever means—one leader than a number of them. However, the duplicity that was often employed in dealing with individual chiefs led to ever increasing divisiveness among the Cherokee people. This resulting conflict of purpose and conduct among the Cherokees would haunt them throughout their three-century struggle to resist white domination.

CHAPTER 2

Under British Rule

When Virginians James Needham and Gabriel Arthur reached the Cherokee Overhill settlements in July 1673, they found a village protected on one side by a high cliff. The other sides of the Cherokee town were fortified by twelve-foot walls with scaffolds and parapets. The Cherokees were also well equipped with 150 canoes, each of which could carry twenty warriors into battle.[1]

The two Englishmen had been sent over the Appalachian Mountains by trader Abraham Wood of Fort Henry (located near present Petersburg, Virginia), who wished to open a trade path with the Cherokees. The first white contact between the Cherokees and Virginians had taken place thirty-nine years earlier in 1634.[2] Conflicts soon developed, and in 1654 men of the Virginia Colony, supported by a force of Pamunkey Indians, attacked a village of six to seven hundred Cherokees who were located at the site of present Richmond. The colonists and their allies were severely defeated after a bloody fight, and the Britons were forced into making a treaty with the Cherokees.[3]

But now the Cherokees proved to be peaceful. They received Needham and Arthur royally, ceremoniously entertaining them and supplying ample corn, pod vegetables, fish, wild game meat, and bear oil. Numerous horns like those of a bull covered the village dung heaps—likely an indication that the buffalo was still one of their game animals. The Cherokees were so impressed by the white men that they were placed on a scaffold in exhibition, and their one horse was tied to a pole for the villagers to come and view in awe. The king—the title used by the British in lieu of chief—of the town was very amiable with the visitors.

The villagers possessed some sixty Spanish flintlock muskets and other European-manufactured implements, clear evidence that the Cherokees had been in contact with the Spanish of Florida. In fact, the Cherokees told the Englishmen that when twenty of their men had recently gone there to trade, ten of them had been killed and the rest captured. Two had escaped to tell their people of the Spanish treachery, and since then the Cherokees had been deadly enemies of the Spanish.

After a short visit, Needham returned to his employer's post for more trade goods, leaving Arthur at the village to learn the Cherokee language. Accompanying Needham was a Cherokee named Hasecoll, whom the Britons called Indian John. They were on their way back to the Cherokee village when Indian John shot and killed Needham during a quarrel. Afterward he cut out the Englishman's heart and held it toward the east as a symbol of his contempt for the British.

Indian John then sent runners to the village demanding that Arthur be murdered as well. It happened that the king of the town was away at the time. Though some of the villagers were against harming their guest, others tied him to a stake and prepared to burn him to death—as the Cherokees then did to captive enemies on occasion. Arthur was saved, however, by the timely arrival of the king, who immediately shot and killed a man who was bringing forth a firebrand. He then cut the Englishman loose from the post and dared anyone to touch him. Clearly, the chief was in control of the village.

In ensuing months the king took Arthur on raids against the Spanish and other Indian villages in Florida, the coastal areas of the east, and the Ohio country to the north. After Arthur was captured and then released by the Shawnees, the Cherokee king returned him to his employer in Virginia during the spring of 1674. Unfortunately, the name of this Cherokee chief is not given in the Needham-Arthur accounts.

Though Wood made no further effort to establish a trade with the Cherokees, other Englishmen soon penetrated the wild country beyond the Allegheny Mountains. Henry Woodward of Charlestown, South Carolina, an acquaintance of Needham, visited Cherokee towns on the upper Savannah River in 1674.[4]

The first permanent English settlement in South Carolina was made in 1670, and the oldest Cherokee treaty on record was made in 1684 between that colony and chiefs from two villages in far western South Carolina. Signing this document with their own particular mark rather than with the usual cross mark were Corani, Raven of Toxawa; Canacaught, the Great Conqueror of Keowa; Sinnawa, or Hawk, head warrior of Toxawa; Nellawgitehi of Toxawa; Gohoma of Keowa; Caunasaita of Keowa; Gorhaleke of Toxawa; and Owasta, the Beloved Man of Toxawa.[5]

Between 1711 and 1713 some three hundred Cherokees helped colonial forces drive the Tuscarora Indians northward to the Great Lakes region. In 1721 a group of chiefs representing thirty-seven Cherokee towns met at Charlestown with Sir Francis Nicolson, the first British governor of South Carolina, and reached agreements concerning territorial boundaries. There being no supreme head among the Cherokees, Nicolson appointed a chief named Wrosetasatow as such.[6] The Cherokee was also known as Outacite, or Mankiller.

One of the first Cherokee war chiefs to emerge into the realm of modern history was Uskwalena—the name being interpreted as Bull Head or Big Head. He led the Cherokees in defeating the Creeks at Pine Island, near present Guntersville, Alabama, in 1714. The site later became the Cherokee settlement of Creek Path.[7]

With the appointment of Col. George Chicken as British supervisor of Indian trade in the colonies at Charlestown, the records begin to reveal much more concerning the Cherokees and their leaders. Chicken, who had been in the Cherokee country in 1715, returned ten years later on a peace-and-trade mission to the Cherokee country. After conferring with a group of Overhill Cherokees at Quanassee (near present Murphy, North Carolina), he continued on with traders Eleazar Wiggan and Joseph Cooper past the Cherokee valley town of Tamantley (Tomantley) to Elejoy.

The headmen of five towns in the area received the Englishman in a very friendly manner, entertaining him with songs and fanning him with eagle tails. One of the leading men present was the head warrior of Great Terriquo (Tellico). When he later visited the Cherokee town, Chicken found it defended by a surrounding ditch filled with sharp wooden spikes. He also visited Tunisee (Tenassee, Tonasee, Tennessee), where the "King of the Upper People" lived.[8]

Sir Alexander Cuming arrived among the Overhills five years later. An energetic young Englishman of the nobility, Cuming had come to Charlestown in 1729 hopeful of recuperating his family fortunes, which had fallen on hard times. There he became involved in borrowing money with promissory notes and buying up large quantities of silver, gold, and produce, which he shipped abroad. Cuming made a daring, extended journey among the Cherokees and with great dash and aplomb won the friendship of their chiefs and warriors.

Accompanied only by a guide, Cuming proceeded to Keowee (near today's Clemson, South Carolina). There, against the advice of traders, and armed with guns and sword, he brazenly entered the town council house during a meeting of some three hundred elders. When Cuming wildly threatened to burn down the council house if the Cherokees did not recognize King George II, traders such as Ludovic Grant expected the worst. Cuming's audacity, however, overwhelmed the Cherokee leaders, and they on bent knee pledged their loyalty to the Crown of England against the French in North America.[9]

Wrosetasatow had died the previous year, and the Cherokee Nation had no single head of government. Accordingly, Cuming appointed Chief Moytoy (meaning Water Conjuror or Rainmaker) of Tellico as "emperor" of the Cherokees. He also recruited a delegation of seven Cherokee leading men and warriors to travel with him to Charlestown and thence to England to meet King George II.[10]

The two most notable of these were the head warrior of Tassetchee, who was the highest ranked of the group and was generally accepted by the English as king of the Cherokees—the Oukah Ulah—and Ookounaka (Oukandekah), who later became famous as a Cherokee chief under the name of Attakullakulla, or the Little Carpenter. Others were Ketagusta, Tathtiowie, Clogittah, Collanah, and Ounakannowie. The party was accompanied to England by interpreter Eleazer Wiggan.[11]

Departing Charlestown on May 4 on the man-of-war *Fox*, the party arrived at Dover, England, on June 5. Cuming went ahead to prepare King George for the visit, and an audience was arranged for June 18 at the installation of three noblemen as Knights of the Garter at Windsor Castle. The seven chiefs presented a stark contrast to the gorgeously dressed king and court.

Oukah Ulah wore a scarlet jacket, but the rest of the Cherokees wore only their loin cloths, with a horse's tail hanging down behind. The faces and upper bodies of the tribesmen were painted with red, blue, and green, and their shaved heads were bedecked with colored feathers. Oukah Ulah carried a musket, the others their bows.[12]

As Cuming had coached them, the chiefs properly kneeled as instructed and kissed King George's hand, "and there in the presence of the Indian chiefs then kneeling, Sir Alexander declared to his majesty the unlimited power he had acquired at Nequassee upon the 3d, 4th, and 5th days of April, 1730, by the unanimous voice of the Cherokee nation, then declaring in the most solemn manner that his word would be their law."[13]

The chiefs then laid before the king the tribal "crown of Tannasee," which "consists of the tails of the female opossum, put together in the form of a wig," plus four scalps of their enemies and five eagles' tails of peace.[14] King George expressed his pleasure with the gift. He afterward escorted the American visitors to a gallery overlooking the castle terrace. When one of them spied a huge elk grazing in the park, he offered to display his skill with a bow and arrow. The king declined to have his stag shot.[15]

At the king's expense, the Indians were given a banquet of mutton at the Mermaid Inn, then provided lodging at Covent Garden. The status-conscious English press noted that the Cherokee "king" slept on a table above the others, who slept on the floor, scorning to be on the same level with them. They were soon given English-style clothes to replace their forest garb.

During their four months' stay in England, the Cherokees were roundly toasted, driven about in fine coaches, entertained at levees, given gifts, taken to fairs, and ogled at by curious crowds. They competed with the king's archers, witnessed "lunatics" chained to walls at Bethlehem Hospital, attended miracle plays to be awed at the sham fights and acrobats, marveled at displays of English firelocks and cannons, visited an organ builder and heard his instruments, and by order of King George had their portraits painted.[16]

Finally, on September 7 they met with the king's lord commissioners and signed an agreement of friendship and trade. One by one the commissioners listed the king's commands to the Cherokees, and after each they presented the chiefs with a gift: the Cherokees would always be ready at the governor's command to fight for the English—"hereupon we give Twenty guns." The Cherokees would keep the trading path clean—"four hundred pounds weight of gunpowder." The Cherokees would return runaway slaves—"a box of vermillion, ten thousand gun flints and six dozen hatchets." The Cherokees would deliver up any Indian who kills an Englishman—"twelve dozen knives, four dozen brass kettles and ten dozen belts." There would be peace and friendship between the English and the Cherokees "as long as the Mountains and Rivers shall last or the sun shine—a belt of wampum."

Ketagusta was directed to speak for the delegation. Expressing the Indians' admiration and love for Cuming, who had not been invited to the meeting, the Cherokee vowed King George's enemies would always be their enemies. "We came hither naked," he said, "and poor as the worm out of the earth. But you have everything, and we that have nothing must love you and can never break the chain of friendship that is between us."[17]

After an agreement had been signed, the Indians danced and sang the rest of the evening. A few days later they left London for Portsmouth and in five more days sailed for America. They did so reluctantly, especially so because Sir Alexander was not permitted to return with them.[18]

The trip to England did much to win the loyalty and military support of the Cherokees for the British in their fight against the French and their Indian allies in North America. It also caused England to recognize the value of maintaining Cherokee friendship and support. The

French had established closer contact with the Cherokees when a party of Frenchmen visited the Overhill towns in 1736. Though shunned by Attakullakulla—who strongly relished his visit with King George—Oconostota, the Great Warrior of Chota, and some others flew the French flag from atop their houses.[19]

Emperor Moytoy was killed in battle in 1741, and the Cherokees were again without a central head when the newly appointed royal governor of South Carolina, James Glen, arrived at Charlestown in 1745. The new governor was greeted by a delegation of some two hundred Cherokees who had been summoned there for the occasion. British officials had appointed Moytoy's thirteen-year-old son, Ammonscossittee, to succeed his father.[20] He was provided a royal reception, with cannons booming as the governor's coach carried him to the capitol to be enthroned as the new emperor of the Cherokees in the eyes of the British. After placing a silk and fur crown on the boy's head and then receiving Cherokee headmen of various towns, the governor displayed the treaty that had been made in London in 1730.[21]

The effects of the London trip were of great influence on the life of Attakullakulla. For the most part this important Cherokee chief remained a lifelong friend to the English, even when others of his nation warred against them. Several years after his return from England, in about 1738, he was captured by the French-supporting Ottawas and spent some six or seven years in their captivity. His contacts with the French of Canada during that period caused him to be suspect when he returned to his nation.[22]

Born into a high family, Attakullakulla as a boy had been attended by the tribal elders and trained for leadership. A small, thinly built man, he became noted for his diplomatic and negotiating skills. A leader in most of the councils and treaties of his day, he was a good orator and possessed a shrewd mind.[23] However, Attakullakulla had his enemies, both within and without the Cherokee Nation. Some whites believed him to be hypocritical, at times professing peace while promoting bloodshed. He often faced dangerous opposition from his own people for supporting the British, as was illustrated when he and a half blood named Johnny's Brother became engaged in a quarrel. The half blood, who was well soaked with rum, knocked the civil chief to the ground and severely stomped his chest. For a time it was thought that Attakullakulla would lose his life, but he recovered in a few weeks.[24]

Aided by a rumor that Ammonscossittee had tried to sell the Cherokee northern hunting grounds to Virginia, Chota's Old Hop

(Connecorte) had wrested the title of emperor away from the Tellico youth. In August 1751 the new Beloved Man led his own delegation to Williamsburg in an effort to open a trading path with Virginia. The Chota Uku told Gov. Lewis Burwell that he and his people had traveled a long way "thro' bushes and briar" to see their friends.

The desire for and dependency upon European manufactured goods had now grown strong. Cherokee warriors wanted guns and the necessary powder, lead, and flints with which to contest tribal enemies. The women wanted cloth goods, knives, needles, and a whole variety of items that had severely altered their domestic life. Trade was a powerful force that not only modified the Cherokee way of life but also brought them time and again to council with the English, and later the Americans, and make concessions in terms of affiliation and territory.

"We are a poor People," the Raven told Glen, "and can make Nothing for ourselves, nor have we anything but what we get from the white People."[25] Raven complained that the governor of Carolina had given ammunition and other necessities to their enemies; and he argued that the Cherokees could provide the people of Virginia with a barrier against the French Indians by guarding the roads. Burwell gave the chief and his interpreter presents and promised to encourage any inhabitant who wished to trade with the Cherokees.[26]

Attakullakulla was at the lead of a delegation of Cherokees that arrived at Charlestown in June 1753 in response to Governor Glen's request. The Cherokees also wanted to improve their relations with South Carolina. To assure Governor Glen of his loyalty, the Cherokee leader said that he had lately been out warring against Indians allied with the French. He and his party had killed eight people, some of whom were French, and had taken two prisoners.[27]

Glen stated that his main purpose for calling the council was to conclude a treaty between the Cherokees and Creeks. Attakullakulla replied that when he was in England, King George had asked the Cherokees to avenge the lives of his people "whose bones lay white upon the ground," killed by the Creeks. When Glen insisted that he could talk for the king now, Attakullakulla replied that he would be glad to go to England and talk to the king himself. The governor refused. Attakullakulla pointed out that there were other places from which he could go to England, meaning Virginia. Glen was annoyed. He had heard reports that this chief was a troublemaker. He insisted that only he could send anyone to see the king. Attakullakulla changed the subject to his own concern, still shrewdly playing the Virginia card against Glen.

"When I was in England," Attakullakulla noted, "I remember the great King George's talk, for the paper said the governor of Carolina was to supply us with all kinds of goods, but if he did not, we might have them in Virginia."[28]

Glen replied that he, too, had read the paper and that it said nothing about Virginia. Attakullakulla complained that the traders in the Cherokee country treated his people badly, and they dared not complain. "If we do," he said, "they take our skins and throw them on the ground and deny us goods. If we do not give them their prices we must go without any."[29]

In their final talk on July 7, the governor promised to send the Cherokees a great quantity of goods and repeated a promise he had made before — to build a fort in their country as they had been requesting for several years. Attakullakulla indicated that he would take the governor's talk concerning peace with the Creeks back to Old Hop.[30]

Glen was assured that white people would be safe in Cherokee country. Gifts were made to all of the Cherokee delegations, including Attakullakulla and the other six headmen, who were each given a scarlet suit, ruffled shirt, laced hat, shoes, garters, stockings, buckles, silk handkerchief, ribbons, saddle and bridle, fine gun, and blanket. The same prizes were to be taken back to Old Hop. Lesser presents were given to the three headmen of inferior rank, thirty warriors, and four women of the Cherokee entourage. Also distributed among the party was a large amount of gunpowder, bullets, flints, vermilion, domestic goods of all sorts, a drum, and a Union Jack.

The threat of French advancement south from Canada had become even more alarming to the British in the spring of 1754, when French forces seized the forks of the Ohio and began building Fort Duquesne (present Pittsburgh) at the conflux of the Ohio and the Allegheny. Newly arrived Virginia governor Robert Dinwiddie dispatched twenty-one-year-old George Washington to warn the French away, but to no avail. Dinwiddie, a former Scot merchant, then called the Virginia militia into service. He also sent emissaries into the field to make alliances with various Indian tribes, including the Cherokees, and secure the support of their warriors for a spring campaign against the French.[31]

Among these emissaries was twenty-one-year-old Nathaniel Gist, who on the recommendation of George Washington was sent to Chota to make an offer — Virginia trade for Cherokee fighting men. When Gist arrived in the spring of 1755, Old Hop and the other chiefs were more than willing to provide a sizable force. However, a delegation of French-favoring northern Indians arrived at Chota and convinced the Cherokees that neutrality was a much wiser course.[32]

Another meeting was held between Glen and the Cherokees in 1755. Glen wished to persuade Old Hop to sell the Cherokee landholdings in South Carolina, where no active Cherokee towns were still located. Old Hop was in favor of the cession, but other chiefs were not. Because of his advanced age and infirmity the Chota Beloved Man did not wish to travel to Charlestown. However, by reiterating his willingness to build forts in the Cherokee country, Glen was able to get the Cherokee leader to meet him at the former Cherokee town of Saluda, located some twenty-five miles northwest of present Greenville, South Carolina.

Old Hop called a council of his headmen to select someone to speak in his stead. He was not accustomed to talking with white people, he said, and he thought it necessary to choose a person who could best represent the welfare of the Cherokee people. Accordingly, the council chose Attakullakulla and issued him instructions on how to behave and what to say.[33]

There were 506 Cherokee chiefs, headmen, and warriors who took their places in a grove of trees near Saluda on July 2, 1755. Governor Glen, his party, and Old Hop were seated under a brush arbor as Attakullakulla stood before them with a bow in one hand and a sheath of arrows in the other. The Cherokee then spoke, as a British account described him, "with the dignity and graceful action of a Roman or Grecian orator, and with all their ease and eloquence."[34] Following this speech, Attakullakulla was looked upon as the principal spokesman for the Cherokee Nation.

A young Cherokee boy was brought forward and presented to the governor. "I have brought this child," Attakullakulla said, "that when he grows up he may remember our agreement this day and tell it to the next generation that it may be known forever." The Cherokee orator also asked that the governor put all that passed between them in writing so that it could be read to the Cherokee headmen and kept forever. "What I now speak the great King should hear. We are brothers to the people of Carolina, and one house covers all."[35]

Attakullakulla took some earth and corn from a small bag, requesting that they be sent to the king. They were to be a token that the Cherokees recognized his authority over the Cherokees' land and property. Then raising his bow and sheath of arrows above his head, the Cherokee continued. "These are all the arms we have for our defense.

We hope the Great King will pity his children the Cherokees, and send us guns and ammunition. We fear not the French. Give us arms, and we will go to war against the enemies of the great King."

Lastly, Attakullakulla presented Glen a string of white wampum beads as confirmation that every word he had spoken had been accepted by the Cherokee headmen. It was agreed that the Cherokees would provide warriors to fight with the British—with provisos. The British would supply them with arms and ammunition, and they would build the forts that would protect the Cherokee women and children while the warriors were away.[36] The Cherokees in return made their first important cession of land, giving up to South Carolina what is virtually the western fourth of the state today.[37]

Following the Saluda meeting, Oconostota led a warring expedition against the French and their Indians in the Illinois-Wabash country, netting five French prisoners. A tall, big-boned man, his face pitted from a youthful bout with smallpox, Oconostota would become known as one of the Cherokees' greatest warriors but also as a leading civil figure of his time, his life and history coinciding with that of Attakullakulla.[38] The Chota first warrior made no pretense at being a great statesman. Still he would sit quietly through the councils and listen carefully before speaking his mind bluntly and emphatically.

"Why you know you are telling lies!" Oconostota had once told some whites who were trying to buy land from the Cherokees. "We always told you these lands were not ours; that our claim extended not beyond Cumberland mountain; that all the lands beyond Cumberland river belonged to our brothers, the Chickasaws. It is true you gave us some goods for which we promised our friendship in the affair, and our good will. These you have had according to bargain, and more we never promised you; but you have deceived your people!"[39]

Also during 1755 Oconostota commanded some five hundred warriors in a great mass attack upon the Creeks and drove them from northern Georgia. During the key battle at Taliwa, Nancy Ward performed her daring feat that won her the title of "War Woman of Chota." She had gone to the battle site at Taliwa in support of her first husband, a Cherokee named Kingfisher. When he was killed, she took up his musket and joined in the fight. Nancy, who was said to be the niece of Attakullakulla, later married Irish trader Brian Ward.[40]

Glen's inability to improve trade relations as he had promised left Old Hop and his chiefs frustrated. Still, despite pressure from the northern Indians, the Cherokees remained loyal to the British. Ostenaco

(Outacite or Mankiller, also known as Judd's Friend because he saved the life of a white man) and 130 of his men went north to help protect the Virginia frontier from the Shawnees. However, when Attakullakulla visited Charlestown at the end of 1755 and failed to get Glen to act on building the fort he had promised, the unhappy Cherokee orator headed off for Williamsburg to shore up his connections with Dinwiddie and Virginia.[41]

Early in 1756 the Virginia governor sent commissioners Peter Randolph and William Byrd to visit the Cherokees and Catawba Indians for the purpose of recruiting more fighting help. After making a treaty with the Catawbas in February, the commissioners continued on to the French Broad River in North Carolina, where they met with the Cherokees. The Cherokee delegation was headed by Ammonscossittee— who still held a high position as a Tellico chief—and included Attakulla-kulla and Oconostota. Again, it was Attakullakulla who spoke for the Cherokees.

The commissioners presented the usual string of wampum beads and then made a speech warning the Indians against the French. As proof of their friendship, they offered to build a school for the education of Cherokee boys and eventually employ them in settling disputes. The Indians, however, were much more interested in securing a fort for their Upper Towns in present Tennessee. They argued that if their warriors went off to fight, their women and children would not be safe from the French and their Indian allies. Attakullakulla expressed their dismay that Governor Glen had made no move to build the fort he had promised. "I have a Hatchet ready," he said, "but we hope our Friends will not expect us to take it up, 'til we have a Place of Safety for our Wives and Children."[42]

When the fort had been built, he said, the Cherokees would send a great number of warriors. But he also complained that the Virginians still had not been willing to trade with his people as the king had promised him in England. The French, he noted, supplied their Indian allies with firearms.

During the council it was learned that some Cherokees then serv-ing with Virginia troops had been killed and scalped by white settlers. Angry relatives of the dead men threatened the lives of Byrd and Randolph. Attakullakulla told the two men to stay in their tents while he extended apologies and gifts and made a speech in their behalf.[43] Because Old Hop could not cross the mountains, Attakullakulla asked for another meeting closer to where the Cherokee headman lived.

However, Randolph and Byrd had little desire to make another trip into Cherokee country. They presented the Cherokees with a written agreement to consider overnight. On the following day, Attakullakulla returned to say it had been interpreted to him and his chiefs and that they were agreeable to its terms.

The Cherokees would supply four hundred warriors to fight with the Virginians—after the fort was built. The two commissioners and twelve chiefs signed the pact, after which the Virginians presented them with presents and treated them to a banquet. All joined in toasting King George's health. The chiefs departed much pleased; not only had they secured a fort, but they had finally opened a trading path with Virginia.[44]

At the same time these treaty talks were underway, Chief Ostenaco and his warriors joined in an expedition against the Shawnees. The attempted foray failed when the 250-man Virginia force fell apart after their canoes overturned and dumped much of their armament and supplies in the river. For his efforts, Ostenaco was invited to visit Williamsburg again. There he was given a royal reception and the feeling that he was now a key player in Cherokee-British relations.[45]

Governors Glen and Dinwiddie had different intentions regarding the Cherokees. Glen saw them as a protection against attack on South Carolina; Dinwiddie wished to use them in an offensive campaign to drive the French from the Ohio country. The two governors also quarreled over the building of a fort among the Overhills. Dinwiddie responded with only one thousand of the seven thousand pounds requested by Glen as Virginia's share of the fort construction.

In the spring of 1754, as Glen had promised, South Carolina constructed Fort Prince George among the Lower Cherokees near Keowee. Upon its completion, Glen made the arduous journey there to emphasize its importance.[46] In 1756 he ordered a complete rebuilding of the fort and dispatched an agent to Chota to reassure the Overhill Cherokees that a second fort would soon be built there.

Taking personal charge of assembling and outfitting a three-hundred-man expedition, Glen was preparing to march in early June when he was succeeded as governor of South Carolina by thirty-four-year-old William Henry Lyttelton. In the meantime, Dinwiddie had learned of Glen's plans. Not wanting to miss the opportunity of getting fighting help from the Cherokees, he hurriedly sent Maj. Andrew Lewis with sixty men, most of them laborers, with orders to build a fort near Chota under the terms agreed to the year before.[47]

Lewis and his men were welcomed by Old Hop and his chiefs, but

This portrait of Ostenaco was painted at his "palace" abode on Suffolk Street, London.
British Magazine, July 1762.

dissension soon arose. Some of the chiefs demanded two forts—one to guard them from enemies by land and another from those by water. There were others who were convinced that a fort in their country would lead to British domination, persuaded by the French agents that the British meant to enslave them. With the French and Indian War underway, the support of the various tribes had become a matter of fierce competition.

Not waiting for the arrival of the South Carolinians, the Virginians constructed a log fort on the north bank of the Little Tennessee a mile above Chota. When it was completed in August, Lewis found the chiefs reluctant to send the warrior help that Dinwiddie was expecting. Lewis could get only seven men and three women to accompany him back to Virginia. He recommended to Dinwiddie that a military expedition be sent to crush the Cherokees into submission.[48]

Attakullakulla and other Cherokee leaders had maintained their contacts with South Carolina through visits to Fort Prince George. Before leaving office, Glen had sent Capt. Raymond Demere to Prince George to repair that post. When that was done, he was to move on to Chota and build the fort promised for the Overhill Cherokees. While repairing Prince George's defenses and waiting for more troops, Demere met with the visiting Cherokees. He did much to win their friendship and persuade them to remain loyal to Britain.

When Demere arrived at the Little Tennessee on October 1 with two hundred troops and a long packhorse train loaded with materials, supplies, and presents, he was well received by Old Hop and his people. Demere fired his swivel cannons in greeting; and the Cherokees, painted and dressed in their finest attire, came forth to embrace their visitors with great affection.

The reception, however, overlaid a seething conflict between Old Hop and Attakullakulla, who had risen in power dramatically. When Demere complained about Old Hop having entertained Frenchmen in his home (French John, the chief's captive servant, was looked upon as a French agent), Attakullakulla replied that the old chief was a fool who could do nothing without his help.[49]

Demere had brought two men of special importance with him. One was William De Brahm, a German engineer who was assigned the task of building a fort to protect Cherokee women and children. Another was Capt. John Stuart, commander of a company of South Carolina provincials, who would ultimately play a significant role in the affairs of the Cherokees and other Indians of the region.

Demere distributed his presents, and De Brahm—winning a bitter argument with Demere over the site—immediately set about constructing a fort on a narrow ridge near the conflux of the Tellico River with the Little Tennessee south of present Knoxville. The project went slowly, and Demere's troops would work on it through the winter and into the early summer of 1757. When finished, the 105-foot-square log enclosure featured bastions at the corners, each mounting three sixteen-caliber cannons. The fort, which was protected by a steep forty-foot cliff, was left open on the river side. Thick rows of thorny locust trees were planted around the other three sides.[50]

A trading store, a house for the commanding officer, and a building to hold military stores were located at the center of the compound. The post was named Fort Loudoun in honor of the earl of Loudoun, then the commander of all English forces in America. Fort Loudoun was preferred of the two forts, and the Cherokees soon destroyed the one built by the Virginians. However, when De Brahm deserted the project in December, Loudoun was still incomplete and wanting of even barracks for the provincial troops. It was good only for keeping horses, cows, and pigs, the Cherokees claimed.[51]

With Fort Prince George and Fort Loudoun the British had established their presence in the very heart of Cherokee country. But hopes of a happy period of friendship and trade relations were not to be.

CHAPTER 3

Come the King's Men

The desire of Attakullakulla for a compatible relationship and trade with the British had helped the Cherokees maintain a shaky and uneasy peace through the first half of the eighteenth century. Despite the efforts of the French and northern Indians to enlist support of the Cherokees against England and the vacillation and threatened defection of Old Hop and Mankiller of Tellico, Attakullakulla stood firm in his support for the British. When the suspicious Demere accused him of being in league with Old Hop in conspiring with the French, Attakullakulla replied, "I am not a boy but the headman of this nation. I give talks to the Governor of Chota [Old Hop] and not he to me. My mind has always been straight. I always think one way and now I take you by the hand and you hear what I have to say. If I do not perform it, when I come back make me a liar."[1]

Indeed, Attakullakulla had now become the most powerful man in the Cherokee Nation. And it would be he who virtually alone held the Cherokee Nation to its ties with Britain, often in extremely difficult and dangerous circumstances. Leaving Demere at Fort Loudoun to deal with Old Hop and Mankiller, the chief headed off for Charlestown to press for trade and to shore up Cherokee relations there.

During the several days of conferences, the Cherokee leader won Lyttelton's promise to curb the abusive practices of English traders—in particular that of the corrupt Carolinian John Elliott—and to recognize Chota's Cherokee supremacy by sending Tellico's presents through himself. In return Lyttelton repeated a call for Cherokee warriors to help fight the French and their Indians in Virginia.[2]

Upon his return to Chota, Attakullakulla, joined by a force under Oconostota, lead a strike against the French—not in Virginia, however, but against French transportation on the Mississippi and Ohio Rivers. While he was away, the devious Elliott did all he could to undermine Attakullakulla's authority and prestige and enhance that of rival Ostenaco. Learning of this, Attakullakulla had Elliott's scales and measuring sticks seized and taken to Demere. The scales read two pounds light, and the measuring stick was inches short. The Cherokees were infuriated with Elliott; but traders were badly wanted, and he survived for the time.[3]

Mankiller and other Tellico chiefs were still sympathetic to the French cause. Some of them had paid a visit to Fort Toulouse (present Montgomery, Alabama) and were later escorted on to New Orleans. There the French governor had incited them to "Attack some Fort of Strength Knock the Head of 5 or 600 then you will get slaves and Plunder in Plenty."[4]

Even as Capt. Paul Demere arrived to replace his brother in command of Fort Loudoun, the Tellicos murdered the pregnant English wife of a Fort Loudoun man. They hoped to cause a break with England. Attakullakulla held off a reprisal attack by the British until Old Hop could censure the Tellico head warrior. He then placated Demere by forcing all the Overhill headmen to come to Loudoun and pledge their loyalty to the British Crown.[5]

To further bolster the sagging Cherokee-British relations, Attakullakulla organized five war parties to go against the French and their Indian allies where a fort was being built near the mouth of the Ohio. He was saluted by salvos of the Fort Loudoun cannon as he departed on

Old Fort Loudoun stands restored near Vonore, Tennessee.

Photo by author.

September 24, 1757. It would be four months before he and his party would return to Chota and bring back the scalps of a French lieutenant and several soldiers, and two Frenchmen and a woman as prisoners.[6]

The Cherokees' trade with the British had improved greatly during his absence, and Attakullakulla found that his importance to colonial officials had become much diminished. To reestablish his prestige, he traveled to Charlestown. Though uninvited and his presence a discomfort to Lyttelton, the Cherokee was given a state reception. Backing the accounts of his warring exploits and loyalty with two French scalps, he requested more ammunition for his people. He also asked that Elliott be removed.

Receiving the governor's promise of compliance on these matters, Attakullakulla returned home to organize a sizable force of Cherokees to defend Virginia and help fight the French and their Indian allies in the Ohio country. Though the Cherokees were welcomed and much appreciated by George Washington, the British officers belittled their contribution and scorned their custom of asking for presents as compensation for their services. The Virginia legislature offered a seventy-five-dollar bounty for the scalp of any Frenchman or any Indian fighting with the French. Unfortunately, at times the Cherokees were mistaken for the enemy and were either imprisoned or killed. Further, unscrupulous Virginians, knowing that Cherokee scalps would bring a reward as well as any, waylaid, murdered, and robbed some of the allied warriors. "A barbarous method of war introduced by the French, which we are obliged to follow in our own Defence," Dinwiddie observed of scalp taking.[7] Because of the murder of the Cherokees, however, the Virginia legislature was forced to retract their bounty practice.

The news of the murder and scalping of their young men in Virginia caused great dismay and anger among the Cherokee people. Attakullakulla's warriors had served well alongside the British redcoats. But, not wanting to antagonize the Shawnees, with whom he wished to make peace, the Cherokee chief refused to join Gen. John Forbes in an attack upon Fort Duquesne. Forbes ordered him arrested, stripped of his arms, and escorted out of Virginia. The wily chief, however, had heard that the French and Creeks were urging the Cherokees at home into an all-out war against the British. He hurried to Williamsburg to talk with the new governor, Francis Fauquier, arguing that a war could be prevented and good relations restored if a trade path with Virginia could be opened.[8]

Though Fauquier berated him severely, the governor said that the

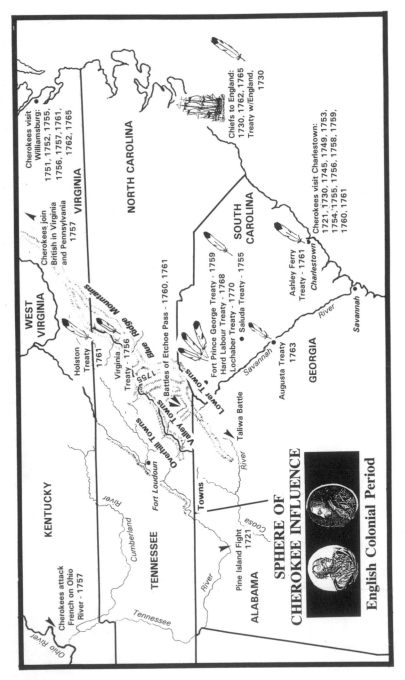

Map labels (rotated):

Ohio River

Cherokees attack French on Ohio River - 1757

KENTUCKY

Cherokees visit Williamsburg: 1751, 1752, 1755, 1756, 1757, 1761, 1762, 1765

Cherokees join British in Virginia and Pennsylvania 1757

VIRGINIA

WEST VIRGINIA

NORTH CAROLINA

Chiefs to England: 1730, 1762, 1765 Treaty w/England, 1730

Cherokees visit Charlestown: 1721, 1730, 1745, 1749, 1753, 1754, 1755, 1756, 1758, 1759, 1760, 1761

SOUTH CAROLINA

Holston Treaty 1761

Blue Ridge Mountains

Virginia Treaty - 1756

1755

Battles of Etchoe Pass - 1760, 1761

Valley Towns

Lower Towns

Fort Prince George Treaty - 1759
Hard Labour Treaty - 1768
Lochaber Treaty - 1770
Saluda Treaty - 1755

Ashley Ferry Treaty - 1761

Charlestown

Savannah River

Savannah

Cumberland River

Overhill Towns

Fort Loudoun

Little Tennessee River

Taliwa Battle

Augusta Treaty 1763

GEORGIA

TENNESSEE

Towns

Coosa River

Pine Island Fight 1721

Tennessee River

Tennessee

ALABAMA

SPHERE OF CHEROKEE INFLUENCE

English Colonial Period

Sphere of Cherokee Influence.

Virginia House of Burgess had already voted to open trade with the Cherokees. Elated with the news, Attakullakulla returned home, avoiding a North Carolina plot to ambush and kill him. Despite this attempt on his life, he promoted the English trade alliance in an address to the Chota council. Then, in response to a request by Lyttelton to see him, he hurried off to Charlestown again. There Lyttelton accused him of being a deserter to the British cause. The Cherokee replied, "I am not a rogue, nor given that way. Many bad and false talks have been sent your Excellency of the Cherokees and many such have also been sent me of the white people, but I believe them not. My love for my own people and their young ones has always determined me to do everything in my power to prevent their falling out with the white people."[9]

But keeping the peace was now beyond his control. The Setticos in particular were on a murderous rampage. While in Virginia, war leader Moytoy of Settico had stolen some horses to replace those he and his men had lost. A battle with the Virginia militia resulted, the Cherokees losing nineteen warriors. Determined to have revenge, Moytoy and his warriors raided the North Carolina frontier and took nineteen white scalps to compensate for their losses. To show the Cherokees' disapproval of Moytoy's action, Demere ordered Old Hop to secure the scalps and bring them to Fort Loudoun for a proper burial. The Setticos turned over some of their trophies but kept others.[10]

Hoping to reinforce relations with the British and, perhaps, to keep his warriors occupied, Attakullakulla led a warring expedition down the Tennessee River. But he had no sooner departed than Old Hop reopened communications with the French. On August 14 Lyttelton ordered the supply of ammunition to the Cherokees halted, a move that only fueled the wrath of the young men. Soon after, Chilhowie trader William Neal was murdered and other traders began fleeing the Cherokee country. Their Indian wives helped them avoid the ambushes that had been set for them.[11]

The Lower Towns, too, were on a rampage. Middle Town chief Round-O of Stecoe (Sticoy) went to Keowee and called the headmen together. With sarcasm he asked if they had found a mountain of gunpowder, if their women had learned to make clothes, and their men knives and hatchets. Just where, he wondered, was their store from which they could get supplies.[12]

Fort Loudoun became more and more threatened. Demere sent for Old Hop, Oconostota, and Standing Turkey for discussion of the situation. Oconostota declared that the hostilities had been caused by

Lyttelton's ammunition embargo. Because the Lower Towns were largely to blame for the order, Demere suggested that the chiefs talk with Lt. Richard Coytmore, commander at Fort Prince George. When Oconostota and Ostenaco arrived there, Coytmore said they would have to talk with Lyttelton in Charlestown.

Ostenaco returned to Chota to keep things quiet while Oconostota joined a party of Lower Town chiefs headed for the South Carolina capital to arrange a settlement, picking up Chief Round-O en route. In Charlestown, Oconostota told Lyttelton that Old Hop had sent him to "make the path straight, to brighten the chain, and to accommodate differences."[13] "Old Hop, my governor, has always loved the white people, and I am come hither to prove it. The path has been a little bad, but I am come to make it straight from your Excellency to my governor. There has been blood spilled, but I am come to clean it up. I am a warrior, but want no war with the English."[14]

Lyttelton may well have been able to work out a peace arrangement with the Cherokee chiefs, but dire reports from Coytmore and Demere had made him suspicious of any Cherokee peace offer. Having already mustered an army of fourteen hundred militiamen, Lyttelton refused to accept Oconostota's plea for peace or hear the other chiefs. Instead he forced the delegation of more than eighty Cherokees to travel with his army to Fort Prince George, promising, "You, Oconostota, and all with you, shall return safely to your country, and it is not my intention to harm a hair of your heads."[15]

The difficulty of the journey plus an outbreak of smallpox demoralized the militia, which began to suffer desertions. In order to reassure other Cherokees that he was not mistreating his captives, Lyttelton dispatched Elliott to Chota. He also sent demands for surrender of Cherokees who had murdered whites. At Chota, Elliott found that Attakullakulla had returned from his warring venture with eight French scalps.

Lyttelton's demands stirred great anger when they were read in the Chota council house. Old Hop called Attakullakulla a traitor for his support of the British. Attakullakulla responded by arguing that Old Hop had failed his fundamental duty as First Beloved Man in not standing for peace. He declared himself to be the new principal man and headed off to meet with Lyttelton, who after going into camp at Fort Prince George had released all but twenty-eight of his hostages. Among those still held were Oconostota and Round-O.[16]

The North Carolina governor received Attakullakulla and his delegation in friendship on December 19. Lyttelton's demands, however, were severe. He called for the surrender of twenty-two Cherokee warriors who were guilty of murders in the Carolinas.[17] As Oconostota pointed out, many would be hard to find or catch; it would be impossible to bring them all in. After much bartering, Attakullakulla persuaded Lyttelton to release Oconostota, Ketagusta, Round-O, and Killianca (Killeannakea).[18]

Despite the Britisher's promise to treat the remaining hostages well, they were crammed into a small cabin at the fort. On December 26, 1759, a treaty was drawn up and the captive chiefs headed by Attakullakulla and Oconostota signed it. By it they agreed to trade an equal number of Cherokees who were guilty of English murders for twenty-two whom Lyttelton retained as hostages. Further, the Cherokees would put to death all Frenchmen coming into their territory.[19] This done, Lyttelton departed for Charlestown, where he was toasted as a great hero for the victory that he claimed he had won over the Cherokees.

However, the Cherokee war leaders—particularly Oconostota, who felt he had been badly betrayed in being seized while on a peace mission— felt no compunction to follow a treaty signed under duress. At this point, in January 1760, Old Hop died. Had innocent Cherokees not then been held prisoner at Fort Prince George, Attakullakulla likely would have been chosen as the new Beloved Man of the nation. But he, more than anyone else, had pushed to support the interests of King George. Instead, Chota's Standing Turkey (his Cherokee name is given variously as Connetarke, Kanagatucko, Cunnacatoque), who leaned strongly toward the French, was named as the new Beloved Man and Cherokee emperor.[20]

With Lyttelton and his army gone, Cherokee warriors struck in blind fury against the white traders and frontier settlements. At Hiwassee, trader John Kelly was murdered, his body quartered and his head and hands displayed on stakes. At Keowee, only a short distance from Fort Prince George, Elliott's trading house was assaulted, and the detested trader was felled with a tomahawk to the head as he ran for his life. Traders throughout the Cherokee country fled their posts, many taking refuge at Fort Prince George.[21]

A group of Cherokee warriors attempted to push their way into the fort to rescue their captive tribesmen, but they were repulsed. In South Carolina, a group of settlers fleeing to Fort Moore were attacked while crossing a stream in wagons. Twenty-three were killed and many taken prisoner. A like number were massacred on Stevens Creek, while other bloody assaults were carried out all along the frontiers of South Carolina and Georgia. Fort Prince George was cut off from outside communication.[22]

In mid-February 1760, Attakullakulla and Oconostota returned to the fort to secure the release of the hostages. There they learned that Round-O, who had rejected freedom in order to stay with his captive son, had died of smallpox along with four other hostages and several soldiers. At the fort's gate, Oconostota called to Coytmore to release the Cherokee prisoners. When the Britisher stubbornly refused, the Great Warrior disavowed the agreement he had signed under duress and stalked away.[23]

On the following day two Indian women appeared on the bank of the Keowee River opposite the fort. When an Englishman from the fort came out, they were joined by Oconostota who said he wished to speak with Coytmore. Lieutenant Coytmore came forth with a junior officer and an interpreter. Oconostota said that he wanted to go to Charlestown and talk with the governor and would like to have a white man accompany him.

Coytmore agreed to this, whereupon Oconostota answered that he would go catch a horse for the man. As he rode off, the Cherokee war chief waved a bridle over his head. It was a signal to some twenty-five or thirty of his men who were hidden in the bushes nearby. They opened fire on the four white men. The interpreter was hit in the buttocks, the junior officer in the calf, and Coytmore in the chest. The lieutenant was dragged back into the fort, where he soon died.[24]

Ensign Alexander Miln, who was now in command at the fort, ordered the hostages to be placed in irons. But when this was attempted, the Cherokees fought back with weapons they had concealed about them. One soldier was killed instantly with a tomahawk, and another mortally wounded. Despite Miln's efforts to stop them, the incensed soldiers of the fort began shooting the hostages, killing them all.

Many of the Lower and Middle Towns lost their headman in the action. It was no longer possible for the peace-minded chiefs such as Attakullakulla to hold back the warriors. The entire Cherokee country became a hostile ocean surrounding the small British outpost at Fort Loudoun. Oconostota led a raid against a South Carolina frontier fort, only to be repulsed with the loss of five Cherokees. In his report of the affair, the exuberant commanding officer of the fort commented, "We have the pleasure to fatten our dogs upon their carcasses, and to display their scalps, neatly ornamented, on our bastions."[25]

At Fort Prince George neither soldiers nor the traders who had taken refuge there dared to venture out. Matters were even worse at Fort Loudoun. The Cherokees placed the fort under a siege that would last from February into August. One of the leaders of the siege was Ostenaco, who declared that if peace were made seven times, he would break it seven times.[26]

With a garrison of some two hundred regulars, fourteen cannon, plenty of ammunition, and a hundred hogs in early January, Demere thought the fort would be able to hold out until relief broke through. Capt. John Stuart, second in command, wrote hopefully on January 12 that the post had at least six months' provisions.[27]

From Charlestown, where a bill had been introduced to declare all captured Cherokees as slaves, a call went out for assistance from the British army. Accordingly, a force of twelve hundred Highlanders and Royal Scots under Col. Archibald Montgomery was shipped to Georgia from Canada. After marching to relieve Fort Prince George, Montgomery began an advance northward against the Lower Towns of the Cherokees. Town after town was surrounded by the British troops, and everyone except the women and children were put to death by the bayonet. The towns and crops were then torched. Second in command Col. James Grant wrote in his report, "I could not help pitying them a little; their villages were agreeably situated, their houses neatly built, and well provided, for they were in the greatest abundance of everything . . . After killing all we could, we marched to Keowee."[28]

After decimating the Lower Towns, Montgomery pushed on north toward the Cherokee Middle Towns. Oconostota was waiting for him at Etchoe Pass on the Little Tennessee River just east of present Franklin, North Carolina. The Cherokee warriors severely damaged the British forces, killing 20 and wounding 76 more. After losing a total of 140 men, Montgomery retreated back to Fort Prince George, the Cherokees harassing him as he went. Claiming a victory in his report, the Britisher argued that he had already punished the Cherokees enough to make them sue for peace and that burning a few more villages was not worth the cost.[29]

It was planned that while Montgomery attacked from the south, Virginia militia would march from the north to relieve Fort Loudoun. A thousand men were assembled under the command of Col. William Byrd, the former commissioner. By the time the expedition reached the upper Holston River, however, Montgomery had already departed the field. Fearing to march against the Cherokees alone, Byrd and his men turned back, forsaking their besieged countrymen at Loudoun.[30]

South Carolinians felt that Montgomery had done far more to inflame the war than to stop it. Gov. William Bull, who had replaced Lyttelton, feared that now the Fort Loudoun garrison would be lost.[31]

He arranged for ribbons and paint, with which food could be purchased from Cherokee women, and slipped through the Indian lines.[32]

Events would soon prove Bull's concern for Loudoun to be valid. As the days, weeks, and months passed, the situation of the garrison there became more and more desperate. Despite the food brought in by Indian women, a number of whom were married to white men at the post, the individual ration of corn was reduced to a third of a quart a day.[33] Word reached the fort that troops were marching in relief. But as the men of the garrison became weak and ill from lack of food, their hope of being rescued faded. By August they had had no word from outside for more than two months, and all felt "abandoned and forsaken by God and man."[34]

Still loyal, Attakullakulla, who during the outbreak had taken his family to the woods for safety, returned to Loudoun and provided the garrison with information to the extent he could. Expelled from the Cherokee council, he finally admitted to Demere that "I am not the man to ask for news. The Indians hide everything from me, and say I am the white man's friend."[35]

On August 6, 1760, the five officers of Fort Loudoun met and issued a statement. Their provisions were entirely exhausted, they said, and they had been subsisting on horse flesh and what little food the Indian women supplied them. They had had no bread since July 7. The men were so weakened they were unable to perform their duties, and many had deserted to either throw themselves upon the mercy of the Indians or take their chances in the woods. They recommended that the fort be abandoned.

Demere agreed. On August 7 he sent Stuart, who was married to a half-Cherokee woman, along with another officer and some friendly Indians, to Chota to arrange a truce with the Cherokees. Meeting with Oconostota and other chiefs, Stuart settled upon the terms of capitulation. The Cherokees were more than generous.[36] They agreed that each soldier could keep a gun in order to secure food on the 140-mile trek to Fort Prince George. They would provide as many horses as possible for the garrison to use on their march. Soldiers who were lame or ill would be cared for at the Cherokee towns. The Indians' only demand was made in the last article of the agreement: "That the fort, great guns, powder, ball, and spare arms, be delivered to the Indians, without any fraud, on the day appointed for the march of the troops." Demere signed the agreement, and on the day before leaving the fort he penned a letter to the governor of South Carolina: "Tomorrow morning we set out," he wrote, "and we flatter ourselves the Indians mean us no harm. We shall make all the dispatch that our starved condition will admit of."[37]

At seven o'clock the following morning, the Fort Loudoun gates were opened and the exodus of some three hundred enfeebled soldiers, women, and children marched out with drums beating and the Union Jack flying. The Cherokees did not interfere, most of the warriors rushing with delight into the conquered military post. A few of the chiefs accompanied the march for a time until one by one they began to drop out for one reason or another. The refugees marched some forty miles, camping near the conflux of Cane Creek and the Tellico. They did not realize that behind them a deadly complication had developed.[38]

On the evening before departing, in a total betrayal of the agreement they had made, Demere and Stuart agreed to bury some of the fort's ammunition. This was done at midnight, with only the two of them and the gunner, who dug the hole, present. But somehow Demere's housekeeper, a Mrs. Glotler, learned of it. In an effort to place herself better with the Indians, she told them of the act. Fortunately for Stuart, the interpreter did not mention his name when repeating the woman's story.

The information sent the Indians into an uproar. A howl for revenge went up, and the Cherokee warriors were soon charging down the trail in pursuit of the retreating garrison. When Attakullakulla learned of this, he was greatly alarmed for the safety of Stuart, with whom he had once taken a blood oath of brotherhood. He called upon a young warrior in whom he held great trust and ordered him to save Stuart if he possibly could. It was said that the Cherokee chief gave his rifle and all of his clothes to save Stuart.[39]

The Cherokee warriors attacked at daybreak of August 10 as the British caravan was preparing to march. The advance guard, consisting of a sergeant and twelve men, led off while the rest of the people were still getting ready. Several Indians were spied on the opposite side of Cane Creek, apparently running to cut off the march. Stuart called out for his charges to stand to arms, but at that moment the war whoop was sounded, throwing the refugees into confusion. Immediately thereafter a mass of Indians, who had crept to within two hundred yards in the tall grass, made their charge from all sides. Stuart described his part in the affair: "One soldier, the interpreter, and my servant, were all that remained with me on the spot where we were encamped. We snatched up soldiers muskets and discharged them. My servant put one of my pistols into my hand; when, almost at the same instant, we were both seized, pinioned, and hurried off the field; in the struggle my pistol went off."[40]

Stuart was the only officer of the five to survive. Demere, Adamson, Bogges, and Wintle were killed in addition to twenty-six soldiers and three women. Demere was held responsible for burying the ammunition, and once he was captured the fighting was halted by Ostenaco. It was said that Demere, being only wounded at the first fire, was scalped and dismembered while still alive. Dirt was stuffed into his mouth as warriors taunted him by saying, "You English want land; we will give it to you."[41]

Stuart was taken to Attakullakulla, who claimed him as his own prisoner. Soon after, the Indians came and dug up the buried gunpowder. During the last of August, Attakullakulla pretended to take Stuart on a hunting trip, delivering him to safety in Virginia. The other prisoners were not so fortunate. Some of them were badly abused, though they were eventually returned unharmed otherwise. Two garrison soldiers and a young boy, however, were taken to Settico. One soldier, Luke Croft, was burned to death; the other, Frederick Mouncy, was saved by a runner sent by Oconostota. The boy was also released.[42]

Following the capture of Fort Loudoun, Oconostota laid plans to use its captured guns to take Fort Prince George. He was offered assistance by the French, who at the same time made an effort to occupy Loudoun. However, the attack was called off when a large French supply boat failed to make it up the Tennessee River.

Many Cherokees had now tired of the war, and a great meeting of some two thousand tribesmen took place in September at Nequassee. Oconostota and Ostenaco both spoke for peace with the British. A captured Fort Loudoun soldier was sent to Governor Bull carrying word of the Cherokees' desire to end the war.[43] With the end of war fever among the Cherokees, Attakullakulla regained his lost position among his people. His high standing with the British was enhanced when he brought ten survivors of the Fort Loudoun garrison to General Byrd's field camp in November 1760. He delivered twelve more to Fort Prince George in March 1761.[44]

The Cherokees were ready for peace, but the British were preparing to enlarge the warfare. On Governor Bull's request Col. James Grant, who had been with Montgomery, was sent to Charlestown with two thousand Highlander troops, adding to the Royal Scots and militia already in place. Accumulating an army of some twenty-six hundred men, Grant marched to Fort Prince George. He was met there by

Attakullakulla, who urged further peace efforts and begged that Grant would proceed no further.[45]

But the British were convinced that the Cherokees must be taught a strong lesson. Grant marched his army northward along the same route Montgomery had taken the year before. Again destroying the Lower Towns, which had been rebuilt, Grant pushed on to Etchoe Pass. In a second battle at the pass, the Cherokees were soundly defeated, opening the way for the British army to ravage the Middle Cherokee settlements: "All their towns, amounting to fifteen in number, besides many little villages and scattered homes, have been burnt; upwards of fourteen hundred acres of corn, according to moderate computation, entirely destroyed; and near five thousand Cherokees, including men, women and children, driven to the mountains to starve; their only subsistence for some time past, being horseflesh."[46]

With this victory, Grant retired to Fort Prince George. On August 28, 1761, Attakullakulla and several other chiefs arrived at Grant's camp to treat for peace. The Cherokee second man said he spoke for the whole nation in expressing a desire to bury the hatchet, never more to use it against their English brothers.

Grant responded with a set of conditions. The Fort Loudoun cannon would be given up; the English would be allowed to build forts in Cherokee country; any Cherokee who killed a white man (with the Chickasaw and Catawba Indians considered as whites) would be put to death by the headman of his town; whites who killed Indians would be turned over to the British; no Frenchmen would be allowed in Cherokee country; traders would not be molested; and all of the Cherokees' prisoners would be given up.

Attakullakulla could accept most of the demanded terms, but there was one he could not. The first of the requirements was that either four Cherokee Indians be delivered to the British and put to death in front of the camp or four "green Cherokee scalps" be brought in. The Cherokee chief refused to give in to this and requested permission to travel to Charlestown to talk with the governor regarding the matter.[47]

On September 15, Attakullakulla met with Bull and other South Carolina officials at Ashley Ferry. "Our women and children are in great distress," he told them, "and dying on account of their towns and corn being destroyed . . . I am sent as a messenger from the whole nation, and hope the path (as the great King told me) will never be crooked, but straight and open to every one to pass."[48] Bull replied, "I have always heard of the good behavior of you the Little Carpenter during the war, therefore I have given orders for your being well taken care of."[49]

Attakullakulla later met with the governor at Charlestown and secured the peace agreement that he wanted. The pact stipulated that other Cherokee headmen come to Charlestown and sign the treaty "so that our old friendship may be renewed, and last as long as the sun shines and rivers run."[50] Attakullakulla further requested that John Stuart be named the "chief white man in their nation." Accordingly, Stuart was appointed as British superintendent of Indian affairs for the Southern Department. A treaty was eventually signed by Attakullakulla and nine other chiefs on December 30, 1761, at Charlestown.[51]

Simultaneous to these negotiations in South Carolina, still another treaty between a different group of Cherokees and the British of Virginia was being conducted on the Holston River near present Kingsport, Tennessee. There on November 19, 1761, at the lead of some four hundred Cherokees, the old tribal patriot Standing Turkey signed a pact of peace and friendship with representatives of Virginia.[52] With this pact, the main body of the Cherokee Nation ended its resistance to British expansion. The destiny of the Cherokee Nation was now largely in the hands of leaders who realized the futility of opposing British military might.

CHAPTER 4

"My Tongue Is My Pen"

Young Lt. Henry Timberlake had been one of the participants at the Holston River treaty in 1761. When Old Hop requested that an Englishman be sent back with him as proof of the good intentions of the British, Timberlake volunteered to go. During his six months' stay with the Cherokees, he cultivated the friendship of several chiefs, in particular Ostenaco, at whose home he resided for a time. He also fathered a son, Richard Timberlake, by one of Ostenaco's daughters.[1]

Ostenaco was highly capable both as a warrior and a diplomat. He had been a strong protector of English traders, once heading a force of forty-seven warriors to patrol the trading routes into the Cherokee country. Governor Glen heaped praise on the Cherokee and entertained him lavishly in Charlestown, lodging him in the governor's own house.[2]

Ostenaco and two other chiefs—Stalking Turkey and Pouting Pigeon—were persuaded by Timberlake to travel to England with him to meet King George III. Ostenaco said that his reason for going was that he wished to know if Attakullakulla, his "violent enemy," had told lies about his visit to England.[3] The visiting Englishman had noted the rivalry between the two chiefs: "The overhill settlement is by these two leaders divided into two factions," he observed, "between whom there is often great animosity, and the two leaders are sure to oppose one another in every measure taken."[4]

Ostenaco and a party of seventy Overhill Indians accompanied Timberlake to Williamsburg, where still another pact was signed on April 23. During the visit they were treated to a banquet at William and Mary College. Among those present to hear Ostenaco speak before the council in the Virginia capitol was nineteen-year-old Thomas Jefferson, then a student at William and Mary. Jefferson later noted that he knew the great "warrior and orator of the Cherokees" well, the chief having often been a guest at the home of Jefferson's father on his trips to and from Williamsburg: "His sounding voice, distinct articulation, animated action, and the solemn silence of his people at their several fires, filled

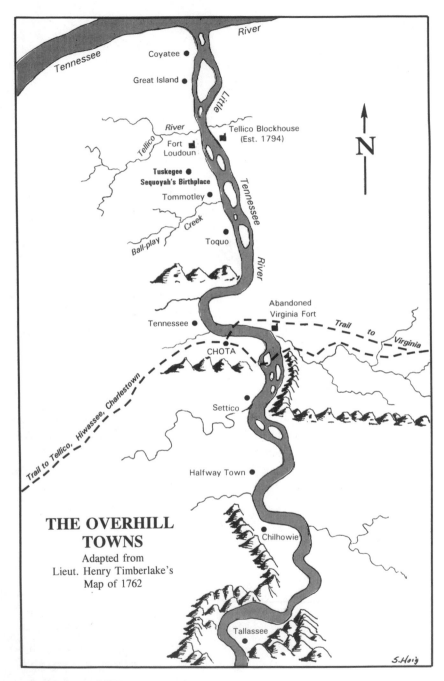

Cherokee Overhill Towns.

me with awe and veneration, although I did not understand a word he uttered."[5]

Ostenaco first lighted his pipe, then passed it to the governor and council before sending two or three large puffs toward the heavens. He then began his talk, saying he was glad to see his elder brethren and that now the darkness (war) had passed and it was light he could see clearly and was ready to make a lasting peace. Upon being shown a picture of King George, Ostenaco expressed his pleasure, saying that now he had seen the king's dead picture he would like to see him alive.[6]

On May 15 Timberlake, Ostenaco, Pouting Pigeon, Stalking Turkey, and interpreter William Shorey set sail on the sixteen-gun British frigate *Epreuvre*. Shorey, who had a Cherokee wife and several children by her, died during the voyage (from consumption—earlier his wife had thrown him into the river to sober him up but couldn't pull him out until help arrived), but the chiefs survived despite suffering extreme seasickness before landing at Plymouth on June 16.[7] As Ostenaco was brought ashore, he sang a loud dirge of praise to God for bringing him safely to land again. As with the delegation of 1730, the Indians drew large crowds of gaping people wherever they went.

An Englishman noted with begrudging humor the attraction of British women to the chiefs. He wrote lyrics for a song of the day, a verse of which went:

> How eager the Folks at Vauxhall, or elsewhere, Sir,
> With high Expectation and Rapture repair, Sir;
> Tho' not that all of them can produce the real Reason,
> Save that M[onste]rs of all Sorts are always in Season.
> If so, let the Chiefs here awhile have their Station,
> And send for the whole of the Cherokee Nation.[8]

An English journal described the chiefs as "tall, well-made men, near six feet high, dressed in their own country fashion, with only a shirt, trousers and mantle round them, their faces are painted a copper colour, and their heads adorned with shells, feathers, ear-rings, and other trifling ornaments."[9]

On the way to London, the chiefs and their escort stopped at Exeter. They displayed little interest in the town's beautiful cathedral, but they took great alarm at a statue of Hercules with a raised club. During the three weeks before meeting with the king, the Cherokees were taken to see all the public buildings and curiosities in and about London. They dined with royalty, toured castles, visited warships and arsenals, witnessed plays, heard concerts, met famous people such as Oliver Goldsmith, and were entertained constantly.

As they continued to draw huge crowds, the inns and taverns gladly invited their presence and plied them with drink. The dining and wining soon had its effects. The intoxication of the Indians began to draw complaints from journals such as *The St. James Chronicle*, which blamed the inn proprietors for the besotted condition of the chiefs. On one outing, Ostenaco fell into an orchestra pit with a lady of the evening at Vauxhall. Then, while being loaded into a coach after having passed out prone on the ground, he made a wild grab at a gentleman's sword and cut his hand badly. Finally, he was tossed bodily into the coach and carted off to his place of lodging.[10]

The three chiefs finally had their audience with King George at St. James's Palace on July 8. Ostenaco was dressed in a blue cloak overlaid with lace and wore a silver gorget bearing the king's arms and the legend "Loyal Chief Outacite Cherokee Warrior."[11] Timberlake was called upon to act as an interpreter, but he had forgotten most of his Cherokee. Without a capable interpreter the king was unable to ask many questions. He presented Ostenaco with a parchment certificate that indicated his regard for the Cherokee people.[12]

The chiefs visited the palace once more before leaving London on August 20 for Portsmouth, where a few days later, laden with gifts, they set sail for Charlestown. There Governor Bull feted the returning chiefs lavishly, and Ostenaco again addressed the South Carolina council. He vowed his loyalty to the Crown and protection for all Englishmen in America.[13]

In November 1763, Ostenaco, along with Attakullakulla and others, attended a large intertribal council between seven hundred Indians and three colonial governors at Augusta, Georgia. Speaking first, Ostenaco proudly displayed the testimonial presented him by King George. In his talk, Attakullakulla asked that better trading relations be established by the British. He also apologized to the other nations — Chickasaws, Choctaws, Creeks, and Catawbas — for troubles caused by some of his young men, who he admitted had been rogues. He warned them, however, that whenever the other tribes did any mischief they were certain to be found out because "a little bird always tells from the top of a tree."[14]

After this meeting, John Stuart escorted Attakullakulla, Oconostota, and the Raven of Nequassee to a council at Fort Stanwix, New York. There they agreed to give up all of their land north of the Tennessee River to their old enemies, the Iroquois, with whom they had been warring. Oconostota then went on to Fort Pitt in an effort to persuade his lifelong enemies, the Shawnees and Delawares, to make peace. His pride was badly hurt when the effort proved to be a failure.[15]

In 1765 Timberlake escorted still another Cherokee party to England. The three-man Cherokee delegation was headed by Cheulah, the Fox, of Settico. This visit, however, had not been authorized by British authorities. Not only was Timberlake snubbed by the king, who evidently had tired of Indian visitors, but he was discredited to the point of penury. The Cherokees, too, were given no kingly audience and were virtually ignored by the British press.

In February the deserted Cherokees were discovered in a deplorable condition on the streets of London by the earl of Hillsborough. Using his own money and tradesmen, the earl clothed them "in the English fashion." Further, he took them to see the British agent for Virginia and introduced them to the lords of trade and plantations. After declaring their affection for the British, the chiefs requested that the problem of whites invading their territory, which had been defined by treaty, be addressed.[16]

The chiefs then did one of the most risky things they could have done in the cause of Cherokee sovereignty. They displayed samples of gold and silver that had been discovered in their country. When the king heard of this, he sent the Cherokees lavish presents and arranged for their safe journey home. Accompanying them were English mineral experts to investigate their mines.

Though now supervising several tribes, John Stuart had not forgotten his debt to Attakullakulla. Accordingly, he sent two fellow Scots, Alexander Cameron and John McDonald, to work among the Cherokees as his deputies. Both men soon married Cherokee women and sired children by them. Oconostota reported to Stuart that Cameron had "done the Cherokees justice, told them the truth, and they all loved him."[17] The chiefs rewarded Cameron with a large tract of land.

Young McDonald, who had been among the Cherokees earlier as a trader, married Anna Shorey, half-blood daughter of the deceased William Shorey. They would eventually become the grandparents of future chief John Ross through the marriage of their daughter Molly to Daniel Ross. Both McDonald and Cameron were stout defenders of the

Indians against the white "villains and horse thieves" who infested the Cherokee country.[18]

Oconostota and Attakullakulla were now old men. In 1768 they were signatory to a treaty at Hard Labour, South Carolina. It was called by John Stuart in response to the Cherokee desire to have a definite boundary set in order to halt white encroachment onto their lands. By this agreement the Cherokees ceded all claim to lands in Virginia and agreed to a point thirty-six miles east of Long Island on the Holston River as the extension of the southwest boundary of Virginia.

Two years following the Hard Labour agreement, another treaty council was held at Lochaber, South Carolina, with over a thousand Cherokees present. On October 18, 1770, Attakullakulla, Oconostota, Ketagusta, and thirteen other chiefs agreed to a new boundary point thirty miles farther west. Once again the Cherokees sought to avoid trouble "removing as far as possible all cause of dispute between them & the said inhabitants on account of encroachment on lands reserved by the said Indians for themselves."[19] In return they were to receive "his Majesty's paternal goodness, so often demonstrated to them," plus an unspecified amount of goods.

The American Revolutionary War period marked the end of British governmental influence on the Cherokees and other tribes of the South. The raw culture of the frontier, wherein whites conducted themselves relatively free from the restraints of formal law, would still have a strong bearing on Indian-white relations. And, with most American colonists being of English-Scot descent, there would continue to be a transition of Anglo culture in modified form. However, the replacement of the colonial governments by American states and a developing new national federalism would mark an ending to many aspects of Cherokee-white relations and the beginning of new ones.

Several important conditions had been true of the Cherokees during the century of colonial rule. It had been a period of preeducation, pre-Christian influence, preindustrialization, and largely preremoval from their ancestral land. It was unique also in that the ruling chiefs were full bloods of the old tribal upbringing, as contrasted to the post-Revolution Cherokee leadership in which the mixed-blood offspring of the British era, many of whom spoke or wrote English, played a major role in Cherokee history.

Even some full bloods had begun to see the value of formal education. The making of pacts confirmed in writing alone fostered the need.

Cherokee leaders found that they were at serious disadvantage in dealing with whites on important matters affecting their homeland and existence. Verbal agreements, they discovered, did not work in their favor. Even more primary was the ability to count and measure when bartering and receiving promised goods. "Do what we can," Attakullakulla insisted, "the white People will cheat us in our Weights and Measures, and make them less. What is it a Trader can not do? They cheat us in the Measure of our Powder. Some of the white Men borrowed by Yeard (yardstick) and cut it, and then gave it back for which I was blamed."[20]

Oconostota, too, came to see the need for education among his people. When a son was born to Alexander Cameron and his Cherokee wife, the chief told John Stuart, "We desire that he may educate the boy like the white people, and cause him to be able to read and write, that he may resemble both white and red, and live among us when his father is dead."[21]

In 1756 commissioners Randolph and Byrd, addressing the Cherokees' concern that they were not getting all of their goods, broached the subject of schooling for some Cherokees:

> To remove these Jealousies for the future we would fain have you send some of your Boys to Virginia, where we have a School [William and Mary, then known as the Brafferton] erected for their Education. We promise you that all due Care will be taken of them, both with Respect to their Cloaths and Learning. When they have come to be Men, they will be acquainted with the Manners and Customs of us both, and our Children will naturally place such Confidence in them as to employ them in settling any Disputes that may hereafter arise.[22]

The Cherokees did not respond to this offer, and nothing had yet been done by 1765. The chiefs who were in London that year said they had often heard that learned people would be sent to help their children read, write, and understand things better, but no one had yet appeared.[23]

Actually it was to the Crown's advantage, as well as the traders', for the Indian to remain untutored, and the British gave no further consideration to his education. For the most part, the native state of the Indian belied his innate intelligence and retarded the interest of whites in providing him formal education. It would be left to the altruistic missionaries to initiate schooling among the tribes.

During all of the British colonial period, only one Christian missionary spent any appreciable time among them. A Jesuit priest named Priber came among the Cherokees in 1736 and spent five years with them, learning their language and serving as an aid to the Cherokee emperor. He wrote a Cherokee dictionary and even drew up a plan of government for the tribe.

Fearing Priber's pro-French influence, the English sent an officer to the Cherokee country to arrest him. This effort was thwarted by the Cherokees; but on a trip to Alabama, the priest was captured and sent off to Georgia. There he was thrown into prison, where he eventually died.[24]

Some small amount of Christianizing resulted from the private influence of intermarriage. Lah-to-tau-yie, a full-blood Cherokee woman, was converted to Christianity by her husband, Edward Graves. She in turn told Biblical stories to other Cherokees and even held prayer meetings in her cabin.[25] By the end of the colonial period, however, no denomination had yet established itself inside the Cherokee territory.

When the British first appeared on the American scene, the Cherokee men were primarily hunters. They scoured the abundant forests to obtain meat from a wide variety of animal and fowl life. The women, largely, planted and harvested maize, beans, and squash and collected nuts, seeds, and berries. They also manufactured baskets, mats, sieves, and some pottery for their domestic use.

As their recorded treaty discussions reveal, conservation of their vast land area was not a prime concern for Cherokee chiefs until near the end of the British period. Treaty considerations were mostly related to war-and-peace alliances and trade. The loss of Cherokee land was commenced under the British, who undertook several treaties to secure large tracts of Cherokee land. But the Cherokees did not yet comprehend the threat they faced. When their chiefs signed the Treaty of Lochaber in 1770, they were still willing to give up most of their Virginia land in order to remove themselves from white encroachment.

At that time white settlers had not crossed the Allegheny Mountains in such great numbers. Following the Lochaber treaty, however, an avalanche of emigrants poured into western Virginia. Still, it was not until the American Revolution began that the loss of their hunting grounds and game became a serious concern to the Cherokees. It was then that the Cherokee chiefs became acutely aware that the appetite of whites for land under the new American states and federal government was insatiable.

Old Corn Tassel, one of the last important chiefs during the British tenure in America, made a poignant statement on the matter at the Treaty of Long Island in 1777:

The great God of Nature has placed us in different situations. It is true that he has endowed you with many superior advantages; but he had not created us to be your slaves. *We are a separate people!* He has given each their lands, under distinct considerations and circumstances: he has stocked yours with cows, ours with buffaloe; yours with hogs, ours with bear; yours with sheep, ours with deer. He has, indeed, given you an advantage in this, that your cattle are tame and domestic while ours are wild and demand not only a larger space for range, but art [skill] to hunt and kill them; they are, nevertheless, as much our property as other animals are yours, and ought not to be taken away without our consent, or for something equivalent.[26]

James Adair, who published his history of American Indians in 1775, saw the colonial period as extremely destructive of Cherokee society, largely because of "a long train of wrong measures, the consequences of which were severely felt by a number of high assessed, ruined, and bleeding innocents."[27] Chief William P. Ross described it as a "period when tribe was against tribe and nation against nation, when cunning met cunning, cruelty retaliated cruelty, and perfidy circumvented perfidy and deeds of heroism defied the sword, the scalping knife, the fagot and torture."[28]

There were, of course, many ways in which the British period exercised positive effects upon the Cherokees and their way of life. One was the consolidation of the Cherokee people in a political sense. Under the British, the tribe began to evolve from a loose confederacy of widely separated villages controlled by local chiefs into a more unified nation organized under a principal leader and subordinate chiefs. The emergence into a single political unit was further impelled by the need for collective protection from white pressure.

As it was with all native tribes, the discovery and appreciation of the white man's manufactured goods exerted immeasurable influence upon the Cherokees. At first, the items brought to their villages were mostly trinkets and wampum, the strings of colorful glass beads that fascinated and delighted Indian people and became a standard friendship offering among the tribes. And, of course, there was the rum and whiskey, which enhanced the white trader's advantage in dealing with the Indians.

Trade was a potent weapon for colonial governors. A threat to cut off trading relations was often enough to bring a chief into line. But by the time of the American Revolution, the Cherokees still had little to offer for trade other than beeswax, bear oil, and the pelts they took from animals—"leather," as it was referred to by the British, who purchased it by the pound weight. The Cherokees had eventually become rich in horses, that is until they were forced to eat many during their war with England. But the Indian horses were not effective trade items because of their tendency to return to their native range. Trader Adair wrote: "Before the Indian trade was ruined by our left-handed policy, and the natives were corrupted by the liberality of our dim-sighted politicians, the Cheerake were frank, sincere, and industrious. Their towns then, abounded with hogs, poultry, and every thing sufficient for the support of a reasonable life, which the traders purchased at an easy rate, to their mutual satisfaction . . ."[29]

Traders usually owned the day in dealing with the Indians: "The Traders are very cross with us Indians," Attakullakulla had complained to Governor Glen. "We dare not speak to them. If we do, they take our Skins, and throw them on the Ground, and deny us Goods. If we do not give them their Price we must go without any."[30]

Adair opined that cheap goods made the Indians proud and lazy; but a far worse consequence took place about 1738. Goods arriving from New Guinea via Charlestown infected the Cherokees with smallpox, wiping out an estimated half of their population. In addition, it was reported that many of them became so despondent over their disfiguration from the disease that they committed suicide.[31]

Under the British the establishment of trading factories in the Lower Towns and their spread northward into the backcountry increased the Cherokee dependency upon trade goods. They were now provided metal-bladed hatchets to replace the old stone-headed war axes, working tools such as hoes and adzes, beautiful cloth material, foodstuff such as sugar and coffee, and an increasing number of other items new to their world—even hats, shoes, breeches, and shirts that effected a trend toward dressing like white men.

The development of a sociopolitical group of mixed bloods within the Cherokee Nation combined with other factors, such as the diminishing of tribal hunting grounds and loss of game, to effect significant cultural and economic changes. Both their food supply and their products of trade diminished as their residential and hunting ground areas lessened. Under the British the Cherokees had already begun to show an inclination for planting, the cultivation of livestock and poultry, and other adaptations of white existence.

It is believed that the Cherokees obtained their first firearms before 1700 and that guns were owned by half of the Upper and Middle Cherokees by 1715.[32] A rifle that could strike a deer or an enemy from a distance was a warrior's most prized possession. At first the British were reluctant to place explosive weaponry into the hands of Indians, and most guns and ammunition were obtained from the French to the south. In order to win the friendship and alliance of the Cherokees, however, the British relaxed their restriction. In 1751, Raven asked Governor Glen for fifty-eight more guns "for his own People, not for the Lower People," as protection against the Creeks. The governor refused, saying they had been given 113 guns already. Two years later, Glen promised a delegation of Cherokees who were visiting Charleston that he would give them the arms and ammunition they requested and a cart to carry them in.[33]

Thus, during the British colonial period the Cherokees had undergone considerable change. Even as they became more advanced in both their hunting and warring capacities, their modes of livelihood and governing structure were adapted to English influence. With the beginning of the American Revolution in 1776, however, Cherokee leaders would find themselves faced with the difficult decision of where to place their loyalty. Further, they would have to deal with the new masters of the Atlantic seaboard, who would prove to be even more demanding of Cherokee lands than their European cousins.

CHAPTER 5

A Wall to the Skies

In late May of 1777, forty chiefs, warriors, and women of the Cherokee Nation arrived at the capital of Virginia: Williamsburg. The Indians made their camp on the green of the capitol under the curious gaze of villagers. Eventually the leading men, headed by Oconostota and Atta-kullakulla, were given an audience inside the stately building. There the Cherokee leaders told Gov. Patrick Henry and the Virginia privy council that they had come to make a peaceful arrangement by which a boundary line could be drawn to prevent the intrusion of whites onto their lands. After the talks were agreeably concluded, the Cherokees entertained the public by holding a dance on the capitol grounds.[1]

Even then the Revolutionary War was underway, and armed brigs blocked the James River against British intrusion. At this point in history, as the United States was being born, the native Cherokees held to an empery that included portions of what are now the states of Virginia, West Virginia, Kentucky, Tennessee, North Carolina, South Carolina, Georgia, and Alabama. In little more than half a century, the Cherokee homeland would be reduced to a small reserve in far western North Carolina, and the main segment of their population removed to what is now eastern Oklahoma.

The ending of British colonial rule in America deeply affected Indian relations. More and more Indian matters were decided by separate colonial governors, whose decisions were enforced largely by colonial militia. Not only did the personality and character of the governors create wide variance in Indian policy, but the actions of poorly disciplined, Indian-hating militiamen often exacerbated the conflict between races. Now Indian leaders would begin to deal face to face with white leaders on a far more personal level.

During their reign, the British had whittled away at the Cherokee lands with treaties, each of which subtracted more and more Cherokee territory. Thus far, with such an abundance of land and with other problems to attend to, the chiefs had not become concerned. During the

1770s, private entrepreneurs began to take a hand in this reduction. Among them was Jacob Brown, who traded a packhorse load of trade goods for a Cherokee tract along the Watauga and Nolichucky Rivers in 1772.

But an even more significant purchase of Cherokee territory was made in 1775 by the Transylvania Company, an enterprise organized by Richard "Carolina Dick" Henderson. This affair would eventually awaken the Cherokees to the acute threat they faced from white advancement and the inevitable loss of their hunting grounds, upon which they still depended greatly for sustenance and raw materials for trade.

Henderson employed Daniel Boone to make an exploratory tour of that portion of the Cherokee Nation that is now Kentucky and central Tennessee. He then persuaded the Cherokee chiefs to treat with him and others of his company at Sycamore Shoals in far eastern Tennessee during March 1775. There he plied the chiefs, including the old and nearly blind Oconostota, who had now become the principal chief of the Cherokees, and Attakullakulla, with generous supplies of whiskey.

A deposition by John Reid, who attended the meeting, stated that he found the chiefs all drunk—that when Oconostota's wife saw the treaty document, she was so upset she went to talk to other chiefs about it. Another witness stated that interpreter James Vann stayed the hands of both Oconostota and Raven Warrior as they prepared to sign, cautioning them to take care of what they were about to do.[2]

The Henderson treaty called for the Cherokees to give up vast amounts of land in exchange for guns, ammunition, blankets, beads, and trinkets to the value of fifty thousand dollars. Dragging Canoe (Tsiyugunsini), son of Attakullakulla, was particularly incensed about the sale of Cherokee hunting grounds. He angrily refused to sign, telling the whites that a dark cloud hung over that land. Stamping the earth, he promised that it would be "bloody ground" and difficult to settle.[3]

The Transylvania purchase marked not only the beginning of Cherokee resistance to the loss of their land but also the decline of tribal influence for the old chiefs. Led by Dragging Canoe, a younger generation of Cherokees would take over as the tribal war leaders. Hot blooded and ready to fight to keep their lands, these young chiefs held an intense enmity for white settlers—the Wataugans, or "Long Knives," as the Indians called them—who had begun to settle west of the Appalachian Mountains along the Holston, Nolichucky, French Broad, Clinch, and Watauga Rivers of eastern Tennessee.

It was partially coincidental that the Cherokee clash with the Wataugans developed at the same time the American Revolution erupted. The two conflicts soon became incorporated, however, by the desire of the British to establish an Indian threat to the Americans.[4] Early in 1776, a party of Cherokees made a long trip to St. Augustine, Florida, to procure arms and ammunition from Superintendent Stuart. In support of their request, they indicated their allegiance to Stuart and the king.[5]

Stuart responded by dispatching a caravan of sixty horses loaded with arms and ammunition to the Cherokees, under escort of his brother Henry Stuart. Dragging Canoe provided an eighty-man warrior escort up the Tennessee River. Soon after the arrival of Stuart, the Cherokees held a big council at Chota. There the young chiefs under Dragging Canoe issued a letter denying that they had sold or given up any of their land to the Wataugans. They demanded removal of the white settlers. "They gave us guns," Oconostota said on one occasion, denying that there had been an absolute sale, "but they made a great deal of grain, raised stock, and destroyed our hunting ground."[6] Therefore, he told the Wataugans, he could not take pay for the lands, only the rent. Dragging Canoe raged against the Wataugans and threatened to attack the white settlements. He was opposed by Attakullakulla, Oconostota, and Nancy Ward, who now participated in Cherokee war councils.

Dragging Canoe might have been restrained had it not been for the arrival at Chota of a deputation of northern Indians who came painted black for war. They indicated their desire to persuade the Cherokees to join them and the British in warring against the Americans. Among the visitors were Delawares, a tribe the Cherokees looked upon with great respect as their "grandfathers."

Attakullakulla and Oconostota were silent throughout the meeting and at the end refused to accept the war belts offered by the northern Indians. Nancy Ward, too, remained unreceptive to the idea of going to war. But the fiery Dragging Canoe was joined by other war-ready young men in striking the village war pole. Among them were men such as Doublehead and John Watts, the brother and nephew of Old Tassel. The two would ultimately play prominent roles in the Cherokee wars.[7]

To prove his intentions, Dragging Canoe led a war party off to the Kentucky road. He returned with four fresh scalps, which he presented to the northern Indians when they departed. He then began making preparations for a three-pronged attack on the white settlements. By

*The only known image
of Nancy Ward is this
statue that once stood in
the Arnwine graveyard
north of Knoxville but
has since vanished.*

Carolyn Foreman,
Indian Women Chiefs.

plan he would lead the major strike along the Holston of eastern
Tennessee and southwestern Virginia; Old Abram of Chilhowie would
lead a war party up the Watauga; and Raven of Chota would attack an
area known as Carter's Valley in present Hawkins County, Tennessee.[8]

Desiring to protect those whites who had shown friendship for the
Cherokees, Nancy Ward secretly divulged the war plans to some traders
who were at Chota. They quickly carried the word to the white settlements. The Wataugans, forewarned of Cherokee threats against them,
had already begun building forts, sending their families off to places of
safety, and rounding up Tories who might join the Indians against them.
Capt. Nathaniel Gist, then working for the British, had been sent to the
Nolichucky region for the very purpose of recruiting the Tories.[9]

The entire Indian force moved eastward to the Nolichucky, where
Raven broke off toward the Holston. Dragging Canoe and Abram continued on to jointly attack a civilian post. Finding the place deserted,
they burned it and then divided their forces. Dragging Canoe, with nearly
two hundred warriors, headed north for the settlements on the Holston.

The militiamen at Fort Lee were waiting for them, as was a like force
at Island Flats near present Kingsport. After a small skirmish with an

advance unit of some twenty warriors on July 20, the militia fell back to a stronger position. From there they successfully repulsed Dragging Canoe's attack, killing thirteen Cherokees and wounding others. When Dragging Canoe himself was wounded in the hip by a ball, he ordered a withdrawal. His men fell upon the isolated cabins in the region, looting, burning, and taking the scalps of eighteen people.[10]

After leaving Dragging Canoe, Abram continued along the west side of the Appalachians. His force of nearly one hundred men moved in small squads toward Fort Caswell on the Watauga River, where they reunited. Early on the morning of July 21, they made a whooping charge on the fort, being driven back with a considerable loss. Instead of renewing the costly attack, Abram placed the fort under siege for nearly two weeks before retiring.

Raven fared little better than the others. He broke his warrior band of a hundred or so into small groups and fanned out to ravage homesteads along the Clinch River into Virginia. They burned cabins, destroyed livestock, and committed some murders before returning to Chota.

The Cherokees under Abram returned home to Tuskegee with two prisoners. One of them was Mrs. William Bean, whom Abram's warriors had captured en route to Caswell; the other was a young boy named Samuel Moore, who had left the safety of the fort to find wood. The boy was tortured and eventually put to death in the terrible old tribal way— by burning at the stake. The same fate almost befell Mrs. Bean. She, too, was taken to a burning mound; but Nancy Ward interceded, took the woman into her home, and eventually saw to her safe return to her family. It was said that while in the Beloved Woman's home, Mrs. Bean taught Nancy Ward how to make butter and cheese.[11]

Militia forces from Georgia, South Carolina, North Carolina, and Virginia struck back in retaliation for this outbreak by the Cherokees. In one attack, a unit of two hundred Georgians captured and burned several Lower Towns on the Chattahoochee and Tugaloo Rivers. Other abandoned towns near Fort Prince George were ravaged by a larger force of South Carolinians, who then joined with two thousand militiamen from North Carolina to render death and destruction among the Middle Towns. Still another army of eighteen hundred Virginians marched on the Overhill Cherokees and easily overran the towns and destroyed large supplies of foodstuff. The Cherokees, driven from their homeland, fled south into the Creek country, to Florida, or to the safety of the woods.[12]

The atrocities that whites claimed the Indians had committed against them were matched by ruthless murder and even torture of Indian women and children by the moblike militiamen.[13] The Cherokees were forced to sue for peace on two fronts. Even as a Cherokee delegation was visiting Williamsburg in May 1777, a group of Lower Cherokees was making a treaty of peace with South Carolina and Georgia at Dewit's Corner, South Carolina. This treaty, by which the Lower Cherokees ceded all of their land in South Carolina, was signed by Ostenaco and eight other chiefs.[14]

The Treaty of Long Island that followed in July at Fort Patrick Henry on the Holston River was attended by authorities of Virginia and North Carolina. Nathaniel Gist, now on the side of the United States, was sent out to the Cherokee towns to bring in the Cherokee chiefs. A celebration was held by the Americans on July 4, it being explained to the Indians that the day marked their independence from Great Britain. The treaty council was almost canceled, however, when an unidentified white man murdered a Cherokee named Big Bullet.

Though Attakullakulla and Oconostota were present, Corn Tassel and Raven spoke for the Cherokee Nation.[15] A stout, mild-mannered but resolute man with a round face and a pleasant countenance, Tassel was noted for his sagacity and profundity of thought. He was also widely reputed for his honesty, one observer noting that "through a long and useful life, he was never known to stoop to a falsehood."[16] As one who sought the best for his people through peace, there is no doubt that Corn Tassel (or Old Tassel as he is also known on record) was one of the most beloved of all the Cherokee chiefs.

In his talks, Tassel stressed the Cherokees' desire for peace but expressed great reluctance to accept the new boundary lines drawn up by the commissioners. He said he suspected they were asking for so much land so that he would refuse, which would give them an excuse for more war. Tassel asked them to write a letter about the matter and send it to Gen. George Washington by Colonel Gist. A delegate from North Carolina objected to contacting Washington, saying that this was a matter between the Indians and North Carolina alone. A special demand was made that no white men be allowed to settle on the favored site of Great Island, opposite Fort Henry—no one except Gist, who was married (in Cherokee terms) to Tassel's sister Wurteh, mother of the famed Sequoyah.[17]

The North Carolinians further refused to offer any payment at all for Cherokee lands on the grounds that their state had already gone to enough expense in protecting their settlements during the war. The Virginia representative offered two hundred head of breeding cows and a hundred sheep in compensation for Cherokee land in his state. This offer was accepted by Raven after consultation with Tassel and other chiefs. Raven said he wanted the new boundary line to be "as a wall to the skies, so that it should be out of the power of all people to pass it."[18]

William Tatham was present at the Long Island council and recorded Tassel's speech to the Americans, answering their demand for more cessions of their territory with great dignity and clarity of logic.

> It is a little surprising, that when we entered into treaties with our brothers, their whole cry is *more land!* Indeed, formerly it seemed to be a matter of formality with them to demand what they knew we durst not refuse. But on the principles of fairness, of which we have received assurances during the conducting of the present treaty, and in the name of free will and equality, I must reject your demands.
>
> Indeed, much has been advanced on the want of what you term civilization among the Indians; and many proposals have been made to us to adopt your laws, your religion, your manners and your customs. But we confess that we do not yet see the propriety, or practicability of such a reformation, and should be better pleased with beholding the good effect of these doctrines in your own practices than with hearing you talk about them, or reading your papers upon such subjects.[19]

Oconostota was the lead signer of the chiefs, followed by Tassel, Raven, and eighteen others, including Attakullakulla. This was essentially the last important diplomatic involvement for both Oconostota and Attakullakulla. The former resigned as a chief in July 1772 and died in the spring 1773. Attakullakulla died, it is believed, around 1780 or 1781. The destiny of the Cherokee Nation had been passed on to a new generation of younger leaders.[20]

By the Treaty of Long Island, the Cherokees were forced to give up all of their land in upper east Tennessee and western North Carolina. Noticeably, Dragging Canoe, who now claimed that Oconostota had offered a reward to have him killed, was not one of those who signed.[21] Declaring the older chiefs to be nothing less than "Virginians and rogues," he led a number of Overhill chiefs in abandoning their towns along the Little Tennessee and establishing several new towns farther to the south along the Tennessee River.

Following Dragging Canoe with the main force of Cherokee warriors were such notable chiefs as Bloody Fellow (Nenetooyah, Nenetuah),

Glass (Tauquotihee), and Middlestriker (Jahleoonoyehka). From this remote area, the dissident element of the Cherokee Nation raided frontier settlements in Georgia, Tennessee, and the Carolinas. They soon became known by the dreaded name of "Chickamaugan Cherokees."

An invitation was issued by the governor of Virginia, Thomas Jefferson, to Tassel and other Cherokee chiefs to visit the Continental Congress. However, before this could happen, in April 1779, a militia army comprising Virginia and Watauga men under Col. Evan Shelby came down the Tennessee River in canoes as far as Chilhowie. At the time, all of the fighting men of the Cherokee towns were with Dragging Canoe warring in Georgia and South Carolina.

The militia force burned eleven or more villages of the peaceful northern Cherokees, including some one thousand homes, and destroyed an estimated fifty thousand bushels of corn. At Talassee they captured the baggage, letters, copies of treaties, and "other archives of the nation" belonging to Oconostota.[22]

In the fall of 1780 Col. Arthur Campbell and militia leader John Sevier led two hundred mounted men on an incursion to penetrate the area and ravage the Cherokee settlements. At the same time, a force of four hundred men from Georgia struck other Cherokee Lower Towns.[23] During his campaign, Campbell was visited in his camp by the "famous Indian woman Nancy Ward." Campbell later noted: "She gave us various intelligence, and made an overture in behalf of some of the Chiefs for peace; to which I then evaded giving an explicit answer, as I wished first to visit the vindictive part of the nation, mostly settled at Hiwassee and Chistowee (Chestowee), and to distress the nation as much as possible by destroying their habitations and provisions."[24]

Col. William Christian reported that the Cherokees were in desperate condition. Many had no clothing, except some old bearskins, and so little to eat he feared they would die of hunger. There were numerous widows and fatherless children.[25] Tassel sent a letter to Gov. Alexander Martin of North Carolina imploring him to show his people mercy: "We are a poor distressed people, that is in great trouble, and we hope you, our Elder Brother, will take pity on us and do us justice. Your people from Nolichuckey are daily pushing us out of our lands . . . We have done nothing to offend our Elder Brother since the last Treaty and why should our Elder Brother want to quarrel with us?"[26]

Destruction of the Chickamaugan towns—plus his people's suspicion that the towns were infested with witches[27]—caused Dragging Canoe to move still farther down the Tennessee River and establish five new towns grouped about the northern end of Lookout Mountain, where present Tennessee, Alabama, and Georgia meet, the site of present Chattanooga. These included the towns of Nickajack, Running Water, Lookout Town, Long Island, and Crowtown. The new locations were less accessible by land and protected from intrusion by the famous Suck and the Narrows of the Tennessee River. From this base, Dragging Canoe and his warriors raided the American frontier settlements. Eventually, the Cherokees would occupy other towns, such as Creek Path, Willstown, Turkeytown, and Doublehead's Town, in northern Alabama on lands once held by the Creeks.[28]

Even as the Chickamaugans continued their war against frontier whites, Tassel and his chiefs of the Upper Towns continued to work for peace. During the fall of 1773, he and Hanging Maw (Scholauetta, sometimes called Hanging Man) visited the home of Col. Joseph Martin at Sullivan, Tennessee, hoping to arrange a visit to the Virginia Assembly when it met.[29] Martin was not there, and the chief returned home. The problem of white encroachment continued until Tassel wrote to Governor Martin in exasperation, "I am going to speak to you once more. I hope you will hear me . . . We fear you have throwed us away."[30]

It became more and more difficult for Tassel and the other chiefs to keep the peace, particularly with the formation of the unrecognized state of Franklin by the Wataugans under the flamboyant John Sevier, who had become known to his followers as "Nolichucky Jack." The Franklin men laid claim to all of the Cherokee lands north of the Little Tennessee River and aggressively promoted settlement of the area. Whites now began to clear land and build their houses virtually to the edge of the Cherokee's beloved village of Chota.

CHAPTER 6

New Elder Brother

To this point the Cherokees had had to deal with individual colony-states both in war and treaty making. The United States entered into its first treaty negotiations with the Cherokees at Hopewell, South Carolina, in November 1785. Though he worked constantly for peace, Corn Tassel demonstrated his ability to stand up firmly for the rights of his people. In his opening speech, he told the commissioners:

> I am made of this earth, on which the great man above placed me, to possess it; and what I am about to tell you, I have had in my mind for many years.
>
> This land we are now on, is the land we were fighting for, during the late contest, and the great man made it for us to subsist upon. You must know the red people are the aborigines of this land, and that it is but a few years since the white people found it out. I am of the first stock, as the commissioners know, and a native of this land; and the white people are now living on it as our friends.[1]

When the commissioners attempted to defend the Henderson Watauga purchase, Tassel defied them: "I know that Richard Henderson says he purchased the land at Kentucky as far south as Cumberland, but he is a rogue and a liar. He requested us to let him have a little land on Kentucky river, for his cattle and horses to feed on, and we consented."[2]

He charged that Oconostota had not signed the treaty, that Henderson had put the chief's mark there himself. Tassel was particularly concerned about the settlement of almost three thousand whites in the fork of the French Broad and Holston Rivers. He insisted that the settlers should be removed. The commissioners said that the Cherokees should have had the British do it at the start. Tassel countered that argument by asking, "Are Congress, who conquered the King of Great Britain, unable to remove those people?"[3]

Nancy Ward also addressed the commissioners, saying:

> I am fond of hearing that there is a peace, and I hope you have now taken us by the hand in real friendship. I have a pipe and a little

tobacco to give the commissioners to smoke in friendship. I look on you and the red people as my children. Your having determined on peace is most pleasing to me, for I have seen much trouble during the late war. I am old, but I hope yet to bear children, who will grow up and people our nation, as we are now to be under the protection of Congress, and shall have no more disturbances. [She then presented a string, a little pipe, and some tobacco to the commissioners.] The talk I have given, is from the young warriors I have raised in my town, as well as myself. They rejoice that we have peace, and we hope the chain of friendship will never more be broke. [She put forth a string of beads.][4]

By the Treaty of Hopewell, the Cherokees accepted themselves to be under the protection (a white euphemism for "under the rule"—they would get scant protection) of the United States and agreed to an exchange of prisoners. A new definition of the Cherokee lands was determined, and the United States promised that no whites would be permitted to settle on them. A unique provision of the Hopewell agreement gave the Indians the right to send a deputy to the U.S. Congress to ensure justice for them. Corn Tassel was the lead signatory, followed by thirty-six others.

As with all other treaties, Hopewell failed to resolve the essential problem of white intrusion onto Cherokee land. Conflicts between Indians and frontier whites continued. In August 1786 Sevier, acting as governor of Franklin, organized a militia force of 250 men. Under the command of colonels William Cocke and Alexander Outlaw, the militia marched to Coyatee, burned the council house, and destroyed the corn of those whom they believed were responsible for some recent depredations.

After meting out this punishment, the Franklin men went on to Chota. There they held a council with Tassel and his chiefs, falsely accusing them of killing Colonels John Donelson and William Christian. In truth, the two men had been burned at the stake by Ohio River Indians in 1782. "I loved Col. Christian, and he loved me," Tassel said. "He was killed going the other way over the big river."[5]

Cocke and Outlaw stated further that North Carolina had sold them all the country on the north side of the Tennessee and Holston Rivers. If any Cherokee interfered with white settlement north of the Little Tennessee, they said, the perpetrators' town would be burned.

Tassel refused to concede the Franklin claim to the land. "You say that North Carolina sold you the land over the river . . . I never heard

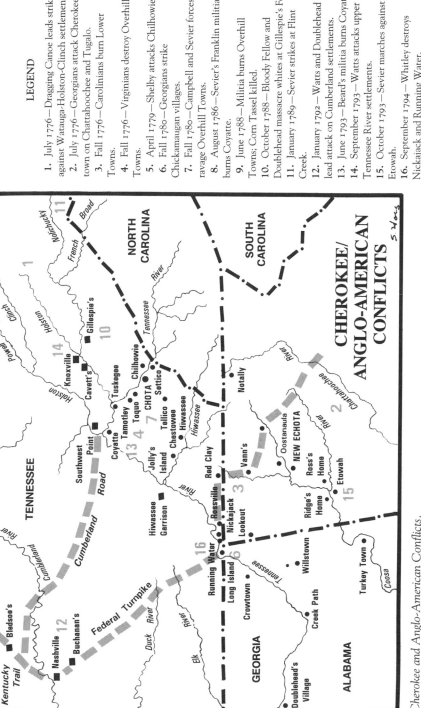

Cherokee and Anglo-American Conflicts.

of your great Council selling you the land you speak of. I talked last fall with the Great Men from Congress, but they told me nothing of this."[6] He said he intended to talk to Congress about it again, but the Franklin men refused to listen. At virtual gunpoint they forced Tassel and Hanging Maw to sign the so-called Treaty of Coyatee, by which the Cherokees supposedly surrendered all their remaining land north of the Little Tennessee.[7] The illicit treaty only increased invasion of the Cherokee country by whites. A Franklin land office began selling homesteads on the very banks of the Little Tennessee at forty shillings per hundred acres.

Colonel Martin, a Hopewell treaty commissioner, protested to no avail. In June 1787, Virginia governor Edmund Randolph wrote the Cherokee principal chief a harsh letter accusing the Cherokees of burning a white woman to death at Chickamauga. He threatened retaliation by the sword and by fire. Tassel replied immediately, denying the charge and saying that such a thing had not happened in the Cherokee Nation in the past ten years. The governor, he said, should inquire into matters before making such rash charges. "I suppose," Tassel observed, "some person has told my Elder Brother this in order to have us driven off, as they may take what little land we have left, which is very little, not sufficient to keep us much longer from perishing."[8]

In another talk to the governor, Chief Long Fellow (Tuskegetchee or Tuskegatahu) said that he had formerly been a Chickamaugan but Colonel Martin had persuaded him to come north and keep the peace, which he had done for the past six winters. He said he commanded seven towns, while thirteen others listened to him. "I have long taken the Virginians by the hand," he said, "and have at this time one of their medals around my neck. I should be sorry to throw that off, but you suffer your people to settle to our towns and say nothing about it."[9]

These talks and that of Chief King Fisher (Chutlob) were carried to Randolph, who was in Philadelphia, by a Cherokee war captain named Sconetooyah. He was accompanied by trader-interpreter Alexander Dromgoole, who had married a sister of Corn Tassel's nephew, John Watts (Kunoskeskie). On Dromgoole's urging, Randolph sent a reply and gifts—a silver pipe and a small medal.[10]

From Philadelphia, Dromgoole and Sconetooyah went on to New York, at that time the U.S. capital, to demand that the Treaty of Hopewell be observed and white infringement on Cherokee land be stopped. The secretary of war gave them reassurances of help, along with presents and medals to take back to the Cherokee chiefs.

Tassel also appealed to the governors of North Carolina and

Virginia. In a letter from Chota on September 19, 1787, he pleaded for them to remove the disorderly whites that had settled within sight of Cherokee towns. "I am an old man and almost thrown away by my elder Brother," he wrote. "The ground I stand on is very slippery, tho' I still hope my elder Brother will hear me and take pity. We were all made by the same Great Being above."[11]

But try as he would, Tassel could not hold back the tide of whites spreading daily onto the Indian lands. Nor could he have prevented the disaster that befell him and other chiefs of the Upper Towns during the summer of 1788. According to Colonel Martin, who was in Chota at the time, the trouble began when a party of whites killed an old Cherokee woman and wounded two Indian children without provocation and then plundered a nearby Cherokee town.[12]

Chief Hanging Maw, suspecting treachery from them, placed Martin and the son of Nolichucky Jack, who was also in Chota, under guard for three days. Later, when some whites appeared and began firing on Chota, all of the Cherokee families fled the town, taking down the white flag that had flown there for three years. Martin and young Sevier also departed.

In the meantime, a command of 150 mounted frontiersmen under Sevier, organized for the purpose of chastising the Indians, was on its way down the Tennessee River. As the Wataugans headed for the Upper Towns, they were met by Martin, who tried to dissuade Sevier from attacking the Cherokee towns. But Sevier would not be deterred. He had avowed to drive all the Cherokees out of their settlements east of the Cumberland Mountains. Marching as far as the Hiwassee River, the militia attacked several undefended Cherokee towns. They killed a number of Indians and drove others into the mountains "without the loss of a man, horse or gun."[13] Reported to be either evacuated or in flames were Talassee, Hiwassee, Chilhowie, Settico, Chota, Tellico, Big Island, and Coyatee.

Sevier's campaign of destruction and murder reaped a gory retribution against a white frontier family. A family named Kirk resided at a forward settlement on Little River twelve miles southwest of present Knoxville. It was visited by a Cherokee named Slim Tom, who asked for something to eat. The father and one son of the thirteen-member family were away, but the family knew Slim Tom and gave him food. Seeing the house to be poorly defended, Slim Tom left and returned with a party of friends to attack it. All of the Kirk family who were present were killed, their bodies left strewn about the yard of their home.

Learning of this on his return march, Sevier turned eastward along the Little Tennessee to Toquo, where Corn Tassel resided. In front of his home, Tassel flew a U.S. flag given him during the Hopewell council, signifying the federal protection promised by the treaty. While Sevier was reportedly away on business, Maj. James Hubbard came to Tassel's house and requested that the chief attend a council with other Cherokee chiefs.

The meeting was to be held in the home of Chief Abram (or Abraham, Ooskwha) at Chilhowie, which was located just upstream on the opposite side of the river. Tassel agreed and went with the militiaman, accompanied by an elder son. It was necessary to cross the river on a ferry to reach Abram's house, and in doing so Hubbard raised a white flag of truce.

The officer waited until all the chiefs were assembled in Abram's small house before he gave the sign for his men to take positions at all of the doors and windows. Then Hubbard called forth one of the men with him. It was John Kirk Jr., who had been away from home during his family's massacre. He stepped forth with a tomahawk in his hand, prepared to take his revenge.

Tassel knew there was no escape, that his end had come. He was old, and his elder brothers were throwing him away. He bowed his head and took the fatal blow from Kirk. One by one the chiefs were axed to death: Tassel; his son; and chiefs Fool Warrior, Long Fellow, and Abram, brother to Hanging Maw. Sevier's militia rode off leaving the bodies unburied.

The willingness to compromise and work out peaceful solutions had reaped only death for Corn Tassel and his chiefs and more encroachment onto the Cherokee homeland. Alexander McGillivray, the half-blood Creek leader, reacted with great anger when he learned of Tassel's murder. "That barbarian," he wrote, referring to Sevier, "I am told, is meditating another expedition for accomplishing the total extirpation of the Cherokees . . . Really, I don't know what to think of a government that is compelled to wink at such outrages."[14]

The *Maryland Gazette* angrily reported: "Indian chiefs remarkable for their good offices and fidelity, in the darkest situation of our affairs, raised a flag on their part, and came out; they came under the protection of a flag of truce, a protection inviolable even amongst the most barbarous people, sacred by the law and custom of nations, and by the consent of mankind in every age: But under this character, and with the sacred protection of a flag, they were attacked and murdered."[15]

When the Wataugans returned home, they were lauded with great acclaim. Sevier gained hero status on the frontier from his exploit. However, the Virginia legislature voted to make an inquiry into Sevier's actions at Chota, and in the U.S. Congress there were calls for posting troops at various places to help carry out the Treaty of Hopewell.[16] Absolutely nothing, however, was done to censure the Wataugans or protect the hapless northern Cherokees.

While most Wataugans basked in their victory, some realized that Sevier's attack would undoubtedly touch off a murderous war on the frontier. And it did. Anger at the Americans raged among the Lower Towns. Virtually all warrior-age Cherokees left the Upper Towns to join forces with Dragging Canoe in striking back.

In August a party of thirty-one men under Capt. John Fain rode unsuspectingly into abandoned Settico and began picking fruit from the trees then ready for harvest. They were suddenly attacked from all sides by Cherokee warriors and driven away after several were killed or wounded.[17]

On October 15, 1788, a Cherokee war party attacked a small settlement called Gillespie's Fort, recently established just below the mouth of Little River on the Holston. Led by Bloody Fellow, the Cherokees demanded that the occupants surrender. When the demand was rejected, the Cherokees stormed the fort, killing twenty-eight people, most of them women, and capturing others.

Bloody Fellow left behind a note for Sevier and Martin saying that the killing of women and children of the fort was unintended: "The Bloody Fellow's talk is that he is now upon his own ground. He is not like you are; for you kill women and children, and he does not . . . you beguiled the head man (Tassel), that was your friend and wanted to keep peace; but you began it, and this is what you get for it. When you move off the land, then we will make peace . . . Five thousand men is our number."[18]

Also signing the note were war captains Taken Out of the Water (Tekakisskee, Categiskey, Kettegiskey), Glass, and John Watts.[19] Watts had such a close attachment to Corn Tassel that he was known as Young Tassel. He was reported "to be in great trouble" about Tassel's murder. There were times when the memory of it affected him so that he could not speak in council.[20]

The chiefs and warriors of the Upper Towns met on November 1 at their town of Ustinaire and sent a letter to Joseph Martin, now a general at the head of North Carolina forces: "Your people provoked us first to war, by settling on our lands and killing our beloved men; however, we have laid by the hatchet, and are strongly for peace."[21]

Sevier, however, was still determined to carry the war to the Cherokees. In late 1788 he led a 450-man militia against the winter camp of Watts and other Cherokee leaders on Flint Creek in present Unicoi County, Tennessee. In a mounted charge against the Indian camp on January 10, 1789, the Wataugans killed a large number of warriors and captured twenty-seven women and children. Sevier used these to bargain for the return of the Gillespie's Fort captives and others.[22]

Following a Cherokee council in May 1789, Taken Out of the Water addressed a message to the president of the United States, imploring him to extend his pity toward his people: "we hope you won't let any people take any more [land] from us without our consent. We are neither birds nor fish; we can neither fly in the air, nor live under water . . . We are made by the same hand, and in the same shape with yourselves."[23]

The Chickamaugan Cherokees were now receiving support from both the Creeks and the Spanish, who then owned Florida as well as the Louisiana country. Seeing the American advancement as a threat to their interests, Spanish authorities willingly supplied the Chickamaugans with guns and ammunition. Conflicts between Indians and whites continued throughout the southern frontier.

The thrust of white intrusion extended even as far as Muscle Shoals on the Tennessee River in northwestern Alabama, where white men were attempting to establish a settlement. During March 1790, a party under a Major Doughty was ascending the Tennessee at that point. A party of Cherokee, Creek, and Shawnee Indians fired on them from the banks, killing six of the party and forcing them to turn about.[24]

During 1790 the United States bolstered its position by separating Tennessee from North Carolina and establishing the new division of Territory South of the Ohio River under Gov. William Blount. Even as it did so, Secretary of War Henry Knox was reporting to President Washington that more than five hundred families had intruded on Cherokee land in disgraceful violation of the Treaty of Hopewell.[25]

Blount sent word out to all of the Cherokee towns, calling for a new treaty council. It would convene in late June 1791 near White's Fort. Blount promised to make amends and right the wrongs done to the Cherokee Nation. His principal purpose was to eliminate the cause of friction between the Cherokees and whites. However, he did so not by removing the intruding whites but by securing title to the land upon which they had intruded.

Blount's emissaries were able to persuade even the Chickamaugan Cherokees to attend the meeting held on the high, tree-shaded banks of the Holston. Forty-two chiefs signed the treaty document. Dragging Canoe, who did not attend, was the significant exception. Leading the signers and indicating his position as principal chief was Boots (Chuleoah). Hanging Maw was next in line, while other notable names included Taken Out of the Water, King Fisher, Black Fox (Ennone or Inali), Bloody Fellow, Watts, and two Chickamaugans who would later play prominent roles in Cherokee affairs—Chuquilatague (Chequlalaga), better known as Doublehead, and Tahlonteskee (many variations but translated as the Common Disturber or Upsetter).[26] Both men were fierce warriors, but Doublehead—a short-statured, compact man with piercing eyes, commanding countenance, and explosive temperament—held a special penchant for violence.

Inking the pact as a witness was a man who would also become deeply entangled in the destiny of the Cherokees. He was John D. Chisholm (John Chisolm on the treaty), a red-headed Scotsman who had transported supplies and treaty presents to the council site for Blount and who served the governor on occasion as an emissary to the Indians. He would return with Blount to the treaty site the following year to help found the town of Knoxville.

The treaty—in addition to providing for the exchange of prisoners, permission for the Americans to build roads through Cherokee country and make use of the Tennessee River for navigation, and the usual promises of peace and Indian subservience to the United States—called for Cherokee cession of extensive territory in western North Carolina and eastern Tennessee. In return the Cherokees were to receive only a few supplies and an annuity of a thousand dollars.[27]

It did not take the Cherokees long to realize they had let themselves be badly swindled. As a result, Bloody Fellow, Northward (Nontuaka), and four other Cherokee chiefs arrived at Philadelphia on December 29 in the company of Indian agent Leonard Shaw, a young graduate of Princeton who had been assigned as the new U.S. agent to the Cherokees; interpreter James Carey, who had been captured as a boy and had been raised to manhood by Chief Little Turkey; and Jane Dougherty, the white wife of one of the chiefs.[28]

After they had been reclothed, the chiefs were taken to meet briefly with President Washington, who requested they conduct their business with the secretary of war. To Knox, the Cherokees complained that they had been tricked and bullied by Blount into signing and that the payment was much too small. Further, whites were already settling on land beyond the boundary set by the Holston treaty. "Among us," Bloody

Fellow pointed out, "we have two kings to look up to; but you have only one who, we hope, will extend his eye over all, both red and white. We have put ourselves under the protection of the United States, and from them only do we expect justice."[29]

The Cherokee insisted that the thousand dollars annually offered by the Holston treaty would not buy even a breech clout for each member of his nation. He would be satisfied, however, if they would give him half again as much, fifteen hundred dollars each year. Also, his people needed plows, hoes, cows, and other items with which they could plant corn and raise cattle.

Knox saw this as a small price to pay for the potential help of the Cherokees in fighting other tribes in the Ohio country, and he agreed to increase the annuity another five hundred dollars.[30] The chiefs were also given silver medals and decked out in scarlet coats trimmed with lace and bedecked with silver epaulets.

In signing the revised treaty agreement of 1792, Bloody Fellow was given the new name of Eskaqua (Iskaqua), or Clear Sky, and designated by authority of the president as General Eskaqua. The war chief left Philadelphia as a stout friend of the Americans, and the delegation returned home fully satisfied and pleased.

Still another peace move was made by the Cherokees when Hanging Maw, John Watts, and John Taylor visited Blount in Knoxville and gave him strong assurances of their peaceful intent.[31] Such was evident when Blount arrived at Coyatee (near the conflux of the Tennessee and Little Tennessee Rivers) to meet with them on May 20, 1792, and deliver the goods representing the first annual payment under the Treaty of Holston. Blount was met by a young warrior on horseback and asked to wait until his hosts were ready to receive him. After a short wait, he entered the town through a path made by two lines of some two thousand gala-dressed chiefs, warriors, and others representing both the Upper and Lower towns. Blount was greeted with shouts of joy and the firing of guns as he rode through the 300-yard corridor to where a house had been prepared for him. He described the scene that followed:

> At the house built there for my reception is erected the standard of the United States [a very elegant stand] on a high pole. To this they [the lower chiefs] were conducted by the Bloody Fellow and John Watts, Kittagesta and other chiefs and Captain Chisholm and [Leonard] Shaw walking side by side with the Bloody Fellow and Watts to the great joy of both parties, where volleys were fired by those from the lower towns in honor of it and returned by the upper . . . Chisholm declares he never saw more joy expressed by any people.[32]

The Coyatee meeting was a festival of eating, conversation, whiskey drinking to inebriation, dancing, and ball playing. A great deal of gambling was done on the games, even the chiefs staking their clothing down to their breech clouts on the events. Blount noted that Bloody Fellow recovered previous losses by pouring liquor into the best players among those opposing his group. His men remained sober.[33]

On the third day, Blount addressed the assembly. He enumerated a list of depredations that had been committed on the frontier from Knoxville to Nashville. The chiefs and warriors of the Lower Towns had arrived at Coyatee, their blackened bodies sprinkled with flour—indicating they had been at war but were now for peace. No longer did they have Dragging Canoe to lead them. The fiery Cherokee war chief had died at Lookout Town on March 1, 1792, shortly after returning from a visit to the Chickasaws regarding the formation of a general Indian confederacy.[34]

Blount spoke, saying that it had been reported to him that Glass, a Lower Town chief, had killed and scalped a woman and a child and taken the woman's eight-year-old daughter captive. The governor said that while he could not prove who committed these acts, he had ordered the militia to stand ready if they were continued. He requested the return of any captives held by the Cherokees, promising to deliver up a Cherokee boy who had been held by the whites.[35]

When he finished, Hanging Maw gave notice that the Cherokee National Council would meet in thirty nights at Estanaula and ordered all chiefs to be there without exception. They would then hear Bloody Fellow's account of his trip to Philadelphia and read the book that Knox had given them as a record of the meeting and agreements made there.

Breath, chief of Nickajack, said that he did not know who committed the crimes, but he promised that any prisoners held by the Lower Cherokees would be returned at Estanaula. Cherokee priest and chief of Lookout Town, Dick Justice (Dik-kek, or the Just, hence Dick Justice[36]), expressed concern over the depredations, saying he hoped they would be able to control their young men after the council.

Blount departed the following day with the feeling that Bloody Fellow and Watts, in particular, would prove to be "the champions of peace."[37] He was sorely mistaken, however, for during the ensuing days, the situation for the Chickamaugan Cherokees would undergo a drastic reversal from the promise of peace to the reality of bloody war.

CHAPTER 7

An Effort at Arms

The old chiefs could hold their councils and make their decisions, but the destiny of the Cherokees was now in the hands of a number of younger, more combative men. Many of these were mixed bloods who had been sired by Scot and English fathers some two or three decades earlier during British rule. Officers, soldiers, traders, emissaries, and other men of British origin often married or cohabited with Cherokee women. Often during the early period they did so with the daughters or sisters of Cherokee chiefs.

Some of these offspring would prove to be deadly enemies to the white blood that ran in their veins. This was particularly so in the case of three men, all of whom are said to have been blood related to Corn Tassel. These were John Watts, Doublehead, and Tahlonteskee.[1] Each would become notorious as a fierce opponent of the Americans. Still another was Bob Benge, the red-headed, half-blood son of trader John Benge, who married a niece of Corn Tassel and had been long among the Cherokees. Known as the Bench, he was said by Blount to have killed a large number of whites.[2]

John Watts was the son of a sister of Corn Tassel. Quite likely his father was the John Watts who served as an interpreter at the Cherokee treaty with the British at Augusta, Georgia, in 1763.[3] His contemporaries describe the Chickamaugan chief as an intelligent, clever, capable man who enjoyed eating, drinking, and jocular conversation. Unquestionably a leading character of the Cherokee Nation during the 1790s, he was an excellent orator with a personal magnetism that made him a natural leader.[4] Following the death of Dragging Canoe, Watts was elected as the head war chief of the Chickamaugan Cherokees.

On the day following Blount's departure from Coyatee, a letter arrived addressed to Bloody Fellow and Watts. It contained an invitation from a Spanish merchant, issued in the name of the Spanish governor, to visit Pensacola, Florida. The chiefs were to bring ten packhorses for transporting the arms, ammunition, and goods that the Spanish government wished to give them. It was further promised that the Spaniards would help the Cherokees win back the land the Americans had taken from them.

The two men lost no time in responding. Bloody Fellow said that he had been blind, but now his eyes were open. After going with Watts as far as the Coosa River, however, he evidently changed his mind again and turned back. Watts continued on with the ten packhorses accompanied by Tahlonteskee and Young Dragging Canoe, son of the deceased war chief.

At Pensacola, the Spanish governor entertained them and took them to see his storehouse of arms. He insisted that they should go to war and regain their lands from the Americans, who "first take your land, then treat with you, and give you little or nothing for it."[5] The Spaniard offered to provide all the arms and goods they needed. While there, Tahlonteskee painted himself black and raised the war whoop, declaring himself to be at war with the United States.[6]

Neither Watts, Tahlonteskee, nor Bloody Fellow were in attendance when the Cherokee National Council met at Estanaula on June 26, 1792. Little Turkey (Kanitta), now recognized as the Beloved Man, or principal chief, of the Cherokee Nation, presided over the meeting. Hanging Maw spoke for the northern towns as their Beloved Man, and Badger (Occunna) was the Beloved Man of the southern towns.

Also present were John D. Chisholm, representing Blount, and agent Leonard Shaw. In the absence of Bloody Fellow, it was left to Chief Northward to tell of the trip and the agreements made there. Following this, Shaw took the floor and read from the record book sent by Knox. He then presented Little Turkey with a large belt of white wampum as a token of friendship from President Washington.

On the following day, Shaw read a speech from President Washington, and Chisholm presented the Cherokee captive boy whom Blount had promised to return. After this, the Cherokee council withdrew to consider the agreements made in Philadelphia. Both Little Nephew, who was designated to make the reply, and Little Turkey expressed much concern about several matters.

The chiefs were disturbed that no efforts were being made to remove settlers from their land, that the line established by the Holston treaty had not been changed, and that they were left with less and less room to hunt. They also said that the whole nation was opposed to the passing of boats up and down the Tennessee River through their country and could not, as the government wished, permit a settlement at Muscle Shoals on the Tennessee in northern Alabama. Despite these things, the Cherokee council pledged "to hold the white people fast by the hand hereafter."[7] Further, Little Turkey promised Chisholm that he would send for three white captives held by the Cherokees and return them.

Watts, Tahlonteskee, and Young Dragging Canoe returned from Pensacola around the last of August, going to Willstown (now Fort Payne, Alabama), where Watts resided. Formerly a Creek town, the site was originally known as Redheaded Will's Town for its founder, trader William Webber. Nestled comfortably in Will's Valley between the elongated ridges of Lookout and Raccoon Mountains, it was on the Cherokee trace that led southwestward from Tennessee to Pensacola and New Orleans.

From Willstown, Watts sent out a call for Cherokee warriors to join him, and soon some six hundred men gathered in response. Watts addressed them in the town square beneath a fluttering U.S. flag and read a letter from the Spanish governor promising them all the provisions they needed to make war. The young men were always wanting war, Watts said, and now the time had come. Other chiefs joined him in advocating hostile action. But now Bloody Fellow stepped forward and spoke against them, saying:

> Look here at the things I fetched for myself, likewise for you warriors! When was the day that ever you went to your father and fetched as much as I have? I did not go by myself, others went with me. If I had gone by myself, perhaps you might have thought that I had made it myself. You had better take my talk and stay at home, and mind your women and children.

Tahlonteskee then rose. "I too have been to Pensacola," he said, "and seen the Governor as well as Watts, and heard his talk. I think a great deal of his talk, for it is good. I shall try to do as he directed me." Tahlonteskee sat back down, and Bloody Fellow continued: "Look at that flag; don't you see the stars in it? They are not towns, they are nations; there are thirteen of them. These are people who are very strong, and are the same as one man; and if you know when you are well, you had better stay at home and mind your women and children."

With Bloody Fellow still standing, John Watts got to his feet again and stepped forward. "The day is come," he announced, "when I must bloody my hands again. Tomorrow I shall send off a runner to the Creek nation to fetch my friends in. Then I shall have people enough to go with me to Cumberland or any place that I want to go."

The Cherokee warriors then dispersed, returning a half hour later all stripped to their breech clouts and painted black. They danced their war dance in the square around the flag of the United States, continuing until the evening.[8]

A council was held on the following day. Once again Bloody Fellow spoke in opposition to going to war. But when Watts called for the Cherokee warriors to meet at Lookout Town and make plans to attack the frontiers of Holston, the council quickly voted to join him. Later the warriors returned, again painted black, and danced around the American flag with their guns and hatchets. When the warriors began firing balls through the flag, Bloody Fellow told them to desist or he would kill some of them. The firing stopped.

Watts assembled his force of six hundred men at Lookout Town, mounting a portion of them under half-blood John Taylor on the two hundred horses that were available. Tahlonteskee, Glass, Fool Charles, and Breath were also assigned as war captains and ordered to be ready to march the following morning. However, the planned invasion of the Cumberland was stopped dead in its tracks when Whiteman Killer (Unacala) arrived at the mouth of Lookout Mountain Creek, his canoe loaded with whiskey. The warriors forgot their war preparation and indulged in a drunken orgy until most lay stupefied. This killed their impetus for a major attack for the time.

Still, word of Watts's army and planned invasion had spread through the frontier, reaching the Cumberland and the white settlement of Nashville, Tennessee. There Col. James Robertson responded by threatening to invade the Cherokee country and "sweep it clean" of Cherokee blood.[9] When word of this reached the Cherokee towns, it refueled the smoldering embers of war among Watts and his followers, who once again prepared for an invasion of the Cumberland country. The Upper Town peace chiefs informed Blount of the impending attack while he was attending the Cherokees' Green Corn dance at Chota on September 10. As a result, he ordered an alert and protective measures for frontier settlements.[10]

By late September, Watts had determined his objectives. First he would wipe out the western Cumberland settlements, then turn back and fall upon the detested Wataugans to the east. He would carry out these goals with a well-organized, coordinated plan of military strategy. He himself would lead the main force of three hundred warriors, plus the Creek allies under Tahlonteskee (who was a close friend of the famous Creek leader William Bowles) and some Shawnees, in an attack on Nashville. Doublehead and Bob Benge would take one hundred men and close the road leading from Nashville to Kentucky, preventing militia reinforcement from there. Chief Middlestriker would do the same with a like number of warriors along the road to Knoxville.

Watts made his attack on Buchanan's Station four miles south of Nashville at about midnight on September 30. The station consisted of a main blockhouse enclosed by a stockade. In response to Blount's warning, a number of white families had accumulated there. Though there were only fifteen fighting men among them, they were successful in holding off the Indians and inflicting heavy damage on the attackers.

Several of the Cherokee war leaders were killed, and Watts himself was seriously wounded, shot in both thighs. The Indians were badly demoralized by their inability to overwhelm the station and the loss of Watts's leadership. The Cherokee-Creek army straggled back toward the Lower Towns, carrying Watts on a stretcher between two horses.[11]

On October 2, a ten-man party of Cherokees and Creeks, led by Tahlonteskee and Tail, a brother of Bench, attacked Black's blockhouse on Crooked Creek. They killed three defenders, wounded another, and made off with several horses.

Doublehead found little movement on the Kentucky road. After killing and scalping two travelers, he hurried to join Watts in his Nashville campaign. En route, while he and most of his men were away hunting food, his camp was attacked by a militia unit of thirty-four men. Doublehead regrouped his warriors and launched a daybreak assault on the militia camp.

In fierce hand-to-hand combat, Doublehead suffered a loss of thirteen men to the militia's four. He withdrew and continued on toward Nashville, only to be met by two runners who told him of Watts's defeat and, it was then mistakenly believed, death. It was said that Doublehead cried at the supposed demise of his nephew.

On November 23, Middlestriker's group intercepted a command of forty-two militiamen on their way to reinforce Nashville. He and his men defeated them and captured their commander, Capt. Samuel Handley. Handley was taken to Willstown, where he was held prisoner for two weeks before a Cherokee council concluded that his life should be spared. After that he was treated in a friendly fashion. Middlestriker and eleven warriors escorted Handley back to Knoxville.[12]

Despite his passionate defense of the United States, the issue of

Bloody Fellow's loyalty was not yet settled. Scot pro-Spain traders John MacDonald and William Panton were able to turn him about with promises of arms and ammunition that Spanish governor Arturo O'Neill would provide if he would go to Pensacola. On October 6, 1792, MacDonald wrote to Spanish authorities: "Through arguments I made to him he was drawn gradually to my way of thinking."[13]

Later that month Bloody Fellow, along with chiefs Glass, Breath, and others with their families—one man with eight of his relatives and friends—arrived at Pensacola with packhorses to secure the promised goods. O'Neill soon found his invited guests to be troublesome and expensive. Beyond the proffered bread, rice, beef, tobacco, wine, and Jamaican rum, the Cherokees asked for saddles, hats, coats, shirts, and even cannons. The last were denied on the grounds that the Creeks would ask for the same. Bloody Fellow promised that the Cherokees would declare war on the United States.[14]

Bloody Fellow reportedly advised the Spanish to build forts at Muscle Shoals on the Tennessee River and on the Tombigbee River to halt American advancement.[15] Spanish archives contain a treaty of peace and alliance, dated October 28, 1793, between Spain and the Cherokees and other Southern tribes. By it the Cherokee nation "entreats His Catholic Majesty to take it under his immediate protection."[16] The Cherokees, however, had supposedly authorized Creek leaders to act in their behalf, and the document bore no Cherokee signatures.

When Bloody Fellow and his party returned, they found that Watts's campaign had been a great failure. However, his young men were still abundantly armed and prepared to continue the war. He recovered enough during the winter that by spring he could joke about his trip to the Cumberland and even his wounds.[17] Though he told his warriors he was well enough to return to the warpath, Watts initiated no new attacks.

On February 6, 1793, Watts, Hanging Maw, Doublehead, and other Cherokee leaders met with Governor Blount at Henry's Station, near Knoxville, for peace talks. Blount stated the wish of President Washington that the Cherokee leader pay him a visit in Philadelphia. Watts declined for the time, saying that such a trip would require the approval of the Cherokee council. Standing Turkey arrived with a party to confirm Watts's sincerity, and all were given safe escort back to Chota.[18]

Later that same month, agent John McKee visited Watts at Chattooga, a small village near Willstown to talk peace. En route, McKee had been warned by John Benge that William Webber had been encouraging Watts to kill him. In fact, Webber sent eight Cherokees for that purpose to meet the canoe of trader Arthur Coody (or Coodey), thinking McKee was with him. Watts, however, was friendly with McKee, joked about his wounds, and consumed the agent's rum until he was drunk.[19]

The matter remained unsettled through the spring; but in June, at the request of Blount, a number of Cherokee leaders gathered at Hanging Maw's home in Coyatee to consider the invitation. Early on the morning of June 12, 1793, a party of mounted militia under Capt. John Beard, who claimed to be pursuing Indian horse thieves, made a charge upon the house. The militia killed several people, including Fool Charles, who was a chief of Running Water, and the daughter of Chief Taken Out of the Water. Hanging Maw, his wife, and Betty, the daughter of Nancy Ward, were wounded. Only the pleading of some white men who were present prevented the militia from killing Hanging Maw.[20]

Blount was in Philadelphia at the time, and it was territorial secretary Daniel Smith who had to answer when Hanging Maw wrote a bitter letter of complaint asking, "When is the day that a white man was killed at my house?" Doublehead also wrote to Smith: "I am still among my people, living in gores of blood," he said. "We have lost nine of our people, that we must have satisfaction for. There is some of the first and principal headmen of our nation fell here, and they are not without friends . . . This is the third time that we have been served so when we were talking peace, that they fell on us and killed us."[21]

There was no organized retaliation during the summer, but the Cherokee warriors, Doublehead in particular, were determined to have their satisfaction. It was September before a large body of seven hundred Cherokees and three hundred Creeks swarmed northeastward up the Tennessee River with Watts at their head.

On the morning of the twenty-fifth, the Indian army reached the general vicinity of Knoxville—close enough that they heard the firing of the morning cannon from the town's garrison. Thinking that they had been discovered, Watts and other leaders became undecided about attacking Knoxville. Eventually, it was determined that they would take a blockhouse they had passed on the way. This was the settlement home of Alexander Cavet, known as Cavet's Station.[22]

The Cavet household consisted of only thirteen members, three of whom were men and the remainder women and children. These few had little chance of holding out against the mass of Indians surrounding the station. In desperation they surrendered themselves, Watts agreeing that their lives would be spared and they would be used to exchange for captive Indians. But once the people came out, the vengeance-minded Doublehead began brutally killing them with his war ax. Watts and other chiefs attempted to stop him, but Doublehead's murderous rampage continued until all were dead except one young boy whom Watts managed to save.[23]

Doublehead's savagery had shocked even Watts, chilling his inclination for warring. In October 1793, Sevier set out in hot pursuit of Watts's Cherokee and Creek army, following its trail to Etowah on the Coosa River, near present Rome in northwestern Georgia. There the Indians entrenched themselves on a high bank and stymied Sevier's militia when it attempted to cross. Eventually, however, the Indians were routed, leaving behind their dead and much equipment. Sevier marched on down the Coosa, destroying several towns and killing three hundred head of Indian cattle.[24]

In June 1794 the government sought to pacify the Lower Town troublemakers—and gain more land concessions—by inviting their chiefs to Philadelphia and making new treaty agreements. The Cherokee delegation was headed by Taken Out of the Water and Northward. Other party members of note were Doublehead, John McLemore (McClemore, McLamore, Euquellooka), and interpreter Arthur Coody, whose surnames would become prominent among the Cherokees.

By the pact signed at Philadelphia on June 26, 1794, the Treaty of Holston was reaffirmed, the Cherokees agreed to pay for every horse

Col. John "Nolichucky Jack"
Sevier, the first governor of
Tennessee, was a fierce
opponent of the Cherokees.

Appleton's Annual Cyclopedia and
Register of Important Events. New
York: Appleton, 1862–1903.

stolen by a tribal member, and the United States agreed to pay five thousand dollars in goods suitable to the tribe's use for relinquishments of
lands by the treaties of Hopewell and Holston.[25]

This visit of a Cherokee delegation to the U.S. seat of government
had not interrupted the conflict between Cherokee warriors and intruding whites. During June 1794 a boat loaded with five white men, three
women, four children, and twenty slaves headed down the Tennessee
River from Knoxville with a boatload of goods for trade in Natchez. The
boat, under the command of William Scott, made it through the famous
"Suck" near Lookout Mountain; but as it passed the Cherokee towns of
Running Water and Long Island, it was fired upon by Indians. The men
on the boat returned the fire and wounded two Cherokees on shore
before continuing on downstream.

Incensed enough by white navigation on the river through the heart
of their homeland, the Indians were further enraged by the shooting of
their people. Cutting across land, a large Cherokee war party—led, some
say, by Whiteman Killer—caught up with the boat and attacked it at
Muscle Shoals. All of the white people were slaughtered, the slaves
taken prisoner, and the boat's cargo plundered. Three Cherokees were
killed and another wounded in the fight.[26]

An account by the Reverend Cephas Washburn, missionary to the
Cherokees in Arkansas, states that after the Muscle Shoals fight the
Cherokees loaded the conquered boat with all the women and children.
They allowed each woman a female servant and some furniture, and
with four slaves to work the boat sent them on downriver to New
Orleans. Washburn said that he heard this story from one of the women
survivors, with whom he often stayed in New Orleans. In a September
letter to Watts, General Robertson noted that none of those who murdered the people in the boats had been punished, nor had the slaves
been returned.[27]

In Nashville, Robertson was still determined to punish the
Cherokees, partially for the Muscle Shoals attack and partially for horse
thefts and other depredations. In September he dispatched a force of
550 mounted infantry under the command of Colonel Whitley to strike
the Lower Towns. Nickajack and Running Water were destroyed, and
many of the inhabitants of the two towns were killed—among them
Chief Breath—and nineteen women and children were taken captive.
Some 150 Cherokee homes were burned, and the spoils were divided
among the white militia.[28]

Watts immediately wrote to General Robertson declaring his desire for peace. Robertson responded, demanding proof of the Chickamaugans' peaceful inclinations by releasing the slaves and a white girl held by them. He offered to trade seventeen Cherokee captives for them, telling Watts to come to him with a flag. He threatened that if the Lower Towns did not make peace the white soldiers would strike them again.[29]

On October 20, while on his way home from Philadelphia, Doublehead addressed a letter to Governor Blount from Coosawatee, a point on the Coosa River, saying that it appeared there would now be a lasting peace. He also asked that he and his people be allowed to hunt on the Cumberland and be kept safe from the whites there. He blamed all the past troubles on the Creeks.[30] Doublehead distributed the treaty annuities that he brought back with him to his town at Oconee Mountain only. Hanging Maw complained that the goods were given to Doublehead and his party of murderers, while the peace faction got none.[31]

On November 7 and 8, 1794, Blount held a council at the Tellico Blockhouse, near old Fort Loudoun. The leading Cherokees present included Hanging Maw, Watts, Bloody Fellow, and Glass. When Blount asked that Watts speak first, he did so but gave recognition to the position of Hanging Maw. "There is Scolacutta," Watts noted, "he is old enough to be my father, and from my infancy he was a great man, and is now the great chief of the nation."[32] He continued on to say that he had not gone to Nashville with a flag as Robertson had suggested, for he preferred to deal with Blount in exchanging captives and making a lasting peace. Hanging Maw spoke angrily against the Lower Towns. He said that because of their bad conduct they had drawn war upon him, and he had had to live in the woods all winter. Still, he said, he could not neglect their request of him to make peace in their behalf. Blount set December 18 as the date when they would meet again at Tellico and exchange prisoners.

This marked the last organized Cherokee military resistance against the United States. Watts now gave up his role as a leader of the Cherokee warring elements and became a lesser figure among the tribe. Doublehead became more and more the main Chickamaugan Cherokee to deal with. He, too, soon abandoned the warpath and became a principal player in Cherokee-U.S. civil relations. From this point, the Cherokee struggle for survival would be conducted under the rules of U.S. law and government—rules, the Cherokees would find, that white officials and white citizens themselves often disregarded.

CHAPTER 8

Intrigue and Assassination

During 1795 and 1796 the Cherokees were almost drawn into a grand Burr-like plot to wrest Florida from the control of Spain—a scheme that would have worked seriously against the interests of the United States. Cherokee warriors were looked to as a part of an invading force of southern Indians by the concocters of the plot—none other than John D. Chisholm and Gov. William Blount.

Chisholm, an ambitious, contentious-natured Scot, had led an interesting career as an emissary for Blount, a member of the state of Franklin legislature, a judge, the builder and owner of the first house of entertainment (as inns were then called) in Knoxville, operator of a mail route, surveyor, slave trader, and general opportunist. The red-headed Highlander had been twice married and apparently divorced before marrying Patsy Brown, the mixed-blood sister of a highly regarded half-Cherokee war captain, Richard Brown.[1]

Blount, a member of the Constitutional Convention at Philadelphia from North Carolina and a personal friend of President Washington, was also a man of ambition and enterprise. Behind the front of his office, he was deeply involved in personal land speculations. Though it was he who would ultimately be charged with the prime responsibility for the Florida conspiracy, it was evidently the much-traveled Chisholm who initiated the idea.

In January 1797, Chisholm led a delegation of Cherokee and Creek Indians to Philadelphia. With him were Brown; Watts; James Carey, a white boy who had been raised among the Cherokees; and John Rogers, a white trader with a large family among the Cherokees. Fearing that Blount was going to cut him out, Chisholm hoped to interest Robert Liston, the British minister in America, in the plan. Liston and a Philadelphia merchant agreed to finance Chisholm in a voyage to London for the purpose of persuading the British government to become involved in the overthrow of Florida. Chisholm tried to get Brown to accompany him, but the Cherokee refused.

Upon reaching London, Chisholm found British officials unreceptive to the Florida scheme, in part because it had been publicly revealed
through a letter written from Blount to James Carey at Tellico. The
spurned Chisholm ended up in debtors' prison in London, though he
would eventually return to America and become deeply involved in
Cherokee affairs. Blount would face impeachment proceedings in
Congress but would ultimately survive them.

Continued white encroachment had made it necessary for the government to seek a cession to Cherokee claim of land north of the
Tennessee River in 1798. Hanging Maw had died by then, and Bloody
Fellow had taken his place as principal chief.[2] The latter presided when
the Cherokees and U.S. officials met at Tellico to work out a new treaty.
At the very start of the council, Bloody Fellow delivered a paper stating the firm refusal of the Cherokees to sell any land or to let white
settlers who had been ejected return.[3]

When officials were unable to shake him or the other chiefs from
this position, they postponed negotiations until September. Finally, on
October 2 the commissioners—whether by the usual methods of getting
the chiefs drunk or bribery or both is not recorded—were successful.
Bloody Fellow, followed by Little Turkey, Taken Out of the Water,
Doublehead, Tahlonteskee, and more than thirty other chiefs, signed
the treaty. By it they gave up tracts in Tennessee and North Carolina
and agreed to the opening of the Cumberland Road connecting the east
Tennessee settlements and Nashville.

In 1800 a small group of Moravian missionaries from Salem, North
Carolina, came to Tellico to request that they be permitted to establish
a school among the Cherokees. They were met in council by Bloody
Fellow, Little Turkey, Boot, Glass, and Doublehead, all wearing the
tribal breechclouts and blankets. The chiefs were dubious about the
school and conducted several meetings on the matter. It was one of
Bloody Fellow's final acts. He would die soon after, and Little Turkey
would reign as Cherokee principal chief until his death at Willstown in
1802. Little Turkey was succeeded by Black Fox.[4]

During the fourth meeting, Doublehead delivered a long speech in
which he recommended that they permit the Moravians a trial.
Doublehead, feeling he should be rewarded for his speech, asked the
ministers to supply him with a bottle of good whiskey. The Moravians
were encouraged further by half-blood James Vann, son of the former
interpreter of that name who had become wealthy with a trading store

at Diamond Hill, Georgia. Though he was a brutal, much feared, and hated town chief, the junior Vann helped the Moravians obtain a building near his home at Spring Place, Georgia, and provided them his protection.[5] Another strong supporter of the school was Charles Hicks, the Cherokee second chief who himself would join the Moravian Church as a convert to Christianity.[6]

Doublehead had been savage and vindictive as a warrior. But as the leading chief of the Cherokees located along Muscle Shoals on the Tennessee River in northern Alabama, he was progressive in working to bring trade to the area and in opening a one hundred-mile wagon road from Tennessee.[7] He had also become interested in developing the trade potential of the West, where there were vast areas of unoccupied land, game was abundant, and he and his people would be out of the reach of American expansion. The Cherokee chief was further encouraged in this by Chisholm, who, divorced by his Cherokee wife, Patsy, upon his return to America, had secured permission to reenter the Indian country.

It was not long before Chisholm located at Muscle Shoals, becoming secretary and confidant to Doublehead, whom he also advised and influenced. On November 20, 1802, he penned a letter for Doublehead to Cherokee agent Return J. Meigs indicating the chief's interest in investigating the western country.

> Sir—When I saw you at the Green Corn Dance you Desired me to come and see you & get some goods from you . . . I have now one request to ask of you—that is to have me a boat built. I want a good Keale Boat som 30 to 35 feet in length and 7 feet wide. I want her for the purpose of Descending the River to Orleans & back. I want her to be lite & well calculated to Stem the Streem. I am determined to buy the Produce of this place & then Return Back by Water . . . I shall want two of your big Guns to mount on the Boat—I am determined for to see up the White & Red Rivers on my Boat and oppen a trade with the Western Wild Indians.[8]

There is no evidence that Doublehead ever got his boat. In March 1804, Chisholm wrote in behalf of Doublehead and Path Killer (Neno-huttahe, Ne-nau-to) saying that because of a severe drought their 121 people, plus 15 whites, were about to perish for lack of food. They requested garden and farming tools, seed, and more canoes for transporting corn. Meigs responded by sending a boat loaded with three hundred bushels of corn down the Tennessee River, 250 miles, to Muscle Shoals.[9]

Return J. Meigs worked hard to persuade the Cherokees to abandon their Old Nation homes and remove to the West.

Appleton's Annual Cyclopedia and Register of Important Events. New York: Appleton, 1862–1903.

The Cherokees claimed that during the 1798 treaty council they were promised they would never again be asked to cede more land. Nonetheless, they learned that the government was about to promote another treaty, one that would legitimatize a settlement on their land in Georgia by a Colonel Wafford. The United States also wanted to secure a right of way for a road from Tellico to Athens, Georgia.[10]

The Cherokees resisted, but commissioners Daniel Smith and Meigs would not give in. Calling another council at Tellico in October 1805, the commissioners employed the standard technique of bribery as a method of working out two new treaties with the Cherokees.[11] Doublehead and Tahlonteskee were promised choice tracts of land by Smith and Meigs for help in persuading the other chiefs to approve land cessions. Still other secret awards were issued when a delegation comprising Doublehead, Vann, Tahlonteskee, and fourteen others was escorted to Washington, D.C., in late December for consummation of still another treaty and a visit with President Jefferson.[12]

The delegation drew much attention in infant Washington City and was treated royally. On December 30, they, along with an Indian delegation from the Missouri River, were taken to the unfinished U.S. Capitol building, where, "dressed in their war habiliments," they filled the gallery.

That night the combined party entertained Washingtonians with Indian dances at a local theater, with an unhappy consequence. One of the Indians, evidently not a Cherokee, became overstimulated by his exertions and too much ardent spirits and died.[13] On one occasion the group was taken aboard the frigate *Adams*, which was decked out for the occasion, accompanied by President Jefferson and the secretaries of war and navy. A salute was fired from the ship in their behalf.[14]

The treaty agreements were finalized and signed on January 6, 1806. Of particular interest was a special clause that awarded five other tracts at Muscle Shoals on the Tennessee River to named persons. One of those was Big Half Breed, (Sequechu or Cheh Chuh), Doublehead's brother.[15] Further, by secret agreement the participating chiefs were to receive a thousand dollars and two rifles each.[16]

James Vann was rewarded by the routing of the Federal Turnpike connecting Augusta with Nashville past his trading post on Georgia's Conasauga River.[17] Vann's home at Spring Place was situated on the projected route near where it divided, one branch going north to Tellico

The Joseph Vann house stands restored near Chatsworth, Georgia.
Photo by author.

and the other west to Nashville. When the road was completed, Vann opened a ferry across the Conasauga River and a trading post, both becoming lucrative enterprises.

He developed a plantation, which surrounded his large brick home, with several farms and a mill, all operated by a large contingent of slaves, whom he often abused during drunken rages. On one occasion Cherokee subagent William Lovely released several Negroes from the chains that the drunken Vann had kept them in for some time.[18] His violence was notorious. It is not surprising that while lodged together in a Washington hotel room, he and Doublehead went at one another with knives. It was said that during a drunken spree, Vann had shot one man from his door just to try out a new gun. On another occasion he stabbed a man during a drunken brawl, and killed his sister's husband in a fight over a slave.[19]

Still another special treaty recipient was John Chisholm, who had been chosen by the chiefs of the Lower Towns to represent them in selling their landholdings in Alabama. He was, however, also serving as an agent for Meigs, who wished him to encourage Cherokee migration to the West. Chisholm's hand in, and reward from, the Treaty of 1806 is more than evident. He was among those given land by the treaty, and he later joined Doublehead in leasing property at Muscle Shoals for ten years to a white man for the purpose of building a dam, gristmill, and sawmill.[20]

These dealings, plus the secret treaty benefits, had caused a great deal of rancor against both Doublehead and Chisholm among Cherokees in the Upper Towns of Tennessee, where it was rumored that the two were selling Cherokee land. This was accentuated by the loss of Cherokee territory given up by the treaties of 1805 and 1806. Still another factor of conflict could well have been resentment over the shift of Cherokee power from Tennessee into Georgia and Alabama.

Doublehead charged that trader John Rogers, in particular, was stirring up trouble for him by meddling in Cherokee treaty affairs. Rogers and his family of adult children were located near the mouth of the Hiwassee River, where Hiwassee Garrison (Southwest Point) had been established.[21] Doublehead insisted that Rogers and others were falsely accusing him of selling Cherokee land. Being ill himself in early 1807, the Chickamaugan chief sent Chisholm north to Tennessee to assist in arranging for the sawmill and to make the point that, while he had rented and leased some land, he had not sold an acre.[22]

A pattern-setting event that would have a drastic effect upon

Cherokee affairs and the men who played a part in them now occurred—an event of intertribal murder that would cast a pall of divisive hostility destined to hang over the Cherokee Nation for years. A number of young chiefs of the Upper Towns in Tennessee were so disturbed by the actions of both Doublehead and Chisholm that they concluded the two men should be killed. A meeting was held to promote an assassination plot. Just who was present is not known, but it is believed that among the main schemers were trader James Vann, a town war chief named Ridge, and half-blood George Sanders (Saunders). John Rogers was also involved. Ridge accepted the role of executor.

The most opportune time would be during the ball play and Green Corn Dance at Hiwassee Town in August. This Cherokee celebration drew virtually all the nation together annually to visit, sport, gamble, drink, and barter with the many traders who came with their goods. The officers, men, and other whites at Hiwassee Garrison were usually interested spectators.

Doublehead did, indeed, come up from Muscle Shoals to attend the fete; but whether forewarned or merely fortunate, Chisholm did not. As was his usual habit, Doublehead was drinking heavily at Hiwassee when a Cherokee war captain named Bonepolisher approached him and angrily denounced him as a traitor. Doublehead warned him to go away, but the enraged Bonepolisher rushed at the Lower Cherokee chief with a raised tomahawk. Doublehead took the blow on his left arm and, drawing his pistol with his right hand, shot Bonepolisher through the heart. Later that evening a reeling-drunk Doublehead entered the tavern near the Hiwassee Ferry where Ridge was present with some friends, including Rogers and Sanders. None of them yet knew about the killing of Bonepolisher.[23] Rogers proceeded to revile Doublehead over the land matter. "Be silent and stop your interference," Doublehead told him. "You live by sufferance among us. I've never seen you in council or on the warpath. You have no place among the chiefs. Be silent, and interfere no more with me."[24]

But the trader had also been drinking, and he persisted well beyond caution. Finally Doublehead had had enough. He pulled his pistol and attempted to shoot Rogers in the face. However, the Cherokee had failed to recharge the weapon, and the hammer snapped without result. A melee followed. Someone doused the light, and shots flashed in the darkness. When the light was rekindled, Doublehead lay on the floor of the tavern with his lower jaw shattered by a ball.

Friends attempted to get Doublehead to the safety of the garrison just across the Tennessee River, but instead they were forced to hide him in the loft of a schoolmaster's house. Ridge and his cohorts (probably Sanders and Rogers) followed the trail of blood to the house and found the Chickamaugan leader concealed in a blanket. They fired into it, sending shots through his hips. Though terribly wounded, Doublehead sprang onto Ridge and struggled with him until another Cherokee drove a tomahawk into his skull. The assassins then crushed his head with a spade as they would have a snake they still feared in death.

The Cherokee clans may have also been a factor in the assassination. How much this was involved in the malice that Ridge and the Upper Town people felt for the southern chief will never be known. Nonetheless, the old clan laws protected Doublehead's killers. The Cherokees, though, were now led to revise their old law of clan revenge that required relatives of a slain man to seek satisfaction.[25]

Doublehead's assassination caused even greater dissension between the old chiefs of the Lower Towns and the rebellious Upper Towns. Shortly after the murder, on September 11, 1807, Meigs again employed bribery in getting Black Fox, Glass, and other Lower Town chiefs to alter the cession line of the 1806 treaty. He not only gave personal gifts to the chiefs, but he agreed to cancel their debt of $1,803 to the government.[26] During the following December he negotiated another treaty

Major Ridge, who helped assassinate Chief Doublehead over the sale of Cherokee land, was later murdered over the same issue.

Western History Collection,
University of Oklahoma.

The Major Ridge home near Rome, Georgia, is revealing of pre-removal Cherokee affluence.

Photo by author.

with the Lower Town chiefs, providing a cession of six square miles near Chickamauga Creek for the benefit of a white man, Col. Elias Earle, who wished to operate a mine there.[27]

The Upper Town chiefs immediately responded with a letter to Jefferson, protesting the "sham treaty" and declaring it invalid. Nonetheless, Earle attempted to bring a wagon train of a hundred or so South Carolina families, slaves, equipment, and supplies into the Cherokee country. He was stopped in Georgia by armed Cherokees under James Vann and turned back.[28]

During the spring of 1808, a group of thirty-two Upper Town chiefs and two women paid still another visit to Washington to complain that the Lower Towns were getting far more benefits than the Upper.[29] The members of this delegation were minor chiefs at best: Stone Toater (or Carrier), John of Chilhowa, Crawling Boy, Chilcochatah, and Deer Biter, none of whom are known to have played prominent roles in Cherokee affairs before or after this occasion.[30]

When the delegation suggested their nation be divided into two parts, Jefferson urged them to get together with the Lower Towns and send a delegation to Congress with authority to work out agreements. He also repeated the idea that those who were not pleased with the result might consider resettling on lands beyond the Mississippi.[31] In response, a delegation of six Upper Town and Lower Town chiefs, with two women, was escorted to Washington by Meigs that following December. Their written address to President Jefferson was signed by Seed, Skeuka, Tuchelee (Touchchalee, Toochalar, or Flute), Quolequskee (Quotaquskee or John McIntosh), John Walker, and Ridge.[32]

Jefferson, who was soon to retire from public office at the age of sixty-six, answered their plea politely. For those who wished to take up industrious occupations such as agriculture, he promised continued U.S. patronage. To those wishing to continue to live by the hunt by removing beyond the Mississippi River, he promised every necessary aid in their removal. He recommended that they send an exploring party to reconnoiter the country of the Arkansas and White Rivers: "the higher up the better, as they will be the longer unapproached by our settlements."[33]

Meigs had been working actively among Lower Town chiefs such as Tahlonteskee and Glass on the matter of moving west. Glass wrote to President Jefferson directly to indicate a willingness to migrate. Learning of this, the Upper Town chiefs called a hasty meeting at Hiwassee. Amid a stormy session of charges and countercharges, they deposed Black Fox as principal chief along with Tahlonteskee and Glass.[34]

The Lower Town chiefs refused to abide by the Hiwassee decision, and the animosity between them and the Upper chiefs was reaching a dangerous level. Both groups actively argued their cases concerning removal by sending delegates to Washington to talk with Jefferson. In this setting of conflict, both sides lost important men. John Watts, the former war leader of the Lower Towns, died in 1808. Then in February 1809 James Vann was shot from ambush as he was coming out of a tavern. It was believed that his killer was George Sanders, who had helped murder Doublehead; but no one seemed to really care. His son Joseph, or "Rich Joe," as he became known, inherited the Vann wealth.[35]

Meigs, with the help of John Chisholm, continued to push hard for removal among the Lower Towns. But for many Cherokees his efforts caused great fear that they stood to lose their homeland, the land of their ancestors. The concern was so great that a national council was called at Willstown in September 1809 to reestablish harmony. Black Fox and Glass were restored as dual principal chiefs.[36]

Further, the Willstown council created a national committee of high-ranking chiefs, a move that would provide a basis for the more for-

mal government that would be established later. The national committee would direct the business of the nation, including its financial affairs,
and conduct matters with the U.S. government. Annual meetings would
be held, but the group would also convene when emergencies arose.
Formation of the governing body by the chiefs was of special significance in that it reflected the potential for political unity within the
Cherokee Nation. No longer could the United States as conveniently
connive with individual chiefs to secure Cherokee land.[37]

However, U.S. officials had by no means given up their efforts to
remove the Cherokees entirely from the remaining land they yet held
in Tennessee, Georgia, and Alabama by whatever means it took. The
issue of homeland would spawn the most rancorous split yet known
among the Cherokees, nullifying any hope for tribal equanimity.

CHAPTER 9

"As Long as Waters Flow"

Prior to 1800, the U.S. government had attempted to follow the policy of George Washington, that of integrating Indians into American society. This, too, had been the thrust of the missionaries who came into the Cherokee Nation. But after 1800, a drastic change in thinking took place among political leaders. Spurred more and more by a desire for Indian land, officials increasingly convinced themselves of the imperfection of the Indian and his supposed inability to accept and be accepted into the white world. The purchase of the Louisiana Territory in 1803 annihilated all notion of integration in U.S. policy. Beyond the Mississippi River now lay vast lands to which the eastern tribes could be removed from the presence of Anglo-American settlement.

The Jeffersonian concept, however, was based on the notion of voluntary removal. Efforts were made to persuade the Cherokees and other tribes to exchange their lands in the East for equal amounts in the West. For years the Cherokees had been exhorted to give up their old ways of hunting and become planters and stock raisers like the white people. Now the government began urging them to give up their homes and land and move West, where they could again live off wild game.

Ridge and other Upper Towns chiefs wrote to Jefferson, saying: "Your advise has Been to us to lay by our guns and go to farming. Git hoes, plowes and axes. The young peopel holds your talk fast respecting farming and industrey." The old chiefs, the letter said, wished to throw away the plow and the women's spinning wheel and take up the gun again.[1]

Though Cherokee men had found it hard to give up the hunter's life and adopt farming, more and more they were being forced into it. Encroaching whites had begun to decimate their hunting regions; the buffalo had long since disappeared, and only small game remained. Referring to the Treaty of Holston, Bloody Fellow told Secretary of War Henry Dearborn:

> The treaty mentions ploughs, hoes, cattle and other things for a farm; this is what we want; game is going fast away from us. We must

plant corn, and raise cattle, and we desire you to assist us. . . . In former times we bought of the trader goods cheap; we could then clothe
our women and children, but now game is scarce and goods dear, we
cannot live comfortably.[2]

Forced to depend more and more on agricultural pursuits, the
Cherokees by 1809 had begun deserting their old towns and moving up
the river valleys in search of good, arable land. Many of their former villages became virtually deserted and others much smaller. For the most
part the Upper Cherokees were considered to be planters and herders,
while the Lower Cherokees clung to their hunting habits. It was the latter who, looking to abundant game in the still-pristine West and wishing
to escape from white contact, chose to give up their homes and relocate.

Tahlonteskee had by no means become reconciled by the Willstown
meeting. He sent a letter to Jefferson, speaking for Glass and others and
undoubtedly penned by Chisholm, saying that he was still determined
to migrate to Arkansas: "I and my party are determined to cross the
river towards the West. Our bad brothers may dispute, but with me 12
towns go."[3]

With the death of Doublehead and Watts, Tahlonteskee had become
a leading chief of the Lower Towns. As early as 1792 he had been nomi-
nated by Black Fox as a headman in the place of Corn Tassel: "We have
appointed this man to support his talks, and we hope that both whites
and reds will attend to him."[4] At that time, however, Tahlonteskee was
too much engaged in making war to serve as the peace-seeking diplomat
that Corn Tassel had been. William Blount identified him as a nephew
of Corn Tassel.[5] He is also known to have been the older brother of half-
blood chief John Jolly (Ahu-ludi-ski) and thus was possibly of mixed blood
also.[6] A hard-drinking but forceful man, he had been with the delegation
to Washington in 1806. After shaking hands with Jefferson, he had vowed
"never to withdraw his hand from his Father the President."[7]

From that point, Tahlonteskee essentially gave up his war-making
against the Americans and became the prime leader of the Cherokee
movement westward. In view of the Doublehead assassination, he did
so at considerable personal risk from the Upper Town leaders. They had
continued to resist intensely any move toward giving up their national
lands. When mixed-blood Richard Fields of the Lower Towns indicated
that he planned to go west, Ridge and other chiefs wrote to Meigs insisting that the man had no right to sell his place, which was tribal land.[8]

The decision to uproot his people and move to the raw, unsettled country of the Arkansas and White rivers among enemy tribes was not a particularly easy one for Tahlonteskee. The Cherokees had been crossing the Mississippi River on hunting expeditions long before the United States purchased the Louisiana country. Black Hawk, a Sac and Fox chief, said that in 1787 his father had been killed in a fight with Cherokees on the Merrimac River in Missouri, the Cherokees losing twenty-eight men in the conflict.[9]

As early as May 1782, a delegation of Cherokees had applied to Don Estevan Miro, governor of Spanish-held Louisiana, for permission to settle west of the Mississippi. That he eventually granted their request is borne out by Cherokee chief Konnetue (or Cunnatue), who wrote from the St. Francis River in 1790 that he and a very few followers had settled on a tract given them by the Spanish king.[10] Some scholars say that the Missouri settlement was founded in 1785, following the Treaty of Hopewell by a group of dissatisfied Cherokees.[11] Thus, Cherokees were already residing on the St. Francis River when they were joined by others in 1794.

Other Cherokees, possibly Doublehead's group, applied for permission to occupy a tract of land on the Arkansas River in 1796.[12] Following the massacre of Scott's boat party at Muscle Shoals and the ensuing destruction of Nickajack and Running Water, some Cherokees of the Lower Towns decided that they had had enough of war. They said that they wished to go where it was peaceful—where the Creeks would not incite their "silly young men" to cause trouble.

Accordingly, a small party of Lower Town Cherokees loaded their families and supplies of corn into six canoes and began their long trip down the Tennessee River, the Ohio, and the Mississippi toward Missouri.[13] As they passed through the Chickasaw country, they were spotted. Believing that Chickasaw chief Mountain Leader and his party had been harmed earlier by Cherokees, the Chickasaw mixed-blood warrior William Colbert forced one canoe ashore. Two Cherokee women and two children were captured while Colbert killed and scalped the man.

The Cherokees claimed that the Osages of southwestern Missouri had killed a number of their warriors who had gone on hunting excursions beyond the Mississippi. In January 1805, the Cherokees who resided west of the Mississippi went to war with them. Ten eastern Cherokees led by Red Bird returned from war with Osages of Missouri carrying three scalps that year.

Both Doublehead and Takatoka, undoubtedly at the lead of warriors, are known to have visited the St. Francis settlement and "made times good" by helping fight the Osages.[14] In 1806 Chief Konnetue had indicated that the St. Francis Cherokees were expecting to be joined by a number of families from the Cherokee settlements in Tennessee.[15]

Though Tahlonteskee felt it unnecessary to explore the new country because his people already knew it well, a young mixed blood from the Upper Towns was appointed by Meigs to do so during 1809. Nineteen-year-old John Ross and three companions made the long canoe trip down the Tennessee, Ohio, and Mississippi rivers to the mouth of the Arkansas River. At Arkansas Post they secured a packhorse and explored by foot up the Arkansas as far as the site of present Little Rock. The trip took three months.[16]

In the meantime, Tahlonteskee made his decision. Chisholm wrote to Meigs from Muscle Shoals on the chief's behalf in March requesting permission to "remove or exchange lands for lands west of the Mississippi."[17] He stated Tahlonteskee's understanding that the exchange did not depend on the consent of the Cherokee Nation. The chief also reminded Meigs that the United States had promised to give both advice and aid. Chisholm, who had been quietly promoting the move on Meigs's behalf, added: "It is not best to urge any man. Let the thing speak for itself."

On July 20, 1809, Tahlonteskee and seventeen followers came upriver to Hiwassee and presented Meigs with a list of Lower Town Cherokees who wished to move over the Mississippi under the conditions agreed upon with President Jefferson in Washington. The list was a long one of 1,023 people, including 386 men and 637 women and children. Later, an additional 107 Cherokees joined the group as it made preparations to move.[18]

The numbers of Tahlonteskee's exodus can be viewed against the population of the Cherokee Nation, as cited by Meigs in a December 1809 report: 6,116 males and 6,279 females. Cherokee stock included 6,519 horses, 19,165 black cattle, 1,037 sheep, and 19,778 swine. The Cherokees owned 1,572 spinning wheels, 429 looms, 367 plows, but only 30 wagons. They operated 13 gristmills, 3 sawmills, 1 powder mill, and 2 saltpeter works. Five schools were in operation, attended by 94 children. There were 341 white people in the nation and 583 slaves.[19]

Early in 1810, two more Lower Town chiefs, Sanlowee and Bowle (or John Bowles, Tewulle), requested passports from Meigs for moving with their families—a group consisting of sixty-three people—to the

Arkansas and White Rivers. They planned to make the trip by descending the Tennessee River in twelve canoes and one flat-bottomed boat.[20]

On February 16, Meigs wrote to Governor Blount that Tahlonteskee had departed with a sizable party. How much aid Meigs provided the Cherokees is not clear; certainly it was far short of what Jefferson had indicated. In one report, Meigs stated that he gave one man a rifle; fiscal records indicate that the Sanlowee-Bowle party was provided with twelve blankets.[21]

The details of the Tahlonteskee move are scanty. Just what modes of transportation were used and the route taken were not reported. However, a listing of Lower Town property by Meigs indicates that probably both a water and an overland movement took place. Their possessions included 1,273 black cattle, 369 horses, 868 hogs, 46 spinning wheels, 13 looms, 36 plows, and other smaller items. They also took along 68 black slaves.[22]

It is probable that the stock was driven on a direct land route from Muscle Shoals to the Arkansas River; but, as with the Sanlowee-Bowle group, it is possible that the immigrants may have used the much longer water route. Likely the Cherokees traveled part way by water, then some cut overland to Chickasaw Bluffs (present Memphis), and from there into Arkansas.

In a letter dated June 23, 1810, Tahlonteskee informed Meigs that they had arrived and established a settlement between the Arkansas and White Rivers. He also complained that while en route the Choctaws killed three of his people.[23] Enclosed with the Tahlonteskee letter was another from Konnetue from the St. Francis River settlement, indicating that the two Cherokee groups had made contact.

Tahlonteskee and his party at first moved on to Missouri and lived among Konnetue's band of some two thousand Cherokees. In June 1811, Tahlonteskee wrote to Meigs from the St. Francis saying that he was tired of living in camps and wished to settle down permanently and make farms and houses to live in. He expressed his desire to exchange his "half of the Cherokee Nation" for lands on the Arkansas River.[24]

Between December 26, 1811, and March 16, 1812, the Mississippi valley was struck by a series of severe earthquake shocks that turned much land into swamp areas and changed the course of some rivers. Exhorted by a prophecy of doom by shaman Skawquaw (the Swan), the Cherokees totally abandoned the St. Francis River, many giving up fine farms, and removed to Arkansas. Both Tahlonteskee's group and Konnetue's band relocated, some on the White River but most on the Arkansas River.[25] The presence of a Cherokee settlement on the Arkansas was indicated by a letter from John Chisholm on June 28, 1812. Saying that he could not write extensively for want of paper, Chisholm stated that he had been with Tahlonteskee and his party since leaving the Old Nation and that they were well satisfied with the new country.[26]

One initial location on the Arkansas was at a point where the river passed between two small mountains. They dubbed the site as the Dardanelle. From there the Cherokees spread out up the Arkansas and along inlet creeks, such as Illinois, Pine, Spadra, Horsehead, Frog, and Mulberry. One sizable group took up residence along Petite Jean River, south of the Arkansas.

The Arkansas (or Western) Cherokees soon began to establish themselves on farms, building log-cabin homes, planting fields of corn and vegetable gardens, erecting rail fences for their cattle, and tending their hogs and chickens. The men supported this agrarian produce by trapping and hunting deer, buffalo, and bear that were in plenty among the forested hills south of the Arkansas. The women continued to weave their baskets and work at their looms as was their Cherokee tradition. Hides and produce were taken downriver by canoe and boat four hundred miles to Arkansas Post to trade for the salt, sugar, and other items scarce in the Arkansas wilderness. They were also visited by white traders, whose largest trade item was often whiskey.

Louisiana Creole Louis Bringier, who first visited the Arkansas Cherokees in 1812, held a strong Spanish bias that led him to observe that the Indians under the control of Spain had few vices, while those under U.S. control were extremely corrupted. He wrote of the Cherokees:

> They have cleared about six thousand acres of land with the fire which they have set in the thick canes; but they do not cultivate more than thousand five hundred acres, and that very badly. They raise no other staple except for a few sweet potatoes and pumpkins . . . The Indians spin some cotton, but this hardly amounts to five or six yards per annum . . . The women are very licentious, and the men extremely lazy. The men dress with what we call a morning gown, or a long hunting shirt, a pair of leggings, a calico or a white shirt, and a shawl tied around their heads in the manner of a turban. The women dress with gowns like white women.[27]

One of the pitfalls, in the true sense of the word, of pioneer life was revealed by Tahlonteskee in a letter to Maj. William Lovely at the

Hiwassee agency. He said that he had commenced digging a small well seeking salt. He was drinking heavily as he did so and fell into the well, "very near dieing." The chief swore off drinking whiskey until he finished the well.[28]

Lovely himself arrived on the Arkansas the following July to establish a Cherokee subagency at the mouth of Illinois Bayou. He was delighted with the country, dubbing it the "Garden of the Worlds." But, he pointed out, "We have to pound the Corn into Meal haveing no Mills in all this part of the World every Article is Scarce & very high, flower which is brought by the traders on the Mississippi is from 18 to 24$ p barrel."[29]

Lovely charged that the whites of the region were mostly men who had escaped there after committing the most horrid crimes elsewhere.[30] The Cherokees complained bitterly that whites settled among them without consent, caused disorder, and destroyed game. The whites, on the other hand, strongly denounced the barbarity of the Cherokees. In a petition dated April 12, 1812, they charged that the newly arrived Cherokees had murdered a man named Rector, cut open his corpse, then disemboweled and mangled it. The petitioners asked for the protection of increased troops at Arkansas Post.[31]

In order to avoid armed conflict between the Cherokees and whites, Lovely felt it was necessary for him to take matters into his own hands until the government acted. After meeting with Tahlonteskee and his chiefs, Lovely autocratically defined an area of land north of the Arkansas River and assigned it to the Cherokees. White settlers immediately complained to the government that Lovely had given the Indians "the best and richest part of the Country."[32]

This act was essentially nullified when the Missouri territorial legislature established all of Arkansas as "Arkansas County." Missouri land speculators began buying up large tracts of the best land, surveying it, and putting off Indian "squatters." The Cherokees suddenly realized that they were without any legal claim to the land promised them by Jefferson.

Tahlonteskee and his chiefs were greatly disturbed. They wished to secure legal title to the new country from the U.S. government and have a clear line established to separate them from whites. For this purpose, they dispatched John Chisholm to carry their case to the capital at Washington during the summer of 1814. Though Chisholm was by no means a chief, his ties to Tahlonteskee and the Western Cherokee leadership were so close that he functioned much in that capacity.

En route to Washington City, Chisholm visited Hiwassee Garrison, where he was furnished two hundred dollars by Meigs for the trip. In Washington, Chisholm ran afoul of the English invasion of the infant American capital. On July 22 he wrote that he might well be detained for some time, thanks to the "Damnd Brittish," who had landed and burned the Calvert County, Maryland, courthouse as well as the home of Gen. James Wilkinson, who had fled with his many slaves.[33] With the far-from-completed capitol building likewise being torched and sacked, it was impossible for Chisholm to accomplish anything for the Arkansas Cherokees.

With the Arkansas River country then under the jurisdiction of Missouri Territory, Lovely and Tahlonteskee turned to Gov. William Clark in St. Louis for help in stopping an ongoing conflict with the Osages, who resided to the north and to the west. In May 1815, with Chisholm as a guide, Tahlonteskee led a delegation to St. Louis to talk with Clark personally.[34] "Under the faith of the President of the United States," Tahlonteskee told Clark, "we have been industrious; we have cleared nine miles on each side of the river. We wish to be friendly with our brethren the whites, but at the same time we wish to know that we walk upon our [own] ground."[35]

Through Meigs, Tahlonteskee and his chiefs also applied to the secretary of war for a trading house and a military establishment in their region. They wanted U.S. troops for protection not only from whites but also from the Osages. There had now begun an unending series of horse thefts and murders between the Arkansas Cherokees and the Missouri tribe.

The Cherokees were particularly concerned about a band of that tribe under Chief Clermont, which was located to their west thirty miles up the Verdigris River from its juncture with the Arkansas. This band, which had been persuaded to settle there by Missouri trader Jean Pierre Chouteau, stood between the Cherokees and the buffalo plains.

Upon first arriving in Arkansas, Lovely had led a delegation of eight Cherokees to the Osage village on a peace mission. The Osages responded with a visit to the Cherokees. But the good feelings between the two tribes were short lived. Just who first broke the peace is unresolvable; but Lovely reported that after the Osages had killed a Cherokee chief (unnamed), the Cherokees responded by killing twenty-one Osages.[36]

Once more Lovely and his Cherokee charges turned to Clark for help, and in April 1816 Tahlonteskee and John Chisholm led another delegation to St. Louis. Clark responded by promising to forward their complaints against the Osages to Washington. Also, he said, he had applied for a military post to be established on the Arkansas River.[37] But Tahlonteskee and Lovely were not willing to wait on the slow turn of U.S. government. They arranged for a council with the Osages in early July 1816 at Clermont's village.

On July 9 the two nations signed an agreement by which the Osages gave up their claim to all of the country between the Cherokees and the Verdigris River. This pact, which came to be known as "Lovely's Purchase," was never officially ratified by the U.S. Congress. Nonetheless, it established a division of land that would be accepted in later treaties between the Indians and the United States. This would be Lovely's last act in the Western Cherokee story, however. He had contracted an illness during the trip, one that eventually caused his death on February 24, 1817.[38]

Congress authorized a commission comprising Gen. Andrew Jackson, Tennessee governor Joseph McMinn, and Gen. David Meriwether to conduct a treaty council with both the eastern Old Nation and Western Cherokees. It was to be held at the new Cherokee agency in Calhoun, Tennessee, in July 1817. For some reason—illness or infirmity of old age, perhaps—Tahlonteskee did not wish to attend. John Chisholm was chosen in full council of the Western Cherokees to represent him.[39]

When word of this reached the Old Nation Cherokees, Richard Brown, Chisholm's former brother-in-law, wrote a strong letter of complaint. He charged that "Mr. Chisholm's general character is too well generally known to admit of vindication, and independent of this he is a white man who we conceive has no right to make regulations relative to the internal policy of our nation."[40]

The Western Cherokee chiefs, however, gave Chisholm their full support, writing, "Mr. Chisholm can give every information . . . he understands all the matters of this country and our people."[41] Chisholm did attend the treaty council and played a major role, as evidenced by Andrew Jackson's private note:

> We were compelled to promise to John D. Chisholm the sum of one thousand dollars to stop his mouth & obtain his consent, we have drew a bill in favor of Col. Meigs for this sum—without this we could not have got the national relinquishment. In the course of this conference we were obliged to promise the chiefs from the Arkansas, one hundred dollars each for their expense in coming here—and to three

other influential chiefs, the sum of one hundred dollars in presents—
this sum amounting to six hundred dollars we obtained from Col.
Meigs.[42]

The principal features of the treaty were the cession of more
Cherokee land, an agreement to issue annuities on a population basis
between the Old Nation and Western Cherokees by virtue of a census
to be made in 1818, a definition of Western Cherokee territory, establishment of an allotment of 640 acres in the ceded land for any adult
Cherokee wishing to become a U.S. citizen, and government aid to any
"poor warrior" who removed to the West.[43] That none-too-generous aid
included a rifle and ammunition, a blanket, five pounds of tobacco, and
a brass kettle or, in lieu of the kettle, a beaver trap as full compensation
for the land and improvements they left behind.

Following the treaty council, a delegation of Western chiefs, accompanied by Richard Brown of the Old Nation, set out for Washington for
an interview with President Monroe. En route at Knoxville they met
with Joseph McMinn, who helped them draft a letter to the president
asking for a trade factory where their "poor women and children would
receive clothing and supplies" instead of being at the mercy of unscrupulous traders. They also asked for reimbursement for the horses, saddles,
bridles, blankets, clothing, and money it would take them to make the
long trip to Washington in cold weather.[44]

James Rogers, son of trader John Rogers, went along as an interpreter, and Lt. Sam Houston served as guide for the party as it departed
Knoxville.[45] In addressing Congress thirty-six years later, Houston spoke
of Brown and the delegation's meeting with the president at the White
House. When the Cherokees were presented to the chief executive,
Houston later recalled, they gave him a history of their nation and the
circumstances under which their move west had been made. Monroe
promised them the "constancy, friendship and protection" of the United
States. Then he called upon rhetoric often used in dealings with Indian
tribes to reassure Tahlonteskee and his chiefs:

> He told them, you are now in a country where you can be happy;
> no other white man shall ever again disturb you; the Arkansas will pro-
> tect your southern boundary when you get there. You will be protected
> on either side; the white man shall never again encroach upon you,
> and you will have a great outlet to the West. As long as water flows, or
> grass grows upon the earth, or the sun rises to show your pathway, or
> you kindle your camp fires, so long shall you be protected by this
> Government, and never again removed from your present habitations.[46]

Lovely's purchase had by no means stopped the bloody conflict between the Cherokees and Osages. Under war leader Takatoka, the Arkansas Cherokees had been making plans for a major strike against the Verdigris Osages. During the spring of 1817 young men were recruited from among the Old Nation villages, where fond memories of their Cherokee role in the Battle of Horseshoe Bend in 1814 were still strong. In May, Meigs had warned Chief Jolly that Cherokees going to Arkansas should not do so with a view toward making war on the Osages.[47] Nonetheless, soon after the council at Calhoun had been completed, a letter from the Arkansas Cherokees to Governor Clark was drafted. Claiming that though they had been trying to make peace for nine years, the Osages had persisted in stealing their horses: "Please to inform the President of all this; tell him that we promised not to spill Blood if we could help it, but that at this time the rivers are red with the Blood of the Cherokees . . . Since our last talk to you, we have lost two of our young men, killed by the Osages, we have never attempted to take any revenge whatever, until now."[48] The letter was signed by Tahlonteskee, Takatoka, John McLemore, and four others. Further word on the impending Cherokee attack appeared in a St. Louis newspaper and was reprinted in *Niles' Register*. It claimed that a large coalition of warriors from various tribes had been gathering on the Arkansas: Cherokees, Choctaws, Shawnees, Delawares, Caddos, Coshattes, Tonkawas, and Comanches—all of whom had been victims of Osage marauding. Also present were warriors from Willstown, including Turtle Fields, John Huss, and John F. Boot, all of whom later became Christian ministers among the Cherokees.[49]

The Osages, the Cherokees later claimed, knew of the impending attack and had built forts. However, the Cherokees believed that the Osages, who always fought their battles on horseback, would be at great disadvantage in broken, wooded country. Maj. William Bradford reported it quite differently. He claimed that the Cherokees sent a friendly letter to the Osages inviting them to meet at a saltworks on the Grand River to make peace. Instead, Bradford claimed, they murdered the one chief who came.[50]

This version is supported by Bringier, who claimed that the Cherokee war party compelled the saline operator near the Osage village to lure an Osage out to treat for peace and then killed the old man.[51] Whether or not this is correct, it is apparent that the Osages were not expecting the Cherokees. As the Cherokees surely must have known, the Osages were away on their fall excursion to the buffalo plains. Thus, virtually all of their warrior force was absent when the Cherokee army marched up the Arkansas and Verdigris Rivers. At their lead were Takatoka and Tahlonteskee. John Chisholm, though now an old man, is said to have been there, though the possibility exists that he has been confused with his son Ignatius or one of the other Chisholms then residing in Arkansas.[52]

The Cherokee raiders fell upon the undefended town with merciless fury. They shot and tomahawked virtually all in their path, regardless of age or sex, driving others into the river, where they were slaughtered. When the carnage had been done, they plundered the village and then set it and crops in the field ablaze. By Governor Clark's report, they killed fourteen men plus sixty-nine women, children, and young boys. Over a hundred captives were taken back to the Cherokee villages, along with horses and a large number of scalps. The Cherokees had several men wounded; a Delaware ally was killed.[53]

The event was celebrated in the Old Nation as well as in the West. Sam Houston, then working with Meigs to persuade Cherokee people to join the migration westward, hastened to communicate to his superiors the news of "the most Brilliant success—scalps, Prisoners, horses & baggage" that were the trophies of victory.[54] War dances were held throughout the Cherokee Nation, and Houston surmised that the victory "cannot fail to produce an increase of estimation in the minds of those who heretofore have taken little interest in the Arkansaw country."[55]

Both Tahlonteskee and John Chisholm were nearing the end of their careers and lives. In January 1818, Tahlonteskee, Toochalar, Glass, and John McLemore came to Hiwassee and counseled with the eastern leaders regarding a trip to Washington to clarify the issue of Cherokee ownership of their land. As a result of the visit, the government moved to set boundaries for the western lands.[56]

Also, in an effort to resolve the continuing hostilities between the Cherokees and Osages, Governor Clark was instructed to arrange for a meeting at St. Louis in October. At that time, Tahlonteskee indicated that the Cherokees felt their victory over the Osages had given them the right to claim the country inhabited by Clermont's band. He saw this as a just remuneration for crimes the Osages had committed against his people, adding, "We do not wish to be cramped by them."[57]

During the spring and summer of 1818, a large migration of Cherokees from the Old Nation to Arkansas had taken place, bringing new leaders to replace those who had guided the Western Cherokees' destiny during their first decade. Among them were trader John Rogers Sr. and his sons, John Jr., Charles, James, and Lewis; John Jolly; Bench;

Sam Houston, who once
lived among the Cherokees,
remained their loyal friend.
Lester, *Sam Houston*
and His Republic.

Dick Justice; Glass; and Thomas Chisholm, the son of John Chisholm by his second marriage.[58]

Also on the emigration rolls was a man destined to become famous soon. His name was Sequoyah, or George Guess, inventor of the Cherokee syllabary. However, Sequoyah did not move west at this time. Instead, he, his wife, Sally, and their family moved to Willstown, recanting their wish to remove to Arkansas. On October 17, 1819, he and 836 other Cherokees who had enrolled signed a petition to that effect, declaring that they did so because of injury it did to the Old Nation and because they wished to "bury our bones in the dust which contains the relicks of our forefathers."[59]

In the fall of 1818, John Chisholm died; Tahlonteskee followed him to the grave during the spring of 1819.[60] The new generation of leaders now began to guide the destiny of the Western Cherokees. Their Arkansas lands were still not defined by law, their war with the Osages was far from over, their passage to the buffalo prairie was impeded by hostile Plains tribes, and aggressive whites were pressing them ever closer. This last problem was considered the most serious defect of the Arkansas lands, and some of the Western Cherokees were already considering moving farther away to the mountains or to Mexico's province of Texas to escape once again from the advancing tide of white intruders.

CHAPTER 10

A New Breed of Beloved Men

Following the departure of the Tahlonteskee migration in 1809, a period of compatibility between Old Nation leaders and the United States had spawned an upsurge in cultural improvement. Black Fox died in 1811 and was followed in office by Path Killer, who would prove to be an honorable and capable principal chief. Under his leadership, mission schools were permitted to open inside the nation, and for the first time Cherokee children began learning to read and write.

This social development, however, was interrupted by two major events: a revival of traditional resentment against white influence and a return to the day of the warrior. Many Cherokees still held to the dark myths of supernaturalism, conjuring, and witchcraft. "Shee-lehs" were evil spirits that could take possession of people, stop the rain, and destroy crops. These demons could warn animals against hunters and inflict deadly diseases upon men and other creatures of the world.

Rev. Cephas Washburn stated that he had known of many cases where Cherokees had been put to death by assassins appointed by village headmen.[1] If a man held a grudge against another, if he was tired of his wife and wanted another, if he wished to gain revenge on an enemy, he often made a charge of witchery. Washburn wrote: "This superstition among the Cherokees caused a fearful amount of bloodshed. In one instance a man was killed as a witch who had several brothers. These avenged his death by killing the witchkiller. His relatives avenged his death, and so it went on till seven individuals were killed."[2]

In 1824 the Cherokee National Council took testimony on the matter of witches. The tribunal was told of witches that could possess the bodies of birds and animals as well as those of humans. They could travel far and wide to do their mischief. After hearing these and other stories, the council issued a compromise. It passed a law forbidding the murder of humans to expunge the spirit of a witch but let stand the right to put a bewitched animal to death.[3] In 1829 an Arkansas missionary reported:

The belief in witchcraft which, when we first became acquainted with the people, was almost universal, and the cause of much mischief and several deaths annually, is now fast declining, and will soon be obliterated entirely. Such a belief is already considered as a mark of weakness and ignorance. Conjuring, of course, is now an unprofitable and disreputable business.[4]

Such beliefs were still strong, however, in early 1811, when three Cherokees in northwest Georgia reported that they had been visited by a band of Indians who appeared out of the heavens riding black horses. The visitors said they had been sent by the Great Spirit with instructions for the Cherokees. The people would have to return to many of their old ways, giving up their featherbeds, tables, and non-Indian dress. They were to stop planting the white man's variety of corn, and it should be ground by hand in the old way rather than by gristmills.

The messengers said that the "Mother of the Nation" was very unhappy that the Cherokees had let the wild game be killed off; also that they had let too many bad whites come among them. Some of the goods of whites were needed, however, to help the Cherokees learn to read and write. In essence, the message of the vision was a call for restoration of the old ways but still with acceptance of that part of white influence considered valuable to the Cherokees.[5]

When the vision of the heavenly horsemen was reported to the Cherokee council, Ridge, who had just returned from Washington, jumped to his feet and angrily declared the talk was false. A quarrel ensued, and others rushed upon him in a fury. So great was their passion that they might have killed him, but Ridge was a powerful man and with the help of friends he overcame his assailants.[6]

Though many of the younger chiefs scoffed at the vision, the older ones took it with religious seriousness. The national council responded by ordering a removal of all whites from the Cherokee country excepting only a few teachers, intermarried persons, and others. The threat of heavenly punishment inherent in the vision was strongly reinforced by a great comet display across the skies in August 1811. This was followed in December by the Missouri New Madrid earthquake and aftershocks that rattled and shook structures even in the Cherokee Old Nation.

Still another vision was reported by a Cherokee who was visited by a manlike specter who carried the Great Spirit in the form of a child. The Cherokee was told that if his people did not renew their ancient rituals, religious celebrations, dances, and medicines, the Great Spirit might have to destroy the world. Other prophecies were reported. From all of this there sprang the "Ghost Dance" revival of 1812 in which Cherokees held campfire religious dances, threw their white-style clothing into the blaze, and cleansed themselves with purification baths.[7]

The movement died out when the Cherokees turned from matters of religious revival to those of battle. The tribal call of warriorship that burned yet within the breasts of many Cherokee males was ignited once again in 1813. The Shawnee chief Tecumseh had come south to persuade a majority of the Creek Indians to take up arms against the United States. On August 30 of that year one of the bloodiest Indian forays in American history took place when the Creek Red Stick warriors attacked Fort Mims, Alabama, and killed more that five hundred of its inhabitants. When Tennessean Andrew Jackson was sent to quell the uprising, he accepted the offer of Ridge, John Walker, and John Lowrey to raise a supporting force of Cherokee warriors.[8]

Quickly organized into units of both foot and mounted soldiers, on October 16, 1813, the Cherokees of Chief Junaluska joined Tennessee white militia at Hiwassee Garrison and marched down the Tennessee River under the command of Gen. James White and Col. Gideon Morgan Jr. Even as this portion of Jackson's army gathered at Turkeytown, word came that a band of hostile Creeks was at the town of Talleschatchee, a few miles to the south. When the Cherokees were ordered to advance, they dressed their heads with white feathers and deer tails so they would not be taken for their Creek enemy in battle. Their arms consisted of a mixture of muskets, rifles, swords, tomahawks, lances, bows and arrows, and knives.

At Talleschatchee they found that a troop of white cavalry, among them Davy Crockett, had already wiped out the Creeks to the last man. Afterward White's army of Tennessee militia and Cherokee warriors was sent on to the mouth of the Chatooga River.

White was now ordered to take his militia and Cherokees to the mouth of the Chatooga River to join with forces under Gen. John Cocke. Because of this move, the Cherokees were not with General Jackson and his western Tennessee army when they defeated the Creek Red Stick warriors at Talledega, Alabama. On November 18 they saw their first action when a force of mounted Tennessee militia and Cherokees charged down onto the Creek town of Hillabee. Sixty-one Creeks were killed, and 250 taken prisoner.

Following this victory, the Cherokees were temporarily dismissed and sent home. They took with them captured Creek women, children, and black slaves who were dispensed among the Cherokee population. The five hundred-man Cherokee unit was reenlisted in late January 1814. A white officer promised, "Fifty nights shall not pass ere your swords, your lances, and your knives shall drink the blood of your enemy."[9]

They were again wearing their white feathers and deer tails on March 27, 1814, when Jackson attacked six Creek towns that lay nestled in a horseshoe bend of Alabama's Tallapoosa River. Jackson's small artillery pieces were ineffective against the strong breastwork of pine logs that the Creeks had constructed across the narrow part of the horseshoe, and the Tennessee militia was unable to storm the redoubt.

The Cherokees had been told to take up a position in the rear, their only assignments being to stymie a Creek retreat or prevent any attempt to reinforce them. With virtually no military order or discipline—some said they had more officers than otherwise—the Cherokees soon became impatient to be in the fray. The story was later told that an old man named Shoeboots went to Jackson, struck his breast with his fist, and declared in broken English, "No chicking heart me." Then with bullets whizzing about, he mounted a tree stump, flapped his arms, and crowed to imitate a rooster.[10]

Three young warriors—one of them Charles Reese—plunged into the river and swam to where the Creek canoes were docked along the bank. One warrior was wounded, but the other two each seized a canoe and returned to the Cherokee lines. Other canoes were taken the same way, allowing the Cherokees to cross the river under heavy fire, move close to the barricade, and engage the Creeks in a fierce battle.[11]

This flank attack permitted Jackson's militiamen to overrun and defeat the Red Sticks in a wholesale slaughter. The field count of Creek dead was 557, while another 350 or more were believed to have been killed in the river. The Cherokees lost 18 men, with 36 wounded. Their old friend Sam Houston suffered a leg wound in the fight. "The Cherokee warriors have fought and bled freely," agent Return J. Meigs observed, "and according to their numbers have lost more men than any part of the Army."[12]

When the Tennessee militia had arrived among the Overhills on their way south, the Cherokees had generously shared their corn and livestock to feed the troops. Yet when the war was over and the militiamen returned home, they wantonly marauded homes and plundered the

Cherokees' property, killing hogs and cattle, taking horses, and even stealing clothing.[13]

The Cherokees were extremely proud of their part in Jackson's victory. The names of those who took part would be repeated often in the years ahead in the context of Cherokee leadership and achievement: Ridge (hereafter known as Major Ridge), Richard Taylor, Charles Reese, Young Dragging Canoe, Richard Brown, John Lowrey, John Drew, Going Snake, George Fields, John Walker, and Charles Hicks were those who won laurels for their valor. Also present were John Ross, destined to be the most famous chief of the Cherokees, and Sequoyah, who was determined to take part, despite a game leg, and furnished his own horse. Reese and the two Cherokees who had first crossed the river were awarded silver-mounted rifles by the U.S. Congress.[14]

During the spring of 1816, Secretary of War William H. Crawford requested that Meigs bring a Cherokee delegation to Washington, D.C., for the purpose of extinguishing Cherokee title to land within South Carolina. Led by Col. John Lowrey, the group included Major Ridge, Richard Brown, Cheucunsenee (or Cun-ne-see), John Walker, and John Ross. The *Daily National Intelligencer* noted their presence in the city and lauded them all as having distinguished themselves by their bravery and attachment to the United States.[15]

The delegation was persuaded to sell their South Carolina land for five thousand dollars under a treaty dated March 22, 1816.[16] But at the same time, the chiefs secured U.S. acceptance of the Cherokee claim to four million acres of land in Georgia and Alabama that had been taken from the Creeks by the 1814 Treaty of Fort Jackson.[17]

Andrew Jackson, who had initiated the 1814 pact, was furious with Crawford. Supported by white public opinion in the affected region, Jackson won permission to conduct another treaty with the Indians. In September 1816, he and two other commissioners met with a large group of Cherokee chiefs headed by Toochalar at the Chickasaw council house in northwestern Alabama. Unable to persuade the Cherokees to give up valuable portions of their land south of the Tennessee River, Jackson turned to the tried-and-true method of bribery of the chiefs and interpreters. On September 14 a treaty was signed whereby the Cherokees gave up most of the land obtained by the earlier treaty for the sum of six thousand dollars annually for ten years, plus five thousand dollars upon ratification of the treaty.

The fifteen Cherokee names on the document included that of

George Guess, indicating a leading-man rank for the soon-to-be-famous Sequoyah.[18] Principal chief Path Killer and other important chiefs were not present, and it was stipulated that another meeting would be held at Turkeytown on the Coosa River of Georgia for final approval by the full Cherokee council. The Turkeytown council met on October 4, and the agreement was ratified by Path Killer along with Glass, Sour Mush, Dick Justice, Richard Brown, and others.[19]

But U.S. officials were not done. At the Treaty of 1817, with the Old Nation and Western Cherokees, Jackson was given the mission of obtaining a relinquishment of Old Nation land that equated to the allotment of the thirty-seven hundred Cherokees who had removed west. Jackson attempted to undermine Cherokee resistance by working through friendly chiefs such as Toochalar and Glass. The two chiefs gave in to Jackson's demands by signing a conditional treaty without the approval of the Cherokee council. As a result, the other chiefs refuted the agreement and struck both men from the national council, discarding them as chiefs.[20]

Nonetheless, pressure from Jackson, who pointedly reminded the Cherokees what had happened to the Creeks who defied U.S. power, led to the signing of a treaty on July 8. Richard Brown, a personal friend of Jackson, was the initial signatory for the Old Nation; but the list included leading men Charles Hicks, Going Snake, Sour Mush, and twenty-seven others. The discredited Toochalar and Glass joined John Jolly, who was preparing to move west, in signing with the Arkansas group.[21]

By this treaty, the Old Nation Cherokees ceded two million acres of land in Tennessee, Georgia, and Alabama. They further gave permission for the United States to build military posts, trade factories, and roads inside their territory.[22] However, second thoughts led the Old Nation council to dispatch six delegates under Chief Going Snake to Washington. They were to express complaints regarding their treatment to President Monroe and to arrange for an improved treaty. Audiences with the president and secretary of war failed to produce anything more than promises of brotherhood and friendship.

When a delegation of Western chiefs arrived in the Old Nation on their way to Washington in January 1818, the Cherokee council refused to appoint a delegation to go with them. Despite this, Joseph McMinn — who was then both governor of Tennessee and Indian superintendent — assigned Richard Brown to accompany the delegation of Western chiefs. Lt. Sam Houston served as escort for the group.[23]

After leaving Knoxville, the travelers stopped at the home of Joseph Rogers in Rogersville, Tennessee. While there the forty-five-year-old Brown, who had been ill for several days and still suffered from wounds received at Horseshoe Bend, died on January 26, 1818. Brown was highly lauded as a war leader who had fought in every battle of the Creek war and, further, as a wise counselor in peace. He was buried at Rogersville "with military honors, amidst a very numerous and respectable assemblage."[24]

Neither the white citizenry nor the government had been satisfied by the Cherokee cession of land. At a council called by McMinn in November 1818, the Cherokees were told that the United States could no longer protect them from Americans who encroached on their land, corrupted their women, stole their stock, or made drunkards of their warriors. McMinn attempted to purchase all of their Old Nation territory for one hundred thousand dollars with the expectation that the Cherokees would abandon their lands and relocate west of the Mississippi. The Cherokees would not listen, rejecting the idea in a statement signed by seventy-two chiefs and warriors.[25]

These efforts failing, in February 1819 McMinn escorted a Cherokee delegation headed by Charles Hicks and John Ross to Washington, D.C. There the Indians were persuaded to sign a treaty document that ceded a 6,000 square-mile tract embracing parts of Tennessee, Alabama, North Carolina, and Georgia. Those Cherokees accepting American citizenship in lieu of removing to the West would be awarded 640 acres.[26]

In 1820 the Old Nation Cherokees began to organize a republican form of government modeled after that of the United States, with a national council comprising an upper and lower house and a council president. The previous seventy to one hundred headmen were reduced to thirty-two representatives who were elected rather than chosen by other chiefs. Eleven new laws were enacted, including one that established a judicial system consisting of eight districts with marshals and judges. The legal system was supported by Cherokee Light Horse militia companies. A national superior court was created to review appeal cases that ranged from hog stealing to murder. Taxes were levied for the first time in Cherokee history.[27]

The nation had undergone other important influences, also. The Moravian missionaries had established their religious school at Springplace, Georgia, in 1801. Two years later the Cherokees permitted Presbyterian minister Rev. Gideon Blackburn to open a mission

school near Tellico, followed by one at Sale Creek. Because of illness
that struck Blackburn, the Tennessee schools were closed by 1817.
During the following year, the Brainerd mission school was established
near the Tennessee-Georgia boundary line by the American Board of
Commissioners for Foreign Missions of Boston. At the same time, the
Baptist Board of North Carolina opened a mission school at Valley
Town on the Hiwassee River, followed later by two others in Georgia.

Also, in 1821 Sequoyah revealed his significant invention of a
Cherokee syllabary. It had an immediate and enormous effect upon
learning among the Cherokees. Many adults and children were taught
to read and write in their own Cherokee language within a period of
only a few months. A revolution in learning had been fostered among
the Cherokees. Under instructions from Chiefs Path Killer and Charles
Hicks, the Cherokee council commissioned a medal to be struck to
honor Sequoyah.[28]

By 1824 American Board churches were operating at Brainerd,
Carmel, High Tower, Willstown, and Dwight Mission in Arkansas,
where missionaries worked to teach Cherokee children and convert
elders. Among these were Ard Hoyt, Daniel Butrick, Cephas Washburn,
William Potter, William Chamberlain, Elizur Butler, and Samuel A.
Worcester—and their seldom-mentioned but dedicated wives.[29]

By 1825 a Cherokee half-blood preacher, David Brown, had trans-

The famous Sequoyah, inventor of the Cherokee syllabary, also played a role in Cherokee political affairs.

New York Tribune,
June 29, 1844.

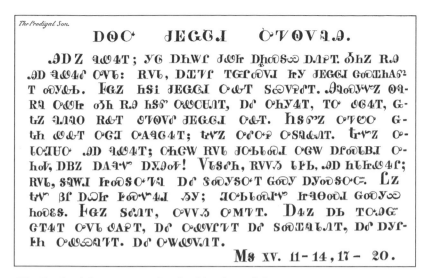

The Prodigal Son, *as printed in the Cherokee syllabary.*

Archives and Manuscripts, Oklahoma Historical Society.

lated the New Testament into the Cherokee syllabary, and in February 1828 a Cherokee bilingual newspaper, the *Tsa'lagi' Tsu'llehisanun'hi,* or *Cherokee Phoenix,* made its appearance. Its editor was Elias Boudinot, an intelligent half blood who as a young man had been sent to an Indian school at Cornwall, Connecticut.

Path Killer and Charles Hicks were the prominent chiefs through the decade of the 1820s. Following the Creek war, Path Killer had become more and more a symbolic Cherokee chief, while the Moravian-educated

Elias Boudinot, original editor of the Cherokee Phoenix, *was assassinated over the issue of removal.*

Western History Collection, University of Oklahoma.

Hicks made most of the important decisions and exercised the real power of principal chief. Though possessed of an Anglo name and accepting the white man's dress and customs, Hicks was deeply interested in Cherokee history and traditions. There is no evidence of any rivalry between him and Path Killer.[30]

A new landed, business class of Cherokees had now emerged, men who had some degree of formal education, were ambitious, and had accumulated wealth. They were in sharp contrast to the larger body of Cherokees, who were still content to live quietly, and largely happily, on their small farms. In a broad sense, the two groups were also separated by full-blood and mixed-blood status. Though the division was not racial, per se, a strong conflict existed between the two regarding traditional and nontraditional social values. Of particular issue were differences in regard to family structure—the old matrilineal pattern versus the patrilineal structure of whites—and the rising individualism that offended the communal aspects of tribalism.[31]

During the 1820s Cherokee entrepreneurship would produce a number of significant figures who in the years ahead would exert great influence upon the fate of the Cherokee Nation. Of particular note were John Ross, Major Ridge, his schooled son John Ridge, Elias Boudinot, his brother Stand Watie, and John and George Lowrey, though there were others. These were men of intellect and ability who could see into and debate issues on a level with the best minds.

Georgia officials were taken aback when they attempted to browbeat the Cherokees, as they had the Creeks, into paying Revolutionary War claims for slaves who had escaped into their country. The Cherokees dug out their 1798 Treaty of Tellico and pointed to the agreement that all thefts and plundering by Indians or whites had been erased. And when U.S. commissioners attempted to claim that the United States owned the Cherokee land by right of *discovery and conquest*, they were asked why time after time the United States had purchased Indian lands and made solemn treaties if the Indian had no title.[32]

Without question, John Ross was the one most significant Cherokee political figure to rise out of the new order. Educated, capable, and stubbornly persevering, he received good leadership training during his prechieftain days of the 1820s. Initially serving as a clerk to the Cherokee council and then as the first president of the Cherokee legislature, his political and communicative skills proved invaluable to the unschooled Path Killer throughout most of the full blood's reign as principal chief.

John Ross, for many years the Cherokees' leading chief, was a determined opponent of removal to the West.

Archives and Manuscripts, Oklahoma Historical Society.

Indirectly, John Ross was another product of Fort Loudoun days. His maternal great-grandfather, William Shorey, was the hard-drinking Scot interpreter who died while accompanying Lieutenant Timberlake and the Cherokee delegation to London in 1762. What became of Shorey's full-blood Cherokee wife, Ghigooie, is not recorded. It is known, however, that two children were produced by the marriage, a son named William, who signed the Treaty of 1805 using the Cherokee name of Eskaculiskee, and a daughter named Anna.

Anna Shorey in turn married Scotsman John McDonald, who settled near Lookout Mountain on the Chickamauga. John McDonald is said to have arrived in America around 1767 and made his way to Fort Loudoun and from there went to Chickamauga, where he met and married Anna. He was serving as the British agent to the Cherokees when he learned that a young Highlander had been captured by the Cherokees and was about to be burned at the stake.

McDonald hurried to the site and cajoled the warriors into releasing their victim. McDonald took the young Scot, Daniel Ross, to his home. Eventually Ross married the McDonalds' daughter Molly and became a trader among the Cherokees. He established a home at the foot of Lookout Mountain and there built a log house in which his children were taught by his old tutor from Inverness, whom he had persuaded to come to America. It is said that Ross's was the first formal school among the Cherokees. Ross later moved to Turkeytown on the Coosa River of Alabama, where John Ross, the third of nine children, was born on October 3, 1790.[33]

Being of small physical stature, he was given the Indian name of Tsan Usdi, or Little John, as a boy; later he would acquire the adult name of Kooweskoowe, reflecting the image of a migratory bird, which was enhanced by his daring trip to the Arkansas country in 1812.

Ross suffered the syndrome of many mixed bloods. He soon learned in life that his being one-eighth Indian would keep him ostracized from full participation as a white; yet his fair skin and largely Caucasian appearance told clearly that he was not totally Cherokee. His home life followed that of white society, with books and newspapers and an interest in world affairs. Further, his parents educated the Ross children through the services of a private tutor. When he was old enough, John was sent off to school at Southwest Point, now Kingston, Tennessee.

Having learned some practical business skills there, Ross worked as a clerk with a trading firm at Kingston upon leaving school. When the second William Shorey, Ross's great-uncle, died in 1809, Ross became a landholder through inheritance of a portion of the big island in the Tennessee River just below Tellico. This was the beginning of his acquisition of considerable land properties in both Tennessee and Georgia.

In 1813, at the age of twenty-three, Ross joined Timothy Meigs, the son of the Cherokee agent, in a joint business venture. Enterprisingly, the two young men established a trading post and warehouse at the north end of Lookout Mountain on the south bank of the Tennessee River. The place became widely known as Ross's Landing, and is now a part of Chattanooga. They supplemented this activity with a profitable ferry that serviced transportation on the Federal route between Nashville and Augusta. Meigs died in 1815, and Ross's brother Lewis took his place in the business.

John Ross took loads of deerskins and other peltry to New York and Baltimore, trading them for the cloth, tools, and items badly needed by the Cherokees. The Creek war was fortunate for the firm, bringing lucrative government contracts in supplying food and other goods to the Cherokees. However, Ross did not simply sit back and profit from the

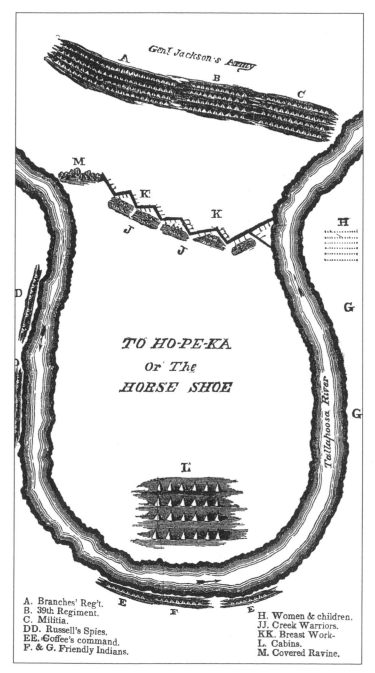

Battle plan at Horseshoe Bend.

Lester, *Sam Houston and His Republic.*

war. In 1813 he volunteered his services as a Cherokee soldier and was
assigned as an adjutant to Col. Gideon Morgan. He rode with the U.S.
and Cherokee forces under General Jackson when the Creeks were
defeated at Horseshoe Bend.[34]

Just prior to his enlistment, Ross had married the former Elizabeth
Brown Henley, whose Cherokee lineage had given her the Indian name
of Quatie. After his brief military service, Ross returned to his occupational pursuits. But now he also became more and more involved in
Cherokee political affairs. His ability to speak and write the English language, a skill that was still rare among the Cherokees, was a great
attribute as the nation began its transition from its old tribal ways to
those of the white man.

Ross was still only twenty-five in 1815 when he accompanied the
delegation to Washington, D.C., to deal with legal matters of treaty
rights, boundaries, war and personal restitution claims, and problems of
Cherokee internal improvement. As the principal communication link
between the Cherokee chiefs and representatives of the U.S. government, Ross was soon dealing with persons at the highest level, including presidents of the United States.

He quickly proved to be mentally adept, tough, and capable in handling Cherokee affairs. He was also fiercely determined to serve the race
to which he had such slight blood relationship; and he was firmly honest. Following the treaty of 1817, the U.S. government exerted immense
pressure upon the Cherokees to migrate west of the Mississippi. Ross
had just been named as the president of the newly created Cherokee
National Council in 1818 when Governor McMinn asked to meet with
the group. During the meeting, McMinn offered large sums of money to
encourage Cherokee removal—money by which members of the council would personally profit. Ross not only resisted the bribery effort, but
he exposed McMinn in an angry letter to a North Carolina newspaper.[35]

It was during the trip to Washington in 1819 that Ross was attacked
in his hotel room by Cherokee John Walker, who was also a delegate.
The incident arose from a new treaty that awarded several Cherokees
special benefits. Those beneficiaries included Walker, who received two
640-acre grants, and his stepdaughter Mrs. Eliza Ross, who received
another. The properties of Lewis Ross at Tellico and that of John Ross
on Big Island were also recognized by the treaty.[36]

Ross saw Walker's reward as a bribe, and told him so. On the night
before leaving Washington, Ross was working late in his hotel room when

Walker, who had been drinking heavily, rushed in with a brick in his hand, yelling that he had come to whip Ross. He threw the brick at Ross, who managed to duck it. When Walker then threatened him with a knife, Ross drew his own. The two men were separated by fellow delegate John Martin, Ross having suffered only a slight cut on the shoulder.[37]

During this same year, Ross undertook a rescue mission to retrieve an Osage child, a boy, who had been captured by the Arkansas Cherokees in their attack on Clermont's village. The young Osage had been passed on to some Alabama whites, who were about to sell him into slavery. At the request of missionaries, Ross went to Mobile and recovered the boy, who was given the name of John Osage Ross. Later, after being adopted by one of the missionaries, the youngster was placed in Brainerd School.[38]

As president of the national committee, Ross was perhaps the leading conductor of Cherokee affairs, carrying out many of the decisions made by the committee. For a time, he served as commander of a Cherokee Light Horse company assigned to the task of removing white intruders from Cherokee land. It was not a pleasant undertaking, often requiring brute force and uncompromising zeal in burning homes and crops to ensure that the squatters did not return.[39]

His resistance to the government pressure for Cherokee removal was so vigorous that officials soon recognized him as a major stumbling block to their plans. In 1822 Ross was instrumental in persuading the Cherokee council to pass a resolution declaring their determination to hold no further treaties that would result in loss of Cherokee land. In an effort to eliminate his opposition, officials deviously sent Creek chief William McIntosh to bribe him and others. During a meeting between a U.S. Indian commission and the Cherokee National Committee in 1823, McIntosh passed a note to Ross. It read:

> If the chiefs feel disposed to let the United States have the land part of it, I want you to let me know. I will make the United States Commissioners give you two thousand dollars, A. McCoy [Cherokee National Committee clerk] the same and Charles Hicks three thousand dollars for present(s) and nobody shall know it. I will get you the amount before the treaty is signed, and if you have any friend you want him to receive, he shall receive.[40]

The infuriated Ross made the note public before the council, and McIntosh was ejected from the meeting. Soon afterward McIntosh was assassinated by his own tribe over treaty issues. Ross's action raised his popularity among the Cherokees considerably. In 1824 he was once more named to a committee to go to Washington and attend to the problem of increasing land demands by Georgia and other matters, such as the division of annuity payments with the Arkansas Cherokees. Making this long midwinter trip by horseback with Ross were George Lowrey, Major Ridge, and Elijah Hicks. Also traveling with the party was John Ridge and his sister Sarah, who was to be situated under the care of a Washington home for her education and social development.[41]

In a meeting with President James Monroe, Secretary of War John C. Calhoun, and Secretary of State John Quincy Adams, the Cherokees were again pressed to sell their homeland and move west to join the Arkansas Cherokees. They adamantly refused. The delegation stayed six months in the capital arguing with Calhoun, defending their rights by treaty, and attempting to get McMinn removed as their agent. Ross penned long letters to Calhoun, the Congress, the commissioner of Indian affairs, the editors of the *National Intelligencer,* and others pressing the Cherokee case for justice. On April 15 he wrote to Congress: "We appeal to the magnanimity of the American Congress for justice, and the protection of the rights, liberties, and lives, of the Cherokee people. We claim it from the United States, by the strongest obligations, which imposes it upon them by treaties; and we expect it from them under that *memorable* declaration, 'that all men are created equal.'"[42]

This plea to the moral premise of American democracy had little effect, the administration and Congress still bowing to the demands of Georgia and others to rid the South of the Cherokees. Ross was back in Washington again the following year, seeking payment of interest due them on delayed rewards under the 1804 Treaty of Tellico and compensation for Cherokee properties from which Indians had been forced by intruding whites.

Ross's deepening involvement in Cherokee affairs as president of the national committee caused him to move from his home at Rossville (the former Ross's Landing) in Tennessee to the head of the Coosa River in Georgia. Now one of the richest men in the Cherokee Nation, he built a comfortable two-story home not far from the residence of Major Ridge and established a successful plantation with gardens and orchards tended by some twenty slaves. Ross also became much better acquainted with Chief Hicks, who instructed him on the oral traditions of the Cherokees and provided him with deeper insight into the thoughts and feelings of the full-blood Cherokees.[43]

John Ross was emblematic of the new Anglicized Cherokee leader whose very being stood against the tribal religious and cultural traditions of the past. He represented one side of an ideological schism that had been growing larger and larger within the nation. These opposing forces came into conflict in 1826, when the Cherokee National Council called a convention to adopt a new constitution and a form of centralized government similar to that of the United States. At the same time, the Cherokees voted to establish a new capital at the confluence of the Coosawatee and Conasauga Rivers in north-central Georgia. The site was at first called New Town, but it was later changed to New Echota, after the old capital of Chota. By the new constitution, the number of chiefs as well as the power of the town councils were reduced considerably.[44] This radical change in leadership was paralleled by some equally significant acts of fate. In January 1827 the elderly principal chief Path Killer died; then two weeks later, Charles Hicks, who had succeeded Path Killer, also died.[45] The nation now faced the pressure of land demands from Georgia and North Carolina without a principal chief.

The change in form of government had been an affront to tribal traditionalists, who particularly resented the Christian-fostered restrictions on their old lifestyle and chieftain system. They rebelled against the proposed constitution by calling their own government-forming council

Buildings of the Cherokee capital have been restored at New Echota, Georgia.

Photo by author.

near the home of Chief White Path, a leader of the insurrection. During the spring of 1827, the entire Cherokee Nation was caught up in the turmoil of a nonviolent revolution that came to be known as White Path's Rebellion.[46]

When members for the constitutional convention were elected in May, a disproportionate number were from the group of wealthier, English-speaking mixed bloods. Only four of twenty-one were full bloods.[47] The election initiated a pattern of political imbalance that would long continue in Cherokee government. Cherokee leadership would be characterized by a pattern of "blood" division. "On the whole," a noted Cherokee scholar observed, "the national committee continued to be predominantly those of experience, of mixed ancestry, wealthy, and English-speaking while the national council was predominantly non-English-speaking and full blood."[48]

The White Path rebellion was ended in June, when a number of the faction, though not White Path, signed a resolution expressing their regret for disturbing the public welfare and agreeing to support the laws of the new constitution. In October the national council elected William Hicks to fill the unexpired term of his deceased brother, and Ross was elected as the second chief.

Though only second chief, John Ross was still the leading spokesman for the Cherokee Nation. Undoubtedly it was he who penned the message to the national council ridiculing the government's offer of a gun, blanket, trap, kettle, and five pounds of tobacco as small compensation for leaving: "our friends, our relatives, our houses, our cultivated farms, our country, and everything endeared to us by the progress of civilization—for what? To tread the barren wilds and dreary waste on the confines of the Rocky Mountains."[49]

When the first election was held under the new constitution in October 1828, Ross was chosen by a wide margin over Hicks as principal chief of the Old Nation Cherokees.[50] During the ensuing decade, Ross would continue to be a towering figure of resistance to U.S. efforts to uproot and remove the entire Cherokee nation to the West. But he would face greatly increased pressure from both the federal government and the state of Georgia. This resulted from two major events: the 1828 election of Andrew Jackson as president of the United States and the discovery of gold on Cherokee land in northern Georgia.

CHAPTER 11

Cherokee Nation West

In August 1819 the Western Cherokees wrote to President James Monroe requesting the "clear opening to the setting of the sun" that had been promised them. The lead signers of the letter were Takatoka, Dick Justice, Glass, and John Jolly, followed by John McLemore, Walter Webber, Thomas Maw (son of Hanging Maw), and Thomas Graves.[1] Glass and Dick Justice, both now quite old, signed mainly to lend the weight of their names. Soon it would be reported that the two chiefs "sleep in death on the Arkansas."[2] The elder John Rogers, who had taken part in the assassination of Doublehead, was soon gone also.

Chief Bowle and his group had settled four miles south of the Arkansas River on Petit Jean Creek. During 1819 the government conducted a survey of the Cherokee lands in Arkansas and instructed those Cherokees living south of the Arkansas River that they would have to move to the north side. Bowle and his people, who were inclined toward a hunting existence rather than that of planting, had no desire to leave the game-rich forests below the Arkansas. Already discontent with increasing white encroachment, Bowle and his band moved south near present Texarkana, Arkansas. They would soon migrate on into Texas.[3]

In July 1820, missionaries Alfred Finney and Cephas Washburn arrived among the Arkansas Cherokees. Selecting a site on the west bank of Illinois Bayou four miles north of the Arkansas, the churchmen felled their first tree on August 25 to begin erection of a mission. They named it Dwight Mission in honor of Timothy Dwight, late president of Yale College.[4] The school opened on January 1, 1822, and soon claimed an enrollment of some forty students under the Lancastrian plan.

Ultimately Dwight would feature a fenced compound containing a boys' schoolhouse, girls' schoolhouse, cabins for the students, dining hall and kitchen, quarters for the missionaries, blacksmith's shop, carpenter's shop, tool house, storeroom, and lumber house. Outside the compound were corn, oat, and clover fields, barn, stable, herding pastures, orchard, and gardens.[5] Here Cherokee children were schooled, indoctrinated with Christianity, and trained in vocational skills.

Also in 1820 the area was visited by Edwin James's group of the Stephen H. Long expedition to the Rocky Mountains, who were returning east down the Arkansas River. As the weary men passed through Arkansas, they were provided the hospitality of various Cherokee settlements along the river. One of those villages visited by the James party was that of Takatoka, who James said had been considered as the principal chief and Beloved Man of the western nation since the death of Tahlonteskee.[6]

When missionary Cephas Washburn first met the chief that same year, Takatoka was about sixty-five years of age. Washburn provided a detailed description of the old man, who he said was descended from ancient priesthood among the Cherokees.

> His hair was of a silver white, and, as usual with the aged among our Indian tribes, it was finer and softer than is common in middle age. His stature was about five feet nine inches, his form erect, and all his movements as easy and agile as those of youth. I never saw a finer face. It was of the Grecian model, with a little stronger marked features. His forehead was high and very well developed, indicating, as the phrenologists have it, intellectual powers of a high order. His mouth and lip expressed great determination and force of character. But his eye was the most striking and awe-inspiring feature in his very fine and interesting countenance. It was the sun in the midst of all the lesser luminaries of his expressive face.[7]

A similar impression was made on a Scottish missionary, Rev. F. R. Goulding, who met Takatoka while the chief was on a visit to the Old Nation to persuade other Cherokees to remove to the West. Goulding noted: "No one could look upon his broad forehead, flashing eye, and expressive face without feeling that he was a born chief."[8]

Takatoka was, indeed, a determined leader. In 1819 he and other Cherokees met with the Osages at Fort Smith, which had been established two years earlier, in an effort to make peace. The Osages demanded the return of the women and children who had been taken prisoner in the massacre of Clermont's village. By then some of the Osage women had married Cherokee men, and Takatoka refused to permit their forced return to their original tribe.

As a result, the war continued, with the Osages killing three Cherokee hunters and taking their furs. The Cherokee war captain, Dutch (Tachee), responded by following the Osages to Nathaniel Pryor's trading house on the Verdigris River, recapturing the furs and killing and scalping one of the Osages.[9] The son of Chief Skyuka who signed the treaties of 1791, 1794, and 1806, Dutch had once lived among the Osages in Missouri. During that time he married an Osage woman, who for some reason was killed by her own tribe. Dutch became a bitter enemy of the Osages, with whom he reportedly fought some thirty battles and took the scalps of twenty-six warriors.[10]

Another peace effort with the Osages was made during the spring of 1820. Four of the younger Cherokee chiefs accompanied the newly appointed Gov. James Miller of Arkansas Territory to Clermont's village. An accord was reached on the basis of the Cherokees' return of four Osage prisoners and the Osages' delivery of the murderers of the Cherokee hunters.[11] The exchange did not take place, however, and hostilities continued into 1821, when Osage war leader Mad Buffalo conducted a foray into Arkansas. After threatening the small military garrison at Fort Smith, the Osages killed three Quapaw Indians before they retreated.

The Cherokees responded with another assault into Osage country, again while Clermont's warriors were away on a buffalo hunt. Led by half-blood merchant Walter Webber, the Cherokees murdered Joseph Revoir, manager of Chouteau's Trading Post on the Grand River and husband to an Osage woman. The reason they gave was that Revoir had been selling arms and ammunition to the Osages. The Cherokees returned home with Revoir's scalp, using it as a pretext for a war dance in celebration of the American Fourth of July.[12]

Webber, the son of Redheaded Will of Willstown, had removed to the St. Francis River as a boy and came with that group to Arkansas. Though he was raised in the old-style Cherokee manner and had no formal schooling, he operated a trading post at the conflux of the Arkansas River and Illinois Bayou. He made trips every spring to Baltimore to procure trade goods and on occasion took his boats up the Arkansas and Canadian Rivers in the Indian Territory.[13]

Buoyed by Webber's feat, the Cherokees laid plans for still another foray against the Osages during their fall buffalo hunt. This time the Cherokees were headed by Thomas Graves. The wealthy Cherokee, who did not speak English, was either a half blood or a white who had been captured as a boy and raised by the Cherokees.[14] His force was sizable, consisting of three hundred men, including some Delawares, Creeks, Choctaws, Shawnees, and whites. Maj. William Bradford at Fort Smith met them en route and was able to persuade all but the Cherokees to turn back.[15]

The Osages, this time with their women, children, and elders, had departed their Verdigris River village and proceeded westward. After crossing the Arkansas River at the mouth of the Cimarron, they divided into three groups. The Osage men pushed on ahead to hunt and to fight off any Pawnees that might be in the vicinity. Following the broad trail of the Osage caravan, the Cherokee war party came upon the lagging women and children. According to their count, the Cherokees killed forty of the group, took thirty prisoners, and captured seventy horses.[16]

The Osages afterward surprised the Cherokees, charged them, and in close-range fighting drove them from the field. Two of the Cherokees were killed, their scalps being taken by their own party to deprive the Osages of that honor. The Cherokees returned to Arkansas with their horses, trophies, and captives. It was reported that Tom Graves held an Osage woman, her child, and a young girl as prisoners for nearly two months before murdering them while in a drunken frenzy. He then threw their bodies to his hogs. He was arrested by a U.S. marshal, who took him by canoe to Little Rock. However, Graves was eventually released.[17]

The Cherokees and Osages made another treaty agreement in August 1822, but the pact did not long hinder the war inclinations of either nation. During the winter of 1822–23, the Osages caught Red Hawk, a nephew of Graves, away from his hunting camp. They killed him and, as was their customary war practice, scalped him and cut off his head.[18]

Just how long Takatoka remained the principal chief is unclear. A letter to President Monroe dated March 17, 1821, was signed first by John Jolly then in turn by John McLemore, Thomas Graves, Raven, John Rogers, and two others. It was delivered to the president in Washington by James Rogers, Walter Webber, and Thomas Maw, who were also listed as chiefs and agents of the Arkansas Cherokees.[19]

Discontented with white intrusion into the Cherokee land in Arkansas, Takatoka led a group of fifty to sixty Cherokees to the Kiamichi River country of present southeastern Oklahoma during the summer of 1823 and established a village. Even there the Cherokee-Osage conflict continued. It was reported that in September Takatoka and his warriors ambushed a party of Osages. For whatever reason, the old war chief and his people soon returned to the Arkansas.[20]

When John McLemore died on July 1, 1824, the *Missionary Herald* referred to the Horseshoe Bend veteran as the late principal chief.[21] On

September 8 following his death, the Cherokee council met at Piney Creek, Arkansas, and organized a new government. The western nation was divided into four districts designated as Point Remove, Illinois, Piney, and Mulberry. John Jolly was chosen as president, Takatoka as vice president, and Black Fox as speaker.[22]

This formalizing of their government was a reflection of other advancements that had been and were being made among the Western Cherokees. The U.S. trade factory at Chickasaw Bluffs (Memphis) had been relocated to Spadra Bluffs in 1818. In May 1822 the factor, Col. Matthew Lyon, took a load of furs to New Orleans, using their proceeds to purchase a cotton gin for the Cherokees. Unfortunately, the seventy-six-year-old Lyon died during a siege of typhoid, and the factory was closed during the fall of 1823.[23]

Steamboats had begun making their way up the winding Arkansas River to Dwight Mission in 1822,[24] then later on to Fort Smith. Eventually, when the river was not too low, the paddle wheelers would inch their way to the Six Bulls area, where in 1824 Cantonment Gibson was established. As slow and undependable as they were, the steamboats were extremely valuable in supplying the frontier Cherokee settlements with foodstuff and other goods, as well as providing much-improved linkage to the outside world.

Other significant changes were also underway. Three companies of Cherokee Light Horse police had been formed in 1820 to control the rampant horse thievery.[25] The Dwight missionaries were beginning to teach Cherokee children the rudiments of white speech and education. Though Takatoka opposed the school and remained aloof from it for some time, he later changed his views and learned to read and write himself.[26]

From the start, Chief John Jolly, a rotund, pleasant-natured man, was a strong supporter of educating Cherokee children. Like his famous forebear Corn Tassel, Jolly was known for his honesty. His generosity was reputed to be virtually unlimited. In Tennessee, Jolly had resided on Hiwassee Island, where he owned and operated a trading post. It was to his village that young Sam Houston came to live for a time, becoming attached to the kindly chief virtually on a father-son basis.

When he moved west early in 1818, Jolly had brought with him sixteen flatboats laden with some 331 Cherokees and their possessions. They settled near Illinois Bayou before eventually moving to Spadra.[27] The English botanist Thomas Nuttall, who came up the Arkansas in

1819, met Jolly and penned a description of him: "Being a half Indian, and dressed as a white man, I should scarcely have distinguished him from an American, except by his language. He was very plain, prudent, and unassuming in his dress and manners; a Franklin amongst his countrymen, and affectionately called the 'beloved' father."[28] Jolly was described by others in his later years as being of a massive frame, though not tall. His hair, which he wore in long locks, was sprinkled with gray. Still speaking no English, he wore the Indian buckskin hunting shirt, leggings, moccasins, and a cloth turban.[29]

The missionaries were now exercising significant influence among the Indians, preaching regularly in the homes of Cherokees, including those of Jolly at Spadra and Webber at Dardanelle, where the Sabbath was spent singing Cherokee songs and socializing. Eventually a second small mission was established on to the west at Mulberry Creek. The Cherokee citizens there voted to erect a school building, furnish books and stationery, board all of the students in private homes, and provide for the teacher and his family.[30]

Takatoka had long been interested in forming an alliance of tribes that had been removed from east of the Mississippi River. His purpose was to better oppose the Osages and other tribes native to the West and to force better consideration from the United States. He and other Cherokees hoped, also, to secure title to the territory west of Fort Gibson, which held the advantages of excellent hunting, good farming land, salt springs, and lead mines.

In October 1824 the old chief led a delegation of Western Cherokees to a grand intertribal council held at Kaskaskia, Illinois. These chiefs included Spring Frog, Young Glass, Witch, Tahlone, John Drew, and Corn Tassel, who was possibly a descendant of Old Tassel. The Shawnees, Delawares, Kickapoos, Peorias, Pankeshaws, and Miamis asked Takatoka to go to Washington with their delegates to help in talks with the president regarding the possible exchange of their land east of the Mississippi for lands in the West.[31]

However, en route Takatoka became very ill. Even as he lay dying, he urged that his followers continue on.[32] As he requested, they journeyed on to Washington, D.C., in hopes of obtaining legal definition of their Arkansas lands. The chiefs found that the government had little interest in their wants. Instead officials demanded the Indians trade their land in Arkansas for the region purchased by Lovely. The delegation rejected the plan out of hand and returned home.[33]

There was great concern among the Arkansas Cherokees regarding the whites who were moving in droves to the Lovely's Purchase area. The Cherokee leaders wrote a memorial of protest to remind officials of President Monroe's vow to provide them the outlet to the west that they had been promised. The issue was intensified in 1827 when Arkansas Territory moved to annex the area that had become known as "Lovely County" of Arkansas.

Much alarmed, the Cherokee council met that December and appointed another delegation to go to Washington. Its purpose would be to secure a survey of both their lands ceded in the East under the Treaty of 1817 and the lands assigned to them between the White and Arkansas Rivers. They also hoped to obtain title to Lovely's Purchase as a western outlet to the buffalo prairies.[34]

The delegation comprised Black Fox, John Rogers, Tom Graves, Thomas Maw, George Marvis, John Looney, and Sequoyah, who had moved west in 1824. James Rogers served as interpreter, and they were escorted by Cherokee agent E. W. Duval. The delegation was empowered only to "arrange and finally adjust with the President of the United States or others all the unsettled matters" between the Western Cherokees and the United States.

There was certainly no intention by the Cherokee council that this delegation should become involved in a treaty that would trade away their Arkansas lands; nor had the delegation any such thoughts. But once they reached Washington, the Cherokees were detained in their hotel for well over a month while government officials cajoled, whiskeyed, and bribed them into signing an agreement for exchanging their Arkansas land for that of Lovely's Purchase.[35]

The government bribery included twelve hundred dollars for Thomas Graves; five hundred dollars for George Guess, plus rights to a saline on Lees Creek of present Oklahoma to replace one in Arkansas; and five hundred dollars to James Rogers. It must be assumed that the others were similarly rewarded.[36]

The Treaty of 1828 also sought to encourage migration of Old Nation Cherokees to the West. Government officials enlisted James Rogers to go to Tennessee and recruit tribespeople for removal. He did not realize the intense rancor that the matter aroused in some Cherokees. While he was at the Calhoun agency, he was attacked by Chief Path Killer. The old chief struck Rogers in the back of the head with a heavy rock and vowed to kill the half blood when he had a chance.[37]

The Treaty of 1828 had momentous consequences for the Western Cherokees, as Agent Duval pointed out in a letter to Secretary of War James Barbour. The Indians, he noted, would be required to "leave their opened fields and improvements, which they have been toiling on for years . . . to settle in a remote area away from conveniences which they now enjoy . . . [they would suffer] the loss of at least one crop . . . and, if no provisions are to be made for them, hardship and suffering in its worse form—hunger, famine and partial nakedness will be the consequences."[38]

Not unexpectedly, there was furious outrage directed at the delegation, several of whom were threatened ominously by having poles erected in their yards—supposedly for the purpose of holding the heads they were soon to lose! Eventually, however, the exchange was accepted fatalistically by the Western Cherokee people, and in the fall of 1829 most of them began their exodus to Lovely's Purchase.

When news that the Cherokees would be awarded compensation payments for their Arkansas lands and for removing, white traders and merchants flocked in from near and far. They used a favorite frontier ploy that had long proved successful—beset the Indians with whiskey to get them drunk and get their money. "Gambling, fighting, debauchery, murder," a missionary wrote, "and every evil work are the concomitants of this prevalence of intemperance. Since last December not less than 50 persons in this nation have gone into eternity, in consequence of intemperance."[39]

Not only did the Cherokees leave behind their homes, gardens, and orchards and take on the task of once again clearing fields, erecting fences, and building houses and barns, but they also faced the inevitable conflicts with whites. These whites often rushed in to take over the Indians' Arkansas farms, forcing residents out and even taking their stock. Then when the refugees reached the new country, they again encountered angry resistance from white settlers who were not prepared or willing to vacate their holdings as the treaty specified they were to do.

Their situation was complicated even further by the fact that the United States had already assigned precisely the same area to the Creeks that the Treaty of 1828 assigned to the Cherokees. When Chief Black Fox wrote to the U.S. government to complain about the animosity that had been created and the suffering of his people, Secretary of War Thomas L. McKinney expressed his regrets that "ignorant people gave you any trouble at home about the Treaty." There was always someone, he complained, who tried to spoil the good work done by others.[40] His answer to Black Fox's plea for help was to send a "Great Medal" to put around the chief's neck.

The dispossessed Cherokees began relocating their families along the Arkansas River from west of Fort Smith to Fort Gibson, forming new communities at places such as Skin Bayou; the Illinois River; Sallisaw River; Webbers Falls, above the mouth of the Canadian; and the Fort Gibson area. Chief Jolly resettled inside the southeast juncture of the Arkansas and Illinois Rivers, where slaves tended his farms and several hundred head of cattle. Three miles up the Illinois from his place, the Western Cherokees had built a council house and established a new capital, which they named "Tahlonteskee." A new Dwight Mission school was erected on the west side of Sallisaw Creek, twelve miles from the mouth and thirty miles east of Gibson. Rev. Alfred Finney died on June 13, 1829, while the mission was being built.[41]

The conflict of land assignments to the Western Cherokees and the Creeks was resolved in a treaty conducted at Fort Gibson on February 14, 1833, with the United States. By it the government agreed to erect eight corn mills, four blacksmith shops, a wagon shop, and a wheelwright shop for the Cherokees. Steel and iron would be furnished along with men to operate the installations. Further, one square mile would be set aside for a Cherokee agency. The pact was signed by Jolly, Black Coat, and Walter Webber, while John Rogers served as president of the attending Cherokee commission.[42]

Walter Webber now operated a trade store at Webbers Falls; a large farm at Fairfield settlement, twenty miles north of new Dwight Mission; and a saltworks. He died April 4, 1834, and was replaced as third chief of the Western Cherokees by Thomas Chisholm.[43]

Among other effects, the move placed the Cherokees in even closer proximity to their inveterate enemies, the Osages. In spite of efforts by U.S. authorities to bring about a peace between the two nations, the Cherokees were still bitter, insisting that "Cherokee blood yet smokes on the ground."[44] Their conflict was lessened, however, by the troubles of both with other warring tribes. The Osages were still conducting raids against the Wacos, Wichitas, Comanches, Choctaws, and other tribes along the Red River. They were also engaged in a bloody war with the aggressive Pawnee Mahas, who came south from the Loup River of Nebraska to hunt and steal horses.

At the same time, the Western Cherokees were pushing aggressively against the tribes native to the buffalo plains. The *Cherokee Phoenix* of

March 18, 1829, recounted one such case by a company of thirty Arkansas Cherokees that a few months before had gone to explore the headwaters of rivers flowing from the Rocky Mountains. The Cherokees, armed with rifles, clashed with a band of Plains Indians armed with bows and arrows. Two of the Cherokees were killed. When seven of the party went forth to seek revenge, two more were lost.

During the winter of 1828–29 a party of Cherokees seventy-five strong rode out to do battle with the Pawnee Picts (the warring branch of the Wichitas, who were also known as the Taovayas) on the Red River.[45] Col. Matthew Arbuckle, commanding Fort Gibson, reported that the Cherokees returned with more than sixty Pawnee Pict scalps.[46]

Still another raid was conducted against the Tawakonis of Texas, despite the strong opposition of Chief Jolly. Jolly had attempted to halt the planned strike, which was being organized at Bayou Menard (eight miles west of Fort Gibson) by war captain John Smith. Being ill himself, Jolly dispatched Sam Houston to attend the war council in his stead. Houston had only recently arrived at Jolly's home from Tennessee, where he had unexpectedly resigned as governor following an unhappy marriage. He was unable to prevent the "raising of the Tomahawk of War" by the Cherokee war party, which joined Dutch and other Texas Cherokees in striking a Tawakoni village on the Brazos River near present Waco, Texas.[47]

Thomas Chisholm, along with John Rogers, Jr., was a leading figure in a council held at Fort Gibson in September 1837 with chiefs of the prairie tribes—the Kiowas, Pawnee Picts, and Wacos. These chiefs had been persuaded by Col. Henry Dodge to accompany him to Gibson following the venture into their country by the Leavenworth-Dodge expedition that summer. Also present at the meeting were Chief Clermont of the Osages and chiefs of the Creeks, Choctaws, and Senecas. During the council, Chisholm and others attempted to end the deep animosity between the tribes of the East and those of the buffalo country. "Our custom is to give beads and tobacco," Chisholm told the prairie guests. "The white beads are emblems of peace and purity. When you smoke the tobacco of friendship, all evil will go off with the smoke."[48]

The council preceded the first treaty made between the United States and the Comanches, Wichitas, and Kiowas. Thomas Chisholm's tenure as a Western Cherokee chief, however, was ended by then. He had perished from typhoid the previous winter, and Joseph Vann had been named to replace him as third chief.

It was Dutch, however, who represented the Cherokees at the Camp Holmes council. In 1831 the U.S. government, having forgiven him for his raid on Pryor's trading post, undertook the expense of moving him and his band north to the Canadian River. There he established a sizable Cherokee settlement on Dutch's Creek (now Dutchess Creek).[49]

Under pressure from the United States and individual states, Cherokees from the Old Nation, many destitute to the extreme, continued to migrate west to the Indian Territory. Arkansas newspapers and missionary journals reported many of these group removals. During the spring of 1829 some 40 to 50 families passed Little Rock, then 65 more, then a smaller group; 200 more in February 1830, 70 in March; then in 1832 contingents of 500 in March, 400 in May, 626 in April. Cherokee agent George Vashon reported that many were so destitute that they were selling their claims to speculators in order to buy food and supplies.[50]

John Rogers, who operated a saltworks on the Spavinaw River, had gained stature as a Western Cherokee leader. When learning of a visit by an Old Nation delegation to Washington to negotiate for land west of the Mississippi in 1834, Rogers himself led a group to the capital in an effort to protect Western Cherokee interests. John Drew, who would later become an officer in a Cherokee Civil War regiment and a Tahlequah merchant, was also a member of the party.[51]

The delegation carried a petition signed foremost by Jolly, Black Coat, and Webber. The paper requested that the annuities of Cherokees migrating west be paid to the Western Cherokees and that their country be enlarged to make it equal to that ceded by the treaties of 1817 and 1819. The delegation also made a plea to President Andrew Jackson for the assistance of Sam Houston, who in 1832 had left the Western Cherokees—and Diana Rogers, daughter of John Rogers, with whom he was living as man and wife. The delegation asked that the president persuade General Houston, "a man who we have long known, to help us and stay with us because he knows all about our country and has lived among us."[52] Houston, however, was busy elsewhere. He was leading an Anglo-American revolution in the Mexican province of Texas.

CHAPTER 12

Dark Clouds Gathering

During the decade from 1828 through 1838, the leadership of John Ross would be tested to the extreme. As the principal chief and most influential man of the Cherokee Nation, his ironlike determination to prevent the loss of the remaining Cherokee lands would be beset by powerful forces from all directions. Arrayed against him from without would be the great political might of the United States as well as aggressive and determined state governments. Georgia, lead by Gov. Wilson Lumpkin, was a particularly fierce opponent of Cherokee interests. From within, Ross would endure opposition from capable and highly respected Cherokee intellectuals who had concluded it was best for their people to give in to white pressure and move west.

Only a man of strong character and dogged will could have withstood the challenges that Ross faced during these years. But even more was required. Without great political skill and powers of persuasion, Ross could never have held out for ten years against his enemies. A short-statured man with features that reflected little of his Indian blood, Ross was intelligent, shrewd, and unswerving. His diminutive physique was offset by an aura of uncompromising dedication to purpose. He was a calm and deliberate combatant whose persistence and skills challenged opponents to the point of angry frustration. Time and again Ross outfought and outmaneuvered the powerful forces of the federal government with the weapons of law and public sentiment. In the end, he lost, not because he himself failed but because his greatest foe, President Andrew Jackson, skirted U.S. laws and manipulated a fallacious treaty against the Cherokees.

On the surface there is a certain irony that the man who led the fight to protect the Cherokee homeland was only one-eighth Cherokee. It could be speculated, however, that this very fact gave him the resolve not to betray the Cherokee being with which he had been raised and felt most akin. Some part of his motivation may well have been the factors of personal aggrandizement and material welfare, as his enemies claimed. Yet it can be counterargued that Ross could have had power and fortune far more easily by capitulating to the United States and taking the bribes that other Indian leaders often accepted.

Despite the warring assistance that the Cherokees had given him against the Creeks, Jackson was committed wholeheartedly to the removal of the Indians from the South. He and his administration would prove ruthless and unrelenting in pursuit of this aim. Jackson adamantly refused to intercede as the state of Georgia pressed aggressively and abusively against the Cherokees. Against this overwhelming force, Ross and other Cherokee leaders stood braced in their attempt to hold back the tide of white aggression by persuading the United States to honor its treaties. At the same time it was necessary to shore up the defection of Old Nation Cherokees who were bending to government persuasion and pressure to give up their homes and relocate. On July 1, 1829, Ross and Chief George Lowrey addressed an appeal to the Cherokees of the Old Nation:

> Don't let the Talk of the President and Secretary of War that is going about scare you. Their say so does not effect our rights to the soil . . . The Treatys entered into between us and the General Govt. are very strong and will protect us in our right of soil . . . It is not the Presidents say so alone but Congress too . . . Friends if you all unite together and be of one mind there is no danger of our rights being taken away from us.[1]

"The clouds may gather," Ross wrote to a friend in 1830, "thunders roar & lightning flash from the acts of Ga. under the approbation of Genl. Jackson's neutrality, but the Cherokees with an honest patriotism & love of country will still remain peaceably on their own soil."[2]

One of Jackson's first acts as president in 1830 was to submit and push through Congress his Indian Removal Bill designed to remove all eastern Indian tribes to unsettled lands beyond the Mississippi River. Further, his administration stood solidly by the power of the states to usurp solemn U.S. treaties with Indian tribes. "The arms of this country," Jackson's Secretary of War John H. Eaton argued, "can never be employed to stay any State of this Union from the exercise of those legitimate powers, which attach and belong to their sovereign character."[3]

There were those white Americans who stepped forward to give Ross and the Cherokees support in their titanic struggle with state and federal governments. Former U.S. attorney general William Wirt, using the pen name of William Penn, wrote a series of pro-Cherokee articles oppos-

Constitutional lawyer William Wirt took the Cherokee issue to the U.S. Supreme Court.

Appleton's Annual Cyclopedia and Register of Important Events. New York: Appleton, 1862–1903.

ing Jackson's Indian Removal Bill for the *Daily National Intelligencer* of Washington, D.C. Vermont representative Horace Everett spoke out angrily on the floor of the House. Missionary leader Jeremiah Evarts worked forcefully in support of the Cherokees. Congressman Theodore Frelinghuysen of New Jersey responded to the argument of Georgia sovereignty on the Senate floor: "Sir," he contended, "the Cherokees are no parties to this issue; they have no concern in this controversy. They hold by better title than either Georgia or the Union."[4]

The political situation that Georgia enacted upon the Cherokees, however, was oppressive to the extreme. Shortly after Jackson's election, Georgia passed a series of laws that included annexing the Cherokee gold-mining territory and denying Cherokees legal rights there. It was made illegal for Indians to testify against white men in court, and contracts made between whites and Indians were declared null and void unless witnessed by two whites. In essence, it stripped the Cherokees of any legal redress whatsoever and opened the door to countless acts of mayhem and theft by whites upon Indian people.

A Wirt-prepared test suit charging Georgia with violations of Cherokee rights was dismissed by the U.S. Supreme Court. The Georgia legislature now issued a law denying residence in the Cherokee country to white men who had not sworn their allegiance to the state. Accordingly, Cherokee missionaries Dr. Samuel A. Worcester and Elizur Butler,

Rev. Samuel Worcester went to prison in Georgia on behalf of the Cherokees.

Archives and Manuscripts,
Oklahoma Historical Society.

along with John F. Wheeler, printer of the *Cherokee Phoenix,* all of whom refused to take the oath, were arrested. The men were put in prison garb and assigned to hard labor with felons.[5]

Ross, who escaped an assassination attempt upon him by a white man during November 1831,[6] was soon to discover that he also faced a serious threat of disaffection within the Cherokee leadership itself. In 1832 the fact surfaced that some of the leading Old Nation men had given in to political persuasion by U.S. officials and were supporting removal. At a general council on July 23, a statement favoring a treaty to sell the Old Nation lands was issued by a group of men opposing Ross. They included Elias Boudinot; John Ridge, son of Major Ridge and president of the national council; William Hicks; William Rogers; William Shorey Coodey; James Starr; John Walker Jr.; and even Andrew Ross, brother to the chief.

A resolution to discuss such a treaty with the Jackson administration, submitted by John Ridge, was quashed by the Cherokee council in October. Instead, Ross won authorization to lead a four-man delegation that included Joseph Vann, John Baldridge, Richard Taylor, and him-

The educated John Ridge was a leader in promoting the Treaty of New Echota, by which the Cherokees sold their Old Nation homes.

Archives and Manuscripts,
Oklahoma Historical Society.

self to Washington. There Ross and the others adamantly rejected a U.S. offer to purchase the Cherokee lands in Georgia, Alabama, and Tennessee for three million dollars.

It was while they were away during the winter of 1832–33 that their homes and those of many other Cherokees were invaded by Georgia whites who had drawn winning lottery numbers for Cherokee land. Ross returned to find his home on the Coosa River and his property taken over by invaders. His wife, Quatie, who was ill, and their children were being held as virtual prisoners in two rooms of the house.

Joseph Vann's brick home, which was surrounded by an eight-hundred-acre plantation consisting of planted fields, gardens, orchards, mills, and slave houses, became a battlefield between two Georgia factions who were engaged in a gunfight over the property. As bullets whizzed back and forth, Vann, his wife, and children trembled for their safety in a room of the home. The family was eventually driven out into the winter snow and cold, fleeing to Tennessee, where they found shelter in a dirt-floored log cabin. John Martin, another wealthy Cherokee, was similarly ejected from his home and farm.[7]

Jackson's passion to remove the Cherokees from the South achieved some results early in 1834. Former congressman Benjamin F. Currey, a friend of Jackson, had been appointed to head the removal program. Through bribery, the use of whiskey, beatings, and even the threat of death, he hauled terrified Cherokees to an evacuation camp near the Calhoun agency. There the Indians, who had been paid compensation for their properties, were besieged by white whiskey peddlers. The camp was turned into an infestation of drunken orgies, fighting, and vice. In mid-February, 457 Cherokees were loaded onto a flotilla of keelboats, barges, and other vessels and sent off down the ice-clogged river in the charge of Lt. Joseph Harris.[8]

Men had been shoved aboard in drunken stupors, and families sometimes were ripped apart in Currey's callous determination to send them west. They were soon victimized even more by the cholera epidemic sweeping the region, an outbreak of measles, and other illnesses that were abetted by exposure to winter elements on the open flatboats. By the time they reached Little Rock, Arkansas, both cholera and measles had decimated the party. During a period of four days, fifty-one people were added to the death toll despite the care of Lieutenant Harris and Little Rock doctor Jesse C. Roberts, both of whom worked heroically among the stricken refugees. All too often, their efforts were in vain. On April 16, 1834—a beautiful, sunshiny day—Harris wrote in his journal of the dying:

> To us it should have been a day of Clouds—Such gorgeous glories seem to mock the wretchedness they shone upon. Notes of lamentation & of woe arose upon the morning air & the Shrieks of the dying! Instant death stalks through our little camp & with an unspairing & awfully disfiguring hand, greedily gathers in his victims to the garner . . . There are three cases of death before breakfast, and eleven in all before the Sun went down . . . A number of my people are now down with sickness of various kinds; and all in panic struck and in scattering through the woods building their Campfires as remote from each other as their several fears direct them . . . At one time I saw stretched around me and within a few feet of Each other, Eight of these afflicted creatures dead and dying. Yet no loud lamentations went up from the bereaved ones here. They are men of true Indian blood . . . Quietly they digged graves for their dead, and as quietly they laid them out in their narrow beds . . . There was a dignity in their grief which was sublime, and which poor & destitute, ignorant & unbefriended as they were, made me *respect them*.[9]

Harris, too, was struck by cholera. Though deathly ill, he carried on, arranging for wagons to carry the pitiful refugees on to their destination. When white teamsters he had hired deserted them, Harris struggled atop a horse and led the way for Cherokees who drove the wagons.

The Cherokees reached Fort Gibson on May 15 in such weakened condition, both in body and spirit, that many died soon after. It is estimated that less than two hundred of the original party that departed Tennessee were still alive a year later. Many of them settled near new Dwight Mission. Even before they arrived, the Reverend Henry T. Wilson Jr. had written a public letter from Dwight concerning the desperate situation of other Cherokee emigrants who were without food, stock, or farming implements: "Driven from the homes of their fathers to the very utmost verge of our country, they know not what to do or where to go. O! Could you see the wrongs which these poor people suffer."[10]

Harris, who would himself die only three years later, warned the government: "For myself I am too well satisfied that if this same course of collection & removing these people is repeated it will be attended by the like disastrous results, not to recommend its immediate & unqualified abandonment."[11]

Despite the intimidation from Georgia and the disaffection of his own leading men, Ross inflexibly opposed U.S. demands, trying all within his power to stymie attempts to force a removal treaty upon the Cherokees. During January 1834, he led still another delegation to Washington in an attempt to work out a compromise, offering a portion of their territory to Georgia and proposing eventual citizenship for the Cherokees. Jackson refused point blank, rejecting any solution except the removal of the Cherokees west of the Mississippi.[12] Ross now attempted to go around Jackson by addressing a lengthy memorial to Congress. In it he detailed the injustices and betrayals that the Cherokees had suffered at the hands of the United States and pleaded for compassion and justice.[13] When Ross's brother Andrew attempted to bypass him with an ad hoc delegation to Washington, the Cherokee principal chief secured a protest petition reportedly with more than thirteen thousand names on it. Ignoring the protest, on June 19, 1834, Secretary of War John Eaton concluded an agreement with Andrew Ross's group providing for Cherokee removal. Congress failed to ratify the treaty, however.

The Old Nation was now so bitterly split that the old specter of assassination unleashed against Doublehead in 1807 returned to further disturb the already poisoned climate. While returning home from a highly emotional council at Red Clay, Tennessee, in the fall of 1834, prominent half blood John Walker Jr. was killed by a shot from ambush. During the council, he had been charged by the Ross people with creating disunity after defecting from them. Ross, who in 1819 had been attacked by Walker's father in a Washington hotel room, was suspected by some of having directed the murder.[14]

The Ridge-Boudinot faction was no less determined to overcome Ross's tenacious resistance to the sale of the Cherokee lands and removal west. On November 27, 1834, a meeting of the Cherokee dissidents gathered at John Ridge's to meet with Agent Currey and organize a party in opposition to the ruling Ross government. Currey promised financial support for a delegation from the group to carry a new treaty proposal to Washington.

Ross responded with his own delegation, and the bitter rancor continued within the Old Nation when the two rival factions arrived in Washington in February 1835. Ross's group was known as the National, or Anti-Treaty, party, while John Ridge, who had been secretly colluding with U.S. and Georgia officials, headed the Treaty party. Jackson ignored Ross but warmly received the latter group. On his orders the Reverend John F. Schermerhorn, recently appointed as a U.S. commissioner, concluded an agreement with the Ridge faction whereby the Cherokees would cede the entirety of their nation east of the Mississippi to the United States for a sum of $3.25 million.

When Ross stymied ratification of the pact by rejecting the price, the government upped the offer to $4.5 million. Ross then responded with a demand for $20 million, which was immediately rejected. On March 14 the Treaty party signed an agreement on the basis of the second figure, with the stipulation that it be approved by a majority of the Cherokee National Council.

Schermerhorn accompanied the Treaty group when it returned home to the Cherokee capital at New Echota. He spent the entire summer and fall working among the feuding Cherokee factions, using coercion and deception to gain enough votes to ratify the treaty. At the same time, Ross was working to find grounds for reconciliation with the Ridge group. On July 30 he wrote to Major Ridge and John Ridge inviting them to a "purely Cherokee" meeting of leading men and "to lay aside all other feelings of a private or a personal character, and duly appreciate any motive, great and lasting good may result in restoring brotherly confidence and harmony among ourselves."[15]

It may well have been this effort by Ross that caused the Cherokee council to vote down the treaty during an October meeting. Even the Ridges and Boudinot voted against it, much to the surprise of Schermerhorn, who laid their action to the powerful resistance of Ross.[16] The council further assigned the making of a new treaty to a delegation headed by Ross. Since Schermerhorn's authority applied only to the rejected treaty, it would be necessary for him to return to Washington for further negotiations.

Troubles were still brewing with the state of Georgia, which was harassing the Cherokees at every opportunity. During the spring of 1835, the council had appointed a committee assigned to the task of ascertaining, for treaty purposes, a list of spoliation claims that could be made on Cherokee property taken or abused by Georgians. The four-man committee was headed by the well-educated Elijah Hicks, the first son of former chief Charles Hicks and a full-blood Cherokee mother. The four men, however, were arrested and imprisoned by the Georgia Guard, who marched them through swamps and mountains for nearly two weeks before releasing them without ever making a formal charge. Numerous other Cherokees were driven away from their homes, farms, and business enterprises. At times women and children were forced away when the man was absent. Alarm and fear swept through the Cherokee communities in Georgia.[17]

Ross himself had fled just across the Tennessee line, he and his family taking up refuge in a derelict log cabin near Red Clay, Tennessee. From there he acted to transfer the press and office plant of the *Cherokee Phoenix* from the Georgia home of editor Elijah Hicks, who was married to Ross's sister Margaret. Having induced the Cherokee council to pass a resolution to move the newspaper to Red Clay, Ross sent a wagon to Hicks's house to pick up the press, type, and other materials. However, Stand Watie, brother of Elias Boudinot, learned of this. Believing that Ross intended to control the *Phoenix* for his own political use and that the press legally belonged to Boudinot, Watie interceded. Supported by a company of Georgia Guard, Watie beat Ross's wagon to Hicks's house and carried off the press materials himself.[18]

On the cold, stormy day of November 7, 1835, the noted poet, playwright, and Cherokee champion John Howard Payne, author of the song "Home Sweet Home," arrived unannounced at the door of Ross's cabin. Payne was welcomed in to supper, after which he and the Rosses sat in front of the fireplace discussing the situation of the Cherokees. Even as they were doing so, the cabin door was thrown open and a squad of armed men rushed in. They were Georgia Guard militia, who had illegally crossed the Tennessee line to arrest Ross.[19]

The Georgians seized his personal and official papers, as well as records of the recent meeting at Red Clay. They then forced both him and Payne onto horses and led them off into the dark, drizzling night.

The two men were held for a time in a sodden log cabin at Spring Place, Georgia, with no charges being made. They were finally released without explanation or apology.

Schermerhorn now went over Ross's head to get still another vote on the failed treaty. He took it on himself to call another meeting of the Cherokee council, though only Ross had the legal right to do so. By threats—Ross claimed Schermerhorn told Cherokees that if they remained east of the Mississippi the "screw would be turned upon them till they would be ground into powder"[20]—and by glowing promises, the U.S. agent persuaded a smattering of Cherokees to attend the meeting. He then pushed them to draw up a new treaty document.

On December 29, 1835, twenty Cherokees—notably including Major Ridge, Elias Boudinot, and Andrew Ross—put their signatures to the treaty. Some of the others, however, would play important roles in Cherokee history. These included Archilla Smith, John A. Bell, James Starr, Charles Foreman, and George W. Adair. Neither John Ross nor any of the elected Cherokee officers, then or ever, signed the pact that most significantly affected the destiny of the Cherokee Nation.[21]

By this agreement, known as the Treaty of New Echota, the Cherokees ceded all of their remaining territory east of the Mississippi River to the United States. In return they would be paid five million dollars and awarded joint ownership of the land already assigned to the Western Cherokees, plus a small tract in present southeastern Kansas. The government would pay for the improvements on the former properties of Cherokee citizens, move them westward at U.S. expense, and subsist them for one year after. Removal would take place within two years after the treaty was ratified by the U.S. Congress. Cherokees who wished to become citizens of the United States would be entitled to purchase preemption rights of 160 acres.[22] Schermerhorn wrote gloatingly to the secretary of war: "I have the extreme pleasure to announce to you that yesterday I concluded a treaty. Ross after this treaty is prostrate. The power of the nation is taken from him, as well as the money, and the treaty will give general satisfaction. Make my respects to the President, and congratulate him on the treaty."[23]

But John Ross had by no means given up the fight. It was still up to him to lead the appointed delegation to Washington for ratification of the Treaty of New Echota. Elias Boudinot and John Ridge resigned from the delegation, Ridge writing that Ross's views were "diametrically opposite to me and my friends."[24] Ridge was replaced by Major Ridge, and Stand Watie went in the stead of Boudinot.

In Washington, Ross used every available means to prevent ratification of the treaty, moving back and forth between the Cherokee Nation and Washington, D.C. He presented two protest resolutions to the government, one signed by some 3,250 Cherokees still residing in North Carolina and another purportedly representing more than twelve thousand Old Nation citizens. On March 8, 1836, he addressed a lengthy plea to the Senate, outlining a history of the abuse and injustice done the Cherokees and imploring their forbearance.[25] Returning home, he worked diligently to incite the Cherokee people against the Ridge-Boudinot faction, held councils, and issued resolutions denouncing the New Echota treaty.

Ross was in Washington again as the Congress prepared to vote on ratification of the New Echota treaty. There he received assurances from solons such as Henry Clay and Daniel Webster that the Senate would not pass the ratification bill. But when it came to a vote, Sen. Hugh L. White of Tennessee, who had spoken out against it in the Senate, unexplainably changed his vote to yea, permitting approval of the treaty by the margin of a single vote. Thus, on May 23, 1836, the U.S. Congress legalized what had clearly been a blatant swindle—nothing less—of the Cherokee homeland by Andrew Jackson.

Further, the government had been well advised of the deception that Schermerhorn had used in obtaining the treaty. On March 5, Maj. William M. Davis, a courageous army officer who was serving as an emigration agent to the Cherokees, wrote to Secretary of War Lewis Cass:

> that paper containing the articles entered into at New Echota, in December last, called a treaty, is no treaty at all, because [it was] not sanctioned by the great body of the Cherokee people, and made without their consent or participation in it, pro or con; and I here solemnly declare to you, without hesitation, that, upon a reference of this treaty to the Cherokee people, it would be instantly rejected by more than nine-tenths of them.[26]

One historian noted: "The details of the graft which crop out in the correspondence of the time as found in the official records prove that the removal of the Indians provided many a fat job for place hunters and friends of influential politicians on good terms with the administration. Many a political debt was paid with the capital furnished by the sale of the Cherokee Nation, East."[27]

In December 1836, John Ross led a group of Old Nation leaders on a visit to the Cherokee Nation West in the Indian Territory. They first visited Chief Jolly, then met with Western leaders at the Tahlonteskee council house. As Ross expressed it, he and his chiefs wished to rekindle the "social fire" between the two Cherokee divisions and "cement our reunion as a nation."[28] His main purpose, however, was to secure total nation support in opposing the Treaty of New Echota. The Western Cherokees complied by issuing a resolution declaring the treaty to be injurious to "the interests and happiness of both parts of the Cherokee family."[29] A lead signature was that of George Guess, followed by those of John Jolly, John Brown, John Looney, John Rogers, Charles Rogers, Dutch, and John Drew.[30] The Western chiefs also agreed to send delegates to accompany those of the Old Nation to Washington in hopes of negotiating a treaty for the best interests of the whole nation. The difficult winter's journey was later described by Ross:

> The long distance, the inclemency of the weather and the obstruction of the Ohio River by ice, delayed our passage and compelled us to change our route and to ascend the Tennessee River and to pass in haste thro' our country. On our arrival at Knoxville [Tennessee] we found that the stages had stopped running owing to the bad state of the roads. We were necessarily compelled to purchase horses at that place and to travel on horse back as far as Salem N. Ca. where we left our horses and took the Stage.[31]

Unable to secure an audience with Jackson, whose eight years in the presidency were about to end, the delegation sent a memorial to both the U.S. Senate and then the president-elect, Martin Van Buren, asking them to reexamine past treaties with the Cherokee Nation and provide redress with a new treaty. They were told by Secretary of War Joel R. Poinsett that because the treaty concerned had been ratified, the government could not now admit it was imperfect.[32]

Former President John Quincy Adams termed the treaty an "eternal disgrace upon the country."[33] The Cherokee Old Nation now stood surrounded and besieged by the irrepressible forces of white America. The U.S. Army and the Georgia Guard were poised against them. They had lost the battle for domain. Now the seeds of an even greater disaster had been sown among the Cherokees. Deep, bitter hostility between the Ross party and the Ridge-Boudinot faction were beginning to rip their nation apart from within.

In 1807, when Ridge had undertaken the principal role in the assassination of Doublehead, he had felt justified in ridding the Cherokee Nation of a man he considered to be a traitor. Many Cherokees felt the same way, and his act of murder brought no retribution. A physically strong, determined man who had the personality and character of a natural leader, Ridge soon rose to higher and higher prominence among his people. His square jaw, firm mouth, and fierce but intelligent visage quickly commanded the respect of other men. In addition to his reputation as a soldier, he had become particularly noted for his stout resistance to efforts to remove the Cherokees from their southern homelands. When appointed by Agent Meigs to accompany a delegation to Washington in 1809, he had taken the floor before the council of chiefs and delivered an eloquent and passionate speech against the abandonment of Cherokee territory.[34]

Ridge's creditable service during the Creek war won him even further recognition, along with the title of major, which essentially became a part of his name from that point on. Ridge was older than John Ross by several years, but he was a stout supporter and mentor of the younger man during his rise to power. The friendship and backing of such a highly regarded leader was invaluable to Ross.

Ridge had never had the benefit of formal education. He could not read, write, or effectively speak English, and, like the other unschooled chiefs, relied heavily upon Ross's ability to read, write, and communicate his views and concerns to white authorities. The two men became close friends and neighbors after Ross settled only two miles from Ridge's plantation on the Coosa River of northwest Georgia.[35]

After Path Killer and Charles Hicks died in early 1827, the main responsibilities of the Cherokee government fell upon Ross as council president and Ridge as speaker of the council until a new government could be organized that fall. This personal alliance was threatened in 1832 after Ridge's resistance to the notion of removal was heartlessly quashed by President Andrew Jackson in a meeting at the White House. At that time, Jackson told Ridge flatly that he would not oppose the despotic laws recently enacted against the Cherokees by the Georgia legislature.[36]

With Jackson clearly setting himself against the Cherokees, Ridge became convinced that further attempts to hold on to their native homelands would bring ruin to the Cherokee Nation. He was joined in this by a small body of Cherokee leading men that included, among others, his son John, Elias Boudinot, David Vann, William Hicks, T. J. Pack, John West, William McIntosh, James Starr, and Andrew Ross, brother of the chief who operated a large farm and gristmill at Willstown.

Spurning the elected Cherokee government under John Ross that favored continued resistance, the group formed a delegation to visit Washington and initiate a removal treaty with the United States. The result of this unsuccessful effort was to intensify animosities among members of the opposing tribal factions and between Ross and Ridge. The break between the two men came in August 1834 when Ross summoned the Cherokee council and people to hear his report on the trip he and a delegation had recently made to Washington. Ridge, who had been with the delegation, listened with increased indignation at Ross's interpretation of what had taken place. He felt that Ross was misleading the people concerning concessions made to the United States. Ridge made a strong objection, and the meeting became heated. Ross supporter Thomas Foreman accused Ridge of hypocrisy, saying that he had tried to give away the Cherokee land while he was in Washington. Foreman argued with great passion that the people should love and hold on to their land. Threats of death were made against Ridge by angry tribesmen, and a petition was submitted in council for impeaching him along with John Ridge and David Vann.

Though the petition was put aside, the factional passions were not. Rumors of plans for the assassination of Andrew Ross and other members of the Ridge group surfaced. Indeed, when John Walker was ambushed stories of other plots against both Ross and the Ridges caused fear and concern in the two political camps. Tensions remained high until September, when Ross met with Major Ridge, and the two onetime friends agreed that they held the other no personal malice.[37]

Ridge was unquestionably the most powerful figure among the Treaty party men. However, the intellect and passion of their cause was most effectively represented by the young intellectuals John Ridge and Elias Boudinot. The two had been among the first Cherokees to attend white schools in the East.

Major Ridge, who had always given support to the establishment of missionary schools in the Cherokee Nation, had seized the opportunity to educate his only son. Both John and his cousin Elias Boudinot, whose original name was Buck Watie, had proved to be bright and willing students in the Moravian mission school at Spring Place, Georgia. There they learned English, studied arithmetic, history, and geography, and were introduced to the white man's work ethic and Christianity. Both boys eventually transferred to Brainerd, just north of the Georgia-Tennessee border.[38]

An invitation for him and Buck Watie to attend the Presbyterian mission school at Cornwall, Connecticut, was issued by American Board missionary Elias Cornelius while on a visit to Brainerd. Major Ridge declined the invitation at first, sending John to an academy at Knoxville, Tennessee, instead. But when this did not work out well, John was sent on to Cornwall, where, Ridge hoped, the boy would get a good education and a God-given "good heart" that would make him useful to his people when he came home.[39]

At Cornwall, the boys' education was advanced into the realms of the Greek and Roman classics, as well as more practical subjects such as rhetoric, geography, and surveying. John, however, became so ill that he was provided a special room at the school. There the handsome eighteen-year-old was tended at times by the daughter of the school steward— blonde, blue-eyed Sarah Bird Northup, then only fourteen. The two fell deeply in love, and the romance failed to subside when John was sent home in 1822 to regain his health. Despite the resistance of her parents and the outcry from Cornwall residents against such a mixed marriage, John and Sarah were married at Cornwall in January 1824. The couple left immediately for Georgia, settling into a newly constructed home not far from that of Major Ridge. There John soon established himself as a well-to-do trader and owner of a slave-operated plantation known as Running Water.[40]

Intelligent and ambitious, the younger Ridge's literacy was more than equal to that of John Ross. In the coming months, he would prove to be a capable challenger to Ross's leadership. Like his father, he had become convinced by the actions of Georgia's white leaders and the federal government that the Cherokee Nation would not long survive on its native lands. He, Major Ridge, and Elias Boudinot became the nucleus of a growing opinion that the Cherokees had no hope of surviving unless they gave in and moved west. This belief, considered by many Cherokees to constitute nothing less than national betrayal, was bitterly resented and opposed by Ross and the bulk of the Cherokee people.

Infuriated at the influence Ross had on the main body of Cherokees, John Ridge wrote to Gov. William Carroll of Georgia asking for the support of the Georgia Guard. From this came the arrests of several pro-Ross men, including the much respected Elijah Hicks.[41]

Elias Boudinot, too, had returned home from Cornwall to become a man of importance. He had grown and changed much from the day when he, as a fifteen-year-old lad still known as Buck Watie, had accompanied

Elias Cornelius north. During the journey, he had had the opportunity of visiting ex-Presidents Thomas Jefferson and James Madison in their homes at Monticello and Montpelier, Virginia. At Washington, D.C., the group was given an audience with President James Monroe in the White House. They met with Secretary of War John C. Calhoun and toured Mount Vernon. In Burlington, New Jersey, they stopped at the home of elderly theologian Elias Boudinot, signer of the Declaration of Independence, Revolutionary War general, and founder of the American Bible Society. On the old man's invitation, Buck adopted his name and thereafter became known as Elias Boudinot.[42]

While at Cornwall, Boudinot grew into a tall, good-looking young man. The studies and discipline of the school, as well as further training at the Andover Theological School, produced an individual of high intellect and strong religious values. Like John Ridge, he fell in love with and married a young Anglo-American girl, Harriet Gold, the daughter of a highly regarded agent for the Foreign Mission School. Prior to his marriage and return home, Boudinot had preached in eastern churches, such as Philadelphia's First Presbyterian Church, where he pleaded the cause of his race's humanness and advancement. However, the uproar of racial prejudice aroused by his marriage—the pair were burned in effigy on the village green at Cornwall—altered Boudinot's belief in the ultimate assimilation of Cherokees into the dominant white culture. The couple made their home at a log-cabin mission known as High Tower on the Etowah River in Georgia. There Elias took up the work of a missionary and teacher.

In 1825 the American Board sponsored a speaking tour of the eastern cities for Boudinot. During the tour he recruited donations for the casting in type of the Cherokee syllabary recently invented by Sequoyah; for the establishment of a Cherokee Nation printing press; and the creation of a Cherokee national academy and library. His trip resulted in the founding in 1827 of the bilingual *Cherokee Phoenix*.

When this first press of a native American people was established at New Echota, Georgia, Boudinot was hired as its editor. The first edition of the newspaper on February 21, 1828, was a historic event. Boudinot quickly proved to be a capable and enterprising editor, not only providing the news and editorial content in English but also translating it into Cherokee. He also worked with his good friend and neighbor, missionary Samuel Worcester, in publishing a Cherokee-language book of religious hymns and a translation of Matthew's gospel from the Bible.

It is fair to say that what Sequoyah did for the Cherokees in language and what Ross did for them in politics, Boudinot did for his people with the printed word. He used it to foster religion, to inform and educate the Cherokees, to express tribal views to outsiders, and to fight against the injustices exerted upon them. When the state of Georgia threatened to extend its jurisdiction and laws over the Cherokees, Boudinot wrote in the *Phoenix:* "What a pernicious effect must such a statement as the report on the joint committee in the legislature of Georgia, have on the interests and improvements of the Indians? Who will expect the Cherokees to make a rapid progress in education, religion, agriculture, and the various arts of civilized life when resolutions are passed . . . to wrest their country from them."[43]

On two occasions Boudinot was called before the commander of the Georgia Guard, accused of printing lies and libelous articles, and threatened with whipping. But when he challenged the officer to cite one instance of false statement, he was released without punishment.[44]

It was not Georgia, however, but John Ross who proved to be Boudinot's undoing with the *Phoenix*. Boudinot fought stoutly against the interference of Georgia into Cherokee affairs. But in the face of a U.S. Supreme Court decision supporting Georgia laws, he came to believe, along with others, that loss of the Old Nation homeland was inevitable. Accordingly, he felt that it was the duty of the *Phoenix* to discuss the possibility of removal westward. Ross autocratically decreed, however, that the paper should print nothing that gave any credence to the idea of removal. The Cherokee principal chief, exerting pressure through the tribal government, forced Boudinot to resign as editor in the fall of 1832.[45] When Ross seized the paper and installed his brother-in-law Elijah Hicks as editor, Boudinot was infuriated. He had personally raised the funds with which the press had been purchased and the Cherokee type cast, and he felt they were his property even if the *Phoenix* was not. This only increased his opposition to the stubborn policies of Ross.[46]

Boudinot became more and more convinced that it was vital for the Cherokees to separate themselves from the white population by removing west. This led him to the conclusion that his intellectual minority could best determine the welfare of the unknowing majority. "If one hundred persons are ignorant of their true situation," he wrote in a letter to the *National Intelligencer*, "and are so completely blinded as not to see the destruction that awaits them, we can see strong reasons to justify the actions of a minority of fifty persons to do what the majority *would* do if they understood their condition, to save a *nation* from political thralldom and degradation."[47]

Like other Georgia Cherokees, Boudinot and his family fell victim to white invaders. In January 1833, Georgians arrived to take possession of Boudinot's home by virtue of their drawing in a Georgia state land lottery. Boudinot fled to safety in Tennessee. The Cherokee world was being turned upside down. Boudinot saw it not as much in terms of loss of land as in the damaging effects the white invasion had upon Cherokee efforts to elevate their level of civilization.

Following the arrest of Ross and John Howard Payne by the Georgia Guard, the two issued a public appeal for Cherokee justice. The Ross-Payne statement declared that the Cherokees did not wish to move west and would, in preference, choose to become U.S. citizens. The appeal further charged that a small group of Cherokees had been guilty of spreading false statements against the tribal leadership. John Ridge, who read the statement while on his way to Washington with a Cherokee Council–appointed delegation to discuss the New Echota treaty, took this as an attack upon himself, his father, and Boudinot. He resigned from the delegation and was soon followed by his father and Boudinot.

Major Ridge had returned from Washington in the spring of 1836 to find that a white man had settled on his land. Under Georgia law, there was nothing he could do about it, though he eventually received over twenty-four thousand dollars from the U.S. government for his home, ferry, and other improvements. John Ridge, who moved to Creek Path, Alabama, preparatory to removing to the Indian Territory, secured an evaluation of nearly twenty thousand dollars on his Running Water plantation.

These three Cherokee leaders were well aware that even greater dangers lay ahead for them as leaders of the Treaty party. There were tribesmen who had already sworn vengeance under the ancient but still-lingering clan codes of the Cherokees. Tragically, a foregone sentence of doom would follow each of them as they moved westward to a new beginning in the Indian Territory.

CHAPTER 13

The Agony of Removal

The decade of the 1830s would prove to be a period of great stress for the Cherokee Nation. Its upheaval and removal west was an ordeal of enormous magnitude. Not only would the leadership of John Ross and others be tested severely, but the whole fabric of Cherokee society would be wrenched with such violent passion as virtually to destroy the Cherokees' sense of tribal being. They arrived in the West, in truth, a people fiercely divided against themselves.

A federal census taken in 1835 provides a statistical overview of the Old Nation Cherokees on the eve of its dissolution in the East. The total population was 16,542, with slightly more females than males. Nearly half the females were under age sixteen, and half the males under eighteen. A slave population of 1,592 existed in the nation, and 201 whites were intermarried into the tribe.[1]

Considering the number of mixed-blood leaders, the nation as a whole contained a surprising number of people of pure Cherokee descent. Of the total population, 12,463 were full blood and nearly 3,000 were either one-half or one-quarter blood. Literacy had gained a significant foothold, with 1,070 who could read in English and 3,914 who could read in Cherokee. There were nineteen schools in the nation, but only 292 schoolchildren.

Though wealth was distributed unevenly between the richer and the poorer tribesman, in comparison to other tribes the Cherokees were well off, with 22,405 cattle and 7,628 horses. Their 8,184 houses provided more than adequate shelter. However, there were but 130 wagons in the entire nation—a scant number to carry more than sixteen thousand people westward.

The New Echota treaty stipulated that the Old Nation Cherokees were to be removed by May 23, 1838. As soon as the treaty had been ratified by Congress, President Andrew Jackson issued a proclamation that the United States no longer recognized the existence of any government among the Old Nation Cherokees. Ross was warned that any further resistance to removal would be put down by the U.S. Army.

Jackson was passionate in his determination that removal of the Cherokees would be underway before his term of office ended in the spring of 1837. He was rewarded in this when a Treaty party group became the first to migrate in response to the Echota agreement they had helped manipulate. The six hundred or more people who gathered at New Echota in January 1837 represented the wealthy elite of the Cherokee Nation. Some of them, such as Major Ridge, had received handsome compensation for their relinquished land, property, and stock. The fine carriages in which the warmly dressed families rode, the stout wagons loaded with personal goods, the finely groomed horses, the fatted oxen, and the numerous black servants were in great contrast to the desperately poor, captive emigrants who would follow. As planned, this group arrived at their new homesites in time to plant spring crops.

In order to attend the wedding of his daughter, Major Ridge dropped out of this first 1837 migration. However, he, along with Stand Watie, accompanied the second contingent of 446 Cherokees, which departed Ross's Landing on March 3. There were few wealthy people in this party. Some of them had been virtually shanghaied or tricked into leaving their homes. Most had been lured into migrating by the expense money paid them by the government—money that was soon thrown away in gambling and drunken revelry while waiting to leave.[2]

This government-supervised group departed with great sadness at leaving their homeland. Eleven flatboats loaded with people, their possessions, and foodstuff—cornmeal, flour, and bacon—set afloat on a water route that followed the Tennessee, Ohio, Mississippi, and Arkansas Rivers. Elijah Hicks accompanied the group as an interpreter; Dr. C. Lillybridge, who kept a diary of the journey, went along as attending physician. The agonizingly long and slow course was fraught with navigational hazards that caused delays. Exposure to cold, rain, and snow in the open boats contributed to numerous colds, pleurisy, fever, and diarrhea. Despite these hardships, the Cherokee party finally reached its boat destination of Fort Coffee, Indian Territory, on March 28 without having lost a member.[3] Most of this group moved on north to the Grand River and Honey Creek region.

Criticism and protest were widespread from the many who saw the Treaty of New Echota as a sham concocted by the administration to achieve its purpose of Indian removal. Among the critics was Gen. John Ellis Wool, who then commanded troops assigned to the removal. Finding it impossible to protect the Cherokees from whites in Georgia and Alabama, he resigned his post in dismay, citing the "white men, who, like vultures, are watching, ready to pounce upon their prey and strip them of everything they have or expect from the government of the United States."[4]

The task was equally distasteful to Brig. Gen. R. G. Dunlap, head of the Tennessee Volunteers. During the summer of 1837 his volunteers were assigned to the building of stockade enclosures, only partially roofed, in which to detain the Cherokees who were to be rounded up at bayonet point and sent west. He, too, saw the Echota treaty as a fraud against the will of the majority of the Cherokees. When he and his Tennessee men, who had long been associated with Cherokee people, found the task of dragging peaceful families from their homes too distasteful to continue, Dunlap also resigned.

Still another migration party of 365 members had departed from the Calhoun, Tennessee, agency on the northward overland trail. Almost immediately they became ravaged by dysentery and fever. The journal of B. B. Cannon, conductor of the expedition, from October 14 through December 28, 1837, is filled with entries of wagon breakdowns, severe rains, roads that were quagmires, and the fifteen burials made along the way.[5]

The John Ridge and Elias Boudinot families, along with the William Lassley family and a woman named Polly Gilbreath, departed Creek Path, Alabama, during mid-October 1837 headed for the Indian Territory. They, too, took the northern route through Nashville, where Ridge paid a courtesy visit to former President Andrew Jackson at his Hermitage home.

Despite these early removals, by the end of the year less than two thousand Cherokees had migrated, leaving over sixteen thousand who still held firm behind Ross. His standing among these Old Nation Cherokees was extremely high. One newspaper noted that "a more popular man with his own people does not live than John Ross."[6]

After accompanying the Western delegation to Washington, Ross remained in the capital until after the inauguration of President Martin Van Buren. Eventually he secured an audience with the new chief executive. Van Buren, however, was a strong disciple of Jackson's Indian policy, and the Cherokee chief made no headway with him. Ross returned home in March 1837 and was pleased to learn that some of his tribal archenemies had already departed.

During August, special agent John Mason Jr. was sent to meet with the Cherokee council at Red Clay in an attempt to persuade Ross and his followers to accept removal. Ross not only ignored the combination of pleas and threats presented by Mason, but also immediately led another delegation to Washington to strongly protest the removal. This time Van Buren refused even to see him.

The determined Cherokee leader remained in the capital through the winter, doing his best to get a new treaty written. He eventually managed to persuade Van Buren to agree to a two-year delay in the removal deadline, but political pressures caused the chief executive to renege on his promise. Ross and his followers suffered still another defeat when a memorial plea signed by more than fifteen thousand Cherokees was rejected by Congress.[7]

Incensed at reports that the Cherokees were making no plans to leave, Van Buren placed some seven thousand army and state troops under the command of Maj. Gen. Winfield Scott, with firm orders to remove the Cherokees by the treaty deadline. On May 10 Scott issued a proclamation warning the Indians to begin preparing for emigration to the West. He also put his troops to rounding up the Cherokees.[8]

Scott admonished the soldiers to use "every possible kindness" in carrying out their task. The ensuing invasion of the Cherokee Old Nation homeland and the capture and imprisonment of more than fifteen thousand Cherokees, however, became an orgy of nefarious behav-

Gen. Winfield Scott directed the collecting and removal of the Cherokees in 1838.
Coombs, The Dawn of the Millennium.

ior by the army. Families were dragged from their homes on the spot, others were hunted down; property was taken from rightful owners at gunpoint; innocent people were abused and degraded; some were killed; and many were caused to die from exposure or illness.

The public press of the day was virtually silent on the behavior of Scott's troops in the roundup, and it is apparent that the country at large had little awareness of how badly the Cherokees were being treated. It was left to the missionaries to report the sordid details of Cherokee capture and incarceration during their roundup of May and June 1838. The private diaries and letters, some of which were published in missionary organs, provide the harsh truth of the event.

The daily journal of missionary Daniel S. Butrick tells of a deaf and dumb man who was shot and killed when he failed to obey a soldier's command; of fathers seized away from their homes and not permitted to return to their wives and children; of mothers dragged away leaving behind children who were still hiding in fear in the forest; and of virtually all the Cherokees being forced to leave behind all of their worldly possessions—clothes, cattle, horses, furniture, bedding, pots and pans—everything except the clothing they wore. Butrick was at the Ross's Landing collection camp on May 31.

> A little before sunset a company of about two hundred Cherokees were driven into our camp. The day had been rainy, and of course all, men, women and children, were dripping wet, with no change of clothing, and scarcely a blanket fit to cover them. Mothers brought their dear little babes to our fire, and stripped off their only covering to dry, their little lips, blue and trembling with cold.[9]

At Calhoun Agency on June 16, 1838, the outspoken Evan Jones wrote in his journal:

> The Cherokees are nearly all prisoners. They have been dragged from their houses, and encamped at the forts and military posts, all over the [Cherokee] nation. In Georgia, especially, multitudes were allowed no time to take any thing with them except the clothes they had on. Well-furnished houses were left a prey to plunderers, who, like hungry wolves, follow in the trail of the captors. These wretches rifle the houses and strip the helpless, unoffending owners of all they have on earth. Females who have been habituated to comforts and comparative affluence are driven on foot before the bayonets of brutal men. Their feelings are mortified by the blasphemous vociferations of these heartless creatures. It is a painful sight.[10]

Once captured, the Cherokees were driven like brute animals into the stockade pens. Horses were taken away from those who had brought them and sold at auction to whites for virtually nothing.[11] Many of the poorly fed and ill-cared-for prisoners were stricken with debilitating illnesses. Already beset with grief from losing their homes, they huddled in fear and confusion. Even so, they had no way of knowing that the worst was yet to come. The bedazzled mass of Cherokee people remained crammed into twenty-three stockade pens without bedding, cooking utensils, extra clothing, or adequate sanitation facilities. They were, as one white minister put it, "prisoners, without a crime to justify the fact."[12]

The few boards and bark that served as the only shelter were wholly inadequate. Most of the Cherokees had only the clothes on their backs during three months of captivity, and these garments did little to protect against the burning heat of summer or the incessant rains and falling temperatures of autumn. Some Indians drank themselves into stupors with smuggled whiskey; guards used liquor and other treats to lure Cherokee girls into the bushes.

Bad sanitation conditions to the extreme, lack of washing or bathing facilities, foul drinking water, and the inadequate, unhealthy food soon led to general poor health and sicknesses. It has been estimated that as many as twenty-five hundred Cherokees perished while being brought in or while being held in the cramped, disease-ridden stockades.[13]

Always present around the confinement camps were whiskey peddlers, unscrupulous whites who married Indian women to profit from government compensations, and those who, as a Tennessee paper declared, strove to destroy every vestige of virtue and morality of the captive Cherokees. One observer noted: "Already have the Shylocks, who hovered over this territory while there remained food for them to prey upon, fixed their gluttonous eyes upon the frontier, and will speedily follow the 'last Indian' to his new home."[14]

Later it was revealed how soldiers marched through the mob of stunned Cherokees and grabbed up enough to load a steamboat and forced them aboard, often dividing husbands and wives, parents and children. Some families were never reunited. Upon arrival at the mouth of the Grand River, the refugees were put ashore among the canebrakes in burning summer heat without shelter or food other than a barrel of moldy crackers that was knocked open and strewed about on the ground.[15]

Three groups of Cherokees were sent west in June 1838. Under escort of Lt. Edward Deas, a party of nearly eight hundred, the first to be forcibly emigrated, embarked from Ross's Landing by double-decked keelboats on June 6. However, by the time the group reached Paducah, Kentucky, more than three hundred of Deas's charges had disappeared. Two other detachments followed soon after. An uncounted group left Ross's Landing by keelboat down the Tennessee River, and another was sent overland to Waterloo, Alabama, before being put on boats.

A severe drought curtailed further removal for the remainder of the summer. It was reported that it was impossible to procure water through the Cumberland Mountains, and many of the rivers were too low for boat travel. By fall the stage was set for one of the blackest chapters in U.S. history, the Cherokee removal over what has become known today as the "Trail of Tears."

The main body of Cherokees was still in the stockades when Ross returned home in July. He was shocked to find how his Cherokee Nation had been ravaged by Scott's troops and white citizens. Ghostly homes and towns sat uninhabited except for scavengers who scurried about looting the houses, fields, and even graves. Earlier in Washington, Ross had paid a visit to Scott. He presented the Cherokees' case, winning the general's admiration and respect. Now upon seeing the pathetic situation of his people, Ross went to meet Scott again at the Calhoun, Tennessee, agency. Arguing that the Cherokees could best manage their own removal, Ross persuaded Scott to provide an allowance of sixty-five dollars per person. He further arranged the appointment of himself as superintendent of removal and subsistence.[16]

When the retired Andrew Jackson learned of this at his Hermitage home at Nashville, he howled in fury. Though feeble of hand, the old warrior penned a scathing letter to Atty. Gen. Felix Grundy demanding that the contract with Ross be terminated and asking, "What madness and folly to have anything to do with Ross . . . Why is it the scamp Ross is not banished from the notice of the administration?"[17]

In August, Ross was permitted to meet with other Cherokee leaders to work out plans for the removal. It was determined that the emigration would begin during September in detachments led by Cherokee conductors and monitored by Cherokee Light Horse police. The land route was preferred, though those who were ill would be transported by boat. Ross submitted a request and won approval for compensation of sixty dollars a person. Lewis Ross, brother of the chief, made arrangements with

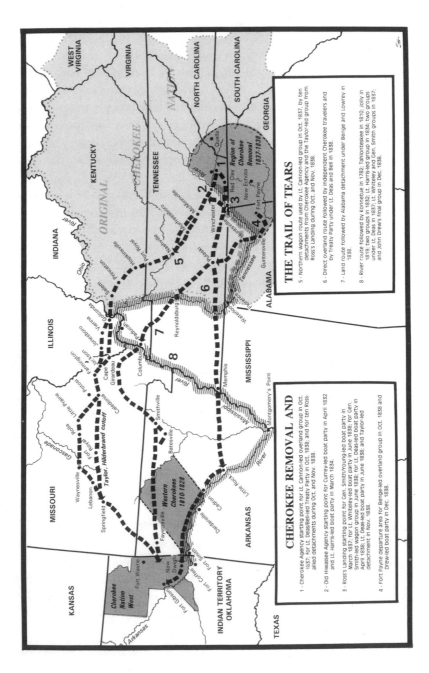

Cherokee Removal and the Trail of Tears.

THE TRAIL OF TEARS

5 - Northern wagon route used by Lt. Cannon-led group in Oct. 1837, by ten detachments from Cherokee Agency and the Taylor-led group from Ross's Landing during Oct. and Nov. 1838.

6 - Direct overland route followed by independent Cherokee travelers and by Treaty Party under Lt. Deas and Bell in 1838.

7 - Land route followed by Alabama detachment under Benge and Lowrey in 1838.

8 - River route followed by Konnetue in 1782; Tahlontetskee in 1810; Jolly in 1819; two groups in 1832; Lt. Harris-led group in 1834; two groups under Lt. Deas in 1837; Lt. Whiteley and Gen. Smith groups in 1837; and John Drew's final group in Dec. 1838.

CHEROKEE REMOVAL AND

1 - Cherokee Agency starting point for Lt. Cannon-led overland group in Oct. 1837; for Lt. Deas/Bell-led Treaty Party in Oct. 1838; and for ten Ross-allied detachments during Oct. and Nov. 1838.

2 - Old Hiwassee Agency starting point for Currey-led boat party in April 1832 and Lt. Harris-led boat party in March 1834.

3 - Ross's Landing starting point for Gen. Smith/Young-led boat party in March 1837; for Lt. Whiteley-led boat party in June 1838; for Gen. Smith-led wagon group in June 1838; for Lt. Deas-led boat party in April 1838; Lt. Deas-led boat party in June 1838; and Taylor-led detachment in Nov. 1838.

4 - Fort Payne departure area for Benge-led overland group in Oct. 1838 and Drew-led boat party in Dec. 1838.

contractors for food and other necessities to be supplied at depots along the way. General Scott agreed to provide wagons, horses, and oxen. And when Ross requested a postponement because of the drought, Scott permitted a delay for the start of the final great removal.[18] The delay was, indeed, necessary; but as a result, the Cherokees remained in their sweltering camp prisons through the summer, undergoing much suffering. On August 1, Ross assembled his Cherokee followers and led them in a pledge that, despite the loss of their homeland, the Cherokee Nation would never die.[19]

The rains came in late September as the mass of Cherokee people were brought to the assembly area at Rattlesnake Springs, near present Charleston, Tennessee. The imprisoned Cherokees named the accumulation camp "Aquohee" or "Captured."[20] On the cold, drizzling morning of October 1, 1838, the first group of wagons pulled into position and the loading began.[21] The chiefs had divided the nearly twelve thousand pro-Ross Cherokees (by official postremoval estimate) at Calhoun into ten groups of equivalent size. An eleventh detachment to form at the Tennessee agency comprised some 650–750 Treaty party members. This dissident group would follow their own southern route directly westward to the Indian Territory.

Another Tennessee-based overland party organized under Richard Taylor at Ross's Landing would follow the northern route. Butrick and his wife, he on horseback and she in a one-horse carryall, were members of this wagon train. His diary—the only daily record of the Trail of Tears yet found—described the difficulties, disturbances, and deaths of the detachment as it traveled up the Sequatchie Valley and turned west across Walden's Ridge onto the northern route followed by the ten groups from Calhoun Agency.

Still another party, made up of twelve hundred or more Cherokees at Fort Payne (the former Willstown), Alabama, would make up a thirteenth overland contingent. The party was led by John Benge, assisted by George Lowrey, second chief of the nation. On September 29, Benge and Lowrey wrote to Ross to say that on the next day they would move out the first of 1,090, with three families yet to come. The commanding officer at Fort Payne had told them to leave by the first of October, as the fort's issuing officer would cease to distribute rations as of that date.[22] There were only eighty-three tents for the entire group. Two-thirds of the detachment were in a destitute condition, many being in want of shoes, clothing, and blankets as well as tents. It was hoped that additional supplies could be picked up at Huntsville. Following down the northerly flow of the Tennessee River, the Alabama Cherokees reached Reynoldsburg, Tennessee (no longer existing, but then situated directly east of Camden), on October 8.

There had been a good deal of sickness among the emigrants. The entourage crossed the Tennessee River at Reynoldsburg and moved on for the Iron Banks near Columbus, Kentucky, where it could be ferried across the Mississippi.[23] After looping through the southeastern corner of Missouri, the Alabama Cherokees drove directly west across northern Arkansas, from Smithville to Fayetteville and on to the Indian Territory.

The tragic exodus of the pro-Ross Cherokees by the northern overland route was the portion of the removal that saw the greatest suffering and did most to create the infamous repute of the Trail of Tears. The human misery, deaths, and brutality of this sorry episode of American history are overwhelming, reflecting both upon the U.S. government and the public character.

William Shorey Coodey, a scholarly Cherokee with Scot blood who had already moved west in 1834, wrote with deep compassion of the removal. He noted that the "pangs of parting are tearing the hearts of our bravest men at this forced abandonment of their dear lov'd country" and recalled how he had felt at his "last lingering look upon the brow of Lookout [Mountain] dimly fading in the distance as the current bore us away, forever."[24] Having returned east to witness the great exodus of 1838, he observed the teams and loaded wagons that stretched at great distance through the forest; the knots of people around each wagon quietly saying their sad farewells; the stately, white-headed form of the aged Beloved Man Chief Going Snake atop his pony, still ready to lead the way.[25] Behind them the flames and smoke rose high from their temporary camp, to which the soldiers had put the torch—a cruel reminder that there would be no going back ever to the life they once knew. Coodey could not restrain the bitterness he felt. "Wretched indeed," he commented, "must be that individual who can fold his arms and look with composure upon scenes like these. I envy not such a being, but despise, aye, loathe him from my very soul whether *white* or *red*."[26]

Many Cherokees had become resigned to their fate. Conductor George Hicks expressed his people's sorrow at being forced to quit the land of their childhood, "but stern necessity says we must go, and we bid a final farewell to it and all we hold dear." They would go, he added, "If the white citizens will permit us, but since we have been on our march many of us have been stoped and our horses taken from our Teams for the payment of unjust and past Demands."[27]

Two famous old chiefs of the Cherokees were still alive to make the trip west. Going Snake, once speaker of the Cherokee council, would he honored by having a district in the new land named for him before he died. Chief White Path, the full blood who in 1828 had attempted to lead a rebellion against the ways of the white man, would fail to make it to the new land.

The first Tennessee detachment was under the lead of conductor Hair Conrad, who because of illness was replaced by Daniel Colston. This group had started earlier but was recalled because of the drought. When the sad farewells had been said and the wagons were ready to roll, John Ross stood on a wagon and spoke a prayer in the Cherokee tongue wishing the party God's guidance. A bugle sounded, and the procession began on what would be a fateful journey for all and a deathly one for many.

Scott had set a course that would use essentially the same route as that taken by Cannon. The overland processions would follow down the Hiwassee River from the Aquohee stockade to Blythe's Ferry on the Tennessee River, then west across Tennessee, then "via Nashville, Colcondo [Golconda, Kentucky], Cape Girauce [Cape Girardeau, Missouri], and the ridge roads of Missouri [westward]."[28] It was Scott's choice, but some blame must be given Ross for agreeing to this much longer northern route that was far more perilous than the direct southern route used by the Treaty people.

The second group under Elijah Hicks departed only three days after the first and soon overtook and passed it. Only a portion of Hicks's group of scantily clad people even had wagon covers to protect them from the wet, cold weather. After two weeks of hard travel, most had grown weary and despondent, and illness had set in. By the time they reached Nashville, the dying had already begun. Four or five Cherokees were buried there, and a week later near Hopkinsville, Kentucky, Chief White Path succumbed to age and illness. He was buried beside the trail, his grave marked with a wooden slab, which had been painted to resemble marble, and a tall pole bearing a white linen flag.[29]

These first two detachments were followed in line from the Calhoun area by nine other Ross groups during the rest of the month and into November. In order, they were Jesse Bushyhead, with 48 wagons and 135 people; Situwakee, 62 wagons and 1,250 people; Captain Old Field and later Stephen Foreman, 49 wagons and 983 people; Moses Daniel, 52 wagons and 1,035 people; James D. Wofford (Chooalooka), 58 wagons and 1,150 people; James Brown, 42 wagons and 850 people; George Hicks, 56 wagons and 1,118 people; Richard Taylor, 51 wagons and 1,029 people; and Peter Hildebrand, 88 wagons and 1,766 people. These counts included a number of slaves who endured the journey alongside their owners. The last overland departure was made on November 7.[30]

The obstacles and misfortunes encountered on the northern route by the eleven overland wagon trains were virtually unending. It would be hard to devise a more difficult scenario or a more tragic one. The situation of moving the elderly and ill many miles along an area with poor roads, which were made increasingly rutted and torn by use and weather; the shortage of adequate transportation, food, clothing, bedding, or shelters; the severe lack of medical care or byway facilities; the need to push forward in disregard of their circumstances and long delays at the ice-clogged Mississippi; the victimizing of the Indian caravans by whites who charged exorbitant fees for provisions and services, including some who committed outright robbery; and excessive tolls to cross land and streams. These things were all exacerbated by weather conditions that ranged from inclement to raging blizzard, by fatigue, by the despair of seeing loved ones perish, and by a sense of lost hope.

A citizen of Maine who was traveling through western Kentucky at the time provided our most poignant account of the Cherokee march. In a letter that appeared in the *New York Observer* on January 26, 1839, he described the plight of a large number of Cherokees he saw encamped in a grove of woods by the roadside. He estimated that there were sixty wagons, six hundred horses, and some forty pairs of oxen. A heavy rain with driving winds had hit the area, and the Indians had only their canvas wagon covers for a shield. They were already weary from the trail, and several of the older ones were suffering badly. Some were quite ill.

Later the New Englander met another group of two thousand Indians, plus that many animals, that filled the road for more than three miles in length. Inside the wagons were the sick and feeble, many near death. A few of the Indians rode horses, but the majority of them, even old women, were on foot carrying heavy packs. Many of the Cherokees had no shoes to protect them from the frozen ground they trod. The observer was told that at virtually every stopping place fourteen or fifteen people were buried. He told of a woman whose youngest child was dying in her arms:

she could carry her dying child a few miles farther, and then she must stop in a stranger-land and consign her much loved babe to the cold ground, and that too without pomp or ceremony, and pass on with the multitude . . .

When I past the last detachment of those suffering exiles and thought that my native countrymen had thus expelled them from their native soil and their much loved ones, and that too in this inclement season of the year in all their suffering, I turned from the sight with feelings which language cannot express and "wept like childhood then."

It has been estimated generally that of nearly eighteen thousand Cherokees rounded up by Scott's troops, fifteen hundred of them are believed to have perished en route to the West, making a total of nearly four thousand who died while being brought in, held at Aquohee and other camps, or on the trail. One Cherokee scholar, however, calculated that the figure was probably closer to eight or ten thousand for the five-year period of removal from 1835 to 1840.[31]

In great contrast to Ross-allied caravans was an October group of seven hundred Treaty party members who, permitted excesses far beyond those allowed others, traveled in comfortable style, drove their own horses and carriages, and enjoyed the benefit of their slaves. This contingent followed its own course, taking a direct westerly course from Calhoun to Ross's Landing to Winchester and Memphis, Tennessee, and from there directly across Arkansas to Little Rock. Having shipped much of their baggage by boat, they moved at a leisurely pace. It took them twenty-one days from Memphis to Little Rock, a distance of 137 miles, or less than 7 miles a day. They still reached the Indian Territory in some sixty-five days on January 7, 1839.

Like the captain of an ill-fated ship, Ross did not leave his beloved Old Nation until the last group of 228 set forth in November 1838. They soon caught up with and joined the 1,613-member company of Peter Hildebrand, which was busy with four boats ferrying its seventy-nine or so wagons and carriages across the Tennessee River. Ross wrote to General Scott, reporting that other detachments were spread along the road to Nashville and that so far things were going well except for some sickness.[32] Soon, however, the weather would turn bad and the road would be filled with broken wagons and hapless people.[33]

Ross's wife, Quatie, was already ill when she set forth in their wagon from the head of the Coosa River in Georgia. Her son James McDonald was now twenty-four, Allen was twenty-one, and daughter Jane was seventeen. They could tend themselves; but Silas was only nine, and George eight.[34] Quatie gave them all the care she could. Yet by the time they reached Kentucky, the rigors of the trail had made her condition worsen into pneumonia. Though she did not complain, Ross became greatly concerned for her. At Paducah, Kentucky, he left the wagon caravan and took his family aboard the *Victoria*, which was carrying the last small group of Cherokees from Alabama under the charge of John Drew. During January 1839 the steamer made its way down the icy Ohio and Mississippi Rivers, then up the Arkansas to Little Rock. There on February 1, Quatie died.[35] Ross buried her in a shallow grave dug from the frozen ground, then moved on upriver to the new home of the Cherokee Nation in what is now eastern Oklahoma. Eventually he would establish his home at Park Hill, near present Tahlequah. Behind him lay defeat and the ashes of the world he and his people had once known.

Ross's great contest with the government of the United States over the Old Nation lands was done. But there still remained the task of keeping alive a nation that was grievously infected by an epidemic of deadly acrimony.

CHAPTER 14

Expulsion from Texas

Even as the Old Nation Cherokees underwent the great trauma of removal to the West, another segment of the nation was reaching the tragic end to a prolonged struggle. The separation of the Fields-Bowle band of Cherokees from the main body of Arkansas Cherokees had established another small but distinct settlement of the nation in Texas, then still a part of Mexico. It also placed the mantle of leadership upon two chiefs and fostered difficult choices concerning the fate of their people. The problems they faced were little short of those known by other Cherokee leaders, and their efforts to establish a settlement removed from white contact would lead to a bloody and tragic end.

Bowle's move into Texas during late 1819 was undoubtedly preceded by Cherokee hunting sojourns to the buffalo prairie of the Brazos River region. Later, supported by temporary permits to take up residence in the province, the group made its first Texas settlement on the Three Forks of the Trinity within the area of present Dallas. The Cherokees, numbering about one hundred warriors and two hundred women and children, remained there for about three years.[1]

Conflicts with resident prairie tribes ensued, however. Bowle claimed that nearly a third of his warriors were killed while there. As a result, the group retreated into the heavy forests of east Texas, locating some fifty miles north of the Spanish fort of Nacogdoches, Texas.[2] For many years after this site was abandoned by the Cherokees, trees could be seen with carved figures of turtles, alligators, snakes, and other figures. Some say they were of Cherokee origin, though they could well have been Caddoan.[3]

Soon after moving to Texas, Richard Fields was chosen to replace Bowle as principal leader of the group. There is some prior indication of Fields's having been prominently involved in Cherokee national affairs. During a council in Georgia between the Cherokees and Moravian missionaries in 1800, he made an address in favor of giving the Moravians a contract to preach among the nation.[4] On December 25, 1801, he wrote a letter to Agent Meigs from Chickamauga in which it was indicated that he had held a government office in relation to the Cherokee Nation.[5]

In 1809, when Fields had declared his intention to "go over the Mississippi," Ridge and other Northern leaders complained to Agent Meigs that Fields had no right to sell his land.[6] Fields, a great-grandson of Scottish trader Ludovic Grant, evidently married, or remarried, after moving west, his wife in his latter years being the daughter of a prominent French trader of Natchitoches, Louisiana, named François Grapp. By her he produced several children who were still minors at the time of his death in 1827. It appears that he may well have left another family behind in the East. His nephew Richard, who was well educated, would later become a leading Cherokee figure.[7]

Just what led to this reduction of Bowle's position in Texas is not known. It may have been that the Cherokees believed that Fields, being more educated, could better deal with Mexican officials in securing rights to the Texas land. American whites were already heading toward the fertile east Texas region, and Fields moved quickly in contacting Mexican officials to secure permanent title to a grant of land to replace the temporary permits. On February 1, 1822, he wrote to the alcalde of Nacogdoches, James Dill, requesting a meeting on the matter.[8] Having had no reply from Dill by November, Fields led a party of twenty Cherokees to San Antonio to seek an audience with the provincial governor, José Felix Trespalacious.[9] The governor received the Cherokees graciously and entered into a treaty with them. By it the Indians agreed to subject themselves to Spanish laws as citizens, to intercede as possible in the movement of stolen Spanish stock to the United States, and to take up arms for the Spanish against other tribes. In return they were granted the right to reside in Texas and enjoy a peaceful existence there.

The governor did not have the power to make grants of land. However, he did issue Fields, Bowle, and six companions—two of them being interpreters—a permit to travel to Mexico City to make a plea for a colonial land grant. The Cherokees' visit coincided with a revolution and change of leaders in Mexico during the spring of 1823. A number of Anglo-Americans, including Stephen F. Austin, who was seeking to renew a grant made previously to his now deceased father, Moses Austin, were also in Mexico City. These men were received much more favorably than were the Indians.

Though Fields and his party were issued promises of a grant by

Mexican officials, the Mexican colonization laws that were passed in 1824 and 1825 failed to include the Cherokees. Even worse, the land they claimed was part of a grant issued to Anglo-American Hayden E. Edwards, a disgruntled colonist who was stirring up a revolt against the Mexican government. Angrily, Fields threatened to join with the Comanches and other tribes in resisting Spanish control in north Texas.

In the fall of 1825 Austin learned that Fields was secretly trying to unite the tribes of northern Texas—known as Norteños—into a confederation to halt the expansion of white settlements. In treaties with the Comanches, Tawakonis, Wacos, and others, he had made a special point of having himself declared to be their "superior chief."[10] However, a reluctance to make enemies of the Mexican government, plus friction between aggressive Cherokee hunters and the prairie tribes, caused Fields to change his mind on unification. During a visit to the alcalde of Nacogdoches in the spring of 1826, the Cherokee leader insisted that he did not plan to war against the Mexicans. He said further that he had some 760 warriors under arms who would help him enforce orders of the Republic.[11] On April 24, Austin, in his capacity as colonel of his colony's militia, sent a message to Fields and other Cherokee chiefs and warriors telling them of plans to attack the Waco and Tawakoni villages on the Brazos River. The attack had been ordered by the Mexican government, and Austin suggested that it would be a good way for the Cherokees to demonstrate that they were good warriors and good citizens.[12]

Fields immediately called a council in which it was agreed that the Cherokees were willing to march with all their forces. However, they were delayed by spring flooding of the Neches and Trinity Rivers. Two weeks after his request was made, Austin sent another message to the Cherokees, saying that Mexico had decided that the Wacos and Tawakonis had indicated their desire for peace. He canceled his call for Cherokee aid.[13]

Members of Austin's colony, however, were fervent in their desire to attack the Brazos tribes regardless of the wishes of the Mexicans. Another call went out to the Cherokees, who indicated that they were waiting only on orders from the government to make their assault.[14] On August 27, Fields wrote to Austin to report that the Comanches were gathering en masse on the Colorado for an attack on Austin's colony. He also said the Texas tribes had been trying to get him to join them but he had refused. He requested permission to go ahead with an attack on the Wacos, who had killed some of his people.[15]

During the previous year, a man who would exert a great influence in their affairs arrived among the Cherokees. John Dunn Hunter was a quiet, well-mannered man with a commanding countenance. He had built a reputation for himself through the 1823 publication of a book in which he claimed great experience among western Indians before retiring to the fashionable life of New York and London. He was lionized in England even as the credibility of his claims was challenged by American publications and western notables.

Whatever the truth of Hunter's earlier life may have been, Chief Fields soon came to hold him in great esteem. Fields afforded the man such high favor and trust as to commission him to travel to Mexico City in an effort to secure a legal title to the land upon which the Cherokees resided in Texas. Fields even sold his own stock to raise money for the journey.[16]

Hunter's effort was unsuccessful. On his return, he painted such a picture of Mexican contempt for the Indians that some Cherokees were ready to go to war. However, he persuaded them to wait until he and Fields rode to Nacogdoches to talk with Mexican officials. There the two men met instead with Edwards. Hunter persuaded Fields to throw in with Edwards, the two promising they would send warriors to aid the Anglo-Americans in their attempt to overthrow Mexican rule. On December 21, 1826, Fields and Hunter joined Edwards and his cohorts in signing a document that declared their independence from Mexico as the Republic of Fredonia.[17] This act and the ensuing events, which have become known to history as the Fredonia Rebellion, would cause severe repercussions on the leadership of the Texas Cherokees.

Edwards's critical act of rebellion came during the following February when he and his men, boldly waving a newly made red and white flag, rode into Nacogdoches and seized an old stone building that had been constructed in earlier times as a fort. The small party held the fort and waited for a response from the Mexican army, which for the moment was occupied in repelling a Comanche raid on San Antonio. The action of Fields and Hunter in joining with Edwards was met with great disfavor by both Chiefs Bowle and Big Mush (or Boiling Mush[18]) as well as others. Hardly more than thirty warriors answered their call to ride to Nacogdoches. And once there, half of them left in disgust upon finding the Anglo-Fredonians engaged in a drunken brawl.[19]

Edwards's attempted strike for independence gained virtually no support from either the Cherokees or the non-Indian public. Austin vigorously opposed the Fredonians. He and his militia joined the Mexican army when it finally marched to quell the rebellion. By this time, it had become clear to Edwards that he had neither the popular nor Cherokee support on which he had counted. He and his compatriots abandoned their fort and fled eastward across the Sabine River to the safety of Louisiana soil.

The Fredonia Rebellion had far more tragic effects among the Cherokees, however. Mexican Indian agent Ellis Bean, who with thirty-five Mexican soldiers had been repelled by Edwards's men when they attempted to put down the rebellion, arrived at the Cherokee villages. There, through promises of fair treatment and a land grant, he had been able to secure the loyalty of Bowle and Big Mush to Mexico and estab-lish Fields and Hunter as traitors to Texas Cherokee interests.

The personal factors behind the events that followed and the rela-tionship between Fields and Bowle have never been clearly established. A Mexican officer reported to his superior in 1827 that Bowle and Big Mush conspired to kill Hunter and Fields as an act of proving loyalty to Mexico. Whether Bowle was motivated by a personal ambition to regain the position of head chief is speculative. It is likely that the decision to punish or remove the two men was either made during a tribal council or by an agreement between Bowle and Big Mush. Bean may well have been of some influence in the matter.[20]

Hunter, it is said, was assassinated by two warriors who were sup-posedly escorting him back to Nacogdoches. He was shot from his saddle while watering his horse in a stream and then shot again and killed as he pleaded for his life. One story has it that Fields went into hiding across the Sabine River, where he was found and killed. A more specific account states that he was killed in northern Rusk County on orders from Bowle and Big Mush. Thus came the end to Richard Fields's career as a leader of the Texas Cherokees. He had worked hard for his people, but he had made the fatal error of trying to lead them in a political direc-tion they did not wish to go.

Much more is known of John Bowle than of Fields. Some accounts have it that he was born around 1756, the progeny of a North Carolina trader and a Cherokee mother. John H. Reagan, who met Bowle when the chief was in his eighties, noted the sandy hair, gray eyes, and Anglo look of the man. One account has it that Cherokee raiders killed his English mother and father and carried him off to their home villages, where he was raised as a Cherokee.

It appears to be purely happenstance that John Bowle came to prominence among the Cherokees in a period immediately following the tumultuous career of William Augustus Bowles among the Creeks. No personal connection between the two has been established; though it is known that Tahlonteskee, of the Lower Towns, like Bowle, was a great admirer and friend of the Creek leader.

Accounts of Bowle's having been involved in the massacre of the Scott party in 1794 and his pre-1800 move to Missouri hang entirely upon the hearsay account by Rev. Cephas Washburn.[21] Bowle's request to Meigs for permission to move west in 1810 places serious question upon the Washburn story. But, as Bowle once told Reagan, he and his people did stop at the St. Francis River en route to Arkansas during 1810 and 1811.[22]

While Bowle had already seen his seventieth year in 1827, he was still a commanding figure and sharp of mind. His decision to sacrifice Fields and Hunter, harsh though it may have been, proved to be highly beneficial to both the Cherokees and himself. He was lauded by the Mexicans, who appointed him as a lieutenant colonel in the Mexican army and presented him with a military hat such as those worn by Mexican officers.

In 1829 a party of six or seven Cherokees and Creeks was discovered while trying to steal horses from a Tawakoni village. Three of them were captured and killed, their scalps being mounted on poles during a Tawakoni scalp dance. When word of this reached the Cherokees in Arkansas, war captain John Smith recruited a revenge party, which rode south to Dutch's village on the Sabine River of Texas.[23] Dutch volunteered to join them with nineteen of his men. Other warriors from the village of Big Mush agreed to rendezvous with them at Marshal Saline two days to the west. From there the Cherokee war party, sixty-three strong, marched for the Brazos. It was early morning and still dark when they reached the Tawakoni village sitting on a low flat among a grove of scrubby elm trees.

By Smith's account—as told to John Ridge—the attack, made on foot, was swift and brutal. Wielding tomahawks and rifles, the Cherokees cut down warriors, women, and children alike, even ruthlessly killing the captives they took. Many of the Tawakonis took refuge in a large, half-buried lodge, twelve feet wide and forty-five feet long. Attempts to burn out the defenders failed. After a time, a large group of horsemen, probably Wacos, came galloping up to engage the Cherokees. They were successful in luring three Cherokee warriors from the others. The bodies of the three were later found pierced with arrows and lances and their scalps taken. But these were the only losses the victorious Cherokees had suffered as they began their return march to Dutch's village with a large number of scalp trophies.[24]

Following the deaths of Fields and Hunter, the Texas Cherokees were in great favor with the Mexican government. Both Bean and Austin, arguing that the assassination of the two men had proven their loyalty to Mexico, exerted strong influence on behalf of the Cherokees being awarded a land grant. Mexican officials agreed. The Texas governor ordered the military command to issue a title for a Cherokee land grant. Before this could be done, unfortunately, the governor died and the military command was changed. The succeeding governor claimed land in conflict with the Cherokees. As a result, the Cherokees remained without legal title to the land on which they resided. Despite his disappointment, Bowle continued his efforts to persuade the Mexican government of the justice and wisdom of supporting a highly civilized Indian tribe of nearly eight hundred, most of whom could read and write and who had prospered with herds of stock and productive farms.

During the summer of 1833, Bowle led a party of Cherokee men to Bexar and from there to Saltillo, then the capital of Texas as well as of Coahuila Province. There they were assured that the matter would be attended to in the near future. However, in a betrayal of his earlier promises, agent Bean persuaded Mexican officials that it was not wise to give the Cherokees title to the lands of east Texas. It would be far better, he argued, to establish them farther west as a buffer against the warring prairie tribes. A resolution to that effect was passed by the Coahuila congress.

Bowle led his people in rejecting the grant. The Cherokees had become strongly attached to the wooded lands of east Texas, and they refused to be sacrificed to the warring between the Norteños and the Mexicans. Further, by 1835 Texas had been thrown into a state of confusion and uncertainty. More and more Anglo-Texans were talking of revolution. Additionally, a new player had come onto the Texas stage in the person of Sam Houston. The man who would emerge as the leader of the Texas revolution and Bowle were old friends, having once lived within seven miles of one another in Tennessee.[25]

In order to protect the Cherokees' position in east Texas, Bowle made every effort to maintain good relations with the Anglo-Americans there. The revolutionists were equally concerned in keeping the goodwill of the

Cherokees, who had the potential of effecting the outcome of their struggle with Mexico. Thus when delegates met at San Felipe de Austin in November 1835 to establish a provisional government, they issued a declaration concerning the Cherokees. By it the convention avowed their friendship for the Cherokees and solemnly guaranteed to recognize their claims to the lands in east Texas. Houston, who recently had been elected as commander in chief of the Texas Revolutionary Army, was a principal proponent and signer of the declaration.

Houston and Bowle had met earlier at Nacogdoches, where they discussed the plight of the Cherokees. Bowle did not return as expected, and Houston heard that the Cherokee leader had called a council of all Indian tribes in northern Texas. On February 5, 1836, Houston wrote requesting that Bowle come to Nacogdoches to meet with officials there, promising, "Your sun will shine bright upon you, and your sleep will not be troubled any more!"[26] When Bowle did not appear, Houston and Col. John Forbes traveled to the Cherokee villages to talk with Bowle and negotiate a treaty. On February 23 Houston signed a treaty document with Bowle, Big Mush, and six others, establishing friendship and trade relations between the Cherokees and the new Texas government.

The pact also clearly defined and recognized Cherokee title to the Texas lands claimed by the tribe. After the treaty was consummated, Houston presented Bowle with a beautiful sword (now held by the Masonic Lodge in Tahlequah, Oklahoma), a silk vest, a sash, and a hat of the day's military style. Bowle responded by decreeing Houston to be a chief among the Cherokees and presenting the Tennessean with his own daughter for a wife. Houston's reaction to this offering is not known, but friendship between the two men led to further social contacts between Cherokees and whites. At Houston's invitation, Bowle traveled to newly founded Houston, where he danced and enjoyed the company of the pretty women there. During one such trip, Texas citizens evidenced their disapproval as the two men boarded a steamer together for a ride to Galveston.[27]

The bond of friendship between Bowle and Sam Houston gave Bowle great reassurance concerning the Cherokee's land claim. Houston was clearly sincere in his support of the grant. On April 13, 1836, eight days prior to the historic Battle of San Jacinto, Houston wrote to the Cherokee chief, saying, "You will get your land as it was promised in our treaty, and you and all my red brothers may rest satisfied that I will always hold you by the hand."[28] After the revolution and his election as president of the new Republic of Texas, Houston continued to give his full support to the treaty he had made with Bowle. He sent it to the Texas congress for ratification with a warning that it was vital for the foundling republic to keep the friendship of the tribe.[29] However, white prejudice against Indians in general and rumors that the Cherokees were organizing to aid the Mexicans created strong opposition to the treaty.

The pact was still hanging unratified in the out-of-session congress during the summer of 1837 when Houston sent a message to Bowle asking him to come to Nacogdoches for a meeting. There Houston prompted the Cherokee leader to visit the Comanches in an effort to persuade them to sign a peace treaty with Texas. Bowle found the prairie tribe in camp along the Red River. But the Comanche abhorrence for the Texans was so strong that Bowle himself was almost murdered before a Comanche chief helped him escape.[30]

The Texas congress reconvened in the fall and debated the Cherokee treaty at great length. Many Texans contended that not only was the Cherokee country a part of a grant made to David G. Burnet, but that Houston's Cherokee pact was detrimental to the interests of Texas and Texas citizens. Much to the chagrin of Houston, the legislators declared the treaty to be null and void. In a speech to congress he bitterly denounced the lawmakers for breaking a sacred pledge to a trusting friend.[31]

Despite the rejection of the treaty, Houston pushed ahead with a personal promise he had made to Bowle that a boundary line between the Cherokees and the whites would be surveyed and marked off. White citizens angrily resisted the effort and made threats against the Indians. Bowle wrote to Houston that "my people from the Bigest to the least have had a little dread on their minds."[32] Houston sent word promising protection and assuring the Cherokee chiefs that the line would be run "before the leaves fall" or he would give them "my life or my land, for I will not tell them a lie."[33]

The Cherokee-Mexican connection that so concerned the Texas government came to a head in August 1838. At that time it was learned that a large body of Mexicans from the Nacogdoches area had organized a rebellion against the Republic of Texas and were encamped on the Angelina River of east Texas. Gen. Thomas Rusk of the Texas militia was assigned the task of locating and putting down the rebels who were commanded by Vincente Córdova.[34] An emissary sent to talk with Bowle returned to report that the Mexicans were encamped near the

Cherokee village. He carried a letter from Houston to Bowle pleading that the Cherokees remain peaceful. "Remember me and my words," he wrote. "We have not asked you to join us to make war but to remain at peace."[35]

Bowle and his men were armed and ready to defend themselves, but it did not appear that they had yet become allied with the Mexicans. When Rusk reached the Cherokee village with his Texas militia army, he found that Córdova's force had fled in disarray. Bowle disclaimed having played any part in the aborted revolution, but few Texans believed him.[36]

Suspicions of the Cherokees were further fueled in early October when eighteen members of a family named Killough of Cherokee County, Texas, were brutally massacred by Indians.[37] Though the identity of the perpetrators was unknown, the Texas public placed the blame squarely on the Cherokees. Fear, resentment, and intense animosity for Bowle and his people exploded across Texas as the expiration of Houston's term of office approached in December 1838.

With Houston's departure, the Indians of Texas not only lost their strongest white ally but also suffered the extremely hostile presence of the new Texas president, Mirabeau Buonaparte Lamar. Lamar, who had migrated from the state of Georgia, where the Old Nation Cherokees had been so severely maltreated, was adamant that the Texas Cherokees

President of the Republic of Texas Mirabeau B. Lamar, a former Georgian, evicted the Cherokees from Texas.

Baker, A Texas Scrapbook.

would have to leave Texas soil. He received strong support for this among the white population of Texas.

In the spring of 1839 there occurred still another incident that incriminated Bowle and his Cherokees even more in the minds of Texans. A pack train of 150 horses and mules sent by the Mexican agent at Matamoros to assist Córdova was intercepted. Its commander, Manuel Flores, was shot and killed. On his body were found letters addressed to Bowle and other chiefs. The Cherokees, the letters promised, would be rewarded with their land if they would raid Texas settlements, burn homes and crops, and steal the Texans' stock.[38] Though some scholars believe that Bowle had made no commitment and was still playing one side against the other, the anger of the Anglo-Texas population was excited to the extreme. Houston still argued Bowle's innocence, but Lamar vowed publicly to eject the Cherokees from Texas. Alleging the danger of a general Indian uprising, Lamar sent two companies of troops to take up a position in Cherokee territory.

When Bowle threatened to fight if the troops remained, Lamar raged at the challenge to his authority. He penned a furious letter, accusing the chief of being in league with the Mexicans and committing depredations against Texas citizens. As a result, he declared, "The Cherokee will never be permitted to establish a permanent and independent jurisdiction within the inhabited limits of this Government."[39] For the time, Lamar said, the Cherokees could live unmolested where they were if they would remain at home "without murdering our people, stealing their property, or giving succor and protection to our enemies." But just as soon as the Texas government could make the necessary arrangements, the Cherokees would be forcibly removed to north of the Red River.

Lamar's message was delivered to Bowle by Indian agent Martin Lacy, accompanied by an interpreter named Cordray, Dr. W. G. W. Jowers, and young John H. Reagan, who had only recently arrived in Texas. Reagan, who would ultimately serve as a Texas Supreme Court justice and U.S. senator, kept a detailed and perceptive journal of his visit to the Cherokee village. He was immediately impressed with Bowle, whose tall, proud bearing reflected great strength and dignity even in his eighty-third year.

The men seated themselves on logs at a spring near Bowle's house, where Lamar's letter was read and interpreted to the chief in Spanish. After digesting the message in silence for a time, Bowle responded by defending his people against Lamar's charges and insisting on their right to the land on which they resided. He also told the emissaries that he had been corresponding with Chief John Ross concerning the possibility of making a united Cherokee migration to California. He ended by recommending that they meet again at the spring in a week or so, after he had time to meet in council with his chiefs and headmen.

When Bowle returned, his countenance was grave. Though he and Big Mush had opposed it, his young men had voted to go to war against the Texans. In a matter-of-fact manner, he explained his situation. He himself knew that if they went to war the whites would ultimately overcome them, and he would undoubtedly be killed. If he refused to fight, his warriors would probably kill him. He was concerned only about his three wives and his children. He knew that either way he would die, and he was ready. But his duty was to stand by his men whatever his fate might be. Thus, with no indication of giving in to Lamar's terms, he departed.

Lamar reacted quickly. He appointed a five-man commission of high-ranking Texas officials that included Vice President David G. Burnet, Secretary of War Albert Sidney Johnston, and General Rusk. His instructions were harsh. The Cherokees would be paid no more than twenty-five thousand dollars for their improvements, goods, crops, and other property. They were to depart just as soon as arrangements could be made. If they did not leave, "nothing short of the entire destruction of all they possess and the extermination of their tribe will appease the indignation of the white people against them."[40]

The commissioners established their camp across the Neches River from Bowle's camp and sent a letter to Bowle requesting a meeting. During talks held in mid-July, the commissioners presented a nine-article agreement for the Cherokees to sign. Two of the articles were particularly unacceptable. Bowle and his men objected to the demand that they give up all but fifty of their gunlocks. Further, they refused to leave the country under escort, as if they were prisoners.

On the morning of July 15, a delegation of officers went to Bowle's camp to urge Bowle to sign the agreement. After conferring with some eighty of his warriors, Bowle told the Texans that he and his men would not sign. He further refused to go to meet with the commissioners again. Later he sent word by his son John Bowle that he was moving his camp.[41]

During these negotiations, General Rusk had shifted his east Texas regiment to the Neches River and established camp. Two other regiments under Col. Edward Burleson and Col. Willis H. Landrum arrived to bolster the Texas strength. To settle the conflict of command, Gen. Kelsey H. Douglas of the Texas militia was named as commanding officer of the combined forces. When Douglas received word that Bowle was moving, he put his units in pursuit. Landrum was ordered to move up the east side of the Neches to cut off the Cherokees on the northeast. Rusk and Burleson marched directly to Bowle's camp. Finding it deserted, they followed the clear trail, which led northwest across the Neches. Scouts were thrown forward with orders to engage the Indians and keep them under long-range fire until the main command arrived.

Late that afternoon six miles west of the Neches, the scouts made contact with Bowle's warriors, who had positioned themselves along a creek not far from where a Delaware Indian village stood. The main Texas force came forward and engaged the Indians in a skirmish that was cut short by darkness. During the brief episode, two Texans were killed and several more wounded. The Cherokees retreated to join their main force north of the Delaware village, leaving behind eighteen dead as well as gunpowder, lead, livestock, corn, and other paraphernalia.

Early the next morning, the Texans set out in pursuit. They put the Delaware village to the torch as they passed, the black smoke of the fire billowing into the sky. Only a short distance beyond, they came face to face with a mile-long line of warriors who were entrenched in a ravine waiting. Texas skirmishers, followed by their main force, pushed forward as a heavy exchange of gunfire erupted. Bowle himself commanded the Indian force. Young Reagan, who was an awed witness to the battle, later described the Cherokee leader:

> During this engagement Chief Bowles was a very conspicuous figure. He was mounted on what we call a paint horse, and had on him a sword and sash, and military hat and silk vest, which had been given to him by General Houston. And thus conspicuously mounted and dressed, he rode up and down in the rear of his line, very much exposed during the entire battle.[42]

Bowle urged his warriors forward, telling them that if they would charge the Texans they would win the fight. But his men were not trained in making mass assault, and eventually they fell back in the face of the enemy's pressure. Finally, Bowle stood alone on the field of battle. Though a prime target for Texas sharpshooters, the old chief had somehow survived. One ball had struck him in the thigh and several more found his horse. Finally, when the animal could go no farther, Bowle dismounted. Sword in hand, the half Scotsman looked almost the ancient Highlander as he began walking away with great dignity. As he did so, he was staggered by a bullet in his back. After a few steps he fell, then pulled himself to a sitting position facing the Texas line. Reagan, who witnessed these events and felt great compassion for Bowle, rushed forward to save him, calling out to others not to shoot. But even as he did so, Reagan's captain fired a pistol shot into Bowle's head, killing him instantly. Afterward, some of the Texans scalped the body and cut strips of skin from his back, supposedly to make bridle reins. It is said that Bowle's body remained unburied and that his skeleton lay at the battle site until the bones had turned to dust.[43]

The Texas attack ended the Cherokee settlement in east Texas. Elements of the group fled in various directions. Some were captured and held prisoner by the Texans until finally in 1840 they were sent to the Indian Territory.[44] Chief Big Mush was among those who escaped, making his way north of the Red River and joining the Western Cherokees, where he took part in a grand council of Indian tribes in 1843.[45]

A large portion of the Texas Cherokees moved to Mexico, being permitted to establish a village near the town of San Fernando. En route Bowle's son John was killed on Christmas Day of 1839 near the mouth of the San Saba River by a Texas command under Burleson. The Texans captured John's mother, two sisters, and three children.[46] A year or two later, according to Reagan, the wives and some of the children of Chief Bowle came to Laredo and requested permission to return to the Indian Territory. Lamar reportedly granted this, furnishing rations and transportation under escort.[47]

Some of the Texas Cherokees went north to the Canadian River and took refuge at the village Dutch had founded when he was moved there by the United States in 1832. Homeless, destitute of clothes, and starving, they were fed for a time by trader Jesse Chisholm, who was located at the conflux of the Little River with the Canadian.[48]

Sam Houston had been away from Texas at the time of the Neches battle. He never forgave Lamar for the killing of his good friend, who he insisted had never drawn one drop of white man's blood. Despite threats against his life, Houston spoke out publicly and bitterly on the matter, his most notable summation being that Bowle was "a better man than his murderers."[49]

CHAPTER 15

Reunion and Conflict

Moving west with the Cherokees and heightened by the soul-wrenching travail of removal was the virulent hostility between the Ross (or Patriot) and the Treaty party groups. The rancor and personal animosities evolving from the forced sale of the Old Nation lands would divide the Cherokee Nation for years to come. Further, once arrived, Ross found there were battles even more severe to fight.

The Western Cherokees gave welcome to their tribal family without complaint; there was, they said, room enough in their land for all. A new capital site was chosen, and it was named Tahlequah, the Cherokee spelling of their ancient town of Tellico, the village that had once been their capital in Tennessee. Said to be the site of an ancient Indian village, Tahlequah sat surrounded by hills of oak and sugar maple. The source of fresh cool water that issued from the foot of a hill was known as Wolf's Spring. When the Old Nation council marked off a public square, surrounded it with a rail fence, and erected a log cabin for its headquarters, the town was little more than a few stores, taverns, and the cabins of public cooks and a few families.[1]

But soon enough, as the Old Nation Cherokees began to rebuild their lives along the Illinois, Grand, Verdigris, and other tributaries of the Arkansas River, a crucial issue would arise. Who would rule here? The government of the Western Cherokees or that of the Old Nation under Ross? The question was not simply a political one. Western Cherokee leaders had long been resentful of Old Nation dominance in treaty matters and annuity distribution. They had organized their governmental system and made treaties in the West separate from the Old Nation. Even as the Old Nation Cherokees were on their way to the Indian Territory during December 1838, Western head chief John Jolly died at his Webbers Falls home. The good-natured chief would be replaced by a more aggressive leadership.[2]

In new elections that spring, John Brown, son of former Old Nation chief Richard Brown, was named principal chief, while John Looney and John Rogers were selected as second and third chiefs, respectively. These men all felt strongly that as the Western Cherokee chiefs they had a mandate to rule over the region assigned by the Treaty of 1828. Though forewarned by members of the Treaty party, they were unsuspecting at first of the political threat presented by John Ross. In early June 1839, the Western chiefs called some six thousand Cherokees together for a three-week unity convention. They met in their new Takatoka council house at Double Springs, north of Tahlequah.

Chief Brown graciously welcomed the newcomers. He told them that they were free to choose their own place to settle, could vote in future elections, and were eligible for political office in the Western Cherokee government. At the same time, Brown noted, they would be subject to the laws of that government. He then invited comments from the newcomers.[3] Ross and John Lowrey were ready. They presented a list of written resolutions calling for the formation of a new Cherokee government west of the Mississippi. This would be achieved, they suggested, by a constitutional committee comprising an equal number of Old Nation and Western Old Settler men. Brown and his fellow chiefs were taken aback and angered by the proposals. They rejected the request, reminding Ross that a government already existed.[4]

The conference would have broken up then had it not been for the efforts of Sequoyah. The famed Cherokee, a son of whom had been killed by a Treaty party member in 1835,[5] now stepped forward as a mediator. Along with Jesse Bushyhead, an educated half blood of the Old Nation group, Sequoyah worked out a compromise. The two factions would meet again in July at the Takatoka council.

Beneath the surface issue of governmental rule, another matter was boiling its way toward violent eruption during the council. The malevolence of Ross men for Treaty party leaders had been incensed by rumors that Ridge and Boudinot had been holding private talks with the Western Cherokee leaders, persuading them against compromise with Ross. Even as the Double Springs conference ended on June 21, more than one hundred determined Ross followers conducted a clandestine meeting to devise a plan for the assassination of the two Ridges, Elias Boudinot, and Stand Watie. Despite suspicions that abounded later, it is doubted that John Ross knew of the meeting. The plotters assigned Ross's son Allen to stay at his father's side and prevent any word of it from reaching him. Twelve names were drawn and volunteers accepted for four execution squads to carry out the old Cherokee clan "law of blood" against the leaders of the Treaty party. On the following night, the squads made their way along the dark paths of the Ozark foothills. Most of the men wore handkerchiefs across their faces, and the lot were armed with guns, hatchets, and knives.[6]

One group arrived at the home of John Ridge on Honey Creek in the far northeastern corner of the new Cherokee territory and dragged him into the yard. While his wife and children watched in horror, Ridge was stabbed over and over. The assassins cut his throat and then ritually stomped him. Thinking him to be dead, the culprits then slipped away into the night. Ridge was still alive, however, as his wife and servants pulled his battered, bloody body inside to his bed, where he soon expired.

Elias Boudinot was overseeing the building of his new home near Worcester's mission, a short distance from Park Hill, when four men approached. They said that they had come for medical supplies from the missionary. They asked for his help. As he headed for the missionary's house, one of the men stabbed him in the back to the knife's hilt. The others then joined in with their war hatchets, raining deadly blows crushing into Boudinot's skull. They then fled to where a group of cohorts waited on horseback and galloped away. A carpenter working on Boudinot's house was sent hurrying to warn Major Ridge, who was on his way to Van Buren, Arkansas, at the time of his son's murder. The warning arrived too late. The body of Ridge, once the assassin of Doublehead, was found lying in the road. He had been shot from ambush and suffered five wounds to his body and head.

Stand Watie, who was at a store at the time, was forewarned and escaped—left by fate to play a large role in future Cherokee affairs. Among those later accused of being involved in the triple killings were Bird Doublehead, son of the famous chief, and James Foreman, a firebrand who had been suspected of killing a U.S. agent in 1834. None of the men were ever brought to trial. The aftershocks of these murders were still reverberating throughout the Cherokee Nation when on July 1 the Lowrey/Sequoyah–arranged council convened at the Illinois River campground. Though the Western chiefs, who had fled to Fort Gibson for safety, scheduled their own meeting to the south at the Tahlonteskee council house, more than two thousand Cherokees answered Sequoyah's call.

Sequoyah sent a letter to the three Western chiefs. He pleaded with them to join other Old Settlers in talking "matters over like friends and brothers." Chief John Looney responded by switching to the Ross faction, but Brown and Rogers remained strongly in opposition. As a result, more than 250 Cherokees led by Sequoyah, his brother Tobacco Will, and Looney signed an "act of deposement" against Brown and Rogers. The two chiefs were charged of having "by their unworthy and unlawful conduct betrayed the trust reposed in them and forfeited the confidence of the Cherokee people." In rebuttal, the Western chiefs claimed that fewer than twenty bona fide Old Settlers were among the petitioners.[7] Under Sequoyah's sponsorship, the reform Old Settlers and Ross's Old Nation party drew up an Act of Union, which they made public on July 12. Elections were set for September 6 at the new "national capital" of Tahlequah. At that time, a new constitution similar to that of the Old Nation was adopted, and John Ross was elected principal chief as expected.[8]

The Ross party had drafted a resolution purportedly designed to establish a stable government. By it, however, members of the Treaty party who had "committed acts of outlawry" were offered amnesty at the price of public retraction of their vows of revenge for the assassinations of the Ridges and Boudinot within eight days. Further, they were to be barred from holding office for five years. Few of them accepted the offer, and Stand Watie swore he would never sign such an oath. Eventually the requirement was revoked.[9]

Accepting defeat, Western chief John Brown went off to Mexico to see about joining the refugee Texas Cherokees there.[10] Rumors made the rounds that John Rogers and his Negro servant had been killed while on the way from his saline to Fort Gibson.[11] Rogers was still very much alive, however, and at the Tahlonteskee council he was elected principal chief by those Old Settlers who refused to accept the new Ross government.[12]

John Smith, the war chief who had led the Cherokees against the Tawakonis in 1830, and the famous warrior Dutch were elected second and third chiefs, respectively. Smith had earlier been forced to flee south of the Arkansas River for a time in fear of the Ross people.[13] Dutch, now known as William Dutch, resided in his settlement along the Canadian River near present Briartown, Oklahoma. In November the three Western leaders issued a protest against the election of Ross, holding to their claim as the rightful Cherokee authorities.[14]

Gen. Matthew Arbuckle, commanding the U.S. military in the area, was strongly opposed to Ross. He provided anti-Ross testimony, convincing Secretary of War Joel R. Poinsett that the longtime chief had instigated and abetted the assassinations of the Ridges and Boudinot. Ross insisted that he did not even know the persons who had been accused of the deed and made no move to arrest anyone despite Arbuckle's insistence.[15]

The explosive state of Cherokee affairs is evident in a resolution issued near Tahlequah on January 16, 1841. It charged that a conspiracy had been formed to take the life of John Ross as well as the chief justice of the Cherokee Supreme Court, the high sheriff, and other public functionaries.[16] Arbuckle placed the Cherokee Nation under martial law, and his influence was felt in the refusal of the Van Buren administration to recognize the Ross government. U.S. officials chose to deal instead with the Treaty party men headed by Stand Watie.

Watie, whose Cherokee name was Degadoga (He Stands on Two Feet—hence, Stand Watie), was born in Georgia in 1806 and was educated at the Moravian Mission School at Springplace, Georgia. For a time he was employed as an interpreter at the Cherokee agency. When he came west in 1837, he settled on Honey Creek east of the Grand River. Sarah Caroline Bell, whom he married in 1843, was his fourth wife.[17] In May 1842, Watie stopped at a grocery store in Maysville, Arkansas, by chance meeting Ross man James Foreman there. Words were exchanged between the two, whereupon Foreman began striking Watie with a horsewhip. As the two men struggled outside of the store, Foreman picked up a board for a weapon. Watie defended himself with a knife, stabbing his assailant. But Foreman was not done. He continued to challenge Watie, who now pulled his pistol and shot him dead. Watie was tried for murder in a Benton County, Arkansas, court and found not guilty on grounds of self-defense.[18]

Though Ross was able to maintain a tenuous hold over Cherokee Nation affairs, he remained in great disfavor with the U.S. government during the Van Buren and Tyler administrations. His efforts to renegotiate the Treaty of New Echota for more money was stymied. Further, at home the Cherokee masses were severely impoverished.

Though still supported by the loyalty of a large majority of the Cherokees, Ross saw the need to reassert his leadership position. In June 1843 he hosted an International Indian Council at Tahlequah. An estimated ten thousand Indians representing seventeen tribes were present to take part in the four-week affair. Gen. Zachary Taylor from Fort Smith paid a visit to the council, and he and Ross were the central figures in a painting of the crowded council house by artist John Mix Stanley.

In an address to the assemblage, Ross stated that his purpose for calling the council was to "adopt such international laws as may be necessary to redress the wrongs that may have been done by individuals of
our respective nations upon each other."[19] His words, however, did little
to ease the seething malice between the Ross and Treaty factions.

Unquestionably, the greatest troublemakers for Ross were the so-
called Starr Gang. James Starr, who had signed the New Echota treaty,
his six sons, and numerous followers resisted the Ross government to
the point of blatant outlawry, often for money or horses as well as blood
vengeance. In part, however, there were purposeful attempts by members of the Treaty party and Old Settlers to disrupt and discredit the
Ross government. That Starr felt justified in such actions, however, is
apparent in a letter that he, Charles Reese, and George W. Adair wrote
to Ross during the spring of 1843: "Several private companies," the letter charged, "have been organized in the Nation under the title of police
companies for the express purpose of killing the Treaty men, as they are
called, including some of the best citizens of our nation." The letter
warned: "War would certainly be the sorest calamity with which our
land can be visited."[20]

But virtual war there would be. Acts of mayhem and murder would
continue to spread a pall of fear over the entire Cherokee Nation. Among
these incidents were the murder of Isaac Bushyhead, who had signed the
1841 resolution warning of such a plot, and the attempted murder of
David Vann, Ross's treasurer, and Judge Elijah Hicks, all of whom were
serving as election officials in the Saline District in August 1843. The
men were on their way separately to inform Ross of election returns when
a party of men surrounded Bushyhead and attacked him with a variety
of weapons, including Bowie knives. Bushyhead pleaded for his life, saying he had done them no harm. It was in vain; the men beat and stabbed
him until he was dead.[21] Forty-three-year-old David Vann was grabbed
as he was mounting his horse, dragged about, and beaten with clubs. He
was so covered with blood that his assailants let him be carted off to safety
by friends. Elijah Hicks was forewarned and escaped harm. The attack
had been led by Treaty party member George West, sheriff of the district, and his father. So great was their fear of retaliation, many Treaty
party people fled from the nation, leaving most of their personal goods
behind.

The gory violence and lawlessness among the Cherokees continued
unabated, propagating a rueful list of murders and countermurders. Many

involved the deaths of little-known Cherokee citizens, but not uncommonly principal figures of the nation were slain. One of the most shocking was the robbery and murders of trader Benjamin Vore, his wife, and a traveler who was visiting their home on September 15, 1843.[22] Vore had operated a trading store at the mouth of the Canadian River for some five years. The killers had entered the house, murdered the three in cold blood, and then burned the place. Vore's charred body was found with an arm extended and an open knife in his hand, indication that he had put up a fight.[23]

Not long after this, a party of ten Cherokee settlers headed by Daniel R. Coodey set out to recover horses and mules that had been lost to thieves. Following a trail to the south, they reached the Washita River, where they visited a settlement of Cherokees who had recently returned from Mexico. There they found shod mule tracks that told them their stock was near. A local resident said that Cherokees Tom, Ellis, and Bean Starr had brought them there.[24] While the posse was searching for the animals, young Bean Starr came galloping up and, as he was trying to get away, was shot from the saddle. He was carried to a house, seriously wounded. The boy confessed to them that he and his brothers Tom and Ellis had stolen the horses. Further, a track made by a horse with a split hoof was considered proof that the group had been guilty of the Vore killings, a similar print having been found at the murder site.

Fearing an attack from the other Starrs, Coodey led his men on south to Fort Washita. There they secured a company of dragoons to help search the countryside for the Starrs. Unsuccessful after three days, Coodey's men put Bean Starr on a horse and took him to the fort, where he could get medical attention. He died a few days later.

With Coodey's volunteers and a company of Cherokee Light Horse police scouring the country looking for them, the Starrs fled into Arkansas, where they had many sympathizers. There they were arrested by state militia. Permitted to keep their guns while being taken to Fayetteville, they easily escaped their guard. They returned to the Cherokee Nation, hovering close to the Arkansas border and prowling the Cherokee country again. In January 1845 John Ross and his government issued notice of a three thousand dollar reward for the capture of Ellis West, Samuel McDaniel, Tom Starr, and Ellis Starr.[25] A company of U.S. Dragoons from Fort Gibson chased the men as far as the Big Bend of the Arkansas before turning back.

Another major disturbance occurred on the night of November 2,

1845, when a band of Treaty party men that included Tom Starr, Ellis Starr, Washington Starr, Suel Rider, and Ellis West came to the home of Return Jonathan Meigs. Meigs, son of the early Cherokee agent and a son-in-law of John Ross, was suspected of having a part in the assassination of the Ridges and Boudinot. The men stuck guns in the window of Meigs's house and demanded entrance. Dodging bullets, Meigs escaped through the backdoor leaving the gang to burn his house down to ashes and brick. The next morning, the bodies of two other murdered Ross men were found nearby.[26]

The Ross faction retaliated a week later when a party led by an elderly Cherokee named Talusky Tuck-quah rode up to the home of Starr's father, James Starr. The elder Starr, who was on his porch wiping his face with a towel, was shot to death immediately. The men also tried to kill and did wound Washington Starr and young teenager Buck Starr, who later died. Suel Rider, who lived nearby, was killed by the group the same day. Anderson Benge and John Downing were among the attackers.[27]

In mid-November another gang of assassins found Tom Watie, brother of Stand Watie, as he had just retired for the night. In 1839 he had been attacked while in bed and had had a hand nearly cut off by a hatchet. Now, being told that he was their prisoner, Watie said he would get dressed. But even as he raised himself in bed, he was shot and his head split open with a tomahawk. His body was afterward mangled with knives.[28]

There was more human slaughter. Watie's murder was followed by those of two Treaty party men near Evansville by a group of fifteen Ross men. One was shot five times, and the other was stabbed through the heart.[29] On December 27, Treaty party member Charles Smith was killed by Col. John Brown (not the Western chief) of the Cherokee Light Horse. Then on January 9, 1846, Granville Rogers, son of John Rogers, was killed at Maysville, Arkansas, by Braxton Nicholson.[30]

In late April 1846, Stand (Ta-kah-tah-kah), a member of the party that murdered James Starr and now an officer in the Light Horse, was at a dance. Some claimed that he was riding a stick around and saying that he was old Jim Starr. Later in the evening he accepted an invitation of a man named Wheeler Faught to go outside and have a drink. There he was waylaid by a group of assassins. He was shot and stabbed to death, then scalped. Before Faught was hanged in April he named Tom, Ellis, Jim, Billy, and Washington Starr as the killers.[31]

When the Starrs next murdered an elderly Ross man named

Cornsilk, the Ross people retaliated by killing a Treaty party man named Turner. Pursued by Cherokee police, Ellis, Dick, and Billy Starr were wounded but escaped across the Arkansas line. When two men of the Ross party were murdered by Jim and Tom Starr, the Light Horse police killed Billy Rider of the Treaty party in revenge.[32]

Western chief John Rogers Jr. placed the blame for such mayhem squarely upon Ross, who he described as "my unceasing enemy produced by envy."[33] In a letter to the *Arkansas Intelligencer* of Van Buren, Rogers pointed out the fact that such acts had not taken place before the arrival of the Old Nation group. The breakdown in law and order, he insisted, was a direct result of Ross's refusal to deliver up accused parties for the murders of the Ridges and Boudinot.

Rogers, now elderly and in ill health, had first settled at Dardanelle when he came west. The year following the Cherokee massacre of Clermont's Osage village he had returned to the Old Nation and brought back two Osage children who were being held captive there.[34] After moving to present Oklahoma that same year, he built the first water mill in the Cherokee Nation West on the Spavinaw River and operated a saline there. Sam Houston had consorted with Rogers's daughter Diana during his stay among the Western Cherokees.[35]

Though Rogers had always been a highly respected man of the region, his efforts to maintain the position of the Western Cherokee government placed him in serious jeopardy. He had, he said, become "an alien in his own land."[36] Learning of a plot to kill him if he were reelected chief, Rogers fled to Virginia, later returning to Arkansas. His son Thomas, a judge for his district, wrote to him from their Spavinaw saline, saying, "If you will take a son's advice, you will stay where you are."[37] Later, Thomas himself was arrested by a company of Ross's police and taken to Tahlequah, where he was held in jail for two days. During that time, John Rogers's saline was occupied by force and leased out at auction.[38] Testimony to the sense of danger that hovered over the Rogers family and others of the nation was given by Chaney Richardson, a slave girl during this period:

> I didn't know nothing else but some kind of war until I was a grown woman, because when I first can remember my old Master, Charley Rogers, was always on the lookout for somebody or other he was lined up against in the big feud.
>
> My master and all the rest of the folks was Cherokees, and they'd been kiling each other off in the feud ever since long before I was

borned . . . We didn't know what we was a-feared of, but we heard the Master and Mistress keep talking 'bout "another Party killing" and we stuck close to the place.[39]

Chaney Richardson's own slave mother was murdered when she went to get bark with which to dye some cloth. Rogers was almost out of his mind with anger and sent his young Cherokee men out to search the woods at night for almost a month, but the killer was never found.

In November 1844, a three-man commission was sent by the Polk administration to get a reading on the intensity of the Cherokee conflicts. After taking testimony at Fort Gibson, the commission made plans to confer with Old Settlers and Treaty party members at the Tahlonteskee council house near the mouth of the Illinois River in December.[40] While still at Gibson, they received a message from John Rogers in Arkansas requesting a military escort for himself and James Carey to attend the proposed meeting. A company of dragoons was provided Rogers.

Chief John Brown, having returned from Mexico, was present at the meeting, along with 286 Old Settlers and 179 Treaty party members, including Stand Watie. John Ross had been invited, but he rejected the offer and sent instead a delegation numbering more than a hundred men and headed by his nephew William Potter Ross.[41]

The Tahlonteskee site had only a few log cabins and a large shed, which was designated as the council house. A few tents had been pitched, and people were gathered around blazing campfires, cooking and warming themselves. The Stars and Stripes floated from the top of an oak tree. A group of Light Horse police appeared, claiming they were searching for the Starrs. The Cherokees at the meeting were greatly concerned at this, as was the commission, who ordered the police to leave. The commissioners wrote to Ross that the presence of the Light Horse was "too well calculated to inspire the fears of the parties called together."[42]

It began to snow heavily on December 6. Because many of the people had no shelter and wished to return home, the commissioners, after enrolling those in attendance, adjourned to the old Cherokee agency between Fort Gibson and Tahlequah. Both the weather and proximity to the Ross headquarters restricted the attendance there. Ross sent a letter of protest concerning the commission's hearing of the opposition parties, but it was rejected out of hand. Still it concluded in Ross's favor that "The complainants [the Old Settler and Treaty party] have not shown in any case that life has been taken or endangered by the Cherokee authorities."[43]

After being ejected from the meeting at Tahlonteskee, the Light

Horse company proceeded up the Canadian River to the home of Dutch. According to a complaint issued by Chief Brown, the horsemen surrounded the house then searched it and the outbuildings, declaring their intention of scalping Dutch if they caught him. The now elderly Dutch, however, had escaped when warned by a friend. The commander of the Light Horse unit claimed that he and his men had been looking for the Starrs and had merely entered Dutch's home to warm themselves.[44]

After playing his important role in bringing about the unity meeting of July 1839, Sequoyah retired from public political involvement. Lt. Col. Ethan Allen Hitchcock, who made a tour of the Cherokee country in 1841, described "the philosopher Guess" as being cheerful, good humored, and intelligent. The Cherokee dressed rudely, "as if not caring for the outward man."[45] His mind ranged over a wide variety of subjects, his observations of which he kept in a daily journal. Sequoyah possessed a natural talent for art, being especially good at human portraits and sketches of animals.

Having now passed his sixtieth year, Sequoyah was in failing health. Still, he was possessed with a great desire to further unify the Cherokee Nation by persuading the tribal refugees in Mexico to return and reunite with the main Cherokee body. He also had a burning curiosity concerning the western prairie and the Indians there. These two impulses led him on a strange and daring odyssey in 1842. With an entourage of young Cherokee men, Sequoyah set out on a route that led southwestward through the famed Cross Timbers and across the Red River. There the group hunted for a time; but becoming quite ill and plagued by a bad cough, Sequoyah was forced to take lodging with the chief of a Kichai band on the Washita River. When he had recovered some, Sequoyah sent all of his escort home except for his son Teesa and a guide named Oo-no-leh, or Worm.[46]

The three men now set out for Mexico. During their long journey across Texas, their horses were stolen by Tawakoni Indians. Being too weak to continue far on foot, Sequoyah was provided refuge in a cave while Teesa and Worm went into nearby San Antonio to procure horses. When the commandant there refused to provide them mounts, the two Cherokees secured Sequoyah in the cave and continued on to Mexico. When they returned with horses, they found the famous Cherokee gone and a note written in Cherokee telling how the cave had become flooded. The Cherokee elder was tracked and found by a campfire, having stayed alive by chewing on his deerskin shirt for nourishment.

Sequoyah was taken on to the Cherokee village near San Fernando,

Mexico, where soon after, in August 1843, he died and was buried. In 1845 the Cherokee Nation, concerned over the disappearance of the great man for whom their council had voted a medal in 1824, sent the Cherokee-Scot frontiersman Jesse Chisholm in charge of a small search party to find Sequoyah. Chisholm made the trip and returned to reveal the fate of the Cherokee intellect. He also brought back the Mexico Cherokees, who resettled on the Brazos River near present Waco, Texas, for a time before moving on north to the lower Washita River.

Even as Sequoyah was attempting to reunify the Cherokees, the nation was on the verge of breaking even farther apart. Before the Texas expulsion of the Cherokees, it was reported John Ross had corresponded with Bowle concerning the possibility of either moving the Old Nation to Texas or making a consolidated migration to California.[47]

In the fall of 1845 a party of fifty-four Western Cherokees and Treaty party members, Teesa Guess being among them, made a winter-long trip through western Texas to investigate it for a possible new home and to enjoy some hunting. On the Brazos they encountered the sixty-three-member village of the Mexico Cherokees and a trading party under Jesse Chisholm.[48]

William Quesenbury (pronounced Cushenbury), a young Arkansawyer, accompanied the party and kept a diary of the trip, from its departure in September 1845 to its return the following March. After a visit to San Antonio, "Cush" met with Jesse Chisholm, who had ranged far south from his home on the Canadian River to conduct trade on the Guadalupe River. The two men traveled together to Torrey's Fort on the Brazos near present Waco, where they found a U.S. commissioner party conducting a treaty council with the Comanches and other Plains tribes. With them were Cherokee agent Pierce M. Butler and M. G. Lewis, commissioners, as well as Elijah Hicks and William Shorey Coodey, president of the Cherokee National Council, whom Ross had appointed as delegates for the Cherokee Nation.[49] The Cherokees assisted in conducting the Treaty of Comanche Peak (where they first met before moving to Council Springs on the Tawakoni River), as did Chisholm, who was immediately hired to help bring in the Comanches. It may have been that in sending delegates Ross was keeping open the possibility of a new Cherokee home on the prairie.

On a political level, matters had been deteriorating badly, and the Cherokee Nation was in severe disarray from outlaw whites and half bloods. An observer of the Cherokees described the dire situation:

there is a wildness growing among these people . . . the knife is in daily use, the stabber is lord of the country: peaceable Indians are shot down in the fields by an unseen and unanswerable foe . . . Not less than seven innocent Cherokees have fallen victim whilst at work in their cornfields . . . the troops here for their special protection cannot leave their camps alone, but in bodies and well armed, lest they are attacked.[50]

In the spring of 1846, President James Polk concluded that in order to arrest the "horrid and inhuman massacres" of the Cherokees it would be necessary to separate them, each with its own government.[51] He would do this by creating a permanent territorial division between the Old Nation group on one hand and the Western Cherokees and Treaty party on the other. A bill to that effect was considered by Congress, but Ross, intensely protective of Cherokee sovereignty, managed to bring about the defeat of the measure.

It was finally decided that representatives of all three groups would meet in Washington, D.C., in June 1846 to work out matters. Ross headed his government's delegation to Washington. He was accompanied by David Vann; John Looney; Stephen Foreman, whose brother Stand Watie had killed in 1842; Tahlequah merchant John Drew; and others. Drew had recently led a posse to recapture a group of Cherokee slaves attempting to escape to Mexico.[52] For the Western Cherokees, or Old Settlers, were Rogers, Brown, Dutch, Richard Drew, E. F. Phillips, and John McCoy. Stand Watie, George Adair, John A. Bell, James Lynch, and John Huss represented the Treaty party. It was, indeed, a strange mix of old enemies.

On May 2 while in Washington, Treaty party delegate Ezekiel Starr died. Soon after, on the fifteenth, John Looney, former Western chief, veteran of the Creek War, and nephew of former chief Black Fox, also passed away. He was replaced by William S. Coodey, who, having recovered from an illness incurred while attending the Comanche Peak treaty council in Texas, hurried to Washington with his wife and servant. Then on June 12, Looney was followed in death by Chief John Rogers, who was subject to epilepsy. Rogers, like Looney, was buried in the congressional cemetery in Washington, his funeral being attended by a large crowd. Stand Watie was a pallbearer.[53]

The Western Cherokees hired lawyers S. C. Stambaugh and Amos Kendall to represent them. These men, both of whom had been involved in Cherokee affairs for some time, presented lengthy arguments tracing the development of Cherokee history and detailing the agreements made with the Western Cherokees in the treaties of 1817, 1828, and 1833. In doing so, they effectively argued the independence of the Western Cherokees from the Old Nation and their sovereignty over the western lands.[54]

The board of commissioners appointed to settle the matter did not agree, however. The treaty they produced declared the Western Cherokees had no exclusive title to their lands. It did offer compensation, however, of a per capita payment to all Old Settlers for release of all claims by them to lands both east and west of the Mississippi.[55]

The treaty thus established the tenet that the Western Cherokee lands were open to all Cherokees, extended amnesty to Cherokee fugitives, and guaranteed due process of law. Inherent in the agreement was the first acceptance by John Ross of the Treaty of New Echota, which had destroyed the Old Nation and moved his people west. On August 6 all three parties willingly signed the agreement, doing so again on August 13 after an executive session of the U.S. Senate had made modifications.[56] The pact did not directly stipulate a choice of any one government, but by agreeing to put differences to one side and being in such a minority, both the Treaty party and the Old Settlers gave tacit acceptance of the majority Ross government. "The Cherokee delegates," a reporter noted at the end, "have all shaken the hand of amity; feuds have been forgotten, and we trust that the long and bloody strife is now forever healed."[57] When President James Polk expressed his hope to Stand Watie that all would now be well, the Treaty party leader replied: "I have entered into this treaty of amnesty in all sincerity; I intend to be peaceable, and have no doubt that others, who have less to forgive, will follow the example which all the leaders have set."[58]

In terms of the welfare of the Cherokee Nation as a whole, the Treaty of 1846 was an overwhelming success. The animosities so deeply embedded in the souls of many Cherokees would by no means dissipate completely. But now for a time the leadership of John Ross would receive little challenge. Most importantly to him, however, was the preservation of Cherokee sovereignty; the Cherokee Nation had survived its most trying moment. With the political rancor quieted and the trauma of the removal behind them, the Cherokee Nation could turn to rebuilding itself.

CHAPTER 16

New Nation, Old Feuds

Following the Treaty of 1846, a much welcomed political tranquillity settled over the wooded hills of the new Cherokee country. With his enemies somewhat pacified and his government fully in power, John Ross had won a major victory. Now he could enjoy not only the blessing of peace but also the new marriage he had made in September 1844. The fifty-five-year-old Ross had wed eighteen-year-old Mary B. Stapler of Wilmington, Delaware, a Quaker girl with whom he had corresponded in secret for some time. The couple made their home in Ross's two-story Rose Cottage at Park Hill near Tahlequah, where daughter Annie was born in 1845, followed by son John Jr. in 1847.

A move to reunite the Cherokee people took place in late 1846 when assistant principal chief George Lowrey, acting in place of the absent Ross, issued a call to all Cherokees to meet in Tahlequah. The purpose was to discuss the recent treaty agreements and to restore good feelings and fellowship. Old Nation as well as Old Settler Cherokees looked to financial compensation for lost property under the 1828, 1835, and 1846 treaties with the U.S. Lowrey advised them that they needed to file their claims with the government.

Now, too, meetings were held by the Indian Mission Conference to consider religious training and schools for the Cherokees, temperance meetings to control the pervasive problem of alcoholism, and assemblies of the Cherokee Bible Society.[1] There were also the beginnings of an abolition movement being sounded in the preachings of missionaries such as Baptists Evan Jones, who had been among the Cherokees since 1820, and his son John B. Jones. These would be severely discordant voices to the Cherokee societal and political establishment, where slavery provided both great economic and private benefits.[2]

A move of much significance to the nation was the 1847 act of the Cherokee council in appropriating funds for two institutions of education for tribal youngsters beyond public school. These were the Cherokee Male Seminary and the Cherokee Female Seminary. Erected on lofty

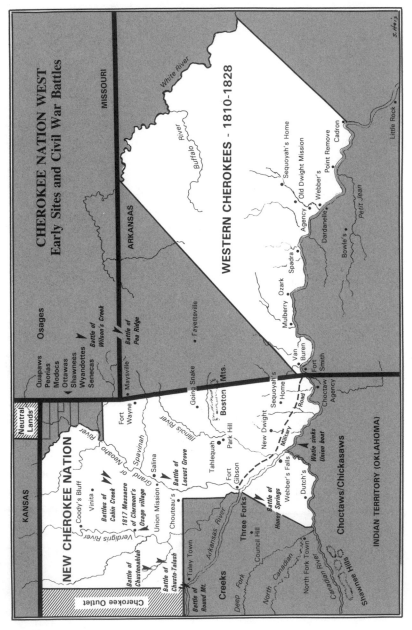

Cherokee
Nation West.

CHEROKEE NATION WEST
Early Sites and Civil War Battles

MISSOURI

ARKANSAS

WESTERN CHEROKEES - 1810-1828

KANSAS

Neutral Lands'

Cherokee Outlet

NEW CHEROKEE NATION

Osages

Quapaws
Peorias
Modocs
Ottawas
Shawnees
Wyandottes
Senecas

Maysville

Battle of
Wilson's Creek

Battle of
Pea Ridge

Fayetteville

Coody's Bluff

Vinita

Battles of
Cabin Creek

1817 Massacre
of Clermont's
Osage village

Union Mission

Chouteau's

Verdigris River

Grand or Neosho River

Spavinah

Salina

Fort
Wayne

Battle of
Locust Grove

Going Snake

Boston Mts.

Illinois River

White River

Buffalo
River

Sequoyah's Home

Agency

Old Dwight Mission

Webber's

Point Remove

Cadron

Petit Jean

Little Rock

Bowie's

Dardanelle

Spadra

Mulberry

Ozark

Van
Buren

Fort
Smith

Sequoyah's
Home

Choctaw
Agency

Military
Road

Watie sinks
Union boat

Tahlequah

Park Hill

New Dwight

Fort
Gibson

Webber's Falls

Dutch's

Battle of
Honey
Springs

Battle of
Chustenahlah

Battle of
Chusto-Talash

Tulley Town

Battle of
Round Mt.

Creeks

Arkansas River

Three Forks

Council Hill

North Fork Town

Deep Fork

North Canadian River

Canadian River

Shawnee Hills

Choctaws/Chickasaws

INDIAN TERRITORY (OKLAHOMA)

S. Heis

rises near Park Hill, the two large brick and stone buildings with their stately columns added to the tribe's Sequoyan fame in establishing the Cherokees as the most advanced Indian tribe in America.[3] The seminaries, though oriented largely toward development of occupational skills, not only created enormous pride among the nation, but they awakened in many an appreciation for formal learning, cultural advancement, and the classic arts.

The Male Seminary was dedicated on a sunny May 6, 1851, and the Female Seminary on the following day. A brass band played "Hail Columbia" before a large crowd as John Ross recounted the trials of the Cherokee people. He told his favorite story of how he had been ridiculed as a boy for wearing a white boy's suit of clothes that his grandmother had put on him. A large number of significant figures of Cherokee history—George Lowrey, Archibald Campbell, John Benge, Steven Foreman, David Vann, W. S. Adair, John Drew, Rev. Samuel Worcester, among others—were present as the first classes of twenty-five Cherokee boys and a like number of Cherokee girls embarked on a four-year study program.[4]

The seminaries were soon joined by churches of the Presbyterians and Methodists and by the lavish Park Hill home of George Murrell, a nephew to Ross by marriage, who had amassed a considerable fortune from a Louisiana plantation and other enterprises. The area was soon being called the "Athens of the Cherokee Nation."

At his Presbyterian church, Worcester worked long hours to print Cherokee translations of the Bible as well as hymn books, almanacs, and temperance broadsides. In the growing settlement of Tahlequah, where the Cherokees erected a two-story Supreme Court building, Princeton-educated Will Ross published weekly editions of the *Cherokee Advocate* in both the English and Cherokee languages—another proud mark for an Indian people.[5] The Cherokee leadership also addressed the situation of the many children who had been orphaned during their removal by the United States. The tribal council voted to appropriate money for care and schooling for them and to erect an orphanage. Ross had hopes for a Cherokee national library, but the funds were never found for it.[6]

Along with this surge of social advancement, the quasi-aristocracy of wealthier, formally educated Cherokees that had been present in the Old Nation redeveloped. Ross himself now entered into a period of renewed personal prosperity in which he enjoyed not only political dominance but a lavish life style similar to that of the plantation owner of the

South. With income from a Park Hill store, trading ventures, and farming to supplement his four-hundred-dollar annual salary as head of the Cherokee Nation, Ross was—certainly in comparison to the average Cherokee citizen—wealthy. A large retinue of slaves tended his fields, orchards, stables, and home, while his socially graceful young wife entertained a constant stream of frontier guests and dignitaries. Ross could regularly be seen riding in his carriage between Park Hill and Tahlequah, black driver in front and a uniformed black youngster in back.[7]

As head of the Cherokee Nation, however, Ross still faced serious problems. The national treasury was seriously depleted; and, though many of the mixed bloods were becoming successful merchants, farmers, and traders—largely through slave ownership—the main body of Cherokee full bloods continued to live in near poverty. Worse still, the social separation between the two groups was growing more and more pronounced. The full bloods rejected schooling for their young, held to the old traditional ways, and rarely spoke anything but Cherokee. Historian Brad Agnew argues that Cherokee schools actually intensified the differences between full bloods and mixed bloods:

> Since there were few qualified Cherokee-speaking teachers, many of the schools were staffed by whites who spoke no Cherokee. Children of full-blood families found it frustrating and humiliating to go to schools where they couldn't understand the teacher and were ridiculed by their mixed-blood classmates. Consequently, it was predominately the sons and daughters of mixed-bloods who attended schools, although over two-thirds of the Cherokees were full-bloods.[8]

Outlawry was a serious matter. The lawless code of the frontier still prevailed in the Indian Territory. Armed robbery, kidnapping of slaves, and horse thievery were rampant. The Cherokee council voted to erect a national jail; however, it would take time, for the nation had no finances to do so. Ross argued that crimes were committed with impunity in part because there was no prison in which offenders could be properly punished. When a U.S. district court was established at Van Buren, Arkansas, and given the power to arraign Indians caught selling intoxicating liquors to other Indians, Ross complained strongly that the act struck at the Cherokees' right of self-government provided by treaty.[9]

Though political assassinations had abated, the personal animosities stemming from political factionalism had not. Knife fights, gun battles, and other causes of violent death were commonplace. Murders occurred mostly out of family feuds, drunken arguments, or in outlawry incidents such as that of Little John Rogers, who was shot by Shadrach Cordrey near Fort Gibson. Rogers was trying to arrest Cordrey for stealing some Seminole-owned slaves.[10]

The Starr clan and their cohorts continued to plague the Cherokee hinterland, committing atrocious murders, robberies, and other crimes.[11] In late May 1848, two U.S. deputy marshals and a posse of some sixty Cherokee Light Horsemen caught up with Ellis Starr, Washington Starr, and a notorious "pirate" named Mat Guerrin. Guerrin had broken into the home of a mixed-blood family at Fort Gibson, kidnapped two free mulatto girls, and sold them into slavery. The posse killed Guerrin and Washington Starr and captured Ellis Starr.[12] Ellis and John Bell, along with eighteen others, were tried for murder, but their trial typified the difficulty faced by the Cherokee courts in bringing law and order to the region. The accused men were acquitted when the main witness failed to appear in court. Everyone understood that it would have meant sure death for the witness to testify. However, the matter was settled extralegally when the two men were lynched without the formality of trial by jury. Tom Starr, who had been arrested for killing an old Arkansas Negro man, escaped jail at Van Buren. He remained at large with a four-hundred-dollar reward placed on his head by the governor of Arkansas.[13]

It was reported that on August 31 Martin Benge, son of Capt. John Benge, brutally murdered George Fields, a former Cherokee sheriff, with a bowie knife as Cucumber Jack and other friends of Benge held the victim. The deed occurred during a dispute over a horse race, but many felt that it was revenge for the killing and hanging of the Starrs. Benge was tried and acquitted.[14]

Selling whiskey within the Cherokee Nation was illegal by U.S. law but practiced extensively. A heavy traffic was plied by dealers between Fort Smith and Fort Gibson overland as well as by boat up the Arkansas River and down the Cowskin and Grand Rivers from Missouri. Occasionally the bootleggers were caught. When U.S. agents intercepted one boat loaded with booze, knocked in the heads of twelve barrels of whiskey, and dumped the contents into the Arkansas, the editor of the *Cherokee Advocate* mused wryly that he feared the "river of grog" might well "get high."[15]

Though far removed from the culture and civilization of the eastern cities, the Cherokees maintained a close association with U.S. affairs. Having long since learned that their welfare and existence were at the mercy of national politics, the Cherokees kept in constant touch with the U.S. government through delegations and representatives who virtually resided in the capital. Ross himself spent much time there.

The Cherokee delegate to Washington in 1848 was Richard Taylor, the grandson of a British major. Taylor, who had commanded a Cherokee company at Horseshoe Bend, was among the several Indian leaders who took part in the grand parade in Washington on July 4 of that year, when the cornerstone for the Washington Monument was laid. He and other Indians were presented silver medals bearing the likeness of George Washington shaking hands with an Indian and bearing the date of 1786. The Cherokee Nation would later join other tribes in contributing a granite block to the construction of that edifice.[16]

In June 1848, Col. A. H. Rutherford arrived from Washington with forty thousand dollars to be distributed among the Treaty party.[17] The claims for these Cherokees had been received much more favorably in Washington than those submitted by the Ross faction, which had so resisted relocation. This inequity agitated old sores and did little for Cherokee internal harmony. Nonetheless, the Old Settlers were still held together by emotional bonds as well as by their own treaty considerations under which they were still owed money by the government. One of their last early headmen, the renowned Dutch, died at his Canadian River home after an illness on November 14. The *Cherokee Advocate* paid him tribute as a great warrior and political leader.[18]

On December 4, 1848, some two hundred Old Settlers met in a council at the mouth of the Illinois in frigid weather—so cold that three people froze to death—to discuss how to get treaty money that was owed them and that they desperately needed. William Shorey Coodey and John Drew were chosen to go to Washington as delegates. While in the capital, Coodey became seriously ill. His daughter Henrietta went to see him there and died in Maryland on her way home. Coodey himself, the brilliant writer and distinguished statesman, succumbed April 16. Like other Cherokees who had died at Washington, D.C., he was buried in the congressional cemetery. The large funeral procession was led by the U.S. Marine Band.[19]

The news of the discovery of gold in California that year excited the Cherokees as much as it did the rest of the nation. Many of them knew the story of how one day in 1828 a Cherokee man in northern Georgia had noticed a shiny particle in the creek near his house and, lifting it on his finger, discovered gold.[20] During the spring of 1849 a California gold rush company headed by James Vann, once editor of the *Cherokee*

Advocate, and David Gunter was formed at Tahlequah and started out on a new trail northwestward up the Arkansas River.[21] En route the party camped on Cherry Creek in Colorado. They found "color" there in the mountain streams but decided to continue on to California. Nearly a decade later, the Cherry Creek find would lead the Cherokee-related Russell party to return and ignite the Colorado gold rush.

Twenty-four-year-old Dennis Bushyhead, son of the Cherokee chief justice, was a member of the 1849 caravan. He would remain in California for nineteen years before returning, eventually to be elected as a principal chief of the Cherokee Nation.[22] His older brother, Edward W., would follow him to California with another Cherokee gold rush party in 1850, becoming a prosperous newspaper editor and publisher in San Diego as well as sheriff of San Diego County.[23]

Also heading for California that year was John Rollin Ridge, son of John Ridge, who was only twelve when his father was assassinated. His mother had taken the boy to Fayetteville, Arkansas, where he was raised and schooled under missionary Cephas Washburn, except for a brief stint in an eastern school. However, it was not gold alone that took him to California. Ridge now held an intense revulsion for John Ross, whom he had sworn to kill to avenge his father's murder, and his followers. In May 1849 the twenty-two-year-old shot and killed Cherokee judge David Kell at Beattie's Prairie in a dispute over his father's estate.[24] For a time he took refuge from arrest in Missouri; but, beset by financial difficulties, he joined the 1850 group of California-bound Cherokees.[25] In California, Ridge would eventually make a name for himself as a poet, newspaperman, and author of the novel *The Life and Times of Joaquin Murieta*. Ridge never returned to his Cherokee homeland, becoming more white than Indian in his lifestyle. He continued to nurse his hatred for Ross, whom he once described in an editorial as the "most loathsome reptile that ever fed upon the vapors of the dungeon."[26]

During that summer of 1850 a Masonic lodge was organized among the Cherokees at Tahlequah, and within a few years a lodge building would be erected on lots provided by the nation. Many of the Cherokee tribal leaders became Masons, as John Ross had done many years earlier.[27]

As midcentury approached, several important players in the Cherokee story would leave the scene. In November 1850, Samuel Downing died during a session of the national council, of which he was a member. General Arbuckle succumbed at Fort Smith on June 11, 1851, during a cholera outbreak that also decimated thirty soldiers who had just recently arrived on the frontier. In November 1852 the trusted, dependable figure of assistant chief and executive councilor George Lowrey was lost to the Cherokees.[28]

Lowrey had served long and well—as a youthful Cherokee warrior; a delegate who visited with President Washington in 1792; a captain of the Cherokee Light Horsemen in 1810; a major in the Cherokee regiment under Col. Gideon Morgan; a member of nearly all the important treaty councils of his time; a framer of the Cherokee constitution and long-standing figure of government; and one of the first Cherokee converts to Christianity and an elder in the Presbyterian church. His tombstone was made to read: "He fulfilled the duty of every office well. An Honest Man, a Spotless Patriot, a Devoted Christian."[29]

Still another longtime Cherokee leader, Richard Taylor, died the following year on June 19. In addition to his Creek war service, Taylor had worked as an agency interpreter, served as a member of the Cherokee governing body since 1817, captained a removal detachment, and was chosen both as a representative to Washington and as a member of the Cherokee Executive Council. In 1851 he was elected to replace Lowrey as assistant chief.[30]

By now it could no longer be said that a Ross or Ridge party existed. Ross, however, continued to be elected to the post of principal chief every four years, each time with an increasing margin.[31] The midcentury census revealed a Cherokee population of more than 17,000, exclusive of 1,844 slaves and 645 free Negroes. The nation could count 27 public schools, 58 churches, 65 blacksmith shops, 14 gristmills, 10 sawmills, 2 tanning yards, 5 salines, 5,770 horses, 28,705 cattle, 35,832 hogs, and 283 mules and asses.

Though the nation's treasury was in difficulty, there was a general prosperity to the Cherokee country. One observer of the Cherokees noted that Ross had

> raised a people from a condition of comparative barbarism to a high
> degree of civilization, morality, and virtue. It would be unjust to other
> enlightened Cherokees, both contemporaries and those who have
> gone before him, to arrogate all the credit of these remarkable achieve-
> ments for him. No one man could have accomplished it. But his has
> been the ruling spirit.[32]

The Old Settler Cherokees received per capita payments in September and October 1851—some $700,000. The issue led to much drinking and celebrating. Merchants of Fort Smith and Van Buren,

Arkansas, reaped a "rich harvest of gold." It was reported that several of the recipients were killed and robbed near Fort Gibson.[33] There was high celebrating again the following spring when after six long years of delay the Old Nation Cherokees were paid the moneys due them under the 1846 treaty. The payments were doled out in hard currency at Fort Gibson for over a month. With the North Carolina Cherokees included in the distribution—unfairly, the Western group felt—the amount came to only $92.79 for each of the 17,530 Cherokees then residing in the West.[34]

Ross and other Cherokee leaders had not given up on their hopes of working out better relations with the tribes of the prairies. In June 1853 they sent a delegation of their "most intelligent men" to meet with the Plains tribes at a point high up on the North Fork of the Canadian River. Employing the plains expertise of Jesse Chisholm, the Cherokees sought to improve relations with the Comanches and others and to "open an intercourse which would tend to civilize and improve their condition."[35] The talks were friendly; however, the buffalo was still plenty, and the Plains Indians were far from ready to take up the white man's ways as had the Cherokees.

Despite their per capita treaty payments, by 1853 the Cherokee national debt had become overwhelming. The noteworthy, bilingual *Cherokee Advocate* had been shut down in 1851. Agent George Butler reported that with no revenue but a small annuity drawn from the United States, the Cherokee government would soon cease to exist if financial help was not provided.[36] An attempt by Ross to enact a tax upon the people was defeated in the national council. He then began looking to the sale of eight hundred thousand acres of land, called the Neutral Lands, that the Cherokees owned in Kansas. Ross led delegations to Washington for talks on the issue, but a price satisfactory to both parties could not be worked out.

A severe drought in 1854 caused extra hardships for the Cherokees. The water in the Arkansas River was so low that it made incoming goods much more expensive. Delivery of schoolbooks for the seminaries was delayed for ten months. Still, in the spring of 1855 the male seminary graduated its first class of five members, and the female seminary graduated twelve. But it was only the following year that the funds upon which the schools had been drawing ran out. With heavy hearts, the council closed the doors of the two seminaries, institutions that had been a major point of pride for them. It would be ten years before the schools would open again.[37]

The internal rancor that still simmered among Cherokee factions exploded into serious conflict during the fall of 1853. A large group of full-blood Cherokees, estimated from seventy-five to two hundred strong, dragged Andrew Adair and his son, George Washington Adair (nephew of George W. Adair), from their homes in the Cherokee Flint District. One report said that the mob was enraged over the murder of Elie Kanasta by Daniel Ross. The story John Ross gave U.S. authorities was that the affair was a neighborhood feud connected to the killing some years earlier of Isaac Proctor by an armed party of which George Adair was a member.[38] Whatever its motivation, the mob took the Adairs out into the night and riddled both with bullets until they were dead. The Cherokees then went after Lafayette Adair, William Foreman, and Thomas Bigby. These men had been forewarned, however, and escaped into Arkansas. Ross sent word ordering the men to disperse, but the full bloods ignored him, claiming that two-thirds of the nation was on their side.[39]

Indian Superintendent Thomas S. Drew of Fort Smith, fearing an insurrection in the Cherokee Nation, asked officials in Washington, D.C., to send out more troops.[40] Daniel Ross, too, was evidently involved in still another killing. After being charged with the murder of Levi Knitts on March 6, 1854, he fled to safety in Arkansas, taking up refuge near Fayetteville.[41]

The thought of great gold deposits waiting to be discovered in the uncharted lands to their west still excited many Cherokees and frontier whites. The drought of 1854 brought near-famine to the Indian Territory, helping to encourage some one hundred Cherokees to join with 278 Arkansas men and eighty teams in a gold-seeking exploration up the Cimarron River of the Cherokee Outlet. Searching for a new "Eldorado," the men followed the river almost to its headwaters in present western Oklahoma and then turned south to explore in the Wichita Mountains. The expedition proved fruitless, as did that of a Missouri company that scoured the Wichita Mountains the following year.[42]

Kept alive by the determined missionaries, the slavery issue would no more go away for the Cherokee Nation than it would for the American union of states. In 1855 the national council advanced a measure outlawing abolitionist teachings. Passed by the Cherokee council, of which Stand Watie was then the speaker, the measure expressed its gratitude to the nation's missionaries but proclaimed the Cherokees "to be a Slave holding People in a Christian like spirit."[43] Had Ross not vetoed the measure out of friendship to the missionaries, it would have been unlawful for them to counsel a slave to the detriment of his owner. Also, it would have been unlawful for the superintendent of public schools to hire a known abolitionist. Missionaries Evan and John Jones, however, continued to dismiss slaveholders from their Baptist congregation even though "threatened with the fist, the cowhide and expulsion from the Nation."[44]

Alcoholism was another serious matter that continued to haunt the Cherokees. A wedding party drank whiskey laced accidentally with poison, and as a result seventeen of them died.[45] D. W. Hitchcock, a mission teacher, wrote, "The country is flooded with whiskey, and that of the vilest sort, producing not only the ordinary effects of spirituous liquors but working death in the drunkard by means of the strychnine and other poisons with which it is adulterated . . . with the whiskey trade, avarice triumphs over every principle of morality, and so the ruinous traffic goes on."[46] To combat the incessant liquor problem, the "Cherokee Cold Water Army" had been formed, enlisting children under the age of sixteen. In 1857, 153 Cherokee youngsters marched in procession around the Tahlequah capital square with banners displaying their vows to resist alcohol. They sang songs, listened to temperance speeches, and then enjoyed a large picnic meal prepared by Cherokee women.[47]

The issue of Cherokee sovereignty underlay all else with Ross; his most adamant purpose was to hold the Cherokees together as a unified, self-determined people. Of particular concern to him was the continued presence of U.S. troops at Fort Gibson. He was disturbed not only by the military's overrule of the Cherokee Nation but also by the horse racing, gambling, drunkenness, and bloodshed that took place regularly in the vicinity of the fort. Further, by treaty, when the fort was closed it was to revert to the Cherokee Nation. Ross saw this as offering potential income for the Cherokees. He requested that the government close the fort so that a "town of respectability might ere long, grow up and flourish."[48] In 1857 the old fort was finally abandoned, and a Cherokee town called "Ketoowha" was laid off and its lots sold to Cherokee citizens.[49] The sale added a badly needed twenty thousand dollars to the Cherokee treasury.[50] By agreement, a cemetery was set aside to hold the remains of U.S. officers and men who had died while serving at the fort.

During that summer John Ross made a tour of the Cherokee country to see for himself its condition. He later reported to the national council that he had been greatly cheered by what he found:

Well cultivated farms, which have yielded abundant crops of grain, and thus affording a full supply for the wants of the people; well filled public schools, large and orderly assemblages, and quiet neighborhoods, which were seen in all the districts, showed marked improvement, and furnish a sure indication of the susceptibility of all classes among the Cherokee people for a thorough civilization.[51]

In his annual report to the commissioner of Indian affairs, Butler echoed Ross's claim of a thriving agriculture among the Cherokees, pointing to the "largest yield of corn, wheat, and oats ever known here."[52] He also noted that the Cherokees were turning their attention to cattle raising, improving their herds by importing stock from Missouri and other states. They were also raising horses. Several thousand head of cattle and a considerable number of ponies, Butler said, had been driven to markets, a large portion of them to California. Though a drought during 1858 restricted the production of crops considerably, Butler could still report that the Cherokees were doing well with stock-raising, many of them moving their herds to the western prairie for winter and summer grazing.[53]

For some time white squatters had been taking up residence on the Cherokees' Neutral Lands in Kansas. The federal government had done little to remove them, and in 1859 Kansas opened the door to increased intrusion by dividing the land into counties.[54] To protest this, to demand payment from the government for damages by the intruders, and to gain permission to tax white traders operating inside the Cherokee Nation, Ross led a delegation to Washington in 1860. There he found the capital astir with anxious talk about the upcoming nominating conventions for the national elections that fall. Talk of slavery and secession were on the tongues of virtually everyone.

The Cherokee proslavers headed by Stand Watie united in a secret organization known as the Knights of the Golden Circle. Mostly these men were educated half bloods who fiercely resented the abolition efforts of some territorial missionaries. The most active of these was Baptist minister Evan Jones. When he learned of the proslavery conclave, he immediately set about organizing the Cherokee full bloods, few of whom had slaves, under an opposing secret group known as the "Keetoowah Society."[55] Roots of the Keetoowahs were deeply embedded in the same factional discontent expressed during the 1853 Adair murders, and the organization's nucleus was first formed by a small full-blood group in 1856. The name was taken from the old Cherokee town of Kituhwa, whose warriors were noted for their fierce defense against invasion by northern tribes and the English colonists.[56] The Keetoowahs were commonly called the "Pins" because of the cross-shaped pins some of them wore. The Pins, however, were a separate group of full-blood militants, many of whom were Keetoowahs.[57]

The essential aim of the full bloods was to wrest political control of the Cherokee government from the half bloods. Jones saw it as a counter against the Cherokee proslavery elements. The group held to the old practices of Cherokee traditionalism. It was also pro-North because of the United States' financial treaty commitments to them. Thus, on grounds of politics, traditionalism, financial support, and abolition, the Keetoowahs saw the slaveholding, mixed-blood planters and merchants as their enemies.

Prominent among the Keetoowahs were Cherokee Baptist converts such as Lewis Downing, who after the war would succeed Ross as the dominant Cherokee political figure; Thomas Pegg; James McDaniels; Smith Christie; and Budd Gritts. Arrayed against them were men such as Stand Watie, who would soon be appointed as a colonel in the Confederate army; E. C. Boudinot, son of Elias, whose hatred of Ross was vehement; James M. Bell, conductor of the Treaty party during removal; William Penn Adair; Richard Fields; and a host of other well-to-do Cherokees and white officials associated with the tribe.[58]

John Ross, himself a slaveholder but long allied with the full bloods of his tribe, made every effort to remain neutral. His foremost concern was still to hold the Cherokees together as a people and as a sovereign nation. Now seventy-one years of age, he had been at the helm of Cherokee destiny for thirty-three years. It would be his fate to live five more years and remain the titular head of the Cherokee Nation through this period of great trial. But in the spring of 1861, he did not yet realize that during the bloody years to follow virtually all that he and other Cherokee leaders had worked for and built over the past decade and a half would be destroyed.

With no military of their own and their destiny long dominated by the federal government, which had now forsaken them by withdrawing its military forces from the Indian Territory, the Cherokees stood totally vulnerable before the crisis created by secession. Not only would the Cherokee Nation be swept into the conflict between the states, but its own penchant for internal strife would once again rip apart its very body and soul.

CHAPTER 17

A House Redivided

The outbreak of the Civil War not only destroyed the status quo in the Cherokee Nation but also drastically redefined the Cherokee leadership roles. Now men of war would take precedence over men of peace, much as they had in the old days of tribal conflict, when the war chiefs held sway. John Ross would find his political authority and power challenged as never before by Stand Watie and his followers.

Positioned as it was in close proximity to the Union states of Kansas and Missouri as well as the Confederate states of Arkansas and Texas, the Indian Territory held a unique position in the Civil War. Both North and South looked to it as a buffer area of protection against invasion. Though its Indian inhabitants were generally considered "too savage" to be used against white men, tribal loyalty was much recruited by both sides as a force to defend the territory from invading armies.

In February 1861, Ross dispatched a four-man delegation to attend a North Fork Town council called by the Chickasaws to discuss what position the tribes would take in the war. At the meeting the Cherokees held back from making any commitment, agreeing only to act together with the other tribes for their common good. Pressure on Ross to act came quickly, however. Officials of the new Confederacy along with those from Arkansas and Texas soon arrived with overtures for Cherokee support of the rebellion. The Union, they insisted, would take away the slaves of the Indians just as it had their land. "Go North among the once powerful tribes of that country," a Confederacy Indian commissioner argued, "and see if you can find Indians living and enjoying power and property and liberty as do your people and the neighboring tribes from the South."[1]

Ross acknowledged the historic affiliation of his people with those of the South, that their "institutions, locality, and natural sympathies are unequivocally with the slave-holding states."[2] But he emphasized the ties of the Cherokees to the United States, citing their commitment under the treaties of Hopewell and Holston to make no treaty with a foreign power or state. The Cherokees, he said, wanted only peace.[3]

Less than two months after the fighting at Fort Sumter on April 12, Ross was visited at Park Hill by Arkansan Albert Pike and rebel general Benjamin McCulloch. Pike, a Harvard-educated schoolteacher turned lawyer and poet, had undertaken an adventurous trek up the Red River to Santa Fe in 1832, when that country was still raw wilderness. Now, as a special commissioner of the Confederacy, he had been assigned the task of making treaties with the Indian tribes of the territory. Ross rejected Pike's generous treaty offer—including the promise of reimbursement for the loss of the Cherokee lands in Kansas—and again declared his determination to remain neutral. Pike, a colorful and strong-willed personality, was highly annoyed; but he had by no means given up. Before he headed west from Tahlequah to treat with the other tribes, he tested the Cherokee political climate. He knew that many mixed-blood Cherokees were fiercely pro-South, particularly Stand Watie, who had already been authorized by McCulloch to raise a Cherokee force for the South.[4]

Pike invited Watie and other mixed bloods to meet with him at the Seminole agency to make a separate treaty. However, pro-Union Cherokees had recently prevented the raising of rebel flags at both Tahlequah and Webbers Falls. The mixed bloods were still unsure of themselves and fearful of Ross and the full bloods. Thus, they did not attend the Seminole agency council, where Pike worked out treaties with the Seminoles, the lower Creeks, Choctaws, and Chickasaws.[5]

Arkansas citizen Gen. Albert Pike initiated treaties with the Cherokees and other Indian Territory tribes for the Confederacy.

Appleton's Annual Cyclopedia and Register of Important Events. New York: Appleton, 1862–1903.

Ross, meanwhile, joined with upper Creek leader Opothle Yahola in sending representatives to talk with the prairie tribes near the Antelope Hills in far western Indian Territory. There an attempt was made to develop an Indian confederacy strong enough to resist the demands of either North or South and protect their neutrality. Most of the prairie tribes were passionately anti-Texas, which in the past had dealt with them harshly in forcing them north into the Indian Territory. It soon became apparent that the weight of loyalty among the other immigrant tribes was with the South. As a result, the effort to unite the Indians of the territory as neutrals failed.

As late as July 1, Ross resisted overtures to join the Confederacy. At that time he wrote Pike, saying that because of the existing treaties between the Cherokee Nation and the Union "no other course is left for us to follow, unless we ourselves set the example of bad faith, which is dishonorable for any Nation, and dangerous to a weak one."[6] But Ross was soon compelled to choose sides. Undoubtedly, he was influenced in his decision by early war developments. On August 10, 1861, the Confederacy won two significant battles. One was the first major battle of the Civil War at Bull Run, Virginia. The other was the Battle of Wilson's Creek, Missouri, in which Stand Watie's band of mostly half-blood Cherokees took part. They greatly aided the South's victory by capturing most of the Union army's artillery. Watie won high praise from the Confederate press for his military leadership.[7] Watie returned to

Though never elected as a chief by the composite Cherokee people, Stand Watie was a fierce competitor for the Confederacy, rising to the rank of brigadier general.

Battles and Leaders
of the Civil War.

Tahlequah firmly in control of the warring element among the Cherokees. One of his men helped arouse the war fever by displaying a scalp he had taken from a Federal soldier he had killed at Wilson's Creek. On July 25 other rebel sympathizers among the Cherokee Light Horsemen charged the mission school at Tahlequah, closing it down and sending most of the Cherokee missionaries fleeing for safety.

When Presbyterian missionary William S. Robinson, who had been among the Cherokees for twelve years, arrived at St. Louis, he told how Watie's men had tried to raise the rebel Stars and Bars over the house of John Ross. However, Mary Ross, the New England Quaker, stood her ground firmly against it, saying she would have her six-year-old son tear it down. The flag was not raised.[8]

While Pike traveled on west to the Wichita agency to make treaties with the Plains tribes, Ross called a meeting of the Cherokee council for August 21. A crowd of nearly four thousand Cherokee men crowded the capital square at Tahlequah. The secession-minded half bloods were in large numbers, well armed, and threatening. Anderson Downing, a pro-Union man, was killed. Cherokee agent John Crawford, a Southerner, gave the tribe a glowing argument on the advantages of secession.[9]

From the mood of the gathering, it was clear to Ross that if he continued to hold out against taking sides, his longtime role as the dominant Cherokee leader would be wrested from him by Watie. Persuaded that he had no other choice, Ross now made a speech in which he stated that neutrality was impossible and that the Federal government, having long since deserted the Cherokees, did not deserve their allegiance. After issuing a passionate appeal for tribal unity, he concluded: "And in view of all the circumstances of our situation I say to you frankly, that, in my opinion, the time has now arrived when you should signify your consent for the authorization of the Nation to adopt preliminary steps for an alliance with the Confederate States upon terms honorable and advantageous to the Cherokee Nation."[10] Ross having thus spoken, the Cherokee council unhesitatingly voted to adopt a resolution abandoning relations with the United States. It was accepted by a resounding voice acclamation of the crowd. On August 24, Ross sent a letter to General McCulloch with a pledge of Cherokee allegiance to the Confederacy, adding, "We hope to render efficient service in the war."[11]

Ross also dispatched Will Ross and Richard Fields to extend an invitation for Pike to return to Park Hill. After a two-hundred-mile ride west they found the Confederate general near Fort Arbuckle and led

John Drew was a Cherokee merchant, soldier, and a conductor on the Trail of Tears.

Archives and Manuscripts, Oklahoma Historical Society.

him back to Fort Gibson. From there Pike was given a gala escort to Park Hill by several companies of newly formed Cherokee Home Guards under the command of Cherokee merchant and militia captain John Drew.[12] Drew, a slaveholder, was married to Ross's niece.

Ross had written to his old friend Opothle Yahola of the Cherokees' decision and invited him to attend the treaty council. Though no longer a chief, the Creek leader still commanded high respect. Almost certainly he had been one of the full bloods who had taken part in the assassination of William McIntosh, father of Creek Chiefs Chilly and Rolly McIntosh, for selling Creek lands in Georgia. At first Opothle Yahola thought Ross's note was a hoax, but even upon verification he remained determined not to join the Confederates. He so decided in part because he was certain that the pro-South, slave-owning McIntoshes were waiting for a chance to kill him. He refused Ross's invitation to come to Park Hill to discuss the matter.[13]

During late September, Cherokee men swarmed into Tahlequah, many of them already under arms with Stand Watie as well as Pins who were eager to enlist in military units under Ross's order to raise twelve hundred men. The commanders of the new units were John Drew, Thomas Pegg, and Will Ross—all of them Ross loyalists.[14] The proslavery men saw that John Ross had shrewdly taken away their advantage. William Penn Adair, a Watie officer and cousin to the George W. Adair whom the full bloods had killed in 1853, saw the treaty convention as an effort by Ross to "put the destiny of everything connected with the Nation in the hands of the Executive." James Bell agreed, writing to brother-in-law Watie, "All of our work will have been in vain, our prospects destroyed and we will be *Slaves* to Ross tyranny."[15]

On October 7 Ross and the Cherokee council signed a treaty with Pike pledging allegiance and military support to the Confederacy.[16] On the Confederacy's part, the pact promised to protect the Cherokees from all enemies, pay them a sum of $250,000, and continue the annuities owed them by the United States. The Cherokees would furnish troops for Cherokee defense. They were not to be used outside the borders of the territory. Pike also initiated pacts with the Osages, Quapaws, Senecas, and Shawnees, whom Ross had invited to the council.

After signing of the Cherokee treaty, Pike presented Ross with a Confederate flag. It was raised above the capital square as an excited crowd cheered and fired salutes. Ross and Watie shook hands, but the enmity for one another was deep and foreboding. There would be no peace between the two strong-willed men nor unity for the Cherokee Nation in the days ahead.

The first serious test of Cherokee solidarity came in November, when the determined Opothle Yahola began a march to Kansas at the head of more than fifteen hundred loyal Creeks plus a number of loyal Seminoles, and several hundred Negro slaves from the various tribes. Creek Chief Motey Kennard and others were especially incensed over their loss of slaves and informed Ross of their intention to attack Opothle Yahola's group. Ross was appalled at this threat to use force against his friend. "Such a conflict," he wrote Kennard, "will bring on a warfare inaugurated by you that will not fail to sever the bonds of peace and friendship between us and the other Tribes of Indians who are not in alliance with Opothleyohola."[17] But Kennard had strong supporters for action. Pike, who had recently been named commanding general of the Confederate military department of the Indian Territory, was then in Richmond. But Douglas H. Cooper, the former U.S. Chickasaw agent, who was second in command, was anxious to use the Indian forces that had been placed under arms. Assembling a force of Choctaw, Chickasaw, Creek, and Cherokee mounted units reinforced by Texas cavalry, Cooper soon had them in hot pursuit of Opothle Yahola's caravan of wagons, horsemen, and droves of horses, cattle, and sheep as it moved northwestward up the Little Deep Fork River.

The first battle of the Civil War in the Indian Territory was fought near the mouth of the Red Fork of the Arkansas on November 19, 1861. It was there that a portion of Cooper's command attacked Opothle Yahola's camp at Round Mountain. After a brief fight, the loyalists were forced to retreat with loss of goods and animals eastward to Bird Creek. When informed of this action, Ross made another plea to Kennard and other Creek rebel leaders for restraint, but with no effect. While at Bird Creek, the refugee forces were engaged again on December 9. After a four-hour battle, darkness came and both sides retired. Opothle Yahola, who suffered heavy losses, moved on north. During these actions, many of Drew's full-blood Cherokees—an estimated 420 out of 480—deserted and went over to the side to fight with the Creeks.[18]

A following engagement, known as the Battle of Chustenahlah, was waged on Hominy Creek just north of the upper Creek village of Tulsey Town (present Tulsa, Oklahoma) on December 26. The rebel forces made a charge that ended in fierce hand-to-hand combat, taking Opothle Yahola's encampment. Having suffered severe casualties and forced to abandon most of their wagons, livestock, and provisions, the loyalists struggled on northward in the face of a sleet storm and numbing cold. During the next morning, straggling elements of Opothle Yahola's badly decimated column were attacked in a running fight by Stand Watie's Cherokee regiment. After that the desperate refugees were left to stagger on to Kansas, some arriving with frozen limbs that had to be amputated. With scant food, clothing, or shelter the Indian loyalists, including the Cherokees who had joined Opothle Yahola, suffered terribly through the winter.

Special agent George W. Collamore reported on the condition of the refugee Indians in Kansas, where among the Creeks alone some 240 people had died and upwards of one hundred amputations of frozen limbs had occurred.

> I found them encamped upon the Neosho River bottom in the timber, extending a distance of some seven miles. Such coverings as I saw were made in the rudest manner, being composed of pieces of cloth, old quilts, handkerchiefs, aprons, &c., stretched upon sticks, and so limited were many of them in size that they were scarcely sufficient to cover the emaciated and dying forms beneath them.[19]

Opothle Yahola's retreat was also disastrous for the Cherokees inside the territory. The deserters from Drew's command aroused the wrath of the Watie half bloods, who demanded punishment. Ross, badly needing Drew's men as a counter to Watie, permitted them to rejoin their unit. But bitter animosity between the groups continued. Occasionally violence resulted, as in the murders of a deserter named Arch Snail and that of Pin leader Chunestotie by Watie's nephew Charles Webber. Despite Ross's angry protest, no action was taken against the killers. Watie's troops became so oppressive that many frightened Cherokees fled north to safety in Kansas.[20]

Despite his enemies, for most of his life Ross had been in firm control of the Cherokee government, the capable champion of their sovereignty as a people. The start of the Civil War—perhaps it could be said his signing of the treaty with Pike—marked an end to that. Abdication of Cherokee military power to the Confederacy and Stand Watie destroyed his ability to manage the course of Cherokee events. Events now controlled him and would continue to do so in a large sense to his end.

Further, the treaty with Pike quickly proved to be a bad bargain for the Cherokee Nation. It soon became apparent that the Confederacy would not, indeed could not, fulfill its treaty obligations. The promised annuities were irregular and sparse. The Confederate agents to the Cherokees were often unavailable or inattentive. The Confederate military command in the region became a nightmare of personal jealousies and backbiting, leading to Pike's being arrested on charges of incompetence and treason. As a result the Cherokees were provided little of the military protection they had been promised. Further, Cherokee troops were not only poorly trained and supplied, but contrary to the treaty stipulation they were taken from the nation to fight in the Battle of Pea Ridge, Arkansas.[21]

Ross found himself adrift in a sea of acrimony—much as the analogy he had once drawn of a man surrounded by floodwaters: a man, realizing that he is about to drown, grabs a passing log, not knowing where it will take him but hopeful that it will keep him alive until be can be saved. Though Ross still professed firm loyalty to the South to a visitor in early 1862, insisting he would "live and die" by his treaty, his actions would disprove the claim.[22] He, too, would grab a passing log.

His old friend, missionary Evan Jones, would provide Ross the opportunity to escape from his deteriorating situation under the Confederacy. Jones, who had earlier been reassigned to Lawrence, Kansas, by the Baptist Mission Board, visited with Cherokees in Opothle Yahola's camp. He firmly believed that Ross had been pressured into signing the Confederate treaty against his will, as he stated in a strong letter to

Commissioner of Indian Affairs William P. Dole: "I could not believe that anything, short of imminent and perilous necessity, could induce him to abandon the position he had taken at the commencement of the contest."[23]

One Union general stated his firm opinion that Ross, whom he said had been hung in effigy three times, had little choice.[24] Jones insisted that, given the chance, Ross would defect to the North. He successfully argued this view with Col. William Weer, commander of the Union's Indian Expedition, which was poised to invade the Indian Territory.[25] Opothle Yahola put it a bit more graphically. During a Lawrence, Kansas, meeting someone commented that one person said John Ross was for the Union and another said he was not. Opothle Yahola answered, "Both are probably right. Ross made a sham treaty with Albert Pike to save trouble. Ross is like a man lying on his belly, watching the opportunity to turn over. When the Northern troops come within hearing he will turn over."[26]

Events would not prove him entirely wrong. Both Jones and Opothle Yahola with his refugee warriors accompanied Weer's command as it marched south from Kansas. After the Union force surprised and routed a Confederate encampment of Cherokees and whites near Locust Grove in the Indian Territory, Weer sent word to Ross asking if he wished to defect to the North.[27] Ross at the time was protected by Drew's two-hundred-man guard at his Park Hill home. At first he was cool to the overture, stating that the Cherokee Nation was honor-bound to the Confederacy by treaty. But when a detachment under Capt. H. S. Greeno arrived at Rose Cottage on July 15, neither Ross nor his guard offered any resistance. Ross was placed under arrest. He and his family were escorted under military guard to Kansas, carrying with them all of the records and papers of the Cherokee Nation as well as its funds and other valuables.[28] There was little question but that Ross could have escaped and avoided arrest; his enemies saw his submission as an abdication of his post as chief of the Cherokee Nation.

From Kansas, Ross and his family were taken to Washington, D.C., where he was granted a pardon and released from custody. Mary Ross had inherited a two-story house in Philadelphia, and the Rosses made it their new home. The U.S. government continued to recognize Ross as the principal leader of the Cherokee Nation, affording him official courtesy as well as subsistence money upon which to live—much too comfortably, it was charged by some.[29]

On September 12, 1862, Ross was granted an interview with President Lincoln. He argued the case of Cherokee loyalty—and thus his own—stating that when the Indian Expedition had arrived in the Cherokee country "the great Mass of the Cherokee People rallied spontaneously around the authorities of the United States."[30] Lincoln was skeptical of Ross at first, but eventually a friendship developed between the two men, affording Ross opportunities to work on behalf of his people—and himself, many said. The fact remained that for the rest of the war, Ross would live in comfort well apart from the agony and destruction of the Cherokee Nation.

At the time of Ross's departure, Stand Watie held the rank of colonel in the Army of the Confederacy and was indisputably the chief war leader among the Cherokees. As the influence of the absent and aging principal chief diminished, that of Stand Watie rose sharply by virtue of his fighting ability. Though he suffered occasional reverses, he and his men always fought tenaciously. At Pea Ridge in March 1862, Watie's Cherokee Mounted Rifle Battalion captured an artillery battery and performed better than other less disciplined Indian troops who became disorganized under fire. Some of the Cherokees committed after-the-battle scalpings and disfiguration of the enemy dead, causing both Union and Confederate military men to look askance at their future use against white troops.

Soon after the Pea Ridge fight, Watie attacked a force of two hundred Union cavalry that was advancing into the territory from Kansas, drove it from the field, then charged into Neosho, Kansas, and tore down the U.S. flag from the courthouse. Forced back by Weer's Indian Expedition in June, Watie again suffered heavy losses in a fight with Union forces at Bayou Menard in July. When the Union army of Gen. James G. Blunt attacked the Confederates under Gen. Thomas Hindman at Maysville, Arkansas, in October, Stand Watie's men not only stood up well against superior numbers but covered the rebels' retreat.

In a mass meeting at Tahlequah on August 21, Stand Watie was elected principal chief of the Cherokee Nation in replacement of the departed Ross. This action was rebutted in February 1863 by men loyal to Ross. Thomas Pegg, who served as head of the Cherokee council, and others voted to depose those Cherokees loyal to the Confederacy and to abolish slavery.[31]

Weer's expedition had not remained in the territory, but in April 1863, Col. William A. Phillips returned with three regiments of loyal

Indian troops to retake Fort Gibson permanently. A Cherokee missionary who witnessed the affair later wrote:

> On April seventeenth, the flag to the American union was raised on Cherokee soil, and the star-spangled banner waved over the nation, and waves there still. The scene was one of unbounded joy.
>
> The whole army was Indian. Two regiments were Cherokees. At least two thousand rich, Indian voices joined in singing "America," "Hail Columbia," and other American airs. There were prayers by the chaplain and by their loved Kanawiski, and there were numerous speeches, while the shouting and the firing of cannon made the earth ring.[32]

During the month following, Watie's men ambushed a federal supply train north of Fort Gibson without success, and in June the Cherokees were driven from the field at Greenleaf Prairie after a hard skirmish. A major fight took place when Watie was sent with five hundred men to intercept a Union wagon train at Cabin Creek. Again his men were overwhelmed by superior Union forces and artillery.

The major Civil War battle in the Indian Territory was fought at Honey Springs on July 17, 1863. Confederate forces under General Cooper were defeated by a Union army under Gen. James G. Blunt, leading to the fall of South-held Fort Smith, Arkansas, in September 1863 and the consequential domination of the Indian Territory by the North.

Watie, who had been sent to make a diversionary move in the direction of Webbers Falls, missed the main action at Honey Springs. Following the Confederate loss, he and his men began operating essentially as guerrillas. In November Watie returned to Tahlequah and sacked the Cherokee capital. Several people were killed, homes were looted, and the general store of Will Ross and Dan Gunter was wrecked. The two men were arrested; only a plea by Watie's wife, Sarah, prevented their being killed.[33]

Some Pin leaders had been meeting in the old Cherokee council house. Watie's men killed them and burned the meeting place. Watie also ordered the torching of Rose Cottage, leaving the charred remains to symbolize the end of Ross's regime of Cherokee power. Some of Ross's more than fifty slaves, now wandering lost without a home or attending master, were taken prisoner.[34]

In her diary, Hannah Worcester Hicks described the severe difficulties faced by the Cherokee women who were ensnared in the web of the

Civil War. Her husband, a Union man, was murdered by a Pin Cherokee while on a trip to Van Buren, Arkansas. "My beloved husband was murdered away from home," Hannah wrote, "and I could not even see him . . . he had been buried twenty-four hours, before I ever heard of it; buried without a coffin, all alone, forty miles from home . . . My house has been burned down, my horses taken, but I think nothing of that. How gladly I would give up everything if only they had spared my husband."[35]

With no means to leave her home, the widowed Hannah watched Indian soldiers of both North and South drive away every available horse and mule; strip the field of their crops; confiscate desperately needed pigs and fowl; and burn fences, barns, and houses. Homes were ransacked and even treasured mementos were taken. Food and clothing became more and more scarce, leaving women, old men, and children vulnerable to the cold of winter and diseases such as smallpox. Communication and transportation between families and communities suffered. There were many deaths, and the surviving lived in dire suspicion of one another.[36]

The Indians were bad enough, a report from Fort Gibson noted in December 1863. But white soldiers, settlers, and wagoners constantly scoured the countryside on roads in every direction and left desolation in their wake throughout the country. "The rebel Indians are scattered throughout the whole nation," the report noted. "They kill all the men and large boys they can catch. They hardly ever kill the women, but they rob them of their horses and provisions when they can."[37]

Watie's hit-and-run raiding tactics produced some dramatic successes during 1864. Only a month after he had been promoted to the rank of brigadier general in the Confederate army, Watie waylaid a Union steamboat on its way up the Arkansas with supplies for troops at Fort Gibson. His capture of a large bounty of clothing, foodstuff, and other provisions was a cheering note to the Confederacy. In August, Watie attacked a Union party at Gunter's Prairie and killed twenty enemy soldiers.

During September he and his men fell upon a Union haying party of white and black troops on the Grand River and massacred a large number of them. Then, in a second battle at Cabin Creek, Watie's unit combined with a Texas force to ambush a large federal wagon train headed for Fort Gibson. The Union escort put up a hard fight, but the Confederates captured the 130-wagon train, its 740 mules, and a huge amount of much-needed food, clothing, arms, and other goods.

In January 1865 Watie was honored with a joint resolution of appreciation by the two houses of the Confederate congress. He would gain further distinction when on June 23, 1865, he became the last Confederate general to surrender.

Watie had long entertained the notion of a flanking movement into southwestern Kansas with the help of the prairie Indians. The Comanches and others, it was hoped, could be used to harass the Kansas transportation routes and cause the Union to withdraw troops from the frontier of Texas.[38] The idea was taken to Texas Gen. S. B. Maxey by Col. William Penn Adair, who commanded the Confederate First Cherokee Division.[39] Adair, the half-blood son of a longtime Cherokee council member, had spent three years in California before returning to study law and become an attorney. As a captain under Watie, he had been captured in 1862 at Pea Ridge but returned to duty in a prisoner exchange and quickly rose in rank.[40]

Early in 1865 Texas military leaders arranged for an intertribal council with the prairie tribes in an effort to secure help in the Kansas harassment. Adair, along with Gen. James W. Throckmorton, represented the rebels at the huge gathering of immigrant and Plains Indians that met at Camp Napoleon on the Washita River on May 24. Even as they were meeting, however, word arrived that Lee had surrendered, and the war was over. As a result, the council produced a document that was a plea for peace and unity among the Indians themselves, laying the foundation for a postwar league of Indian Territory tribes.[41] Adair would prove to be a capable statesman as a principal figure in the reconstruction of the Cherokee Nation.

Another Cherokee who rose to prominence during the Civil War was quarter-blood Elias Cornelius Boudinot.[42] Born near New Echota, Georgia, on August 1, 1835, he was only four years old when his father was assassinated. For his safety, he was taken to live in Vermont, where he was educated. Though partially lame from a childhood accident, he worked for a year as a railroad surveyor. Coming west in 1853, Boudinot studied and practiced law in Arkansas, edited the *True Democrat* newspaper in Little Rock, and took part in Arkansas politics, being chosen as chairman of the state Democratic convention, which opted for secession.[43]

At the outbreak of the Civil War, Boudinot helped recruit the Confederate regiment commanded by Watie. As a major in the unit, he participated in the battles of Oak Hills and Elk Horn, rising to the rank of lieutenant colonel. In 1863 he was elected as a Cherokee delegate to the Confederate congress, serving with that body until the end of the war. In addition to being an excellent writer and a powerful orator, Boudinot was a talented musician. After the war, he would become Ross's most severe postwar critic and political enemy.

New leaders were also standing forth among the Ross political faction. One of the most capable was Will Ross. Born on August 28, 1820, near Lookout Mountain in Tennessee, Ross received his early education at a Presbyterian mission school. As a boy he attended an academy at Greenville, Tennessee; and at the age of seventeen entered Hamil's Preparatory School in New Jersey. Financial help from John Ross allowed him to attend Princeton University. He graduated with honors at the top of his class of forty-four in 1842.[44] Thus well educated when he came west, Ross gained further preparation for a leadership role through his tribal service. Elected clerk of the Cherokee senate in October 1843, he drafted laws and wrote state papers for the chief and council. In 1844 he served with a delegation to Washington, D.C., and became editor of the *Cherokee Advocate* when it began publication on September 26 of that year. In 1849 he joined with his brother D. H. Ross in operating a sawmill as well as a Tahlequah mercantile store. He was also active in temperance activities and served as a Cherokee council member as well as a director for the Cherokee seminaries. In 1850 he and David Vann went east to secure teachers for the two schools.

Will Ross was one of the delegates sent by Chief Ross to the North Fork Town council in February 1861. Soon after, he joined his uncle in signing the Confederate treaty. As a lieutenant colonel in the Cherokee Home Guards under Drew, he participated in the Battle of Pea Ridge. Though he was among those who defected to the North when the Indian Expedition arrived, he was captured in Tahlequah by Watie's men and was nearly assassinated.

Ross went north under a "parole of honor" in 1862, returning the following summer with the Union army as a member of the Third Regiment of Indian Guards. During the remainder of the war, he was a partner in the sutler's store at Fort Gibson and a member of the non-functioning Cherokee National Committee.

Lewis Downing was born in eastern Tennessee, the son of Samuel Downing, a half-blood son of a British army major. Lewis's mother, Susan Daugherty, was half Irish and half Cherokee, thus making Lewis a quarter blood as well. He did not, however, read or write English, and he spoke only Cherokee. As a youth Lewis Downing was schooled at the Valley Town Mission operated by Baptist missionary Evan Jones in

Georgia. He came west in the 1838 removal detachment under Jesse Bushyhead, settling near present Westville, Oklahoma. During the prewar years, he served as pastor of a Baptist church and was a temperance leader. In 1845 he was elected as a senator from the Going Snake District. After moving to a farm on Spring Creek in the Saline District, he was again elected to the Cherokee senate in 1851. That same year he was named as a delegate to go to Washington on tribal business. He represented the Saline District again in 1859.[45]

Though a mixed-blood, Downing was religiously affiliated with Evan Jones, and his Baptist abolitionist views led him to side with the full-blood Pins. He became a chaplain in Drew's regiment and was with the rebel army at the Battle of Pea Ridge. In July 1862 along with a number of other members of Drew's unit, Downing switched to the North, joining the Union's Third Indian Home Guards, in which he rose to the rank of lieutenant colonel. In 1864 Downing was chosen assistant principal chief under Ross, placing him in position to become an important leader in the postwar rebuilding of the Cherokee Nation. He would have a significant political impact on Cherokee politics in the years ahead.

These men—William Penn Adair, Elias C. Boudinot, William P. Ross, and Lewis Downing—would all play key roles in the Cherokees' post-Civil War struggle to preserve their sovereignty in the face of a westward exploding United States. But John Ross was not yet done.

CHAPTER 18

Resisting Dissolution

Prior to the Civil War, John Ross had fought desperately to avoid separation of the Cherokees from their homeland in the South. He had also battled against the disunion of its people, but the war had split them more severely than ever. Following the war, just as it had been following removal, the deep intratribal animosities between half bloods and full bloods would continue for years. This propensity, as widow Hannah Hicks put it, "for destroying each other as fast as they can"[1] would ill prepare them to meet the challenge of postwar reconstruction. In the period between 1865 and 1890, the Cherokees would face powerful, disruptive forces from the United States.

Will Ross, Lewis Downing, W. P. Adair, and others would vie to determine the postwar direction of the Cherokee Nation. Though new political purposes and alliances would arise, the Cherokees were still unable to escape the acrimonious factionalism that had plagued their turbulent past. In part, the course for continuing dissension was set in the final days of John Ross's and Stand Watie's influence as younger men sought to throw off the mantle of the old.

Mary Ross died soon after the end of the war in July 1865. The heart-broken chief buried his child bride in her family plot at Wilmington, Delaware, in August and, now almost seventy-five and in poor health, headed back for Tahlequah. There he was joyously received by a cadre of supporters who reelected him chief for another four-year term. His stated goal remained the reunification of his people. Fate would have it otherwise, however, and Ross himself would become the focus and a virtual symbol of continued divisiveness among the postwar Cherokees. Upon his return to the Cherokee Nation in September 1865, John Ross rode anxiously out to view Rose Cottage. It stood in ruin and desolation. He wrote to his daughter: "The only buildings standing was Johnny's chicken house, the carriage house, and Peggy's cabin. We found the old dun mare and the broken leg horse in the garden, and riding through the orchard, found a few peaches, other fruits being all gone—I cannot express the sadness of my feelings."[2]

Rose Cottage was not alone. The Cherokee Nation itself had been devastated by the war, and the people no less. Not even the enormous tragedy of the removal had created as much death and displacement of family members, destruction of homes, or decimation of farms, cattle herds, and other personal property. "Living off the land, armies stripped the countryside as they went—bivouacking in fields, burning fences, and trampling crops . . . Cherokee soldiers 'requisitioned' supplies from loyal Cherokees they had known all their lives . . . It was Cherokees who robbed and stole and murdered fellow Cherokees."[3]

At war's end, cabins, missions, and schools had been destroyed, their remnant chimneys dotting the countryside; rail fences lay ripped apart; and once-productive fields were overgrown with grass and weeds. In addition to the killing of the war and that of neighbor-against-neighbor, the livestock wealth of the nation had been pillaged by occupying armies of both North and South as well as by a steady stream of horse and cattle thieves, both white and Indian, from Kansas. Left behind were penniless widows, hundreds of orphaned children, a freed slave population void of resources, and an impoverished, bitterly divided populace. Not only was the political structure of the nation in shambles, but it faced a U.S. government that demanded harsh retribution from the Indian Territory tribes that had sided with the Confederacy.

Further, the once-sacred retreat of the Indian was now threatened by railroads, land speculators, and others who wished to exploit the vast Indian domain that lay between Texas and Kansas. Promises of past U.S. presidents, government officials, and solemn treaties of an everlasting Indian sanctuary were either forgotten or, if remembered, now happily nullified in the public mind by the Cherokee participation in the rebellious war.

While in exile in the East, John Ross had continued his long efforts to sell the Cherokees' Kansas Neutral Lands to the United States. During 1864 and 1865 he and supporters from the territory offered proposals that were rejected by the government. However, Ross was successful in obtaining $150,000 held in trust for the Cherokees from the sale of tribal land. Government officials charged that Ross and his family used the money to enjoy a high lifestyle while loyal Cherokees in the West were suffering badly.[4]

On September 8, 1865, the federal government convened a treaty-making conference at Fort Smith, Arkansas, with the Indian tribes of eastern Indian Territory. The government's purpose was to make new treaties in view of the tribes' disloyalty during the war. The Cherokees were represented by two factions. Lewis Downing, Thomas Pegg, and H. D. Reese headed the Northern group and were accompanied by John and Will Ross. Stand Watie, Elias C. Boudinot, William Penn Adair, Richard Fields, and James M. Bell made up the Southern delegation.

The tone of the conference was set when Commissioner of Indian Affairs Dennis N. Cooley charged that John Ross had willingly led the Cherokees to side with the rebels and that he had been a strong influence in persuading other tribes to align with the South.[5] Ross somewhat weakly defended himself by arguing that he had but followed the will of his people in signing the treaty with Pike. It is generally believed that Cooley's attack on Ross was prompted in part by the commissioner's affiliation with railroad and land development promoters.

Colonel Boudinot took the floor to support and add to Cooley's accusations. His long black hair complemented his high cheek bones in giving him much the appearance of a full blood. He charged that, as a leader of the Pins, Ross had been responsible for the "murders and assassinations that covered our land with gloom and dread before the war."[6] He went on to claim that Ross, who had been guilty of duplicity and falsity his entire life, was still an enemy of the United States and not the choice of any sizable portion of the Cherokee people. This was rebutted in a prepared statement by Downing and ten other Cherokees, who asserted that Ross had never, to their knowledge, acted as an emissary of the rebel cause.[7] The Northern delegation refused to sign until the commissioners agreed to incorporate their defense of Ross into the conference records, while the Southerners continued to discredit his character and leadership.

Tentative agreements were eventually worked out at Fort Smith, but the government required that the treaty be signed at Washington, D.C. Deeply humiliated by the commission's refusal to accept him as chief of the Cherokees and bedridden with illness, Ross tendered his resignation to the Cherokee council, which appointed Downing to replace him.[8] However, upon recovering somewhat, Ross was determined to have a part in the finalization of the treaty at Washington. He resumed his office and in January 1866 accompanied Downing, Pegg, and others to the national capital. During a conference with President Andrew Johnson the delegation again defended Ross's action in signing the Confederate treaty.[9] Ross remained in Washington through the spring and summer. Though again forced to his hotel bed by illness, he continued to oppose efforts by Boudinot and his Southern delegation to split the Cherokee Nation through legalizing a separate government for those Cherokees residing south of the Arkansas.

John Rollin Ridge unexpectedly arrived in Washington from California bearing an appointment to represent Stand Watie, with whom he had stayed in touch over the years. Ridge said he had been warned by friends not to return to the Cherokee Nation or even Arkansas, but he intended "some day to plant my foot in the Cherokee Nation and stay there to die."[10] Though he had had virtually nothing to do with Cherokee affairs during the past sixteen years, government officials accepted him as the leader of the Southern Cherokee delegation in lieu of Boudinot.[11]

Ridge was effective in working out a treaty that was favorable to the Southern group and appeared to have the support of President Johnson and Congress. From his Washington sickbed, Ross impugned the credentials of Ridge and Boudinot to represent the Cherokees. Ridge, his detestation of Ross undiminished by time, assailed the character of the old chief in scathing terms and declared him unfit to be a Cherokee leader.

Aided by anti-rebel sentiment in Congress, Ross was successful in undercutting support for the Southern Cherokee treaty proposals and winning government acceptance of his own conditions. Further, during the negotiations, a serious disruption developed among the Southern delegates. Boudinot, bitter at having Ridge (with whom he had gone to school as a boy) take his place as leader of the Southern delegation, accused his fellow delegates—Ridge, Richard Fields and Stand Watie's son Saladin—of trying to cheat him out of his share of their government expense money. Even as he had castigated Ross, Boudinot wrote letters impugning his fellow delegates, especially Ridge—who died not long after returning to California. Boudinot called him "a slanderer and a liar, a thief and a coward."[12] Having insulted both Northern and Southern factions, it was little wonder that Boudinot was unpopular among his own people and when not in Washington resided in Arkansas for safety.

The Treaty of 1866 was Ross's final contest, his final victory. It was signed on July 19, and on August 1 the Cherokee patriarch died.[13] His body was interred temporarily beside that of Mary Ross at Wilmington, Delaware. Under instructions of the Cherokee National Council, a three-man delegation brought Ross's remains to Tahlequah, where he was laid to final rest in the Ross cemetery, near the site of Rose Cottage, the following spring.

Ross was gone, and Stand Watie retired to his farm on Honey Creek, where at age sixty-five his eventful life ended September 9, 1871. A new generation of Cherokee men now came forward to claim leadership of the nation. In November 1866 Will Ross was named principal chief to fill the unexpired term of his uncle.[14] A thin-faced man with flowing mustache and beard, the well-educated Ross dressed and spoke in the vogue of white political leaders of the day. Though he had won election by a large majority of mostly Northern Cherokee votes, Will Ross had long been a John Ross man and was stoutly disliked by the Southern Cherokees. Further, the predominance of his white ancestry in his appearance did him little favor with full bloods.

The Treaty of 1866 and a supplement agreement in 1868 whereby the Kansas Neutral Lands were sold, provided severely needed funds for Cherokee schools, an orphanage, and other uses. But Ross entered office with some serious problems looming for the nation. The treaty had ordained that a railroad could be built across Cherokee land, decreed that a federal court would be established inside the nation, and foreshadowed the organization of the Indian Territory under one federally controlled government.[15] Each of these measures threatened Cherokee autonomy. The railroad could forcibly purchase land, and it would bring more and more white settlers. A federal court would surely replace tribal judicial power, and a territorial government would eradicate tribal rule over their own people.

Though he took up the cause of John Ross in seeking tribal unity, Ross faced intense political opposition, not only from the Boudinot Southerners but also from a political wing led by Lewis Downing. An exceptionally gifted orator, Ross spoke out strongly on the important issues in addresses to the Cherokee council and to a general convention of the Cherokee people. He also stressed the importance of tribal harmony and of a common school education in English for the Cherokee children.[16]

Ross's initial term of office was brief. Not fully trusted by either the full bloods or Southern Cherokees, he was defeated by Downing for the office of principal chief in the elections of August 1867. Downing, the first of several Baptist ministers to hold that office, was supported by Boudinot's faction, who knew they could not elect a candidate of their own. After his election, many former rebel Cherokees who had moved to Texas began returning to the nation and taking part in tribal politics.

Will Ross continued to play a leading role in Cherokee affairs. He served as president of the first intertribal council of the nations of the Indian Territory at Okmulgee in June 1870. With a railroad convention even then preparing to meet at Bentonville, Arkansas, the Cherokees were particularly concerned about the railroad threat to their lands. Ross issued an eloquent plea against railroad intrusion to the president, Congress, and people of the United States stating the Indians' desire for peace and autonomy.[17]

The Cherokees' fears were well founded. During the summer the U.S. government, ignoring tribal treaty rights, gave approval to the Missouri, Kansas, and Texas Railroad Company to build a north-south road across the eastern portion of the Indian Territory. A Cherokee delegation led by W. P. Adair issued a protest to no avail. In 1871 the M.K.T. Railroad Company extended its line from Chetopa, Kansas, to Chouteau Station, inside the Cherokee Nation, eventually continuing on south to Bogy Depot and Texas.[18]

That same year, the U.S. federal court at Van Buren, Arkansas, was moved to Fort Smith. It was originally intended that the court's jurisdiction apply exclusively to crimes committed against Indians in the territory by others in the same tribe. However, the lines of authority between tribal and federal court were often in dispute. Such had been the case in the fall of 1870 with the accidental killing by full-blood Cherokee Zeke Proctor of his wife's sister during an argument between Proctor and her white husband. A Cherokee court was conducting a trial of Proctor at the Going Snake District courthouse when it was learned that U.S. marshals were on their way with a posse to take the accused man to Arkansas for arraignment. By the time the marshals arrived, everyone in the courthouse, including the judge and defendant, were armed and waiting. The posse, among which were some Cherokee men, had no sooner dismounted than a barrage of gunfire erupted. The marshals and their party were driven off, leaving behind seven dead and three mortally wounded—U.S. marshal Jacob Owen among them. The judge, B. H. Sixkiller, was hit in the wrist, and Proctor in the leg.

Downing vigorously objected to the interference of U.S. officials in Cherokee internal affairs, and a Cherokee delegation headed by Will Ross delivered his protest to the secretary of interior. Eventually, the U.S. government conceded the legal sovereignty of the Cherokees in the case. Nonetheless, the gory affair had emphasized the condition of territorial law enforcement and led the Cherokees to write a new legal code for their courts.[19]

After his appointment to the bench at Fort Smith in 1875, Judge Isaac Parker, the famous "Hanging Judge," and his two hundred U.S.

deputy marshals began wielding a strong arm of law over the Indian Territory. The Cherokee Nation had already been subjected to U.S. court jurisdiction when in 1870 U.S. revenue agents, acting on complaints of white tobacco dealers, seized a tobacco factory owned jointly by Stand Watie and Elias C. Boudinot. Boudinot took his case to the U.S. Supreme Court, which held the seizure to be legal. This decision was further supported by Congress, which passed an act nullifying the treaty right of Indians to be excluded from the revenue laws.[20]

Cherokee leaders felt strongly that this was a breach of their treaty rights and stifled the efforts of Indian people to engage in capitalistic enterprise. "The tax gatherer stands ready to enter our country," Downing declared, "and wrench from us, our scanty earnings. Already the manufactories of our citizens have been seized and sold, under the operation of tax laws, from which the United States are sacredly pledged to exempt us."[21] In a proclamation to the Cherokee people, he called for a national day of humiliation, fasting, and prayer for heavenly protection from the "avaricious men, and enemies of the Indian, [who] have opened their batteries on Indian treaties and threaten their annihilation."[22]

With two of their great fears—invasion by the railroads and their autonomy subjected to the jurisdiction of U.S. courts—having come to pass, the Cherokees and other removal tribes of the Indian Territory faced still another threat. It was posed by politicians and government officials who sought to absorb the Indian nations into the Union and, in doing so, extinguish their titles to tribal lands. A number of measures to this effect had been submitted in the Congress, the most significant one being the "Territory of Oklahoma Bill," which was introduced on March 17, 1870, by Sen. Benjamin F. Rice of Arkansas.

Alarmed Indian Territory leaders called an emergency meeting of the Intertribal Council at Okmulgee on September 27, 1870, and requested Will Ross to draft a constitution for a unified Indian Territory. The document Ross produced was a well-crafted instrument of government and included a bill of rights. Congress, however, was unwilling to accept it. In early 1872, the Cherokee council dispatched a delegation headed by Ross to Washington, D.C., to defend its cause. Few men could have made a more eloquent appeal than did Ross in addressing a Congressional committee. A newspaper wrote of the speech:

> As a legal argument we venture to say that there will be few delivered before Congressional Committees this session to equal it in concise and lucid statement . . . It is an appeal to the highest tribunal for

Though a highly regarded orator and statesman, William P. Ross was never elected as principal chief, even though he twice held the office by fill-in appointment.

Mrs. William P. Ross, ed., *The Life and Times of Honorable William P. Ross of the Cherokee Nation.* Fort Smith, Ark.: Weldon & Williams, Printers, 1893.

the existence of a nation—for the preservation of a race . . . Without passion, without maudlin sentiment, yet rising on the height of the subject in strong and weighty words worthy of the purest ideal of English eloquence, it is the more intense for its self-restraint.[23]

Even as this legislative battle was being fought, Chief Downing died at his home on November 8, 1872, less than a year after being reelected for a second term. He was buried near his former farm home on Spring Creek near present Locust Grove, Oklahoma. During his term as head chief of the Cherokees he faced the problems of protecting tribal autonomy, adjudicating the conflict between mixed- and full-blood Cherokees, restraining the powerful railroad interests, evicting illegal white intruders from Cherokee land, finding a just settlement for the Cherokees' landless former slaves, working against the many territorial bills that sprouted in Congress each year, and, as always, finding the finances needed to support the many internal needs of the badly indebted Cherokee Nation. All of these issues were still there when the Cherokee council unanimously named Will Ross to fill the vacated office.

The *Cherokee Advocate,* which had been resurrected in 1870, described Ross as one of the ablest, if not the ablest man of the Nation."[24] After being sworn in, Ross immediately returned to the capital. A Washington reporter noted the presence of "the lofty Adair and the quiet, precise, and gentlemanly Mr. Ross," who "were hard at work trying to defeat any bill organizing their nation into a territorial form of government."[25] The reporter observed, too, that Colonel E.C. Boudinot was also in Washington, working every bit as diligently to have the Oklahoma bill passed. Described as "progressive and very popular" in Washington circles, Boudinot was now employed as a lobbyist for Jay Gould's M.K.T. Railroad Company. Many Cherokees considered him, as the *Advocate* publicly stated, to be a traitor to his people. The paper caustically observed, "Col. Boudinot may comfort his soul with—what? With the reflection that in the general breakup of his people, he may secure a few more eligible lots in the town of Vinita, and a few more acres of the common ground in the common domain."[26]

The battle would remain engaged for the remainder of the decade. In the spring of 1873, Ross issued a lengthy, well-stated protest to Congress; in February 1874 he defended the rights of the Indian Territory nations in a speech before the House Committee on Territories. The Cherokee intellect also led in recommending that the national council recognize the rights of Cherokee freedmen as a "measure humane in spirit."[27] However, he was unable to persuade the council in the matter.

The financial panic of 1873 had been accompanied by a long drought, leaving behind a severe depression. The powerful railroad interests were still pressing against Cherokee borders. Texas cattlemen refused to pay taxes on their herds that passed through the territory. Gangs of white outlaws infested the country, and both the Cherokee law enforcement and courts were badly corrupted. Public drunkenness, gun and knife fights, and killings were commonplace, giving the Cherokees a national reputation as "Indian savages." The infamous Tahlequah riot of November 24, 1874, which took place on the eve of Thompson's taking office, was a prime example. Two inebriated territorial Cherokees shot and killed a Cherokee from North Carolina on Tahlequah's main street in broad daylight. They then moved on to a livery stable, where they emptied their pistols at others in a blazing gun battle. Throughout all this, the city sheriff, who reportedly had been worked into office by a local horse-thief gang, did nothing.[28]

This was followed on Christmas Day by a gun battle at Vinita that may or may not have been politically motivated. A sheriff and several deputies, one of them a Ross party official, interrupted a Downing party meeting, supposedly for the purpose of finding illegal whiskey. A gunfight broke out, resulting in the deaths of a Downing man and a deputy, with the sheriff and others wounded. The affair made national head-lines. An account by the *Cherokee Advocate* expressed the views that the sheriff's posse was the attacking party and that Chief Ross "winks at lawlessness in order to prevent any action favoring a Territorial gov-ernment." On the day following, the *Advocate* office burned to the ground.[29]

Despite his brilliant service, Ross was defeated for the post of princi-pal chief in the election of August 1, 1875, by Baptist minister Charles Thompson. Accordingly, Ross retired from political life. Taking up the editorship of the *Indian Journal* at Muskogee, he continued to champion the cause of Indian rights with perceptive, sharply reasoned editorials against the Oklahoma bill, the 1876 suspension of the Cherokee National Council by the United States, the transfer of Indian affairs to the War Department, military posts being placed on tribal land, and many other anti-Cherokee matters.

The Cherokee name of the newly elected principal chief, Charles Thompson, was Oochalata. The Anglicized name, by which he was known politically, was adopted from Dr. Jeter Lynch Thompson, whom he replaced in the Cherokee council in 1867. Despite his Cherokee name, Thompson was a half blood in an unusual fashion. While his father was a full-blood Cherokee, his mother was a white woman. Believed to have been captured as a child during the early period of con-flict in the Old Nation, she spoke and understood only the Cherokee language.[30] Thompson was fatherless when he accompanied his mother over the Trail of Tears to settle on Brush Creek in present Delaware County, Oklahoma. He received his only education at Evan Jones's Baptist mission near Westville. As a faithful disciple of Jones, Thompson became involved in the politics of abolition. Like Downing, when the Civil War began he enlisted first with Drew, later serving with the Third Indian Home Guard as a corporal.

After the war Thompson returned home to take up the life of a farmer, practicing some law and serving as a Baptist preacher. He also operated a general merchandise store at his home on Spavinaw Creek. In 1867 he entered politics and was elected to a post on the Cherokee National Council. He quickly gained prominence as a lawmaker, being chosen as president of the senate.[31]

When Thompson came to office in 1875, the Cherokee Nation faced a mountain of problems. His term as head chief of the Cherokees, however, was relatively quiet, in part, perhaps, because of his limited capacity to involve himself in the larger issues confronting his nation.

With little formal education and unable to speak or read English, he left the problems created by the federal government, the railroads, and a disturbing influx of whites largely to Ross, Adair, and others. Thompson, an avowed populist, was active in protesting the government's interference concerning the rights of Cherokee freedmen, against whom he held a strong bias. Being conservative on most political issues, however, he did not draw the intense internal hostility as had other, more progressive leaders.[32]

The *Cherokee Advocate* of July 25, 1877, summarized the advancement that the Cherokee Nation had made since the war's end. Its debts had been paid off, a capitol building had been built, along with an orphanage, an insane asylum, and a penitentiary. Repairs and additions had been made to the seminaries, and the nation now had some four million dollars invested. The paper also commented on the Cherokee political condition:

> Old party lines are pretty well rubbed out. North and South sound only in the faintest echoes. Pin and Halfbreed are heard no more. The Slogan of Ross and Downing has lost its magic . . . The "dead past" is busy with its funeral and for once in the history of this country, the people are alive to the living and present issues of the day.

At the time that Thompson took office, there was a growing argument being made, erroneously, by the newly appointed Commissioner of Indian Affairs J. Q. Smith and other white leaders that territorial full bloods preferred a territorial government. It was, the argument went, the half bloods who were holding it back. Thompson worked to offset the idea that the Cherokees were ready to give up their governmental sovereignty, but the idea would continue to enliven the submission of bills to create an Indian territory.

Thompson also faced another federal intrusion into Cherokee autonomy when Smith decreed that the Bureau of Indian Affairs could determine who was a Cherokee citizen and who was not. Thompson defined the situation to the Cherokee council: "We are then informed that there are certain persons, that are classed [as intruders], who have rights that we ignore . . . We are then berated as unfit for self-government . . . guaranteed to us by treaty."[33] The problem would not go away. By the end of Thompson's term of office in 1879, the country had firmly fixed its eyes upon the land that had so earnestly been promised to the Cherokees and other tribes for so long as the grass shall grow and the waters flow.

CHAPTER 19

An End to Sovereignty

Prior to 1880 a number of events occurred in western Indian Territory that would bring the white man and the authority of the United States to the region in strength and ultimately affect the destiny of the Cherokees and all the tribes of the region.

In the fall of 1867 Texas cattle drovers took the first of a multitude of cattle herds northward across the Indian Territory to the new railhead at Abilene, Kansas. The route, which followed in part the wagon road of trader Jesse Chisholm between present Oklahoma City and Wichita, would become known as the Chisholm Cattle Trail. Soon cattlemen began pausing to fatten their beef herds on the grassy pastures of the Cherokee Outlet before taking them on to market, thereby establishing a white presence inside the Outlet.

The Sheridan-Custer military campaign against the Plains Indians in 1868 resulted in the building of Camp Supply on the upper North Canadian River and the massacre of the village of Cheyenne principal chief Black Kettle on the Washita by the Seventh Cavalry. Fort Sill was established in 1869, followed by Fort Reno in 1875, both bringing U.S. troops—as well as wagon commerce and stage transportation—to the region on a permanent basis. Under President Ulysses S. Grant's Quaker Indian policy, agencies and reservations for the Plains Indians were created in the territory, instituting even further non-Indian supervision and influence.

A more serious development began to threaten the sanctity of the "Indian homeland" in 1879. This was the Oklahoma Boomer Movement under the leadership of Kansas native David L. Payne. It had been Elias Boudinot who ignited the craze for non-Indian settlement inside the Indian Territory by authoring an article that appeared in the February 15, 1879, issue of the *Chicago Times*. The article made public the fact that in the postwar treaties of 1866 with the Creeks and Seminoles, nearly two million acres of land at the center of the Indian Territory had been left unassigned to any tribe. The area became known officially as the

"Unassigned Lands" and popularly as the "Oklahoma Lands." Many whites contended that such lands were "government land" and thus belonged to U.S. citizens at large.

In the summer of 1879, Payne initiated the first of numerous intrusions from Kansas and Texas into the Indian Territory. He founded settlements inside the Unassigned Lands only to have them removed by U.S. troops. In the fall of 1884, Payne went so far as to establish the Rock Falls settlement in the Cherokee Outlet—an even greater disregard for Indian sovereignty.[1] In support of Cherokee and cattleman interests, the U.S. army burned the settlement, later taking Payne and eight of his followers on a punishing wagon ride through eastern Oklahoma to Fort Smith. En route, Cherokee citizens had a chance to view the noted agitator when his wagon was driven through the streets of Tahlequah under escort of a squad of black cavalry troopers.[2]

After Payne's death in 1886, the Oklahoma Boomer cause was taken up by his lieutenant, William L. Couch, and a growing body of western leaders who lobbied their cause in Congress. They had strong support from the railroads, particularly the Santa Fe, which connected Arkansas City, Kansas, and Gainesville, Texas, with a line through the Unassigned Lands in 1887, at the same time extending another across the northwestern corner of the Cherokee Outlet from New Kiowa, Kansas, to the Texas Panhandle.

The Cherokees and other territory tribes refrained from physical opposition. Instead, they made their stand on their legal treaty rights in Washington, where they sought to stymie the boomers and defeat their most dangerous enemy of all—the growing national mood to strip the Indian nations of tribal autonomy.

The Downing party and the lingering National party of Ross now dominated Cherokee politics. The National party won its last election when Thompson was defeated in October 1879 by Dennis W. Bushyhead. Born near Cleveland, Tennessee, in 1826, Bushyhead had been educated at home and in mission schools prior to coming west in the great removal at the age of fourteen. He studied under Worcester at Park Hill, later attending a school in New Jersey. He was in his second year at Princeton when his father died. He returned to Tahlequah and worked as a mercantile clerk until he was elected to the Cherokee National Council in 1847.

Having gone to California with the gold rush in 1849, Bushyhead spent nineteen years there as a miner, with modest success. Returning

*Popular Dennis W. Bushyhead
served two terms (1879–87) as
principal chief of the Cherokees.*
Leslie's Illustrated Newspaper,
April 22, 1882.

by boat via Panama and New York City in 1868, he took up the mercantile business of his murdered brother, Jesse. In 1871 he was elected
as national treasurer and served in that office for the eight years pre-
ceding his election as principal chief. Though not a minister, he was a
Baptist.[3] A man of imposing figure and strong character, Bushyhead
would enjoy high esteem as a Cherokee leader and personage.

Even as Bushyhead came into office, the census of 1880 was being
taken. It would reveal that in the decade and a half since the end of the
Civil War, the Cherokee Nation had made a strong recovery. Its population now was virtually the same as it had been at midcentury: 19,720
in 1880, compared to 19,489 (including slaves and free Negroes) in
1850, but the effects of the war were still reflected in a disproportionate nine-to-five ratio of women to men over the age of eighteen. It was
almost purely an agrarian society, with 4,224 families and 4,054 farms,
the principal crops being corn, wheat, oats, and cotton. Its holdings had
increased considerably. The number of cattle was 66,746, compared to
28,705 in 1850; horses, 13,512, compared to 5,770; mules, 1,239, compared to 283; and hogs, 107,721, compared to 35,832.[4]

Bushyhead's annual message in November 1879 discussed the main
problems facing the Cherokees: the railroad demand for Indian land;

the Oklahoma boomers who were invading the territory to the west; dealing with the Negro freedmen, who were demanding land and much-needed economic help; white intrusion; and the continuing threat of territorial reorganization.[5]

At its April–May 1879 meeting at Eufaula, the Intertribal Council, which now comprised thirty-two tribes of the Indian Territory, had issued a strong protest against the establishment of a U.S. territorial government over their nations.[6] Thus far they had been able to prevent passage of the Oklahoma bill despite continuing pressure by persistent whites. All of the Indian nations saw a territorial government as a threat to their independence and treaty agreements.

Bushyhead was destined to serve as principal chief for two terms through most of 1887. During these eight years, the Cherokees would see a continuation of relatively calm domestic times. A serious disruption occurred in 1881 over the killing of a Cherokee citizen by a group of Creek-associated blacks. When approximately one hundred Cherokee men formed a posse and started in pursuit, Bushyhead intercepted them and persuaded them to desist.[7]

The principal historical influences on Bushyhead's tenure as chief were the stern law-and-order efforts of Judge Parker's court, the persistent invasions of the Oklahoma boomers under Payne into the territory, and the initiation and development of the great cattle drives from Texas to Kansas.

The Texas cattlemen began pausing their herds en route to fatten them for market on the grassy meadows of the Cherokee Outlet, the large body of land that stretched across the central and western top of the territory. For a good while, the cattlemen paid nothing for this pasturage. In 1883, when the Cherokee Strip Live Stock Association was formed, the Bushyhead administration arranged an agreement whereby they would pay $100,000 for a five-year lease period.[8] In the years following, Bushyhead's political opponents would issue charges of incompetence and favoritism over the collection and distribution of the grazing-fee moneys. There was also a scandal when accusations erupted over a $22,500 fee paid to attorney Col. W. A. Phillips for his handling of a $300,000 appropriation from Congress.[9]

Despite the relative serenity of his eight years as head chief, Bushyhead's tenure ended in a political squabble. Ineligible to hold office for a third term in 1887, Bushyhead threw his support to second chief Rabbit Bunch, who was defeated by Joel B. Mayes of the Downing party in a bitterly fought contest in August 1887. When the national council failed to make the required canvass of election returns, Bushyhead continued to maintain the duties of chief per designation of the Cherokee Constitution. The situation grew more and more tense, with supporters of Mayes arming themselves for potential action and federal officials arriving to investigate. Finally, in January 1888, an appointed committee invaded the council building, broke into the locked executive office, counted the votes, and installed Mayes.[10] When Mayes began his term of office, the Indian Territory was still the domain of Indian nations and reservations. But its borders had already been shattered to the point of destruction by the white man. Soon this last refuge of the Indian would fall to non-Indian settlement, and with it the autonomous rule of the Indian nations.

A fifty-two-year-old former chief justice, Mayes was born in Georgia in 1833, his mother being a mixed-blood Cherokee and his father a white man. Coming west as a young boy during the Old Nation removal, he attended the Male Seminary, graduating in 1856. He farmed on Grand River and taught school prior to the Civil War. During the war, he served with the Confederacy as a quartermaster, afterward entering Cherokee politics and spending several years as a circuit judge. The *Tahlequah Telephone* newspaper identified him as a lawyer, farmer, and splendid cider maker.[11]

During February 1889, the U.S. Congress was close to passing a bill to open the Unassigned Lands to settlement. Mayes led a delegation to Washington, D.C., to lobby against the measure, which most territory Indians dreaded. "We have come," he told a Senate committee, "to protest any action on your part to extend your territorial jurisdiction over any portion of our country. We refer you to the treaties in which you solemnly agreed not to extend your territorial rights over us without our consent."[12] Mayes and other Indian spokesmen failed to prevent the Congress from passing the Springer Amendment rider to the Indian Appropriation Bill, giving the U.S. president the power to open the contested region by proclamation. Newly elected Benjamin Harrison issued the edict on March 23, 1889, and a month later, on April 22, the first great land rush of homesteaders into the Unassigned Lands took place. It was clear to all, whites and Indians alike, that other areas of the Indian Territory, including the Cherokee Outlet, also would soon fall domino-like to the white man.

The political race of 1891 saw three slates of candidates for

Cherokee national offices: Mayes and Stephen Teehee represented the Downing party; G. W. Benge and Henry Chambers, the National party; and Dennis Bushyhead and Samuel Smith, a new Liberal party. During the campaign, it was charged that Mayes had failed to protect Cherokee interests in the Cherokee Outlet. He was accused of being too friendly with the cattlemen, though his camp circulated his claim that he had once turned down a twenty-five thousand dollar bribe to sign a new lease with the cattle syndicate.[13] Mayes won the election with a comfortable margin, but under the Cherokee system Henry Chambers of the Nationals was elected assistant chief.

Fifty-five-year-old former Confederate colonel Elias C. Boudinot had died at Fort Smith on September 27, 1890, following a short illness. Five years earlier, when he had returned to the Indian Territory, threats upon his life forced him to take up residence in Arkansas.[14] He played a major, if unpopular, role among the Cherokees. Even as he was being given a Masonic burial, the first legislative assembly of the newly created Oklahoma Territory, which he had done much to bring about, was meeting at its capital of Guthrie. His nephew, attorney Elias C. Boudinot, would keep the name much involved in Cherokee affairs in the years ahead.

The loss of many important Cherokee leaders continued into 1891; mostly they were men born in the Old Nation: D. H. Ross, former editor of the *Cherokee Advocate*, who died in Washington; former chief Charles Thompson (Oochilata), who died at seventy, almost totally blind; Judge David Rowe, one-time second chief, said to be the most intelligent full blood in the nation; Will Ross, who was struck by a heart attack at the age of seventy-one as he waited to catch a train on July 2; and Rabbit Bunch, the recent National candidate and a former second chief.[15]

Then at year's end, political disaster struck. Within a four-day period in early December 1891, the Cherokee Nation lost both its principal chief and assistant chief to an epidemic of influenza. Ignoring pleas from his doctor and family, assistant chief Henry Chambers, sixty-five, rose from a sickbed on December 10, put on his boots, and requested his violin. After playing his favorite tune, the Cherokee executive lay back in his bed and died.[16] Four days later, on December 14, in a Tahlequah hotel room where he had been staying during the legislative session, Chief Mayes also died. He had not been feeling well for a few days, but only on the day before his death had there been any cause for concern. With both top leaders gone, the office of chief passed temporarily to the clerk of the senate, Thomas M. Buffington, until a new chief and assistant chief could be chosen by the national council.[17]

A number of men were considered to head the government, but in the final vote it was Col. Johnson Harris who was named principal chief and Stephen Teehee as second chief. Harris, a Downing party man, had served as senator from 1881 to 1887, as executive secretary since 1887, and as a delegate to Washington, D.C., on several occasions.[18] Harris was born in Cobb County, Georgia, on April 19, 1856, the son of a white man and a half-blood mother. He came to the Indian Territory in 1868, settling near present Warner, Oklahoma, where he taught in tribal schools and became a well-to-do rancher. Entering politics in 1881, he was elected president of the Cherokee senate in 1889 and national treasurer in 1891. He was said to be a gentlemanly person, modest and retiring.[19]

Harris's most immediate concern as chief was the sale of the Cherokee Outlet, as the United States was strongly insisting upon. In order to end the cattle leasing agreement, President Grover Cleveland had issued an order for the cattlemen to vacate the Outlet. Though negotiations for the sale had begun under Mayes, it was left to the Harris administration to complete the transaction. In January 1892, Elias Boudinot (the younger) chaired a Cherokee commission that signed an agreement to sell the Outlet; later he led a special delegation to Washington to work out details. On May 17, 1893, Chief Harris and four other Cherokee officials arrived at the capital and signed the contract for sale of the Outlet. By it the United States agreed to pay $8,595,736.12 for 6,574,487 acres of land. Only six months later, on September 16, the area was thrown open to another great land rush into the region that had once been given the Cherokees as an outlet to the buffalo prairies.

A clash of wills between Harris and the council developed over issuance of the money from the Outlet sale to the people. Council opponents of Harris moved to impeach the principal chief for "malfeasance and misdemeanors," the lower house voting twenty-two to ten in favor of it. But the matter was tabled over the end of the year holidays; when the senate reconvened in January, Harris forces managed to defeat the impeachment efforts.[20]

The rapid disintegration of the old Indian Territory as an Indian sanctuary was underway, and tribal leaders knew well that it signaled a dire threat to their governmental autonomy. This fact was virtually assured when the Dawes Commission was created by President Cleveland in November 1893. Headed by Henry L. Dawes of Massachusetts, the commission's mandate was to negotiate the allotment of Indian lands in severalty, abandonment of tribal organizations, and formation of a territorial government or a union with the new Oklahoma Territory.[21]

Meeting with the Chickasaws, Choctaws, and Creeks at Checotah in what was billed as the International Council of Indians, the Cherokees joined in a statement of protest against any change in the status quo, pointing to advancements that the Indians had made economically, socially, and religiously.[22] Putting aside its differences with the chief, the Cherokee council authorized him to appoint a five-man committee to talk with the Dawes party, which had set up its headquarters in ten rooms of a Muskogee hotel. At Harris's invitation, committee members toured the Cherokee Nation during the spring and summer, interviewing Cherokee citizens.

The attention of most Cherokees from June through Aug , however, was diverted by the issuance of Outlet payments at Vi   in the Cherokee Nation. Huge crowds, estimated up to ten thousand, flocked to the town. Roads were lined with horses and wagons for miles around. Trains, even freights, arrived loaded with passengers. Stores were jammed and vendors plied their wares on the streets. A theatrical group played at a large pavilion, and dance halls ran all night. The Vinita *Indian Chieftain* suggested that if the Dawes Commission wished to study the Cherokee in his "native heath," it could have done so during the Outlet payment.

With the Indians came an "army of fallen women who have followed the treasure wagon," and prostitution was practiced openly. There were plenty of armed toughs from the backcountry, but gunplay resulted only when a deputy sheriff took two shots at the sheriff. The sheriff responded by shooting the horse from under the fleeing deputy.[23]

In August the commission wrote to Harris with specific proposals for an allotment plan and, irked that Cherokee officials had not acted, asked for an early reply. Harris responded by saying that the Cherokees first wanted a settlement of all differences between them and the U.S. government, particularly the removal of intruders from Cherokee lands. His reply drew a caustic editorial from the white-owned *Chieftain*, which expressed the sentiment of many full bloods and the U.S. government when it chided: "Now, honor bright, don't every intelligent person in the country know that a few 'first families' have always controlled this country and monopolized it, and that they are to all intents and purposes white people, and is not the chief himself a white man, casually speaking?"[24]

The Dawes Commission's report to Congress in November supported the claim made by a visiting Senate committee earlier that spring: the mixed bloods were controlling the Indian governments, which were openly corrupt, and they were monopolizing the best lands; further, that it was impossible to police the increasing white population in the Indian nations under the existing dual law enforcement of the tribes and the United States.[25]

Harris joined other Indian leaders in defending their right of self-government. In December, he traveled to Washington for the purpose of protesting efforts to make the Indian Territory into a state or U.S. territory.[26] Unable to stop the determined efforts to disband the tribal governments, Harris helped delay a Cherokee response to the commission through the remainder of his term. He would continue to serve the Cherokee government in political affairs after leaving office.

In August 1895, Samuel Houston Mayes, brother to deceased Joel, and his running mate, full-blood George Swimmer, won a close contest over Robert Ross and H. T. Landrum and took office. Mayes, a stockman who owned a great deal of land, had been sheriff of Coowesekeowee District for two years and had served as a senator from there for two terms.[27] During his term as chief from 1895 to 1899, Mayes presided over the Cherokee Nation as it was literally dismantled. There was little he could do to delay the inevitable. During the fall of 1896, a Cherokee delegation headed by former chief Bushyhead was authorized to confer with the Dawes Commission. Negotiations continued into 1897, past even a July special session of the Cherokee council, without resolution of the allotment and other key issues.

At the same time, the old contest between full bloods and mixed bloods in the Cherokee Nation continued. One tribal paper noted: "The full-blood Cherokee's dream is to continue an Indian nation for all time to come, and they will never consent to anything else."[28] Elias Boudinot spoke for most mixed bloods when he admonished the Cherokee people that they should get ready for the change that was surely coming to their country.[29] There was no question that Boudinot was becoming a figure of importance and influence among the Cherokees. As lawyer for the nation, he spent much time defending Cherokee interests in Washington. He had only recently returned from there when on February 20, 1896, he died, six years after the death of his namesake uncle.

Success of the Dawes Commission in getting other tribes to make agreements increased the inevitability that the Cherokees would soon follow. In June 1898, Congress passed the Curtis Act, guilefully titled "An act for the protection of the people of the Indian Territory, and for other purposes." The act accomplished many of the Dawes Commission's objectives. By forcing allotment on the basis of tribal rolls previous to January 1896, it nullified the actions of tribal government. Tribal laws and courts were abolished, and a U.S. Indian inspector was assigned to provide oversight of the Indian Territory for the secretary of interior.

Addressing a special session of the Cherokee council in 1896, Mayes observed: "It is indeed a melancholy reflection to find ourselves at last so near to what seems to be the inevitable conclusion of unknown centuries of national existence."[30] The *Chieftain* had been solidly for Mayes during the 1895 election, but in 1897 that would change drastically. It was then that Frank J. Boudinot, brother of the younger Elias C., gave affidavit testimony that $126,000 of a $400,000 payment to Cherokee freedman had gone into the hands of a party of lawyers and Cherokee officials through a secret agreement. By Boudinot's testimony, these included his now-deceased brother; lawyer R. H. Kern; Chief Mayes; former chief Johnson Harris; and two others.[31] Boudinot's statement was supported by a like affidavit from the widow of Elias, who claimed that the others gave her only $3,500 of a promised $13,500 share. Mayes denied any part in the scheme, however, offering as evidence a July 15, 1896, letter from him to President Cleveland asking for an investigation of Kern. W. J. McConnell, investigator for the U.S. Senate Committee on Indian Affairs, reported that Moses Whitmire, the seventy-year-old freedman trustee who could neither read nor write, had unwittingly approved a document giving Kern a fee of one-third of the total sum rather than the verbally agreed-on one-tenth.[32]

The *Chieftain* continued to hold Mayes culpable. "If ever a poor, ignorant lot of people on earth were robbed with open and shameless effrontery," the paper editorialized, "it was the Cherokee Negroes."[33] Though a Congressional investigation was made of the affair and an accusative report issued, no formal charges were ever made against any of those reportedly involved. The national council appointed a committee to investigate, but Mayes maneuvered it into nonexistence.

In the meanwhile, the council reacted to the Curtis Act by condemning it as a violation of their treaties with the United States. Prevented from successfully challenging the measure's constitutionality in court, the Cherokees authorized Mayes to appoint another seven-man delegation to work out the many complex differences between their nation and the United States. In January 1899, an agreement was reached, and Mayes put it to a vote of the Cherokee people. Though few Cherokees favored the disintegration of their nation, even many full bloods now realized that it was impossible to prevent and that they should take the best deal they could get. The agreement was approved by a two-to-one margin. The U.S. Congress failed to ratify it, however, forcing another round of negotiations.

The Cherokee elections of 1899 pitted T. M. Buffington of Vinita of the Downing ticket against the National candidate, full-blood Wolfe Coon. Buffington, a six-foot-seven, 260-pound former senator, was a good-natured, well-liked man. Born forty-four years earlier near Westville, Cherokee Nation, he had been raised on a farm and educated at the Baptist mission. In 1879 he resettled near Vinita, where he was elected as a judge of the Delaware District and later as a senator. As president of the senate, Buffington served as interim principal chief for eleven days after the deaths of Joel Mayes and Chambers. His political credentials also included duty as a delegate to Washington, a term as a circuit judge, and two terms as mayor of Vinita.[34]

Coon was "a sharp-looking man" of medium size with partially gray hair. Very Indian-like in appearance and mannerisms, he did not speak English.[35] He was not only president of the Cherokee senate but also a leader of the full-blood Keetoowah Society. Being very bitter against the Curtis bill and the U.S. government, the society had even refused to permit any mixed-blood person to address their assembly when it held its every-fourth-year convention north of Tahlequah.[36]

In winning the election of August 1899, on the eve of the twentieth century, Buffington became the first Cherokee principal chief who had not been born in the Old Nation. The main political concerns during his four-year term would involve the size of allotments made to Cherokees under a new treaty, the question of a valid roll for Cherokee freedmen, the growing controversy of single or double statehood for the Oklahoma and Indian territories, and the dissolution of the Cherokee national government under edict of the Harris Act. In his address to the Cherokee council in November 1901, Buffington sought to maintain cohesion in the face of the political and social upheaval his nation faced.

> Who of you desires to remain in the confused condition that prevails in the country now? . . . While the government that we love so well and to which we have clung so tenaciously is fast going, let us give personal support to each other so that it may be said the Cherokee

people are keeping abreast of the times and apace with the onward march of civilization.[37]

Buffington made numerous trips to Washington, D.C., to deal with Cherokee problems. In an effort to secure more than the proposed eighty acres per household-head allotment, the chief, Wolfe Coon, James Keyes, and Redbird Smith appeared before a congressional committee in early 1902. Soon after, Buffington called a special session of the council to consider distribution of relief money for Cherokee full bloods who were starving following a severe drought.[38]

No longer able to stand their ground on a defined homeland and stripped of an organized political body and leaders to protect their interests, the Cherokees were now more defenseless than ever. Though the story of the Cherokee self-government could be said to have ended here, they still faced the ongoing challenge of winning just treatment in a white-dominated America.

CHAPTER 20

The Fourth Phoenix

"We would now commit our feeble efforts," the educated Cherokee editor Elias Boudinot wrote in the February 21, 1828, issue of the *Cherokee Phoenix*, "to the good will and indulgence of the public, praying that God will attend them with his blessings, and hoping for that happy period, when all the Indian tribes of America shall arise, Phoenix like, from their ashes." But that would not be the last rise from ashes for the Cherokee Nation. The Cherokees underwent similar travail following the great removal west and again following the Civil War. Beginning the twentieth century without a government and leaders to fight for their interests, the nation would again fall into the ashes of disarray and ultimately seek a fourth phoenixlike rebirth.

While it has been said that Buffington was the last chief to preside over a Cherokee government (prior to World War II), that honor technically belongs to his successor, William C. Rogers. Chosen by the Downing party as a compromise candidate over Buffington and others, Rogers defeated National candidate E. L. Cookson in the August 1903 election. He was elected to office along with a majority of Downing legislators, but it was to a government with little power or authority. The *Indian Chieftain* of August 8, 1903, observed: "So far as the chief's election is concerned, the last political battle that the Cherokees will ever engage in has been fought out . . . Not a dollar of Cherokee money can be expended without the consent of the [U.S.] government and no interest of the people can be interfered with in the least were the chiefs so minded. As the nominal head of a defunct nation the chief will have little authority."

Like Buffington, Rogers was born in the Indian Territory, on December 13, 1847, near Claremore in the Cherokee Nation. He was the quarter-blood son of Charles Coody Rogers and the grandson of former Western Cherokee Chief John Rogers Jr. He attended tribal schools as a boy, including a year at the Cherokee Male Seminary. After the war he went into farming, eventually opening a general store, around which the town of old Skiatook emerged.[1] Standing six-foot-three with a heavy build and wearing a walrus-style mustache, he was a dominating figure. Upon entering politics he was elected as a member of the Cherokee lower house in 1881, again in 1883, and to the Senate in 1889 and 1895. He was known as a stern, uncompromising, but totally honest man, and his reputation was little damaged when he killed a man in 1893. Rogers evidently became enamored of an attractive young Cherokee girl who worked in his home and jealous of the attention shown her by Deputy Marshal Lee Taylor. When Taylor came to elope with the girl, the infuriated Rogers shot and killed him.[2]

As Cherokee chief from 1903 until his death in 1917, he was responsible for dissolving the affairs of the Cherokee government. He also signed the land titles of the Cherokee people as they took up individual allotments after becoming citizens of the United States in 1901.[3]

Rogers was active in opposing the idea of merging the new Oklahoma Territory and the remaining Indian Territory as a single state. He was a leading figure at a convention of the principal chiefs of the Five Civilized Tribes at Muskogee in August 1905. There the five tribes drafted a constitution for organizing the Indian Territory as the "State of Sequoyah." Though the small percentage of citizens of the five nations who voted gave overwhelming approval to the move, it received little support in Congress, where single statehood was preferred.

The national council chosen in 1903 met during Rogers's first term of office even though it had been rendered essentially irrelevant by the Harris Act. Further, the U.S. Congress had decreed that "the tribal government of the Cherokee Nation shall not continue longer than March 4, 1906." In the face of this deadline, Rogers refused to call what he considered would be a costly and useless election in 1905. One was held nonetheless, and many of those elected were full-blood opponents of Rogers. Rogers bluntly notified the council that he did not consider it to be legally elected. This stirred a great deal of enmity against him among legislators who accused him of being much too cooperative with the federal government in dissolving the Cherokee political body. While he was in Washington in November, the council voted to impeach him and named Frank Boudinot, attorney for the Cherokee full bloods, as principal chief. Secretary of Interior Ethan A. Hitchcock reappointed Rogers to his post, however.[4]

On November 16, 1907, the twin territories were officially amalgamated into the state of Oklahoma by virtue of a proclamation issued by

President Theodore Roosevelt. This gave even further certainty to the end of tribal autonomy and self-government as known in the past by the Cherokee and other Indian nations. The Cherokee legislature and court system no longer existed, but there remained legal matters that required official attention and documents to be signed. Because of this, Rogers maintained the Cherokee principal chief's post in a semiofficial capacity until his death on November 8, 1917. He is buried near Skiatook.

Following Rogers's death, Congress authorized the president of the United States to appoint principal chiefs for the Cherokees. Even these appointees were mere token figures who, after A. B. Cunningham's term of office from November 8 to 25, 1919, served only one day. The presidentially appointed one-day chiefs were Ed M. Frye in 1923; Richard B. Choate, in 1925; Charles J. Hunt in 1928; Oliver P. Brewer in 1931; and William W. Hastings in 1936.[5] No more were appointed until 1942, when Jesse Milam, a Chelsea banker, was given a similar one-day appointment. This was followed, however, by four-year appointments for him in 1943 and 1947. Before he died in 1949, Milam worked to reorganize Cherokee tribal affairs. But it was his successor, William W. Keeler, who began to reinstitute Cherokee efforts to control their own destiny.

For a time Keeler studied toward a degree in petroleum engineering at Kansas University before dropping out to work for Phillips Petroleum

W. W. Keeler worked to bring much-needed reforms to the impoverished Cherokee Nation of the twentieth century.

Archives and Manuscripts, Oklahoma Historical Society.

of Bartlesville, Oklahoma. He soon began a rapid rise in the employment of this company. In 1968 he became chairman of the board and chief executive officer of Phillips. He was responsible for establishing the Cherokee Foundation, designed to serve much-needed Cherokee causes.[6]

Keeler was first appointed principal chief in 1949 by President Harry Truman. He returned to the Cherokee chief post in 1971 through the first Cherokee election permitted by the United States since statehood.[7] He worked to revitalize the Cherokee government, often using his own money in the effort. Under Keeler's tenure as chief, however, the system of delegating Cherokee affairs to a business manager became too burdensome. Keeler's successor in 1975 was University of Oklahoma law school graduate and Tahlequah banker Ross Swimmer. Swimmer undertook the reestablishment of a tribal government with the aim of creating a more direct line of communication between the Cherokee leadership and the Cherokee people. He worked to address the severe need for improved tribal health facilities. Also, aware that Cherokee motivation and pride as a people had suffered badly under the dominance of white authority, he began efforts to enhance tribal identity.[8]

These same concerns remained under the administration of Chief Wilma Mankiller, who was elected to the post of principal chief following the resignation of Chief Swimmer in 1985. During her administration, Mankiller made strong advancements in tribal health care, education, housing, and employment.

Perhaps the greatest threat to the Cherokees, as well as to other Indian tribes, remains the loss of tribal self. Their historic struggle for justice and social advancement has been enjoined by the danger of annihilation through assimilation into the dominating non-Indian culture of America. Today the Cherokees seek to strengthen pride in their own culture. They are teaching young people the Cherokee language, reawakening interest in the ancient tribal crafts, and giving emphasis to native Cherokee art forms.

Still, the essential clash between tribal traditionalism and social improvement has boiled to the point of physical violence in modern political races—evidence that the challenges of leadership among the Cherokees remain as great and as crucial to their survival as a people, perhaps, as those faced by the chiefs of their difficult and troubled past. Like those who preceded them, Cherokee leaders of today and beyond will be required to guide their people along the same precarious path that separates advancement from extinction.

Those Who Stayed Behind

When the United States drained the southern states of Cherokees and poured them mercilessly into the West in 1838, one small but important reservoir of tribespeople remained behind. These were Cherokees who either resided in the Smoky Mountains of eastern Tennessee and western North Carolina or had taken refuge in caves to escape capture.[1] This group had presented a special problem to the troops assigned to bring them in.

On the assurance that all had been found, the Fourth Infantry was reassigned to the Canada frontier. Afterward it was estimated that some three hundred had evaded an initial sweep through the North Carolina country and that some forty or fifty more had stolen away from the emigration depots. Actually there were probably closer to three or four thousand. Indian runners were sent to persuade the Cherokees to come in, but these efforts failed.[2]

A large detachment of mounted soldiers was again sent into the mountains. A camp of sixteen Cherokees was found and arrested. These captives were being escorted down the Little Tennessee River when it was learned that another party of Cherokees was nearby. Lt. A. J. Smith and three men, guided by trader William Holland Thomas, went to collect them. Smith found eight Cherokees in the camp. Upon learning that twenty more belonged to the band, he remained in camp until the next morning, hoping they would all come in. However, when no more Cherokees appeared, Smith started back with five men and seven women, expecting to overtake the other command. There was soon trouble, as he reported:

> On the evening of the 1st, I discovered an unwillingness among the Indians to travel, and, in order to make great speed, I put some of the children on horses; but it was with great difficulty I could get them along. I suspected all was not right, and frequently cautioned the men to be on their guard. Shortly after sunset, I discovered a long dirk knife in the possession of one of our Indians, and ordered it to be immediately taken from him. He turned it over without any hesitation; and we

had proceeded on but a short distance before I spied an axe, which I also ordered be taken from them, but I am sorry to say, too late, for I had scarcely finished the order, before I saw the axe buried in the fore-head of one of our men. This being the signal for attack, the others fell immediately to work, and in less than a minute they killed two, wounded a third, and commenced searching them, and carrying off every article they could lay their hands on. I fortunately escaped unhurt, and owe my life in a measure to the spirit and activity of my horse.[3]

Troops were soon scouring the mountains and, again with the help of Thomas, recaptured most of the band. Among them was the wife and two sons of an older Cherokee named Tsali, though Tsali himself evaded capture for a time. Three of the male prisoners were blindfolded and shot by an appointed Cherokee execution squad. Later, Tsali was captured and executed by Cherokees who were working with the troops on the promise they would not be included in the removal. It was said that the old man faced his death with a calm spirit and courage, asking only that his surviving family be cared for.[4] This was the incident that gave rise to the famous legend of Tsali as a North Carolina Cherokee hero, one that is celebrated by the outdoor pageant, Unto These Hills. In its story, Tsali is portrayed as having willingly submitted to capture and execution in order that the North Carolina Cherokees would be allowed to remain in their homes.

The Cherokees who resided on the mountainous headwaters of the Little Tennessee and Cheoah Rivers in the western tip of North Carolina were known as the Quallatown Cherokees. For the most part, they were poor, illiterate full bloods who followed a quiet, unobtrusive existence removed from outside influence. Largely divorced even from the rest of the Cherokee Nation, they tended their small farms, raising some cattle and sheep without the tribal or federal annuities that other Cherokees received. However, they were not beyond the connivances of whites who were prone to taking advantage of them in trade or seeking to take their land.

The Quallatown Cherokees were headed by Yonaguska, or Drowning Bear. Though a man of imposing stature, dignity of person, and oratorical ability, he drank heavily, often to the point of stupor. Eventually he would be converted to total abstinence by Baptist missionaries—and by the shocking experience once of waking up from a drunken coma to find that his funeral was being prepared. In the main, Yonaguska relied heavily upon the advice and counsel of white trader William Holland Thomas.[5]

At an early age, Thomas had come to work in the Cherokee trading store of Felix Walker. Yonaguska developed an affection for the boy, adopting him into the tribe and considering him virtually a son. Thomas possessed a responding attachment to the Cherokees and became a life-associate to them. Eventually he took over the trading store and opened others. Also, through self-teaching in law he was able to help the tribe greatly in its legal matters.

Yonaguska's faith in him was rewarded when in 1836 Thomas made the first of many trips to Washington, D.C., and won government recognition for rights of the Quallatown Cherokees in the New Echota Treaty. Thomas was also the key figure in the government's exclusion of the North Carolina group from the great removal. It was he who had persuaded the dissident chief Euchella (Oochella or Ursala)—whose wife and son had died of starvation while hiding from the troops—to win exemption from removal for his impoverished band by capturing Tsali.[6]

Yonaguska, who in his later years did much to lead his people away from their rampant alcoholism, died in the spring of 1839. He was succeeded by Flying Squirrel (Call-lee-high). Thomas, however, continued to be the leading political force of the North Carolina Cherokees for two and a half decades until the end of the Civil War. During that time he aggressively defended the rights of his adopted people and fought to gain them the citizenship status that would protect them from further attempts at removal. He encouraged religious pursuits, temperance, and education. Thomas also attempted, unsuccessfully, to improve their economic situation through the cultivation of silkworms and the manufacture of brooms under a Cherokee company he had formed.

Most importantly, in 1842 Thomas took it on himself to begin securing legal protection for the Cherokees' land in North Carolina. As their agent, he used their money to purchase tracts of land from white settlers, land that was eventually laid off into five town districts. He continued this until the Civil War erupted in 1861.[7]

Thomas was such an overpowering influence upon the North Carolina Cherokees that prior to the Civil War there was little pronounced leadership from their native chiefs. Even during the war, Thomas continued to be their de facto head chief. He organized and headed an all-Indian Cherokee Legion in the service of the Confederate states. But Indians suffered the image among Southerners of being savage animals in war, and the Cherokees were permitted to participate only in minor skirmishes during the conflict.

When the war was over, the North Carolina Cherokees were made to pay a price for their disloyalty by federal officials. The tribespeople, like Thomas himself, were physically and spiritually spent with the war. Factionalism and disharmony had spread among them almost like the deadly smallpox epidemic that decimated the tribe during 1866. Thomas was now scorned by many for involving them in the war. His capacity to lead had been further damaged by a series of personal and financial problems. Further, he had begun to develop signs of the mental illness that would eventually lead him at the age of eighty-eight to a pitiful death in a state mental institution.

Coming forth to fill the leadership vacuum were men such as George W. Bushyhead, headman of the Cherokees' Sand Town, and James Taylor, a former Cherokee agent. Bushyhead had also had the prewar experience of visiting Washington, D.C., in relation to Cherokee claims. In 1866 he returned to the capital to make a plea for a reservation where his people could be removed from scheming whites.[8] He argued that the eastern Cherokees were a distinct tribe and wanted the same protection afforded other Indians. This right was acknowledged by Congress in July 1868 and led to a December tribal council organized by Bushyhead. In a meeting held at their town of Cheoah, a new constitution was written and a declaration was issued calling for a convention to elect tribal officers.[9] During 1869, the Cheoah council elected Bushyhead as council chairman, giving him the claim of being principal chief of the eastern Cherokees and the authority to represent them in Washington in 1870.

There was intense opposition to Bushyhead exerted by the Flying Squirrel faction, who challenged the legitimacy of the Cheoah council. When Bushyhead, who had become ill, retired from the political scene and moved to South Carolina, he was succeeded by a Cherokee with the famous name of John Ross. At the same time, a competitive council held at Quallatown elected the elderly Flying Squirrel as principal chief.[10] The government, however, insisted on dealing with Ross as the Cherokee headman.

During this period of great political stress and uncertain leadership, the North Carolina Cherokees were suffering severe problems. One was a gross injustice that was imposed upon them by unscrupulous Washington lawyer Silas H. Swetland. Working in league with former army general James G. Blunt and others, Swetland swindled clients while preparing an official roll for the tribe. Among other nefarious acts, as their tribal attorney he threatened to remove Cherokees from the rolls if they did not pay him a fee.[11]

The Cherokees' situation was further distressed by financial claims upon their land. Years before, in order to protect their ownership, Thomas had purchased much of the land in his name to hold in trust for them. His financial demise had resulted in liens upon the property against which claims could be made. When the Indians sought legal redress to protect their property, they were disallowed the right as citizens to sue. Eventually they were given that privilege, but it would be 1874 before the complex matter was finally resolved by arbitrators.[12]

Efforts to remove the North Carolina Cherokees to the Indian Territory had not died. They were abetted by Cherokee Nation principal chief Lewis Downing, who in 1869 had encouraged them to join their brothers in the Indian Territory. The invitation was reluctantly accepted during the spring of 1871 by some ninety Cherokees under headman Obadiah. However, the impoverished band made it only as far as Loudon, Tennessee, where they became stranded by lack of funds.[13] In assisting the Obadiah group and others to continue on to the territory, government officials chose to work through Ross as their choice of principal chief. Flying Squirrel and his full bloods vigorously opposed all removal operations. This bitter political feud and impasse continued until October 1875. At that time the constitutional amendments of the Cheoah council were adopted, and duties were prescribed for a principal chief and second chief.[14]

With this resolved, Lloyd Welch of the Flying Squirrel faction was elected principal chief for a four-year term.[15] Welch proved to be a successful politician, using his office to build a strong political base in competition with the Ross-Taylor faction. He was easily reelected as principal chief in 1879, but soon after it was learned that he was terminally ill. He died in June 1880 after delivering a poignant farewell address.

The general council replaced Welch with his lieutenant, Nimrod Jarret Smith (Tsaladihi), a man who would become a dominant figure among the North Carolina Cherokees for many years to come. Standing a well-proportioned six-foot-four and wearing a handsome goatee, mustache, and long, wavy hair, the quarter-blood Cherokee was a demanding figure. Fluent in both Cherokee and English, he was a capable politician and a shrewd, determined leader.[16] During the twelve years he served as principal chief of the North Carolina Cherokees, Smith proved his political abilities in fighting for the legal status and land rights of his people and opposing white intrusion. Washington politicians were impressed with the force of his personality and political acumen. All in all, Smith was an outstanding tribal spokesman and leader.

Unfortunately, he was also other things. A church investigation revealed that in his private life he often indulged in rowdy, drunken brawls. It came to light, also, that he had long carried on an affair with a married woman and had caused one of his daughters to cohabit with a white trader for his personal benefit. He was soundly rejected by his people in the election of 1891, dying two years afterward as a disgraced, lonely figure.[17]

Unlike the Oklahoma Cherokees, whose tribal government was essentially dissolved by the Dawes Act and Jerome Commission, the Cherokees of North Carolina continued their legislative form of governance into the twentieth century. A principal chief, who was elected for a four-year term, presided over a legislature comprising two representatives elected from each of five townships. But the eastern Cherokee government, too, was restricted by U.S. authority, and none of the chiefs following Smith were such dominating figures.[18]

The North Carolina Cherokees, however, are an eminent part of the Cherokee existence and have done much to perpetuate and publicize their cultural heritage. Each year thousands of visitors come to the Cherokee ancestral homeland in the Great Smoky Mountains National Park to attend the Cherokee drama "Unto These Hills." They also witness restorations of the Cherokee past in the Oconaluftee Indian Village, Cherokee library and museums, and arts and crafts centers.

Notes

Abbreviations

Prologue: Historical Overview

1. Lowery, "Sequoyah or George Gist," *Journal of Cherokee Studies* 2 (fall 1877): 386.

2. *Colonial Records of South Carolina, 1750–1754*, 164.

3. Williams, ed., "Tatham's Characters," 177–78.

4. Kappler, *Indian Treaties*, 439.

5. Ibid., 442.

Chapter 1: Out of a Mystic Past

1. House, *Final Report of the United States de Soto Expedition*; Monette, Valley of the Mississippi, 2:31–32; Bourne, *Hernando de Soto in the Conquest*, 14–15; Mooney, Myths, 24–29.

2. Serrano y Sanz, *Spain and the Cherokee and Choctaw Indians*, 1–2 n. 5.

3. *Cherokee Advocate*, January 12, 1901.

4. *Scots Magazine*, October 1755, 504–5; *London Magazine*, October 1755.

5. Woodward, *Cherokees*, 20.

6. Reid, *Law of Blood*, 3–10.

7. *Journal of the American Geographical Society of New York* 5, 1874, 217–24.

8. Corkran, "Cherokee Pre-History," 458–60. See also Dickens, *Cherokee Prehistory*.

9. Brown, "Eastern Cherokee Chiefs," 4–5; Corkran, *Cherokee Frontier*, 3. By midcentury traders were adding two more divisions: the Valley Towns and the Out Towns. *Colonial Records of South Carolina*, 1750–1754, 86–87.

10. Corkran, "Cherokee Pre-History," 455–66, citing J. H. Payne, Papers Concerning the Cherokee Indians 7, Newberry Library, Chicago. See also, Mooney, "Cherokee Mound-Building," 167–71.

11. Corkran, "Cherokee Pre-History," 464–65.

12. Williams, "Journal of Sir Alexander Cumings," in *Early Travels in the Tennessee Country*, 122.

13. Identified variously as Chote, Chotah, Choto, Chotto, Chotte, Choate, Chateauke, Echota. A town named "Choty" is mentioned as early as 1716 as a trading center. Described as being between Quanesee and Tougelo, it was evidently a different site. See *Colonial Records of South Carolina*, 1710–1718, 123.

14. King and Olinger, "Oconastota," 222.

15. Williams, *Henry Timberlake's Memoirs*, 1756–1765, 93. In 1754 Peter Williamson, a Scot who had been kidnapped at the age of eight and sent to America as a slave, was captured in his western Pennsylvania home by Indians. After being held for nearly two years, he escaped and returned to Scotland, where in 1768 he published a book telling of his travels among the Indian nations. He plagiarized much of Timberlake's account of the Cherokees. See Williamson, *Life and Astonishing Adventures of Peter Williamson*, 79–80.

16. *American Magazine*, October 1757, 12–13.

17. Williams, *Timberlake's Memoirs*, 59.

18. Dickson, "Judicial History," 46.

19. Ibid, 46.

20. Serrano y Sanz, *Spain and the Cherokee and Choctaw Indians*, 2.

21. Adair, *History of the American Indians*, 152–53.

22. Reid, *Law of Blood*, 53, citing Raymond Demere to W. H. Lyttelton, July 30, 1757, *Third South Carolina Indian Book*, 391–92.

23. *American Magazine*, March 1760, 118–19.

24. Adair, *History of the American Indians*, 428–29.

25. Dickson, "Judicial History," 46.

26. Reid, *Law of Blood*, 145–46, citing Swanton, "The Indians of the Southeastern United States," Bulletin 137 Bureau of American Ethnology, 723. In her *Memoirs*, 11, Narcissa Owen refers to her grandfather, Thomas Chisholm, as the last hereditary chief of the Western Cherokees. Chisholm, third chief of the Western Cherokees in 1834, was elected to that post. McLoughlin, *Cherokee Renascence*, 145, refers to his father, John D. Chisholm, as a chief. This author, however, has found no record of Chisholm's having ever been elected as a Cherokee chief, though he would serve virtually as such among the Western Cherokees.

27. Williams, *Timberlake's Memoirs*, 93.

28. De Brahm, *Philosophico-Historico-Hydrogeography*, 224.

29. Williams, *Timberlake's Memoirs*, 109.

30. Mooney, *Myths*, 384–85.

31. Ibid.

32. "Lieut. Timberlake's Memoirs," *London Magazine*, February 1766.

33. Adair, *History of the American Indians*, 152–53; Reid, *Law of Blood*, 69, citing Minutes of February 9, 1757, *South Carolina Council Journal*.

34. Royce, *Cherokee Nation of Indians*, 376; Brown, *Old Frontiers*, 18–19; C. Foreman, *Indian Women Chiefs*, 72.

35. Williams, *Timberlake's Memoirs*, 60–61.

36. Reid, *Law of Blood*, 17–27.

Chapter 2: Under British Rule

1. Alvord and Bidgood, *First Explorations of the Trans-Allegheny Region*, 78–97, 209–26. Woodward, *Cherokees*, 27–30, gives the Cherokee town as being Chota. However, there is no mention of Chota in accounts of the visit by Needham and Arthur. There are numerous references to the Cherokees as "Tomahaitans"—a name that is somewhat similar to the early town of Tamantly, mentioned by Colonel Chicken in 1825 (Tamatle on Hunter's 1830 map and Tommotley on Timberlake's map). Also mentioned in the Needham/Arthur accounts are the Indian towns of Sitteree, Occaneechi, and Aeno.

2. McLoughlin, *Cherokee Renascence*, 16.

3. Mooney, *Historical Sketch of the Cherokee*, 19–20.

4. Swanton, "The Indians of the Southeastern United States," 111.

5. *Cherokee Advocate*, January 30, 1845.

6. Mooney, *Historical Sketch*, 24.

7. Brown, "Eastern Cherokee Chiefs," 4.

8. Williams, "Col. Chicken's Journal," in *Early Travels*, 90–104; Col. George Chicken's Journal, 1725, Gilcrease Institute transcript. Chicken noted the existence of the Cherokee towns of Elijoy, Cheowee, Tamantley, Tunisee, Terriquo, Coosaw, and Tallasee.

9. Williams, *Early Travels*, 117–29; C. Foreman, *Indians Abroad*, 44–81.

10. The names of the seven are given variously. The English recorded them as Scay-agusta Oukah, Scalilasken Keta-gusta, Tethtowe, Clogoittah, Colannah, Unnaconoy and Oucouacon. *North Carolina State Records*, 3:129. British journals also gave the Cherokees various titles, such as king, emperor, prince, general, etc.

11. According to Henry Timberlake, who knew him well, Little Carpenter gained his name from his excellence in building houses. *London Magazine*,

February 1766, 88. Bartram in *Travels in North America* says it came from his great diplomatic skills whereby, "Like as a carpenter could make every notch and joint fit in wood, so he could bring all his views to fill and fit their places in the political machinery of his nation"; Williams, "Tatham's Characters," 174 n. 6.

12. *Grub Street Journal*, July 2, 1730.

13. Cuming to *London Evening Post* as printed in *London Magazine*, October 1755, 499.

14. Ibid.; *North Carolina State Records*, 3:129; Williams, *Early Travels*, 129.

15. *Grub Street Journal*, June 25, 1730.

16. Ibid., September 17, 24, 1730; *The Daily Post*, August 12, 1730; C. Foreman, *Indians Abroad*, 47–52.

17. *North Carolina State Records*, 3:132–33.

18. During the Cherokees' visit to England, word had arrived of Cuming's American financial manipulations. Suspicious investors in Charlestown broke into his safe and discovered it contained only empty boxes and rubbish. A letter from the colonies telling of his financial dealings was printed in English papers. As a result, Cuming was ostracized by British authorities, and he eventually landed in debtors prison. *Grub Street Journal*, September 10, 1730; Williams, *Early Travels*, 117–21.

19. Kelly, "Oconostota," 221.

20. Brown, *Old Frontiers*, 46.

21. Corkran, *Cherokee Frontier*, 13–16.

22. Affidavit of Robert Gandy, *Colonial Records of South Carolina*, May 21, 1750-August 7, 1754, 71.

23. Williams, "William Tatham," 174; Corkran, *Cherokee Frontier*, 43.

24. Ludovic Grant to Governor Glen, February 8, 1754, *Colonial Records of South Carolina, 1750–1754*, 474–75.

25. Ibid., 196.

26. *London Magazine*, November 1751, 601.

27. *Colonial Records of South Carolina, 1750–1754*, 430–53.

28. Ibid.

29. Ibid.

30. Corkran, *Cherokee Frontier*, 39–40.

31. Allen, *Robert Dinwiddie*, 44–45.

32. Corkran, *Cherokee Frontier*, 54–58; Williams, "The Father of Sequoyah," 3–4.

33. *Scot's Magazine*, October 1755, 505; "Treaty of 1755," 65.

34. *Scot's Magazine*, October 1755, 506–7.

35. Brown, *Old Frontiers*, 55.

36. Milling, *Red Carolinians*, 184; Brown, "Eastern Cherokee Chiefs," 7. See also Landrum, *Colonial and Revolutionary History of Upper South Carolina*, 23–24.

37. Royce, *Cherokee Nation,* 17.

38. Kelly, "Oconostota," 221–34. Oconostota was likely victimized by the smallpox of 1738–39 that was brought to America by slave ships. It was said that nearly half the Cherokee population was wiped out by the plague. Mooney, *Historical Sketch,* 26.

39. Williams, "William Tatham," 175.

40. Starr, *History of the Cherokee Indians,* 468–69; *Cherokee Advocate,* March 23, 1892; *Virginia Magazine* 9 (April 1902): 360–64.

41. Corkran, *Cherokee Frontier,* 63–65.

42. "A Treaty between Virginia and the Catawbas and Cherokees, 1756," 251.

43. Kelly, "Attakullakulla," 11.

44. Ammoscosette (Ammonoscossittee) was the lead signer of an agreement on March 17. *Scot's Magazine,* September 1756, 460–61.

45. Corkran, *Cherokee Frontier,* 66–67.

46. *Scot's Magazine,* June 1754, 297.

47. *London Magazine,* October 1755, 498–99.

48. Hames, "Anglo-French Rivalry," 313–14.

49. Kelly, "Attakullakulla," 15–16.

50. De Brahm, *Philosophico-Historico-Hydrogeography,* 208–9.

51. Hames, "Anglo-French Rivalry," 316–17; Corkran, *Cherokee Frontier,* 108–9.

Chapter 3: Come the King's Men

1. Corkran, *Cherokee Frontier,* 96, citing "Indian Books of South Carolina," 5:308–10.

2. Ibid., 100–108.

3. Ibid., 130–34.

4. Hames, "Anglo-French Rivalry," 319.

5. Ibid., 130–36.

6. *American Magazine,* February 1758, 45.

7. "A Treaty between Virginia and the Catawbas and Cherokees, 1756," 260 n.

8. Corkran, *Cherokee Frontier,* 160–65.

9. Ibid., 166–67.

10. Brown, "Eastern Cherokee Chiefs," 9–10; Corkran, *Cherokee Frontier,* 169–70.

11. Corkran, *Cherokee Frontier,* 173–74.

12. Ibid.

13. *American Magazine,* November 1759, 695–700; *Scot's Magazine,* January 1760, 38–39; Corkran, *Cherokee Frontier,* 175–78.

14. Brown, *Old Frontiers*, 91, citing *South Carolina Journals*, October 15, 1759.

15. Ibid.

16. Corkran, *Cherokee Frontier*, 185–86.

17. Ibid., 187.

18. "Treaty of Peace and Friendship, December 26, 1759," 1760, 144–45; *American Magazine*, January 1760, 35–37.

19. Ibid.

20. Ibid., April 1760, 211; Corkran, *Cherokee Frontier*, 194.

21. *London Magazine*, January 1760, 38–40; March 1760, 155–56; September 1760, 490–93; Corkran, *Cherokee Frontier*, 192–93. Among them was trader John Downing, whose surname would become eminent among the Cherokees. Another prominent name of the day was trader John Vann.

22. *South Carolina Gazette*, February 13, 1760, as reprinted by *Scot's Magazine*, March 1760, 154–56.

23. Report from Charlestown, S.C., *South Carolina Gazette*, February 13, 1760, as reprinted by *Scot's Magazine*, April 1760, 211–13.

24. Report from Charlestown, S.C., February 23, 1760, *British Magazine*, April 1760, 273; *American Magazine*, March 1760, 118–19; Milling, *Red Carolinians*, 300, quotes a similar account by Ensign Alexander Miln, who succeeded in command of the fort.

25. Brown, *Old Frontiers*, 95.

26. Report from Charlestown, June 21, 1760, *Scot's Magazine*, August 1760, 438.

27. *South Carolina Gazette*, February 13, 1760, as reprinted by *Scot's Magazine*, March 1760, 156.

28. Report of Col. James Grant, June 4, 1760, *Scot's Magazine*, July 1760, 378–79.

29. Report from Fort Prince George, *Scot's Magazine*, September 1760, 490–93.

30. Hames, "Fort Loudoun," 452–53.

31. Brown, *Old Frontiers*, 99.

32. Hames, "Fort Loudoun," 453.

33. Ibid.; Report from Charlestown, S.C., June 21, 1760, *Scot's Magazine*, August 1760, 438.

34. Hames, "Fort Loudoun," 454.

35. Kelly, "Attakullakulla," 20.

36. Ibid., 593.

37. Ibid., 592.

38. Captain Stuart letter, *Scot's Magazine*, December 1760, 663.

39. Ibid., March 1761, 123.

40. Ibid., December 1760, 663.

41. Brown, "Eastern Cherokee Chiefs," 14.

42. Brown, *Old Frontiers*, 102. Captain Stuart saw the boy soon after his release. *Scot's Magazine*, December 1760, 664.

43. Brown, *Old Frontiers*, 105–6.

44. Kelly, "Attakullakulla," 21.

45. Report of Grant's March, *Scot's Magazine*, July 1761, 378.

46. Ibid., July, August, 1761, 378, 430.

47. Evans and King, "Historic Document of the Grant Expedition against the Cherokees," 291–92.

48. Report from Ashley Ferry, S.C., September 16, 1761, *Scot's Magazine*, November 1761, 604–5.

49. Ibid.

50. Ibid., 663.

51. Copy of treaty, South Carolina, December 30, 1761, *Scot's Magazine*, February 1762, 103. The Cherokees agreed to permit the regarrisoning of Fort Loudoun, but orders came from England to destroy the post.

52. Williams, *Timberlake's Memoirs*, 36.

Chapter 4: "My Tongue Is My Pen"

1. Evans, "Ostenaco," 53.

2. Ibid., 41–42.

3. C. Foreman, *Indians Abroad*, 65–66; "Report from Williamsburg," *Court Magazine*, July 1762, 515–17.

4. Williams, *Timberlake's Memoirs*, 95.

5. Jefferson, as cited by Williams, *Dawn of the Tennessee Valley and Tennessee History*, 272.

6. Ibid.

7. C. Foreman, *Indians Abroad*, 65–66; Williams, *Timberlake's Memoirs*, 132.

8. Howard, "A New Humorous Song."

9. *Universal Magazine*, June 1762, 332.

10. C. Foreman, *Indians Abroad*, 75.

11. Evans, "Ostenaco," 51–52. The gorget is on display today at the Royal Ontario Museum, Toronto, Canada.

12. *London Magazine*, August 1762, 445.

13. Evans, "Ostenaco," 52.

14. *North Carolina State Records*, 11:179–89.

15. Brown, "Eastern Cherokee Chiefs," 18–19.

16. *British Magazine*, February 1765, 105; Brown, "Eastern Cherokee Chiefs," 18.

17. Brown, *Old Frontiers*, 128.

18. Ibid., 125.

19. "Treaty with the Cherokees at Lochabor, S.C., 1770," 360–64.

20. Ibid., 442.

21. Brown, *Old Frontiers*, 128.

22. "A Treaty between Virginia and the Catawbas and Cherokees," 250.

23. *British Magazine*, February 1765.

24. Bloom, "Acculturation of the Eastern Cherokees," 345–46.

25. Woodward, *Cherokees*, 85.

26. Williams, "Tatham's Characters," 177–78.

27. Adair, *History of the American Indians*, 251.

28. Ross, *Life and Times of the Honorable William P. Ross*, 234.

29. Adair, *History of the American Indians*, 230.

30. *Colonial Records of South Carolina, 1750–1754*, 442.

31. Adair, *History of the American Indians*, 233.

32. Bloom, "Acculturation," 334–35.

33. *Colonial Records of South Carolina, 1750–1754*, 198, 436. "A Quantity of Amunition was ordered for each Indian to use on the Road, viz., 1 Pound of Powder, and 2 Pounds of Bullets to each Man, and it was ordered that 200 Pounds of Powder, and 400 Weight of Bullets should be left for the Upper Cherokee Towns, and 100 Pound Weight of Powder and 200 Weight of Lead Bullets be left for the Lower Cherokee Towns." Bloom, "Acculturation," 449.

Chapter 5: A Wall to the Skies

1. *New-York Journal and General Advertiser*, July 7, 1777.

2. Depositions of John Reid and James Robinson, *Calendar of Virginia State Papers*, 1:284, 285–86.

3. Depositions of Samuel Wilson and Charles Robertson, *Calendar of Virginia State Papers*, 1:282–83, 291–92. Dragging Canoe had been given his name when as a boy he had dragged a canoe, which was too heavy for him to carry, over a portage in order to keep up with his father's war party. Older warriors had shouted "Tsi.yu Gansi.ni," meaning "He is dragging the canoe!" Evans, "Dragging Canoe," 176, citing J. Leonard Raulston and James W. Liningood, *Sequatchie*, 33.

4. Some historians have held that England made no attempt to incite the Indians against the Americans. Williams, *Tennessee During the Revolutionary War*, 25 n. 4, effectively argues otherwise.

5. Ibid., 24.

6. Haywood, *Civil and Political History of the State of Tennessee*, 507.

7. Stuart's Report, *North Carolina State Records*, 10:763–83.

8. Evans, "Dragging Canoe," 181–82.

9. Williams, *Tennessee during the Revolutionary War*, 35.

10. Evans, "Dragging Canoe," 182.

11. *Cherokee Advocate*, March 23, 1892.

12. Report of Colonel Christian, *North Carolina State Records*, 10:844.
13. Mooney, *Historical Sketch*, 41–43.
14. Ibid.; *New-York Journal and the General Advertiser*, September 1, 1777.
15. Corn Tassel's Cherokee name is given as Rayetaeh on the Treaty of Long Island document; as Koatohee on the Treaty of Hopewell; as Onitositah by Williams in "Tatham's Characters"; as Udsidasata by Mooney in *Myths*; as Kaallahnor on a 1787 receipt.
16. Williams, "Tatham's Characters," 176.
17. Haywood, *Civil and Political History*, 501–14.
18. Ibid., 510.
19. Williams, "Tatham's Characters," 175–78.
20. Kelly, "Attakullakulla," 27; Kelly, "Oconostota," 231–32.
21. Brown, *Old Frontiers*, 159.
22. *Pennsylvania Gazette*, February 28, 1781.
23. Mooney, *Historical Sketch*, 50.
24. Report of Col. Arthur Campbell, January 15, 1781, *Pennsylvania Gazette*, February 28, 1781.
25. Christian to Governor Harrison, December 16, 1782, *Calendar of Virginia State Papers*, 3:398.
26. *North Carolina State Records*, 16:415–16.
27. *American State Papers, Indian Affairs*, 1:431.
28. Evans, "Dragging Canoe," 185.
29. *North Carolina State Records*, 17:11.
30. Old Tassel talk, October 10, 1784, *North Carolina State Records*, 17:175–76.

Chapter 6: New Elder Brother

1. *American State Papers, Indian Affairs*, 1:41.
2. Ibid., 42.
3. Ibid., 43.
4. Ibid., 41.
5. Ibid.
6. Ramsey, *Annals of Tennessee*, 344–45.
7. *North Carolina State Records*, 18:696–98.
8. *Virginia Calendar of State Papers*, 4: 306.
9. Ibid., 307.
10. Ibid., 315, 368; *Maryland Gazette*, January 29, 1789; *Pennsylvania Mercury and Universal Advertiser*, June 15, 1787. It was reported that Sconetoyah was the son of one of the Cherokee principal chiefs. Since this name does not appear again in Cherokee records, he may well have been the son of Corn Tassel, who was killed along with his father the following year.

Williams, "Tatham's Characters," 175–76 n. 9, states that Corn Tassel visited Philadelphia in 1787 and talked with Benjamin Franklin. No evidence can be found to support this statement.

11. *North Carolina State Records*, 20: 779–80.

12. Joseph Martin to Governor Randolph, June 11, 1788, *Calendar of Virginia State Papers*, 4: 452. Martin was married to Betsy Ward, daughter of Nancy Ward, the War Woman of Chote.

13. *Maryland Gazette*, July 17, August 28, September 4, 11, 1788; Williams, *History of the Lost State of Franklin*, 206–7.

14. *Pennsylvania Gazette*, October 15, 1788. In giving his memory of this in 1835, Cherokee second chief George Lowrey referred to Old Tassel by the name of Kahn-yah-tah-hee, or The First to Kill. When the villagers returned, he said, carrion birds had devoured the body of one chief, but that of Corn Tassel "was untouched and unchanged even in death. His hand still grasped the violated Flag of Peace, and upon his dead life [lips] lingered a benignant smile." Lowery, "Sequoyah or George Gist," 389–90.

15. September 18, 1788. Whether or not Sevier was responsible for the murder of Tassel and the others, tacitly or otherwise, remains undetermined. See Williams, *History of the Lost State of Franklin*, 208 n. 10, regarding letter of justices July 9, 1778, and contention that Sevier should be held responsible for the murders. At the close of the American Revolution, Sevier was arrested for heading the seceding State of Franklin. He escaped, and eventually the matter was dropped. Today he remains a state hero in Tennessee.

16. *Calendar of Virginia State Papers*, 4:475.

17. *Maryland Gazette*, September 8, 1788; Mooney, "Historical Sketch," 55.

18. *Maryland Gazette*, November 27, 1788; Haywood, *Civil and Political History*, 517–18. Also signing the note was Kettegiskie (or Categiskey—this was probably the Tekakisskee, or Taken out of the Water, who signed the Treaty of 1794), John Watts, and the Glass.

19. It is known that the mother of John Watts Jr. was a sister of Corn Tassel. Quite likely his father was the John Watts who served as an interpreter at the 1763 treaty with the British at Augusta, Georgia, and possibly the John Watts who, along with Patrick Henry, was assigned a land grant south of the Tennessee River in 1789. *American State Papers, Indian Affairs*, 1:114.

20. *American State Papers, Indian Affairs*, 1:48, 204; John Kirk Jr. wrote a letter dated October 17, 1788, to Watts: "I have heard of your letter lately sent to Chudkey John (Sevier)—You are mistaken in blaming him for the death of your uncle. Listen now to my story. For days and months, Cherokee Indians, little and big, women and children, have been fed and treated kindly by my mother. When all was peace with the Tenasee towns, Slim Tom, with a party of Satigo and other Cherokee Indians, murdered my mother, brothers and sisters, in cold blood, when the children just before was playful about them as friends, and the very instant some of them received the bloody toma-

hawk, they were smiling in their faces—This begun the war, and since I have taken ample satisfaction, and can now make peace, except with Slim Tom. Our beloved men, the congress, tells us to be at peace—I will listen to their advice, if no more blood is shed by the Cherokees; and the head men of your nation take care to prevent such beginnings of bloodshed in all times to come. But if they do not, your people may feel something more, to keep up the remembrance of JOHN KIRK, jun., Captain of the Bloody Rangers." *Maryland Gazette*, January 2, 1789.

21. *American State Papers, Indian Affairs*, 1:47.

22. *Maryland Gazette*, February 12, April 2, 1789.

23. *American State Papers, Indian Affairs*, 1:57.

24. *Maryland Gazette*, July 15, 1790; July 29, October 20, 1791.

25. *American State Papers, Indian Affairs*, 1:58.

26. In 1792 Blount referred to Doublehead as a "rising popular character among the young warriors." He also claimed that Doublehead, who had begged him for permission to hunt on the Cumberland, had gone there and killed travelers. *American State Papers, Indian Affairs*, 1:270, 274.

27. Royce, *Cherokee Nation*, 30–31.

28. *Maryland Gazette*, April 5, 1792; *American State Papers, Indian Affairs*, 1:203, 245, 271.

29. *American State Papers, Indian Affairs*, 1:204–5.

30. Kappler, *Indian Treaties*, 32–33.

31. *American State Papers, Indian Affairs*, 1:203, 268; Maryland Gazette, May 10, 1792.

32. White, "John Chisholm, a Soldier of Fortune," 62.

33. *American State Papers, Indian Affairs*, 1:266–70.

34. Ibid., 264–65.

35. Ibid., 264, 268–69.

36. Starr, *Cherokees West*, 218.

37. Ibid.

Chapter 7: An Effort at Arms

1. See Malone, *Cherokees of the Old South*, 40–43, 56, regarding Watts and Doublehead; see notes in chapter 5 regarding Tahlonteskee. Armistead report, August 1807, Records of Cherokee Agency in Tennessee (M-208), NA, states that Sequechu was Doublehead's brother. This would support the statement by Malone, *Cherokees of the Old South*, 56, that Doublehead was of mixed blood. McLoughlin, *Cherokee Renascence*, 116, believes him to have been a full blood on the basis of his charge against John Rogers and his party of "half breeds." Council at Willstown to Meigs, September 19, 1806, Records of Cherokee Agency in Tennessee (M-208), NA. Sequechu, or Big Halfbreed, was a signatory to Cherokee treaties in 1806 and 1817.

2. Goodpasture, "Indian Wars and Warriors," 256–57. At the Treaty of Hopewell, Chief Tassel complained that trader John Benge had been robbed of 150 pounds sterling of leather by whites in Georgia. *American State Papers, Indian Affairs*, 1:43, 438.

3. *North Carolina State Records*, 11:179.

4. Ibid., 443. Governor Blount had a high respect for him. He and other whites were constantly giving Watts clothes and gifts. This amused Watts's brother, Unacata, who thought it made the chief become even more saucy.

5. *North Carolina State Records*, 11:328.

6. *American State Papers, Indian Affairs*, 1:289–94, 327–29.

7. Ibid., 273.

8. Ibid., 289–92, 327–29.

9. Ibid., 184.

10. Ibid., 276.

11. Ibid., 294–95; Brown, "Eastern Cherokee Chiefs," 26–27; Brown, *Old Frontiers*, 360–63; *Maryland Gazette*, November 8, 1792.

12. *American State Papers, Indian Affairs*, 1:434.

13. Serrano y Sanz, *Spain and the Cherokee and Choctaw Indians*, 64.

14. Ibid., 62–64. Other Cherokee leaders with Bloody Fellow were John Taylor, James Shawrey, and Carlos of Chicamoga.

15. Serrano y Sanz, *Spain and the Cherokee and Choctaw Indians*, 54.

16. Ibid., 84–87.

17. *American State Papers, Indian Affairs*, 1:444–45.

18. Ibid., 447; *Maryland Gazette*, February 7, 21, 1793.

19. *American State Papers, Indian Affairs*, 1:444–45.

20. Ibid., 459; *Maryland Gazette*, July 18, 1793.

21. *American State Papers, Indian Affairs*, 1:460.

22. Ibid., 468–69.

23. The boy's reprieve was temporary, however, for only three days after he arrived in the Lower Towns he was tomahawked to death by a Creek Indian. *American State Papers, Indian Affairs*, 1:634.

24. Ibid., 622–23.

25. *Maryland Gazette*, June 5, 1794; Kappler, *Indian Treaties*, 33–34.

26. Mooney, *Historical Sketch*, 66–67, citing Haywood, *Civil and Political History*, 308; and Ramsey, *Tennessee*, 594. That all of the white people were killed appears to be verified by Colonel Robertson's demand of Watts for the return of the slaves only. Watts did not deny they were being held and agreed to an exchange of prisoners. *American State Papers, Indian Affairs*, 1: 531, 536–37. In 1829 Thomas Scott charged that some sixty of the slaves taken by the Cherokees were still in the possession of wealthy half bloods on the Arkansas River. Report from Greenville Mississippi, May 10, 1829, Letters Received, OIA, Cherokee Agency (M-234), NA.

27. Starr, *Cherokees West*, 21. By Cephas Washburn's account, a Cherokee

named Bowl was the leader of the Cherokees of this attack, but there is good reason to doubt that Chief Bowle of Texas history was involved.

28. *American State Papers, Indian Affairs*, 1:632; *Maryland Gazette*, November 13, 1794.

29. *American State Papers, Indian Affairs*, 1:531.

30. Ibid., 532.

31. Ibid., 536.

32. Ibid., 536–38; *Maryland Gazette*, November 26, 1795.

Chapter 8: Intrigue and Assassination

1. "Impeachment of William Blount," 2383, 2386.

2. Ibid., 2390.

3. Royce, *Cherokee Nation*, 52.

4. Journal of Occurrences in Cherokee Agency in 1802, Records of Cherokee Agency in Tennessee (M-208), NA.

5. McLoughlin, *Cherokee Renascence*, 73, 89.

6. Gabriel, *Elias Boudinot*, 23–24.

7. Meigs to Hawkins, February 13, 1805, Records of Cherokee Agency in Tennessee (M-208), NA; McLoughlin, *Cherokee Renascence*, 85–86, 172.

8. Doublehead to Meigs, Records of Cherokee Agency in Tennessee (M-208), NA.

9. Doublehead and Path Killer to Meigs, March 27, 1804, Records of Cherokee Agency in Tennessee (M-208), NA; Meigs to Secretary of War, May 1804, Records of Cherokee Agency in Tennessee (M-208), NA.

10. Royce, *Cherokee Nation*, 55–60.

11. Ibid., 59–60.

12. *National Intelligencer and Washington Advertiser*, December 15, 1805. It was charged that Jefferson had suggested to a trader named Hooker that he get the Cherokees so heavily in debt that they would have to sell their land. His principal agent in encouraging the Cherokees to move west was Return J. Meigs, who as Cherokee agent had established himself at Southwest Point. David Fields to Meigs, November 18, 1807, Correspondence and Miscellaneous Records, Cherokee Agency, 1806–1807 (M-208), NA.

13. *New York Evening Post*, January 8, 1806.

14. *Daily National Intelligencer*, January 10, 1806.

15. Armistead report, August 1807, Letters Received, OIA, Cherokee Agency (M-234), NA.

16. Ibid., 91; Royce, *Cherokee Nation*, 65–69. McLoughlin, *Cherokee Renascence*, 145, refers to Chisholm as a chief. There is no known record, however, of Chisholm's having ever been elected as a Cherokee chief, even though he would serve virtually as such for the remainder of his life.

17.　McLoughlin, *Cherokee Renascence*, 89; Kappler, *Indian Treaties*, 74.

18.　Lovely to Meigs, March 8, 1806, Records of Cherokee Agency in Tennessee (M-208), NA.

19.　McLoughlin, *Cherokee Renascence*, 137, 151, 174. In 1809 Joseph Vann was listed as owning 250 horses, 1,000 cattle, 150 swine, 10 plows, and 115 black slaves.

20.　Doublehead and chiefs to Black Fox and chiefs, August 9, 1805; Meigs to Smith, August 19, 1805; Doublehead to Smith, November 16, 1805; Doublehead affidavit, November 16, 1805; Letters Received, OIA, Cherokee Agency (M-234).

21.　Doublehead to Meigs, October 3, 1806, Letters Received, OIA, Cherokee Agency (M-234).

22.　Ibid., January 14, 1807; Chisholm to Meigs, January 25, 1807, Meigs to Dearborn, February 12, 1807, Letters Received, OIA, Cherokee Agency (M-234).

23.　Armistead report; Hall to Armistead, August 9, 1807, James Phillips to Meigs, August 15, 1807, Letters Received, OIA, Cherokee Agency (M-234).

24.　Claiborne, *Life and Times of Gen. Sam Dale*, 44–49.

25.　Brown, "Eastern Cherokee Chiefs," 30; see also John Howard Payne Papers, typescript, 2:26–30, 43–46, Newberry Library, Chicago, as cited by McLoughlin, "Jefferson and Cherokee Nationalism," 560 n. 32.

26.　Meigs to Dearborn, September 27, 1807, Records of Cherokee Agency in Tennessee (M-208), NA.

27.　Treaty of Cherokee with Mr. Meigs on Behalf of U.S., December 2, 1807, Records of Cherokee Agency in Tennessee (M-208), NA.

28.　Pathkiller and other chiefs to Jefferson, January 24, 1808, Records of Cherokee Agency in Tennessee (M-208), NA.; Lowrey to Meigs, February 8, 1808, Letters Received, Secretary of War, Unregistered Series (M-222), NA.

29.　Riley letter, March 22, 1808, Records of Cherokee Agency in Tennessee (M-208), NA.

30.　McLoughlin, "Jefferson and Cherokee Nationalism," 563 n. 43, citing Sevier Letter, February 9, 1808, Daniel Parker Papers, Box 2, Pennsylvania Historical Society.

31.　Jefferson to Cherokee delegation, May 4, 1808, Letters Sent by Secretary of War Relating to Indian Affairs, 1880–1824 (M-15), NA. Eaton, *John Ross and the Cherokee Indians*, 21–22, citing *Jefferson's Works*, Library Edition, 16:432–35.

32.　Address of Cherokee Chiefs to Jefferson, December 21, 1808, Eaton, *John Ross*; *Daily National Intelligencer*, December 14, 1808. While in Washington, Meigs was appointed as senator for Ohio to fill a vacancy caused by resignation. He took his seat on January 6, 1809; *Daily National Intelligencer*, January 4, 11, 1809. Cherokee chiefs in Washington, December 21, 1808, Records of Cherokee Agency in Tennessee (M-208), NA.

33. Jefferson address to deputies of Upper and Lower Towns, January 9, 1809, *American State Papers, Indian Affairs*, 2:125.

34. McLoughlin, *Cherokee Renascence*, 144–45.

35. Malone, *Cherokees of the Old South*, 150-51.

36. McLoughlin, *Cherokee Renascence*, 109, 156.

37. Ibid., 156–57.

Chapter 9: "As Long as Waters Flow"

1. McLoughlin, *Cherokee Renascence*, 149–50, citing The Ridge, et al. to Thomas Jefferson, Daniel Parker Papers, Box 2, Pennsylvania Historical Society.

2. Malone, *Cherokees of the Old South*, 51.

3. Turtle at Home, Tolluntuskee, and Glass to Jefferson, November 25, 1808, Letters Received, Secretary of War, Unregistered (M-222), NA.

4. *American State Papers, Indian Affairs*, 1:271–72.

5. William Blount letter, September 26, 1792, *American State Papers, Indian Affairs*, 1:291.

6. Meigs to Calhoun, February 19, 1818, Records of Cherokee Agency in Tennessee (M-208), NA; Nuttall, *Journal of Travels into the Arkansas Territory*, 129; Lewis and Kneberg, *Hiwassee Island*, 18.

7. McMinn to Secretary of War, January 10, 1818, Records of Cherokee Agency in Tennessee (M-208), NA.

8. Ridge and others to Meigs, October 23, 1809, Records of Cherokee Agency in Tennessee (M-208), NA.

9. Starr, *Cherokees West*, 129.

10. Ibid.; Konnetue letter, June 17, 1811, Records of Cherokee Agency in Tennessee (M-208), NA.

11. Royce, *Cherokee Nation*, 76,

12. *Territorial Papers of the United States*, 15:179.

13. *American State Papers, Indian Affairs*, 1:539–40.

14. Thompson to Meigs, January 2, 1805, Meigs to Dearborn, May 31, 1805, Hicks letter, March 31, 1805, Tolunteskee and Committee to Meigs, June 23, 1810, Records of Cherokee Agency in Tennessee (M-208), NA.

15. Treat to Dearborn, December 31, 1806, *Territorial Papers*, 14:56–57.

16. Ross, *Life and Times*, 254; Fiscal Records, April 1, 1813, Records of Cherokee Agency in Tennessee (M-208), NA.

17. Chisholm to Meigs, March 1809, Records of Cherokee Agency in Tennessee (M-208), NA.

18. Meigs to Chisholm, November 2, 1809, Records of Cherokee Agency in Tennessee (M-208), NA.

19. Meigs to Secretary of War, December 1, 1909, *American Register or General Repository of History, Politics, and Science*, 6:316–18.

20. Passport signed by Return J. Meigs, January 10, 1810, *American Register or General Repository of History, Politics, and Science*, 6:316–18. As Everett points out in *The Texas Cherokees*, 127 n.23, the much repeated account of Cephas Washburn that Bowle moved West before 1800 is pretty well discounted by this passport.

21. January 10, 1810, Records of the Cherokee Agency (M-208), NA.

22. Meigs letter, August 12, 1809, Records of the Cherokee Agency (M-208), NA.

23. Taluntuskee and Committee to Meigs, Records of the Cherokee Agency (M-208), NA.

24. Bringier, "Notices of the Geology," 39–40; Tahlonteskee to Meigs, June 17, 1811, Records of Cherokee Agency (M-208), NA.

25. Receipt for goods sent to Cherokees on Arkansas River, March 13, 1813, Records of Cherokee Agency (M-208), NA.

26. Chisholm letter, June 28, 1812, Records of Cherokee Agency (M-208), NA.

27. Bringier, "Notices of the Geology," 41.

28. Tahlonteskee to Lovely, March 13, 1813, Records of Cherokee Agency in Tennessee (M-208), NA. The chief also expressed a romantic interest in Lovely's sister, noting "I have courted her, but in vain."

29. *Territorial Papers*, 14:706.

30. Lovely letter, July 10, 1813, *Territorial Papers*, 14:706.

31. *Territorial Papers*, 14:544–45.

32. Ibid., 720–21.

33. Chisholm to Meigs, July 22, 1814, Records of Cherokee Agency in Tennessee (M-208), NA.

34. Lovely to Clark, May 27, 1815, *Territorial Papers*, 15:56–57.

35. G. Foreman, *Indians and Pioneers*, 38.

36. Lovely to Clark, October 1, 1813; Lovely to Clark, May 27, 1815, *Territorial Papers*, 15:49–51.

37. Clark to Lovely, May 2, 1816, *Territorial Papers*, 15:134–35.

38. G. Foreman, *Indians and Pioneers*, 46. Mrs. Persis Lovely, who had once lived in the home of the father of President James Madison, remained in her Arkansas log cabin in order to be near the remains of her husband. Meigs to Graham, Records of Cherokee Agency in Tennessee (M-208), NA; *Territorial Papers*, 21:148–49.

39. Talk by Arkansas Chiefs, 1817, Records of Cherokee Agency in Tennessee (M-208), NA.

40. Grant Foreman Papers, Gilcrease Institute, Box 24, 40:407.

41. Cherokee Chiefs to Meigs, 1817, Correspondence and Miscellaneous Records, Cherokee Agency, 1816–18, NA.

42. G. Foreman, *Indians and Pioneers*, 43–44.

43. Kappler, *Indian Treaties*, 140–44.

44. Delegation and McMinn to Monroe, January 14, 1818, Letters Received, Secretary of War Relating to Indian Affairs (M-271), NA.

45. McMinn to Meigs, January 18, 1818, Records of Cherokee Agency in Tennessee (M-208), NA.

46. Ibid.

47. Meigs to Jolly, May 3, 1817, Records of Cherokee Agency in Tennessee (M-208), NA.

48. Cherokee chiefs to Clark, July 11, 1817, *Territorial Papers*, 15:304.

49. *Niles' Weekly Register*, September 27, 1817; *Cherokee Advocate*, May 26, 1880. Another participant was the educated David Brown. He later wrote: "A few months ago I was in Arkansas, went to war with the Osage Nation. How do you think I felt then, when I was among the cruel savages, I wish then to murder and kill. But O, now I cannot pray enough for the same nation which I much despised"; *Christian Observer*, March 20, 1820.

50. G. Foreman, *Indians and Pioneers*, 58.

51. Bringier, "Notices of the Geology," 33.

52. Thomas Nuttall, the English botanist who came up the Arkansas in 1819, states that a white man "named Chisholm" had bashed an Osage infant to death against a tree; Nuttall, *Journal of Travels*, 192. Bradford mentions that among the attackers were the "Chissoms," of which there were several in Arkansas at the time. Among them was John Chisholm's white son, Ignatius, a former slave trader who had followed his father west. Ignatius's son Jesse, the half-Cherokee namesake of the Chisholm Cattle Trail, was only twelve or thirteen at the time.

53. G. Foreman, *Indians and Pioneers*, 58–59, citing Clark to Sibley, November 11, 1817, Missouri Historical Society, Sibley Ms., III.

54. McMinn to Graham, November 25, 1817, Records of Cherokee Agency in Tennessee (M-208), NA.

55. Ibid.

56. Mooney, *Historical Sketch*, 96; Royce, *Cherokee Nation*, 93–94.

57. G. Foreman, *Indians and Pioneers*, 80.

58. Baker, *Cherokee Emigration Rolls, 1817–1835*, 1–14.

59. Correspondence and Miscellaneous Records, 1819–20, Cherokee Agency in Tennessee (M-208), NA. George Guess, number 316, is listed to have a family of eleven. See also affidavit of Sally Guess, in Chase, *1842 Cherokee Claims, Skin Bayou*, 217–19.

60. A. B. Grubbs to Meigs, October 29, 1818, Meigs to Arkansas Chiefs, June 14, 1819, Records of Cherokee Agency in Tennessee (M-208), NA.

Chapter 10: A New Breed of Beloved Men

1. Washburn, *Reminiscences*, 107–8.

2. Ibid., 110.

3. Hitchcock, A Traveler, 192.

4. Missionary Herald, February 1929, 80.

5. McLoughlin, Cherokee Renascence, 179–81.

6. McKenney and Hall, The Indian Tribes of North America, 1:386–89; Cherokee Advocate, March 12, 1898. See also McLoughlin, "New Angles of Vision on the Cherokee Ghost Dance Movement," 317–45. The McKenney-Hall account tells of a half blood named Charles who came down from the mountains and talked to a gathering at a great feast and medicine dance, saying: "The Great Spirit told me that he is angry and has withdrawn his protection because you are following the customs of the white people. You have mills, clothes, feather beds, and tables—worse still, you have books and even domestic cats! The Great Spirit said to tell you that he is angry and has withdrawn his protection."

That was why, Charles insisted, the buffalo and other game were disappearing. He said the Cherokees must return to the customs of their forefathers. They must kill their cats, cut short their frocks, and dress as Indians again. Also they must stop living in houses and give up the arts they had learned from the white man. "Then your game will come back," the Cherokee soothsayer said, "the white man will disappear, and the Great Spirit will love his people again."

7. McLoughlin, Cherokee Renascence, 182–84.

8. Ibid., 190–94; Green, The Politics of Indian Removal, 40–43; Debo, The Road to Disappearance, 76–83.

9. Wilkins, Cherokee Tragedy, 71.

10. "Battle of the Horseshoe," Wheeler's Daily Independent, May 2, 1879.

11. Daily National Intelligencer, April 12, 1817.

12. Wilkins, Cherokee Tragedy, 78.

13. List of Claims for Spoliation on Their Property by the Militia of Tennessee in 1824, Special Files, Correspondence of Office of Indian Affairs (Central Office) and Related Records, NA.

14. Daily National Intelligencer, April 12, 1817; "Battle of the Horseshoe," Wheeler's Daily Independent, May 2, 1873.

15. Daily National Intelligencer, February 21, 1816.

16. U.S. Statutes at Large, 7:138–39.

17. Royce, Cherokee Nation, 77–78.

18. Ibid., 81–82; U.S. Statutes at Large, 7:148–49.

19. U.S. Statutes at Large, 7:148–49.

20. McMinn to Secretary of War, November 13, 1817, Letters Received, Secretary of War re Indian Affairs (M-271), NA.

21. Ibid.

22. Kappler, Indian Treaties, 140–44.

23. Speech of Sam Houston, Daily National Intelligencer, March 3, 1854.

24. Ibid., February 14, 1818.

25. *American State Papers, Indian Affairs*, 2:466–67.

26. Moulton, *Papers of Chief John Ross*, 1:31–35.

27. *American State Papers, Indian Affairs*, 2:279–83. See also *Laws of the Cherokee Nation Adopted by the Council at Various Periods*.

28. The medal was completed in 1825; but because Sequoyah did not return from the West, it was not presented until 1832. Ross to George Gist, January 12, 1832, Moulton, *Papers of Chief John Ross*, 1:234.

29. *Cherokee Advocate*, April 18, 1864.

30. Moulton, *John Ross*, 31. An April 26, 1823, letter to Joseph McMinn signed by Pathkiller and twenty-two other Cherokees refers twice to "our Head Chief Mr. Charles R. Hicks." Moulton, *Papers of Chief John Ross*, 1:47–48. On April 29, 1824, in a letter to Thomas L. McKenney, John Ross and others refer to instructions given them by "Path Killer and Charles R. Hicks the two principal chiefs of our nation."

31. McLoughlin, *Cherokee Renascence*, 301, 326–27.

32. Ibid., 304–5.

33. *Daily Oklahoman*, September 10, 1922.

34. Eaton, *John Ross*, 28; Moulton, *John Ross*, 2–12.

35. Moulton, *John Ross*, 20.

36. Treaty with Cherokees, 1819, *U.S. Statutes at Large*, 7:195–99.

37. Eaton, *John Ross*, 32, citing Payne Manuscripts, 2:450; Moulton, *John Ross*, 22.

38. Cornelius, *Little Osage Captive*, 64–74; Washburn, *Reminiscences*, 130–31.

39. Moulton, *John Ross*, 23.

40. McIntosh to Ross, October 21, 1823, in Abel, "Cherokee Negotiations of 1822," 188–221.

41. Moulton, *Papers of Chief John Ross*, 1:55.

42. Ibid., 76–78.

43. Moulton, *John Ross*, 31.

44. McLoughlin, *Cherokee Renascence*, 388–96.

45. *Niles' Weekly Register*, June 9, 1827.

46. G. W. Featherstonhaugh, who visited the Cherokees in 1837, described White Path as an "old chief remarkably cheerful and light of step, although seventy-six years old" and gave his Indian name as Nennenóh Oonáykay. Featherstonhaugh, *A Canoe Voyage*, 235.

47. McLoughlin, *Cherokee Renascence*, 394.

48. Ibid., 407.

49. *Niles' Weekly Register*, November 22, 1828.

50. Eaton, *John Ross*, 55–56.

Chapter 11: Cherokee Nation West

1. Baker, *Cherokee Emigration*, 1–14. Meigs to Arkansas Chiefs, June 14, 1819, Letters Received, OIA, Cherokee Agency (M-234), NA; Western Chiefs to Monroe, August 1819, Letters Received, Secretary of War Relating to Indian Affairs (M-271), NA. Timothy Flint met Dick Justice when the Cherokees were still in Arkansas. He described the full-blood Cherokee as being a small man then between eighty and ninety years old. The chief had a number of wives and more than thirty children. Flint, *Recollections of the Last Ten Years*, 147.

2. Cherokee Delegation to Secretary of War, March 12, 1825, Letters Received, OIA, Cherokee Agency (M-234), NA.

3. Miller to Calhoun, June 20, 1820, Letters Received, Secretary of War Relating to Indian Affairs (M-271), NA; Clarke, *Chief Bowles and the Texas Cherokees*, 14–15.

4. Finney and Washburn to Calhoun, September 1821, Letters Received by Secretary of War Relating to Indian Affairs (M-271), NA.

5. *Missionary Herald* 18 (January 1822): 107; map of Dwight Mission, Harvard Collection, ABCFM 18.3.1, v. 3.

6. James, *Account of an Expedition from Pittsburgh to the Rocky Mountains*, 2:272–73.

7. Washburn, *Reminiscences*, 75–76.

8. G. Foreman, *Indians and Pioneers*, 223 n. 20, citing Rev. F. R. Goulding, *Sal-o-quah; or Boy-life among the Cherokees*, 234 ff.

9. Arbuckle letter, July 29, November 4, 1826, Letters Received, AGO (Main Series) (M-567), NA; G. Foreman, *Indians and Pioneers*, 85–87.

10. McKenny and Hall, *Indian Tribes of North America* 1: 330-43.

11. G. Foreman, *Indians and Pioneers*, 76-79.

12. *Missionary Herald* 18 (January 1822): 71–72.

13. *Cherokee Advocate*, September 17, 1879.

14. Graves hosted the James party in 1820. "His house . . . is constructed like those of the white settlers, and like them, surrounded with enclosed fields of corn, cotton, sweet potatoes, &c., with cribs, sheds, droves of swine, flocks of geese, and all the usual accompaniments of a prosperous settlement." Graves also held a large number of slaves. James, *Account of an Expedition*, 2:267.

15. G. Foreman, *Indians and Pioneers*, 122–26.

16. *Arkansas Gazette*, December 29, 1821.

17. *Missionary Herald* 21 (August 1825): 246; G. Foreman, *Indians and Pioneers*, 126–27 nn. 13, 14. U.S. Marshall Henry L. Briscoe arrested Graves, placed him in irons, and took him to the Crawford County, Arkansas, courthouse. When Graves's friends threatened reprisal, Briscoe slipped him away down the Arkansas by canoe to Little Rock. There a court eventually decided

that as a Cherokee, Graves was not liable to the laws of Arkansas Territory, and he was set free. *Arkansas Gazette*, February 19, 1822; March 11, 1823.

18. G. Foreman, *Indians and Pioneers*, 148–49.

19. Letters Received by Office of Secretary of War Relating to Indian Affairs (M-271), NA.

20. *Arkansas Gazette*, August 13, September 16, 1823; *Missionary Herald* 20 (February 1824): 46.

21. *Missionary Herald* 21 (February 1825): 48.

22. Ibid., 50.

23. *Arkansas Gazette*, May 14, August 13, September 24, 1822.

24. *Missionary Herald* 18 (September 1822): 289.

25. *Arkansas Gazette*, January 13, 1821.

26. Starr, *Cherokees West*, 76–78.

27. Meigs to Calhoun, February 19, 1818, Records of the Cherokee Agency in Tennessee (M-208), NA.

28. Nuttall, *Journal of Travels*, 182.

29. Washburn, *Reminiscences*, 141.

30. *Missionary Herald* 23 (December 1827): 384.

31. Cherokee resolution, October 27, 1824, Letters Received, OIA, Cherokee Agency West (M-234), NA.

32. Spring Frog to Secretary of War, February 27, 1825, Letters Received, OIA, Cherokee Agency West (M-234), NA.

33. Cherokee chiefs to Secretary of War, March 12, 1825, Letters Received, OIA, Cherokee Agency West (M-234), NA.

34. Cherokee West resolution, December 28, 1827, Letters Received, OIA, Cherokee Agency West (M-234), NA.

35. Series of letters between U.S. government and delegates of Cherokees West, February through July 1828, Letters Received, OIA, Cherokee Agency West (M-234), NA.

36. McKenney to Duval, May 28, 1828, Letters Sent by Office of Indian Affairs, 1824–1831 (M-21), NA.

37. Rogers letter, December 28, 1828, Letters Received, OIA, Cherokee Immigration (M-234), NA.

38. Duval to Barbour, April 24, 1828, Letters Received, OIA, Cherokee Agency West (M-234), NA.

39. *Missionary Herald* 26 (September 1830): 298–99.

40. McKenney to Chief Jolly, November 22, 1828, Letters Sent, OIA (M-21), NA.

41. *Missionary Herald* 26 (January 1830): 12.

42. *U.S. Statutes at Large*, 7:414–16.

43. *Missionary Herald* 28 (January 1832): 9; 31 (January 1835): 23.

44. *Cherokee Phoenix*, October 14, 1829.

45. Ibid., March 18, October 14, 1829.

46. Arbuckle letter, July 24, 1830, Letters Received, AGO (Main Series) (M-567), NA.

47. Houston to Arbuckle, July 8, 1829, Williams and Barker, *Writings of Sam Houston*, 1:136–38; C. Foreman, "The Cherokee War Path," 252–67.

48. "Proceedings of a Council Held at Fort Gibson, Arkansas, in September 1834," T. B. Wheelock Journal, September 1834, Record Group 75, NA.

49. Claim presented by Dutch to United States on March 19, 1833, Letters Received, Cherokee Agency (M-234), NA.

50. Vashon to Eaton, August 28, 1830, Letters Received, Cherokee Agency (M-234), NA.

51. Cherokee delegation, April 24, 1834, Letters Received, Cherokee Agency (M-234), NA.

52. Ibid.

Chapter 12: Dark Clouds Gathering

1. Moulton, *Papers of Chief John Ross* 1: 166.
2. Ibid., 195–96.
3. Ibid, 162–63.
4. *U.S. Register of Debates*, reel 2, 312.
5. Mooney, *Historical Sketch*, 111–13.
6. Moulton, *Papers of Chief John Ross*, 1:236–39.
7. Ibid., 432–34.
8. Journal of Lt. Harris, sect. 10, Cherokee Removal File, OHS/AMD.
9. Ibid.
10. *Cherokee Phoenix*, May 24, 1834.
11. Journal of Lt. Harris, sect. 10, Cherokee Removal File, OHS/AMD.
12. Mooney, *Historical Sketch*, 152.
13. Moulton, *Papers of Chief John Ross*, 1:290–93.
14. King and Evans, "Death of John Walker, Jr.," 4–16.
15. Moulton, *Papers of Chief John Ross*, 1:349.
16. Royce, *Cherokee Nation*, 158.
17. Moulton, *Papers of Chief John Ross*, 2:410–11.
18. Ibid., 353, 357.
19. *Cherokee Advocate*, March 10, 1862.
20. Moulton, *Papers of Chief John Ross*, 2:400.
21. Kappler, *Indian Treaties*, 439–47, 448–49. John Ridge and Stand Watie, along with James Rogers and John Smith representing the Western Cherokees, joined in signing a supplement to the Treaty of New Echota on March 1, 1836.
22. Mooney, *Historical Sketch*, 117; Royce, *Cherokee Nation*, 125–30.

23. *Daily National Intelligencer*, May 22, 1838.

24. Moulton, *Papers of Chief John Ross*, 2:376–77.

25. Ibid., 394–413.

26. *Daily National Intelligencer*, May 22, 1838.

27. Eaton, *John Ross*, 99.

28. Moulton, *Papers of Chief John Ross*, 1:498–99, 712.

29. House, *Memorial Remonstrating against the Treaty of 1835*.

30. Ibid.

31. Moulton, *Papers of Chief John Ross*, 1:508–9.

32. Ibid., 498–99, 507–9, 713. The Western delegates included John Looney, Aaron Price, Dutch (who was now known as William Dutch), and William S. Coodey.

33. *Congressional Record*, May 25, 1836.

34. McKenney and Hall, *Indian Tribes of North America*, 1:189; 2:77–106.

35. Eaton, *John Ross*, 55.

36. Wilkins, *Cherokee Tragedy*, 228–29.

37. Moulton, *John Ross*, 56–58.

38. Wilkins, *Cherokee Tragedy*, 104–14.

39. *Report of the Secretary of War on Indian Affairs*, 1822, 162.

40. Wilkins, *Cherokee Tragedy*, 132–52.

41. House, *Memorial and Protest of the Cherokee Nation*.

42. Perdue, *Cherokee Editor*, 6–7.

43. *Cherokee Phoenix*, March 6, 1828.

44. Perdue, *Cherokee Editor*, 22–23.

45. Gabriel, *Elias Boudinot*, 128–33.

46. Boudinot's views are stated at length in Senate, *Documents in Relation to the Cherokee Treaty of 1835*.

47. *Daily National Intelligencer*, May 22, 1838.

Chapter 13: The Agony of Removal

1. McLoughlin and Conser, "The Cherokees in Transition," 678–703.

2. Carter, *Cherokee Sunset*, 206–7.

3. G. Foreman, "Journey of a Party of Cherokee Emigrants," 232–45.

4. G. Foreman, *Indian Removal*, 271–72.

5. Ibid., 280–83.

6. *Daily National Intelligencer*, September 22, 1838.

7. Carter, *Cherokee Sunset*, 228.

8. *Army-Navy Chronicles* 5 (May 3, 1838): 285, 372–75.

9. Butrick Journal, OHS/AMD.

10. *Baptist Missionary Magazine* 18 (September 1838): 236.

11. *Niles' Weekly Register* 48 (August 18, 1838): 385.

12. G. Foreman, *Indian Removal*, 289.

13. Carter, *Cherokee Sunset*, 245.

14. *Daily National Intelligencer*, November 14, 1838.

15. Wiley, *Tale of Home and War*, 10.

16. Carter, *Cherokee Sunset*, 246–47.

17. Brown, *Old Frontiers*, 511.

18. Moulton, *Papers of Chief John Ross*, 1:649–51.

19. Starr, *History*, 104–5.

20. Senate, *Report of C of IA in Relation to Claims against the Cherokees*.

21. Carter, *Cherokee Sunset*, 250.

22. Moulton, *Papers of Chief John Ross*, 1:673–74.

23. *Daily National Intelligencer*, October 25, 1838.

24. C. Foreman, "Coodey Family," 329.

25. Featherstonhaugh, *Canoe Voyage*, 235, described the chief as a fine old man, with a good deal of Indian dignity," and gave his Cherokee name as "Innatáhoolósah."

26. Ibid., 323.

27. Hicks to Ross, November 4, 1838, Moulton Collection, OHS/AMD.

28. *Daily National Intelligencer*, October 25, 1838.

29. G. Foreman, *Indian Removal*, 303.

30. *American State Papers, Indian Affairs*, 10:296–310.

31. Thornton, "Cherokee Population Losses," 289–300.

32. Ross to Scott, November 12, 1838, Moulton Collection, OHS/AMD.

33. Ibid., 262.

34. Moulton, *John Ross*, 13.

35. *Arkansas Gazette*, February 6, 1839.

Chapter 14: Expulsion from Texas

1. In both his *Memoirs*, 30, and "The Expulsion of the Cherokees from East Texas," 40, Reagan states that the Cherokees were on the Trinity for about three years. In 1969 the Cherokee Nation placed a historical marker in Dallas commemorating the event. Clarke, *Chief Bowles*, 14 n. 45, citing *Dallas Morning News*, July 19, 1969. Sam Houston later insisted that the Cherokees entered Texas at the request of the Mexican government; Williams and Barker, *Writings of Sam Houston* 1, 333.

2. Woldert, "Last of the Cherokees in Texas," 192–93.

3. Clarke, *Chief Bowles*, 15 n. 49.

4. McLoughlin, *Cherokees and Missionaries*, 45–46.

5. Fields to Meigs, September 25, 1801, Correspondence and Miscellaneous Records, Cherokee Agency (M-206), NA.

6. Cherokee chiefs to Meigs, October 23, 1809, Correspondence and Miscellaneous Records, Cherokee Agency (M-206), NA

7. *Handbook of Texas*, 1:597.

8. Fields to Mexican Governor, February 1, 1822, "Cherokees in Texas" File, Foreman Collection, OHS/AMD.

9. Trespalacious to Lopez, November 8, 1822, "Cherokees in Texas" File, Foreman Collection, OHS/AMD.

10. Austin to Saucedo, September 8, 1825, McLean, *Papers Concerning Robertson's Colony in Texas*, 2:365–67.

11. Commandant of Texas to Commandant of Eastern Interior States, April 14, 1826, McLean, *Papers Concerning Robertson's Colony in Texas*, 2:539–42.

12. Austin to Fields, April 24, 1826, McLean, *Papers Concerning Robertson's Colony in Texas*, 2:543–46.

13. Austin to Cherokee Chiefs, McLean, *Papers Concerning Robertson's Colony in Texas*, 2:565–56.

14. Expedition against the Waco Indians, August 5, 1826; Austin to Saucedo, August 15, 1826, McLean, *Papers Concerning Robertson's Colony in Texas*, 2:621–22, 624–25.

15. Fields to Austin, August 27, 1826, McLean, *Papers Concerning Robertson's Colony in Texas*, 2:635–36.

16. Clarke, *Chief Bowles*, 34, citing Bennet Lay, *The Lives of Ellis P. Bean*, 114.

17. *Courier des Natchitoches*, January 2, 16, 1827. Signing the document, which is published in full in the January 16 issue, were Richard Fields, John D. Hunter, Ne-ko-lake, John Bogs, and Cuk-to-keh.

18. John Smith, a prominent man among the Western Cherokees, referred to Boiling Mush as the head chief of the Texas Cherokees in 1829–30; C. Foreman, "Cherokee War Path," 240.

19. Barker, *Life of Stephen F. Austin*, 168–69.

20. Clarke, *Chief Bowles*, 50–51, citing Yoakum, *History of Texas*, 2:250; Starr, *Cherokees West*, 153; Foote, *Texas and the Texans*, 1:250; Gulick et al., *The Papers of Mirabeau Buonaparte Lamar*, 3:263; Woldert, "Last of the Cherokees in Texas," 193.

21. Starr, *History*, 38–39.

22. Passport issued by Meigs January 10, 1810; Bowle letter, January 26, 1820, Correspondence and Miscellaneous Records, Cherokee Agency, 1801–35 (M-208), NA. Reagan, *Memoirs*, 29–36.

23. Houston to Arbuckle, July 8, 1829. Williams and Barker, *Writings of Houston*, 1:136–38.

24. C. Foreman, "Cherokee War Path," 233–63. Two other accounts in Brown, *Indian Wars and Pioneers of Texas*, 10–14, parallel Smith's story. One, however, states that it was the Waco village that the Cherokees attacked and the Tawakonis, living three miles below on the Brazos, who came to their rescue.

25. Williams and Barker, *Writings of Houston*, 2:333.

26. Houston to Bowles, February 5, 1836, Williams and Barker, *Writings of Houston*, 2:355–56.

27. Reid, "Extracts from the Diary of W. Y. Allen," 46.

28. Gulick et al., *Papers of Lamar*, 2:69.

29. Winkler, *Secret Journals*, 35–36.

30. Houston to Bowles, July 3, 1837, Williams and Barker, *Writings of Houston*, 1:131–32. Clarke, *Chief Bowles*, 71, citing *Telegraph and Texas Register*, June 13, 1837, and R. B. Blake Collection, Fort Worth, 125–27.

31. Williams and Barker, *Writings of Houston*, 2:319.

32. Bowles to Houston, forwarded under letter dated August 12, 1838, Williams and Barker, *Writings of Houston*, 2:273–74.

33. Houston to May, August 12, 1838, Williams and Barker, *Writings of Houston*, 2:273.

34. Winfrey and Day, *Texas Indian Papers*, 1:8; DeShields, *Border Wars of Texas*, 293–94.

35. Houston to Bowl, August 14, 1838, Williams and Barker, *Writings of Houston*, 2:277.

36. Clarke, *Chief Bowles*, 84–86.

37. Moore, *Killough Massacre*, 4–20.

38. Wilbarger, *Indian Depredations in Texas*, 157–64.

39. Gulick et al, *Papers of Lamar*, 2:590. In a paper written in 1897, Reagan claimed that the communication delivered to Bowle was considerably different from the one supposedly delivered and then held by the secretary of state. Reagan, "Expulsion of Cherokees," 38–39.

40. Winfrey and Day, *Texas Indian Papers*, 1:67–70.

41. Reagan, "Expulsion of Cherokees," 43.

42. Ibid., 45.

43. Clarke, *Chief Bowles*, 110, citing Noah Smithwick, *The Evolution of a State; or Recollections of Old Texas*, 280.

44. Starr, *History*, 222.

45. *Arkansas Intelligencer*, July 15, 1843. Interestingly, on October 1, 1828, a letter by Richard Taylor and James Brown from the Cherokee Agency East to John Ross had listed Big Mush as one of several removal conductors complaining against a group that was stirring up trouble in the migration camps.

46. Brown, *Indian Wars*, 69.

47. Reagan, "Expulsion of Cherokees," 46.

48. Robertson to Mayfield, April 7, 1841, in Winfrey and Day, *Indian Papers of Texas*, 1:122–23; Senate, *Encroachment of Indians*, 57–58.

49. James, *Raven*, 309.

Chapter 15: Reunion and Conflict

1. Ross, *Life and Times*, 2 (unnumbered page).

2. Moulton, *Papers of Chief John Ross*, 2:32.

3. Ibid., 9.

4. Brown, Looney, and Rogers letter, June 19, 1839, Letters Received, OIA, Cherokee Agency (M-234), NA; Starr, *History*, 110–11.

5. House, *Indian Chiefs*, 5.

6. McLoughlin, *After the Trail of Tears*, 15–16; Bell-Watie account, *Arkansas Times and Advocate*, August 28, 1839; Arbuckle to Grayson, June 6, 1839, Letters Received, OIA, 1839; Wilkins, *Cherokee Tragedy*, 322–24.

7. Senate, *Discontents and Difficulties*, 115–19.

8. Ibid. See also *Constitution and Laws of the Cherokee Nation*.

9. Cherokee Decree, July 7, 13, 1839, Commissioner of Indian Affairs, 1839, 363–92.

10. House, *Cherokee Indians*, 3.

11. Wharton to Freeman, July 9, 1839, Letters Received, Cherokee Agency, 1839, NA.

12. House, *Cherokee Indians*, 41.

13. Ibid., 26–27.

14. Ibid., 25.

15. Ibid., 26–27, 54–55; House, "Memorial," 107–8.

16. Cherokee Nation Papers, M943-1-30, F18, WHC/UO. The resolution was signed by a number of men that interestingly included Treaty man James Starr.

17. Franks, *Stand Watie*, 2–8.

18. Ibid., 80–88; Paschal, "A Report of the Trial of Stand Watie," Cherokee Nation Papers, M943-2-1-E, Box 1, WHC/UO.

19. *Arkansas Intelligencer*, July 15, 22, 1853; list of tribes at council, June 19, 1843, Letters Received, OIA, Cherokee Agency (M-234), NA.

20. McLoughlin, *After the Trail of Tears*, 41–42; letter to Ross, March 21, Cherokee Nation Papers, 1843, M943-2-7, Box 2, F32, WHC/UO; McLoughlin, *Champions of the Cherokees*, 236–37.

21. *Arkansas Intelligencer*, August 19, 1843.

22. C. Foreman, "Israel G. Vore and Levering Manual Labor School," 198.

23. Senate, *Discontents and Difficulties*, 38–39.

24. Coodey letter, *Cherokee Advocate*, December 26, 1844.

25. Ibid., January 16, 1845.

26. House, *Cherokee Disturbances*, 231; *Arkansas Intelligencer*, November 15, 1845.

27. Senate, *Message of the President of the U.S. Regarding the Internal Feuds Among the Cherokees*, 262–64; House, *Cherokee Disturbances*, 230–31.

28. *Arkansas Intelligencer*, November 22, 1845.

29. Ibid.

30. House, *Cherokee Disturbances*, 185–86, 231.

31. *Arkansas Intelligencer*, March 7, 1846; McKisick to Medill, March 23, 1846, House, *Cherokee Disturbances*, 225–27.

32. *Arkansas Intelligencer*, June 27, 1846.

33. Rogers to Butler, August 1, 1843, Letters Received, OIA, Cherokee Agency (M-234), NA.

34. Starr, *Cherokees West*, 69. The story of one of the children, an Osage girl, is told by Elias Cornelius in *The Little Osage Captive*.

35. See Hoig, "Diana, Tiana or Talihina?," 52–59. Houston wrote to John Rogers on May 30, 1843, saying, "You have known me since I was a small boy." Williams and Barker, *Writings of Houston*, 3:398–99.

36. *Arkansas Intelligencer*, October 14, 1843.

37. Thomas Rogers to John Rogers, May 26, 1843, Letters Received, OIA, Cherokee Agency (M-234), NA.

38. Rogers, February 12, 1844, Letters Received, OIA, Cherokee Agency (M-234), 1844, NA.

39. Rawick, *The American Slave*, 257.

40. Senate, *Discontents and Difficulties*, 54–55.

41. *Cherokee Advocate*, December 26, 1844.

42. Senate, *Discontents and Difficulties*, 61–62.

43. Ibid., 66–67.

44. Ibid., 141–42.

45. House, *Report of Lt. Col. Hitchcock*, 6–10.

46. *Cherokee Advocate*, June 26, 1845. A detailed account of Sequoyah's journey was provided by Worm.

47. Arbuckle report, Letters Received, Office of AG, 1840, NA; Reagan, "Expulsion of Cherokees," 38–39.

48. William Minor Quesenbury Diary, 1845–1861, Manuscript Collections, University of Arkansas.

49. "Journal of Elijah Hicks," 68–99. William Shorey Coodey was a scholarly Scot-Cherokee mixed blood who had moved west in 1834. After losing his first wife, he eloped with the young daughter of Richard Fields and established a handsome home at Frozen Rock, a steamboat landing on the Arkansas River just below the mouth of the Grand. He drafted the Constitution of the Cherokee Nation in 1839 and was elected speaker of the national council. He died at Washington, D.C., in 1849 at the age of forty-three and was buried in the congressional cemetery; C. Foreman, "Coodey Family," 323–41.

50. *Daily National Intelligencer*, June 27, 1846.

51. House, *Cherokee Disturbances*, 160, 231; *Arkansas Intelligencer*, November 15, 1845.

52. Moulton, *Papers of Chief John Ross*, 2:312.

53. *Arkansas Intelligencer*, May 2, 1846; *Cherokee Advocate*, June 18, 1846;

New Orleans Picayune, June 21, 1846. A correspondent gave his impression of the Cherokee leaders who were in attendance:

There was John Ross with his Scotch face, followed by the fat, aldermanic old gentleman Richard Taylor, his genteel nephew W. S. Coodey, Walker, McNair, David Vann, Foreman, John Drew and Richard Field. Then came the treaty party, headed by a remarkably handsome man six foot high, George W. Adair, their chief, who was followed by that fierce and brave brother of the lamented Elias Boudinot, Stand Watie, John A. Bell, Joseph M. Lynch (the latter are a couple of keen merchants, neither of whom would ever be suspected of having Indian blood,) and lastly the amiable and intelligent face of the Rev. John Huss, a pure Christian, who reads and speaks his own native tongue, and no other. In this he preaches to the Indians and teaches their children.

Next came the delegation of "Old Settlers," the very finest specimens of true pioneers. They were headed by their old chiefs, John Brown and Dutch, men of remarkable bravery and unconquerable perseverance, as this controversy has proved. They were accompanied by Ellis Phillips, John L. McCoy and Richard Drew. *Arkansas Intelligencer*, September 4, 1846.

The reporter was also highly impressed with John West, a six-foot-ten-inch member of the Treaty party. But these men were not the only Indian presence in Washington that summer. A large delegation of Comanches and other Plains Indians had been brought to visit the president following the Treaty of Comanche Peak. Cherokee half blood Jesse Chisholm accompanied them as an interpreter. *Baltimore Sun*, June 27, 1846; *Daily National Intelligencer*, June 29, 1846. Dutch died at his home on November 12, 1848. *Fort Smith Herald*, November 22, 1848.

At the time of this visit, a group of George Catlin paintings were on display in the Capitol. These Indians, as well as the Cherokees, were pleased to see portraits and scenes made by Catlin while visiting their home regions twelve years earlier. Further, it so happened that even the Cherokees' old friend Sam Houston, now a U.S. Senator from Texas, was in town. *Cherokee Advocate*, August 6, 1846; *Columbian Fountain*, July 3, 1846.

54. House, *Cherokee Disturbances*, 19–29.
55. "Treaty with the Cherokees," August 6, 1846, U.S. *Statutes at Large*, IX, 8: 74–77.
56. *Cherokee Nation*, 176–77.
57. *Arkansas Intelligencer*, September 5, 1846.
58. Ibid.

Chapter 16: New Nation, Old Feuds

1. *Cherokee Advocate*, October 29, 1846.

2. See McLoughlin, *Champions of the Cherokees*, for an excellent account of the efforts made against slavery among the Cherokees by these two Baptist missionaries.

3. *Daily National Intelligencer*, September 17, 1850.

4. *Cherokee Advocate*, May 5, 1880.

5. C. Foreman, *Park Hill*, 88–108.

6. Moulton, *John Ross*, 158–59.

7. McLoughlin, *After the Trail of Tears*, 77.

8. Agnew, "Indian Territory on the Eve of the Civil War," 36.

9. Moulton, *Papers of Chief John Ross*, 2:410; *Commissioner of Indian Affairs*, 1852, 40; *Daily National Intelligencer*, November 5, 1853, citing Ross's message to the national council.

10. *Cherokee Advocate*, June 5, 1848; *Arkansas Intelligencer*, June 10, 1848.

11. *Cherokee Advocate*, June 12, 1848.

12. *Arkansas Intelligencer*, June 10, 1848; *Daily National Intelligencer*, June 29, 1848.

13. *Arkansas Intelligencer*, September 8, 1849; *Cherokee Advocate*, August 27, 1849; *Daily National Intelligencer*, November 3, 1848; *Cherokee Advocate*, November 4, 1847, July 3, 1848.

14. *Daily National Intelligencer*, September 30, 1848; *Arkansas Intelligencer*, June 10, 1848.

15. *Cherokee Advocate*, December 9, 1847.

16. *Daily National Intelligencer*, July 6, 7, 1848.

17. *Arkansas Intelligencer*, June 10, 1848.

18. *Cherokee Advocate*, November 27, 1848.

19. Ibid., April 9, May 12, 1849.

20. Ibid., October 6, 1882.

21. Ibid., January 15, 1849.

22. Ibid., February 12, 1898;

23. C. Foreman, "Edward W. Bushyhead and John Rollin Ridge," 299–311.

24. *Cherokee Advocate*, May 21, 1849.

25. Ellis, "'Our Ill-Fated Relative,'" 376–95.

26. Ibid., 388.

27. G. Foreman, *Five Civilized Tribes*, 402–3.

28. *Daily National Intelligencer*, December 2, 1850; June 26, 1851; November 23, 1852.

29. *Cherokee Advocate*, March 26, 1879.

30. *Daily National Intelligencer*, July 19, 1853.

31. Ibid., September 17, 1850, November 20, 1851.

32. Ibid., February 21, 1852.

33. Ibid., November 10, 1851, citing *Fort Smith Herald; Cherokee Advocate,* October 15, 1851.

34. Moulton, *John Ross,* 153; G. Foreman, *Five Civilized Tribes,* 407.

35. *Daily National Intelligencer,* May 3, 1853; *Commissioner of Indian Affairs,* 1853, 384.

36. *Commissioner of Indian Affairs,* 1854, 322–23.

37. G. Foreman, *Five Civilized Tribes,* 414; Moulton, *John Ross,* 160.

38. *Daily National Intelligencer,* October 8, 1853, quoting the *Arkansas Intelligencer;* Ross to Drew, September 26, 1853, Moulton, *Papers of Chief John Ross,* 2: 384–85. The *Arkansas Intelligencer* story would seem to imply the mob's anger was related to tribal politics, indicating perhaps that this was Daniel Hicks Ross, John Ross's nephew who compiled the Laws of the Cherokee Nation in 1867. However, on August 16, 1856, Chief Ross wrote to Agent Butler asking that he demand to the governor of Arkansas that Daniel Ross, who was then residing near Fayetteville, and two other men who had committed murder upon Cherokees be returned to the Cherokee Nation for trial. This appears to indicate it was not Ross's nephew. *Commissioner of Indian Affairs,* 1856, 58.

39. *Daily National Intelligencer,* October 8, 15, 18, 20, 1853; Letters Received, Cherokee Agency (M-234, M-208), 1853–54, NA.

40. *Daily National Intelligencer,* October 25, 1853; Ross to Drew, September 26, 1853, Moulton, *Papers of Chief John Ross,* 2:384–85.

41. Ross to Butler, August 16, 1856, Letters Received, OIA, Cherokee Agency (M-234), NA.

42. *Southwest Independent,* June 23, August 3, 1854; *Daily Missouri Democrat,* July 28, 1855.

43. Act of the Cherokee National Council, October 24, 1855, Letters Received, OIA, Cherokee Agency (M-234), NA.

44. Letters Received, Cherokee Agency (M-234, M-208), 1855; Letter, September 8, 1860, Letters Received, OIA, Cherokee Agency (M-234), 1860, NA; Moulton, *John Ross,* 162–63.

45. *Daily National Intelligencer,* June 3, 1847.

46. *Commissioner of Indian Affairs,* 1857, 500–501.

47. G. Foreman, *Five Civilized Tribes,* 385–86.

48. Ross to Belknap, December 12, 1850; Ross to Butler, September 8, 1851, Moulton, *Papers of Chief John Ross,* 2:344–45, 387.

49. Ross to Woodford, May 7, 1858, Moulton, *Papers of Chief John Ross,* 2:412–13.

50. Eaton, *John Ross,* 160.

51. *Commissioner of Indians Affairs,* 1857, 561

52. Ibid., 499–500.

53. Ibid., 492–94.

54. Moulton, *John Ross,* 158–59.

55. *Commissioner of Indian Affairs*, 1860, 447.

56. McLoughlin, *Champions of the Cherokees*, 346–49.

57. Hendrix, "Redbird Smith," 24.

58. McLoughlin, *After the Trail of Tears*, 155.

Chapter 17: A House Redivided

1. David Hubbard to John Ross, June 12, 1861, *Official Records* 13, 1:497–98.

2. John Ross to Henry M. Rector, February 22, 1861, *Official Records* 13, 1:491–92.

3. Ross to Hubbard, June 17, 1861, *Official Records* 13, 1:498–99.

4. Pike to Toombs, May 29, 1861, *Official Records* 4, 1:359–61.

5. *Report of Albert Pike*, 7–11.

6. Ross to Pike, July 1, 1961, Cherokee Nation Papers, M943-2-7, Box 3, F26, WHC/UO.

7. Franks, *Stand Watie*, 118.

8. *New York Times*, October 6, 1861.

9. Eaton, *John Ross*, 184.

10. Ross's address to the Cherokees, August 21, 1861, Moulton, *Papers of Chief John Ross*, 2:479–81.

11. *New York Times*, October 6, 20, 1861.

12. Thoburn, "The Cherokee Question," 175–78.

13. Ross to Chiefs and Headmen of Creek Nation, August 24, 1861; Ross to Opothle Yahola and Others, September 19, 1861, Moulton, *Papers of Chief John Ross*, 2:482, 487–88.

14. Stapler to Ross, September 25, 1861, Moulton, *Papers of Chief John Ross*, 2:488–89.

15. Adair to Watie, August 29, 1861, Cherokee Nation Papers, X, 3, WHC-UO. William Penn Adair was the son of George Washington Adair, the elder.

16. *Report of Pike*, 26–27; *Official Records* 4, 1: 669–87. Signing with Ross were assistant principal chief Joseph Verner and executive councilors James Brown, John Drew, and William P. Ross. Lewis Ross, Thomas Pegg, and Richard Field signed as special treaty commissioners.

17. Moulton, *Papers of Chief John Ross* 2: 497-99.

18. Debo, "Site of the Battle of Round Mountain, 1861," 187–206; Trickett, "Civil War in the Indian Territory," 266–80; Fischer and Franks, "Confederate Victory at Chustotalasah," 452–76.

19. Collamore to Dole, April 21, 1862, *Official Records* 2, 4:11–13.

20. McLoughlin, *After the Trail of Tears*, 195–97.

21. Moulton, *John Ross*, 173–74.

22. Ibid., 172–73; James McIntosh to S. Cooper, January 4, 1862, *Official Records* 1, 8:732.

23. In contradiction to this, Pike claimed that after the Battle of Pea Ridge, Ross had sent William P. Ross to him to say that the Cherokee chief would "be gratified to receive the appointment of Brigadier General in the Confederate service." Pike to Commissioner of Indian Affairs, February 17, 1866, Thoburn, "Cherokee Question," 178.

24. Wyman to Halleck, November 30, 1861, *Official Records* 1, 8:395–96.

25. McLoughlin, *Champions of the Cherokees*, 402.

26. *Lawrence Republican*, February 6, 1862.

27. Furnas, *National Cyclopedia of American Biography*, 12:1; Ross to Weer, July 8, 1862, Moulton, *Papers of Chief John Ross*, 2: 515–16.

28. Ibid.

29. Moulton, *John Ross*, 178–79.

30. Ross to Lincoln, September 16, 1862, Moulton, *Papers of Chief John Ross*, 2:516–18.

31. Franks, *Stand Watie*, 129–30.

32. E. P. H., *Tale of Home and War*, 120.

33. Stand Watie to Sarah Watie, November 12, 1863, Cherokee Papers, WHC/UO.

34. 1860 Census Slave Schedule, Arkansas plus the Indian Territory West of Arkansas, 26, OHS/LIB. Ross was one of the largest slaveholders in the Cherokee Nation with fifty-one slaves and eleven slave houses.

35. C. Foreman, *Park Hill*, 123.

36. Confer, "Indian Territory Homefront," 110–16.

37. Report from Fort Gibson, December 7, 1863, Letters Received, OIA, Cherokee Agency (M-234), NA.

38. Smith to Pike, April 8, 1865, *Official Records* 48, 2:1267.

39. Adair to Maxey, February 5, 1865, *Official Records* 1, 34:945–46.

40. *Cherokee Advocate*, November 10, 1880.

41. *Official Records* 1, 48, 2:1102–3; Lewis, "Camp Napoleon," 359–64.

42. *Indian Chieftain*, October 2, 1890; Cherokee Nation Papers, M943-1-30, F45, WHC/OU, citing *National Illustrated Magazine* 1 (1884): 169–73.

43. Speer and Brown, *Encyclopedia of the New West*, Indian Territory section, 9–10; Moulton, *Papers of Chief John Ross*, 2:717.

44. Meserve, "Chief William Potter Ross," 21–29. Ross, *Life and Times*; Moulton, *Papers of Chief John Ross*, 2:734–35.

45. Meserve, "Chief Lewis Downing and Chief Charles Thompson (Oochalata)," 317–18; Moulton, *Papers of Chief John Ross*, 2:720–21. Downing's personal life is interesting for its romantic aspects. After his first Cherokee wife, Lydia Price, died, Downing married Lucinda Griffin, also a Cherokee, and by her had several children. During his many trips to Washington he met and had an affair with a wealthy widow named Mary

Eyre. Though she knew Downing was married and had a family, she moved to Tahlequah and patiently bided her time. Eventually Lucinda died, and after a time, two years before his death, Downing and the persistent widow were married.

Chapter 18: Resisting Dissolution

1. McLoughlin, *After the Trail of Tears*, 212.

2. Moulton, *Papers of Chief John Ross* 2: 649.

3. Confer, "Indian Territory Homefront," 114–16.

4. Moulton, *John Ross*, 180.

5. *Commissioner of Indian Affairs, 1865*, 304; Abel, *American Indian under Reconstruction*, 198–200.

6. *Commissioner of Indian Affairs, 1865*, 306; *Daily National Intelligencer*, October 5, 1865.

7. *Commissioner of Indian Affairs, 1865*, 308; *Daily National Intelligencer*, October 25, 1865. See also *Communication of the Delegation of the Cherokee Nation*.

8. *Daily National Intelligencer*, November 18, 1865.

9. Moulton, *Papers of Chief John Ross*, 2:665–67.

10. Ridge to Watie, September 22, 1853, Cherokee Nation Papers, M943-2-1-B, Box 1, F9, WHC/OU.

11. Ellis, "'Our Ill-Fated Relative,'" 388–90.

12. Ibid., 391.

13. *Daily National Intelligencer*, August 2, 4, 1866.

14. Ibid., November 7, 1866; Ross, *Life and Times*, 7-8.

15. Kappler, *Indian Treaties*, 942–50, 996–97.

16. Ross, *Life and Times*, 55–57.

17. *Cherokee Advocate*, June 18, 1870.

18. Ibid., October 22, 1870; August 3, 1872.

19. Wardell, *Political History*, 307; G. Foreman, "The Tragedy of Going Snake Court House"; Littlefield, *Cherokee Freedmen*, 42–43.

20. U.S. Supreme Court Reports, 20, 227–30; *Cherokee Advocate*, October 21, 1871; April 29, 1876; Speer and Brown, *Encyclopedia of the New West*, Indian Territory section, 9–10.

21. *Cherokee Advocate*, October 22, 1870.

22. Ibid.

23. Ibid., March 2, 1872, citing the *Neosho Journal*.

24. *Van Buren Press*, November 19, 26, 1872; Meserve, "Downing and Thompson," 321. Meserve incorrectly gives Downing's date of death as November 9, 1872.

25. Ibid., December 24, 1872.

26. *Cherokee Advocate*, January 10, May 11, 1878.

27. Littlefield, *Cherokee Freedmen*, 80.

28. McLoughlin, *After the Trail of Tears*, 301–2.

29. Ibid.

30. Meserve, "Downing and Thompson," 322.

31. *Cherokee Advocate*, June 10, 1876.

32. Littlefield, *Cherokee Freedmen*, 87–88. In its November 9, 1878, issue the Cherokee Advocate noted that Chief Thompson had raised eight thousand bushels of corn, plus crops of sweet potatoes and Irish potatoes, and commented, "He is a good farmer as well as a good chief."

33. McLoughlin, *After the Trail of Tears*, 357–58.

Chapter 19: An End to Sovereignty

1. Hoig, *David L. Payne*, 187–206.

2. *Cherokee Advocate*, September 5, 1884.

3. Ibid, February 12, 1898; Meserve, "Chief Dennis Wolfe Bushyhead," 349–59.

4. *Cherokee Advocate*, September 22, 1880.

5. Ibid., November 4, 1879.

6. Ibid., April 20, 1879.

7. Meserve, "Bushyhead," 356–57. In "Problems of a Cherokee Chief," Keith outlines some of the problems of Bushyhead's constituency, as revealed by his correspondence.

8. Meserve, "Bushyhead," 355–56.

9. *Indian Chieftain*, June 18, 1885; Wardell, *Political History*, 341.

10. Ibid., 344.

11. *Tahlequah Telephone*, May 21, 1891. During the 1887 Mayes-Bunch election contest, editor B. H. Stone of the *Telephone* made some derogatory remarks about Elias C. Boudinot, editor of the *Cherokee Advocate*, which supported Bunch and the National party. The incensed Boudinot, son of William P. Boudinot and nephew to Col. Elias C. Boudinot, purchased a pistol at a hardware store and went to Stone's office. When Stone refused his demand for an apology, he shot the editor in his chair and killed him. Boudinot escaped punishment on the claim that Stone had made a move for his gun.

12. *Tahlequah Telephone*, March 1, 1889.

13. Ibid., June 11, 1891. This figure was later enlarged to $50,000 by a man who claimed he had personally witnessed Mayes's rejection of the offer. *Fort Gibson Post*, October 21, 1897.

14. *Indian Chieftain*, October 2, 1890.

15. Ibid., December 17, 1891.

16. Ibid.

17. Wardell, *Political History*, 345.

18. Dewitz, *Notable Men of the Indian Territory*, 74.

19. Meserve, "Chief Colonel Johnson Harris," 17–21.

20. *Indian Chieftain*, December 14, 21, 28, 1893; January 11, 18, 1894.

21. Ibid., February 15, 1894.

22. Ibid., March 8, 1894.

23. Ibid., June 21, August 30, 1894.

24. Ibid., September 13, 1894.

25. Wardell, *Political History*, 315, citing Senate, *First Annual Report of the Dawes Commission*, 90.

26. *Indian Chieftain*, December 27, 1894.

27. Dewitz, *Notable Men*, 73.

28. *Indian Chieftain*, November 28, 1895.

29. Ibid., February 13, 1896.

30. Ibid., August 13, 1896.

31. Senate, *Report of Payment of Cherokee Freedmen*; *Indian Chieftain*, November 21, 1895, December 9, 1897; Littlefield, *Cherokee Freedmen*, 190–96.

32. Senate, *Report of Payment of Cherokee Freedmen*; *Indian Chieftain*, December 16, 30, 1897.

33. *Indian Chieftain*, November 10, 1898.

34. Ibid., August 10, 1899; Meserve, "Chief Thomas Mitchell Buffington and Chief William Charles Rogers," 135–40.

35. *Fort Gibson Post*, August 31, 1899, January 11, 1900.

36. Ibid., May 7, August 11, 1898.

37. *Cherokee Advocate*, November 14, 1901.

38. Ibid., December 26, 1901, February 20, 1902.

Chapter 20: The Fourth Phoenix

1. Caywood, "Administration of William C. Rogers," 29–37.

2. *Purcell Register*, June 23, 1893.

3. Meserve, "Chiefs Buffington and Rogers," 140–46.

4. Wardell, *Political History*, 348–49.

5. Litton, "Principal Chiefs," 270.

6. Lowe, "W. W. Keeler," 116–29.

7. West, *Among the Cherokees*, 149–50.

8. *Daily Oklahoman*, August 4, 1975.

Afterword: Those Who Stayed Behind

1. *Daily National Intelligencer*, November 17, 19, 1838.

2. Forster to Scott, November 15, 1838, House, *Capture of Reputed*

Indian Refugees. Report of General Scott, November 6, 1838, as published by the *Daily National Intelligencer*, November 19, 1838. One officer, who considered the refugee Cherokees to be outlaws, rather curiously claimed that he would use the Indian runners only to bear invitations of kindness, "deeming it against the honor of the United States to employ, in hostilities, one part of the tribe against another."

3. Report of Lt. A. J. Smith, November 5, 1838, as published by the *Daily National Intelligencer*, November 19, 1838.

4. Finger, *Eastern Band of Cherokees*, 26–27.

5. Ibid., 11–19.

6. Ibid., 24.

7. Gulick, *Cherokees at the Crossroads*, 14–15.

8. Finger, *Eastern Band of Cherokees*, 102–3.

9. Carrington, "Eastern Band of Cherokees," 18; Mooney, *Myths*, 173.

10. Carrington, "Eastern Band of Cherokees," 19–20; Litton, "Principal Chiefs of the Cherokee Nation," 253–70.

11. Finger, *Eastern Band of Cherokees*, 108–11.

12. Ibid., 118–21.

13. Ibid., 115–16.

14. Litton, "Principal Chiefs," 259.

15. Finger, *Eastern Band of Cherokees*, 131.

16. Ibid., 139–40.

17. Ibid., 152–71.

18. The Eastern chiefs in succession were Stilwell Saunooke, 1891–95; Andy Standing Deer, 1895–99; Jesse Reed, 1899–1903; Bird Saloloneeta, 1903–7; John G. Welch, 1907–11; Joseph A. Saunooke, 1911–15; David Blythe, 1915–19; Joseph A. Saunooke, 1919–23; Sampson Owl, 1923–27; John A. Tahquette, 1927–31; Jarrett Blythe, 1931–39.

Bibliography

Books

Abel, Annie Heloise. *The American Indian under Reconstruction.* Vol. 3 of *The Slaveholding Indians.* Cleveland: Arthur H. Clark, 1919.

Adair, James. *The History of the American Indians.* London, 1775; reprint with introduction by Robert F. Berkhofer Jr. Johnson, New York: Reprint Corp., 1968.

Allen, John Richard. *Robert Dinwiddie: Servant of the Crown.* Williamsburg: Colonial Williamsburg Foundation, 1973.

Alvord, Clarence Walworth, and Lee Bidgood. *The First Explorations of the Trans-Allegheny Region by the Virginians, 1650–1674.* Cleveland: Arthur H. Clark, 1912.

Anderson, William L., ed. *Cherokee Removal, Before and After.* Athens: University of Georgia Press, 1991.

Appleton's Annual Cyclopedia and Register of Important Events. New York: Appleton, 1862–1903.

Baker, DeWitt C. *A Texas Scrapbook.* New York: A.S. Barnes and Co., 1875.

Baker, Jack D., trans. *Cherokee Emigration Rolls, 1817–1835.* Oklahoma City: Baker Publishing, 1977.

Barker, Eugene C., ed. *The Austin Papers.* Austin: University of Texas Press, 1927.

———. *The Life of Stephen F. Austin, Founder of Texas.* Austin: Texas State Historical Association, 1949.

Bartram, William. *Travels in North America.* New Haven: Yale University Press, 1958.

Battles and Leaders of the Civil War. New York: Castle Books, 1956.

Bourne, Edward Gaylord. *Narratives of the Career of Hernando de Soto in the Conquest of Florida, As Told by a Knight of Elvas.* 2 vols. New York: Allerton Book Co., 1922.

Brown, John Henry. *Indian Wars and Pioneers of Texas.* Austin: L. E. Daniel, Publisher, 1890.

Brown, John P. *Old Frontiers, the Story of the Cherokee Indians from Earliest Times to the Date of Their Removal to the West, 1838.* Kingsport, Tenn.: Southern Publishers, 1938.

Carselowey, James Monford. *Cherokee Pioneers*. Adair, Okla.: n.p., 1961.

Carter, Samuel, III. *Cherokee Sunset: A Nation Betrayed*. New York: Doubleday & Co., 1976.

Chase, Marybelle W., comp. *1842 Cherokee Claims, Skin Bayou District*. Nashville: n.p., 1988.

Claiborne, J. F. H. *Life and Times of Gen. Sam. Dale, the Mississippi Partisan*. New York: Harper & Brothers, 1860.

Clarke, Mary Whatley. *Chief Bowles and the Texas Cherokees*. Norman: University of Oklahoma Press, 1971.

Coombs, *The Dawn of the Millennium*. New York: F. Combs, 1869.

Corkran, David H. *The Cherokee Frontier: Conflict and Survival, 1740–1762*. Norman: University of Oklahoma Press, 1962.

Cornelius, Elias. *Little Osage Captive, an Authentic Narrative*. Boston: S. T. Armstrong and Crocker & Brewster; New York: J. P. Haven, 1822.

Cotterill, R. S. *The Southern Indians*. Norman: University of Oklahoma Press, 1954.

Debo, Angie. *The Road to Disappearance*. Norman: University of Oklahoma Press, 1941.

De Brahm, William Gerard. *Philosophico-Historico-Hydrogeography of South Carolina, Georgia, and Florida*. In *Documents Connected with the History of South Carolina*., edited by Plowden Charles Jennett Weston. London: 1856.

DeShields, James T. *Border Wars of Texas*. Tioga, Tex.: Hearld Co., 1912.

Dewitz, Paul W. H. *Notable Men of the Indian Territory*. Muskogee, Okla.: Southwestern Historical Co., 1906.

Dickens, Roy S., Jr. *Cherokee Prehistory: The Pisgah Phase in the Appalachian Summit Region*. Knoxville: University of Tennessee Press, 1976.

Drake, Samuel G. *Biography and History of the Indians of North America*. Boston: O. L. Perkins and Hillary Gray & Co., 1834.

E. P. H., substantially written by Rev. Worcester Willey and revised by Mrs. E. P. Howland. *A Tale of Home and War*. Portland, Maine: Brown Thurston Co., 1888.

Eaton, Rachel Caroline. *John Ross and the Cherokee Indians*. Menasha, Wisc.: Collegiate Press, George Banta Publishing Co., 1914.

Ehle, John. *Trail of Tears: The Rise and Fall of the Cherokee Nation*. New York: Doubleday, 1988.

Everett, Dianna. *The Texas Cherokees: A People between Two Fires, 1819–1840*. Norman: University of Oklahoma Press, 1990.

Featherstonhaugh, G. W. *A Canoe Voyage of the Minnay Sotor*. 2 vols. London: Richard Bentley Publisher, 1847.

Finger, John R. *The Eastern Band of Cherokees, 1819–1900*. Knoxville: University of Tennessee Press, 1984.

Flint, Timothy. *Recollections of the Last Ten Years Passed in Occasional*

Residences and Journeyings in the Valley of the Mississippi. Boston: Cummings, Hilliard and Co., 1826.

Foote, Henry Stuart. *Texas and the Texans.* Philadelphia: Thomas, Cowperthwait & Co., 1841.

Foreman, Carolyn. *Indian Women Chiefs.* Muskogee, Okla.: n.p., 1954.

— — —. *Indians Abroad.* Norman: University of Oklahoma Press, 1943.

— — —. *Park Hill.* Muskogee, Okla.: Star Printing Co., 1948.

Foreman, Grant. *The Five Civilized Tribes.* Norman: University of Oklahoma Press, 1934.

— — —. *Indian Removal: The Emigration of the Five Civilized Tribes of Indians.* Norman: University of Oklahoma Press, 1953.

— — —. *Indians and Pioneers.* New Haven: Yale University Press, 1930.

— — —. *The Last Trek of the Indians.* Chicago: University of Chicago Press, 1946.

Franks, Kenny A. *Stand Watie and the Agony of the Cherokee Nation.* Memphis: Memphis State University Press, 1979.

Gabriel, Henry Ralph. *Elias Boudinot, Cherokee, and His America.* Norman: University of Oklahoma Press, 1941.

Green, Michael D. *The Politics of Indian Removal, Creek Government and Society in Crisis.* Lincoln: University of Nebraska Press, 1982.

Gregory, Jack, and Rennard Strickland. *Sam Houston with the Cherokees, 1829–1833.* Austin: University of Texas Press, 1967.

Gulick, Charles A., Jr., Winnie Allen, Katherine Elliott, and Harriet Smither, eds. *The Papers of Mirabeau Buonaparte Lamar.* 6 vols. Austin: Pemberton Press, 1968.

Gulick, John. *Cherokees at the Crossroads.* Chapel Hill: University of North Carolina Press, 1960.

The Handbook of Texas History. 3 vols. Ed. by Walter Prescott Webb and Eldon Stephen Branda. Austin: Texas State Historical Association, 1952–76.

Harper, Francis. *The Travels of William Bartram.* New Haven: Yale University Press, 1958.

Haywood, John. *The Civil and Political History of the State of Tennessee.* Nashville: House of the Methodist Episcopal Church, South, 1915.

Hitchcock, Ethan Allen. *A Traveler in Indian Territory.* Edited by Grant Foreman. Cedar Rapids: The Torch Press, 1930.

Hodge, Frederick W. *Handbook of American Indians North of Mexico.* Bureau of American Ethnology *Bulletin* 30. 2 pts. Washington: GPO, 1905.

Hoig, Stan. *David L. Payne: The Oklahoma Boomer.* Oklahoma City: Western Heritage Books, 1980.

— — —. *Night of the Cruel Moon: Cherokee Removal and the Trail of Tears.* New York: Facts on File, 1996.

— — —. *Sequoyah, the Cherokee Genius*. Oklahoma City: Oklahoma
    Historical Society, 1995.

Horsman, Reginald. *Race and Manifest Destiny*. Cambridge and London:
    Harvard University Press, 1981.

James, Edwin. *Account of an Expedition from Pittsburgh to the Rocky Mountains*.
    2 vols. Ann Arbor, Mich.: University Microfilms, 1966.

James, Marquis. *The Raven*. Indianapolis: Bobbs-Merrill, 1929.

Kappler, Charles J., comp. and ed. *Indian Treaties, 1778–1883*. New York:
    Interland Publishing, 1972.

King, Duane H., ed. *The Cherokee Nation: A Troubled History*. Knoxville:
    University of Tennessee Press, 1979.

Landrum, J. B. O. *Colonial and Revolutionary History of Upper South Carolina*.
    Greenville, S.C.: S. C. Shannon, 1897; reprint, Spartanburg, S. C.:
    Spartanburg Reprint Co., 1959.

Lewis, Thomas M. N., and Madeline Kneberg. *Hiwassee Island, An
    Archaeological Account of Four Tennessee Indian Peoples*. Knoxville:
    University of Tennessee Press, 1946.

Littlefield, Daniel F. *The Cherokee Freedmen: From Emancipation to American
    Citizenship*. Westport, Conn.: Greenwood Press, 1978.

Logan, John M. *History of the Upper Country of South Carolina from the Earliest
    Periods to the Close of the War of Independence*. Charleston: S. G.
    Courtenay & Co., 1859.

McKenney, Thomas L., and James Hall. *The Indian Tribes of North America*.
    Edited by Frederick Webb Hodge. 3 vols. Totowa, N.J.: Rowman and
    Littlefield, 1972.

McLean, Malcom D., comp. and ed. *Papers Concerning Robertson's Colony in
    Texas, 1823 through September 1826*. 2 vols. Fort Worth: Texas
    Christian University Press, 1975.

McLoughlin, William G. *After the Trail of Tears: The Cherokees' Struggle for
    Sovereignty, 1839–1880*. Chapel Hill: University of North Carolina
    Press, 1993.

— — —. *Champions of the Cherokees: Evan and John B. Jones*. Princeton:
    Princeton University Press, 1990.

— — —. *Cherokee Renascence in the New Republic, 1794–1833*. Princeton:
    Princeton University Press, 1986.

— — —. *Cherokees and Missionaries, 1789–1839*. New Haven: Yale University
    Press, 1984.

Malone, Henry Thompson. *Cherokees of the Old South: A People in Transition*.
    Athens: University of Georgia Press, 1956.

Milling, Chapman J. *Red Carolinians*. Columbia: University of South
    Carolina Press, 1969.

Monette, John Welsey. *History of the Discovery and Settlement of the Valley of
    the Mississippi*. 2 vols. New York: Harper & Bros., 1846.

Mooney, James. *Historical Sketch of the Cherokee.* Chicago: Smithsonian
Institution Press, 1975.

— — —. *Myths of the Cherokees and Sacred Formulas of the Cherokees.*
Nineteenth and Seventy-Seventh Annual Reports of the BAE. Nashville:
Charles Elder, 1972 reproduction.

Moore, Jack. *The Killough Massacre.* Jacksonville, Tex.: Kiely Printing Co,
1966.

Morse, Jedidiah. *Narrative of a Tour by the Rev. Jedidiah Morse in the Summer of
1820.* New Haven: S. Converse (Printer), 1822.

Moulton, Gary E. *John Ross, Cherokee Chief.* Athens: University of Georgia
Press, 1978.

— — —, ed., *The Papers of Chief John Ross.* 2 vols. Norman: University of
Oklahoma Press, 1985.

National Cyclopedia of American Biography. 50 vols. Ann Arbor: University
Reprints, 1967-71.

Nuttall, Thomas. *Nuttall's Journal of Travels into the Arkansas Territory,
October 2, 1818–February 18, 1820.* Vol. 18, *Early Western Travels,*
edited by Reuben Gold Thwaites. Cleveland: Arthur H. Clark Co.,
1904–7.

Odell, Marcia Parson. *Divide and Conquer: Allotment among the Cherokees.*
New York: Arno Press, 1979.

Owen, Narcissa. *Memoirs of Narcissa Owen.* Washington: Private Printing,
1907.

Parins, James W. *John Rollin Ridge, His Life and Works.* Lincoln: University of
Nebraska Press, 1991.

Perdue, Theda, ed. *Cherokee Editor: The Writings of Elias Boudinot.* Knoxville:
University of Tennessee Press, 1983.

*Proceedings, War and Reconstruction in Indian Territory: A History Conference
in Observance of the 130th Anniversary of the Fort Smith Council.* Fort
Smith, Ark.: National Park Service, Oklahoma Historical Society,
Arkansas Historical Association, 1995.

Ramsey, J. G. M. *The Annals of Tennessee, 1797–1884.* Kingsport, Tenn.:
Kingsport Press, 1853.

Rawick, George P. *The American Slave: A Composite Autobiography.* Westport,
Conn.: Greenwood Publishing Co., 1972.

Reagan, John H. *Memoirs.* Edited by Walter F. McCaleb. New York: Neale
Publishing Co., 1906.

Reid, John Phillip. *A Law of Blood: The Primitive Law of the Cherokee Nation.*
New York: New York University Press, 1970.

Report of Albert Pike on Mission to the Indian Nations, Richmond, 1861.
Facsimile reprint by order of The Supreme Council, 33 (degree), A.&
A.S.R., S.J., U.S.A. Washington, D.C., 1968.

Ross, Mrs. William P., ed. *The Life and Times of Honorable William P. Ross of the Cherokee Nation*. Fort Smith, Ark.: Weldon & Williams, Printers, 1893.

Royce, Charles C. *The Cherokee Nation of Indians*. Chicago: Smithsonian Institution Press, 1975.

Serrano y Sanz, Manuel. *Spain and the Cherokee and Choctaw Indians in the Second Half of the Eighteenth Century*. Translated and Annotated by Samuel Dorris Dickinson; edited by Mary Herron. Sevilla: Tip. de la Guia Official, 1916; reprint in English, Idabel, Okla.: Museum of the Red River, 1995.

Speer, William, and John Henry Brown, eds. *Encyclopedia of the New West*. Marshall, Tex.: The U.S. Biographical Publishing Co., 1881.

Starkey, Marion L. *The Cherokee Nation*. New York: Russell & Russell, 1946.

Starr, Emmet. *Cherokees West, 1794–1839*. Claremore, Okla.: Emmet Starr, 1910.

———. *History of the Cherokee Indians*. Millwood, N.Y.: Warden Co., 1921.

Strickland, Rennard. *Fire and the Spirits: Cherokee Law from Clan to Court*. Norman: University of Oklahoma Press, 1975.

Walam Olum or Red Score, the Migration Legend of the Lenni Lenape or Delaware Indians. Indianapolis: Indiana Historical Society, 1954.

Wardell, Morris L. *A Political History of the Cherokee Nation, 1838–1907*. Reprint, Norman: University of Oklahoma Press, 1938.

Washburn, Cephas. *Reminiscences of the Indians*. Van Buren, Ark.: Press-Argus, 1955.

West, C. W. Dub. *Among the Cherokees*. Muskogee, Okla.: Muscogee Publishing Co., 1981.

Wilbarger, J. W. *Indian Depredations in Texas*. Austin: Steck Co., 1935.

Wiley, Worcester. *A Tale of Home and War*. Portland, Maine: Brown, Thurston & Co., 1888.

Wilkins, Thurman. *Cherokee Tragedy: The Story of the Ridge Family and the Decimation of a People*. New York: Macmillan, 1970.

Williams, Amelia W., and Eugene C. Barker, eds. *The Writings of Sam Houston, 1793–1863*. 8 vols. Austin: University of Texas Press, 1938–43.

Williams, Samuel Cole. *Dawn of the Tennessee Valley and Tennessee History*. Johnson City, Tenn.: Watauga Press, 1937.

———. *Early Travels in the Tennessee Country, 1540–1800*. Johnson City, Tenn.: Watauga Press, 1928.

———. *Henry Timberlake's Memoirs, 1756–1765*. Marietta, Ga.: Continental Book Co., 1948.

———. *History of the Lost State of Franklin*. New York: Press of the Pioneer, 1933.

— — —. *Tennessee during the Revolutionary War*. Nashville: Tennessee Historical Commission, 1944.

Williamson, Peter. *The Life and Astonishing Adventures of Peter Williamson*. Fairfield, Wash.: Ye Galleon Press, 1978.

Winfrey, Dorman, and James W. Day. *The Texas Indian Papers, 1825–1843*. 4 vols. Austin: Texas State Library, 1959.

Winkler, Ernest William, ed. *Secret Journals of the Senate, Republic of Texas, 1836–1845*. Austin: Austin Printing Co., 1911.

Woodward, Grace Steele. *The Cherokees*. Norman: University of Oklahoma Press, 1963.

Yoakum, Henderson. *History of Texas, from Its First Settlement in 1685 to Its Annexation to the United States in 1846*. 2 vols. New York: J. S. Redfield, 1855.

Articles

Abel, Annie Heloise. "Cherokee Negotiations of 1822." *Smith College Studies in History* 1 (July 1916): 188–221.

Agnew, Brad. "Indian Territory on the Eve of the Civil War." In *Proceedings, War and Reconstruction in Indian Territory: A History Conference in Observance of the 130th Anniversary of the Fort Smith Council*, 35–40. Fort Smith, Ark.: National Park Service, Oklahoma Historical Society, Arkansas Historical Association, 1995.

"The Battle of the Horseshoe as Told by the Cherokees." *Wheeler's Daily Independent*, May 2, 1873.

Bearss, Edwin C. "The Civil War in Indian Territory and the Fort Smith Council." In *Proceedings, War and Reconstruction in Indian Territory: A History Conference in Observance of the 130th Anniversary of the Fort Smith Council*, 5–10. Fort Smith, Ark.: National Park Service, Oklahoma Historical Society, Arkansas Historical Association, 1995.

Bloom, Leonard. "The Acculturation of the Eastern Cherokee: Historical Aspects." *North Carolina Historical Review* 19 (October 1942): 323–58.

Boeger, Palmer H. "The Indians' Decision to Go with the South in the Civil War." In *Proceedings, War and Reconstruction in Indian Territory: A History Conference in Observance of the 130th Anniversary of the Fort Smith Council*, 41–49. Fort Smith, Ark.: National Park Service, Oklahoma Historical Society, Arkansas Historical Association, 1995.

Bringier, L. "Notices of the Geology, Mineralogy, Topography, Productions, and Aboriginal Inhabitants of the Regions around the Mississippi and Its Confluent Waters." *American Journal of Science and Arts* 3 (1821): 15–46.

Brown, John P. "Eastern Cherokee Chiefs." *Chronicles of Oklahoma* 16 (March 1938): 3–35.

Carrington, Henry B. "Eastern Band of Cherokees." *Eleventh Census of the United States, 1890: Extra Census Bulletin.* Washington, D.C.: GPO, 1892, 11–21.

Carter, Kent. "Deciding Who Can Be Cherokee." *Chronicles of Oklahoma* 49 (summer 1991): 174–205.

Caywood, Elzie Ronald. "The Administration of William C. Rogers, Principal Chief of the Cherokee Nation, 1903–1907." *Chronicles of Oklahoma* 30 (spring 1952): 29–37.

Confer, Clarissa. "Indian Territory Homefront: The Cherokee Nation in 1862." In *Proceedings, War and Reconstruction in Indian Territory: A History Conference in Observance of the 130th Anniversary of the Fort Smith Council,* 110–17. Fort Smith, Ark.: National Park Service, Oklahoma Historical Society, Arkansas Historical Association, 1995.

Corkran, David H. "Cherokee Pre-History." *North Carolina Historical Review* 34 (October 1957): 455–66.

Dale, E. E. "Additional Letters of General Stand Watie." *Chronicles of Oklahoma* 1 (October 1921): 131–49.

Debo, Angie. "The Site of the Battle of Round Mountain, 1861." *Chronicles of Oklahoma* 27 (summer 1949): 187–206.

De Filipis, M., ed. "An Italian Account of Cherokee Uprisings at Fort Loudoun and Fort Prince George, 1760–1761." *North Carolina Historical Review* 20 (July 1943): 247–58.

Ellis, Clyde. "'Our Ill-Fated Relative': John Rollin Ridge and the Cherokee People." *Chronicles of Oklahoma* 48 (winter 1990–91): 376–95.

Evans, E. Raymond. "Notable Persons in Cherokee History: Dragging Canoe." *Journal of Cherokee Studies* 2 (winter 1977): 176–89.

———. "Notable Persons in Cherokee History: Ostenaco." *Journal of Cherokee Studies* 1 (summer 1976): 41–54.

Evans, E. Raymond, and Duane H. King. "Historic Document of the Grant Expedition Against the Cherokees." *Journal of Cherokee Studies* 2 (summer 1977): 272–96.

Fischer, LeRoy H., and Kenny Franks. "Confederate Victory at Chustotalasah." *Chronicles of Oklahoma* 49 (winter 1971–72): 452–76.

Foreman, Carolyn Thomas. "The Cherokee War Path." *Chronicles of Oklahoma* 9 (September 1931): 233–62.

———. "The Coodey Family of Indian Territory." *Chronicles of Oklahoma* 25 (winter 1947–48): 323–41.

———. "Edward W. Bushyhead and John Rollin Ridge, Cherokee Editors in California." *Chronicles of Oklahoma* 14 (September 1936): 295–311.

———. "Israel G. Vore and Levering Manual Labor School." *Chronicles of Oklahoma* 25 (autumn 1947): 198–217.

Foreman, Grant. "John Howard Payne and the Cherokee Indians." *American Historical Review* 37 (July 1932): 723–30.

— — —. "The Murder of Elias Boudinot." *Chronicles of Oklahoma* 12 (March 1934): 19–24.

— — —. "The Tragedy of Going Snake Court House." *The Daily Oklahoman*, October 7, 1934.

— — —. "The Trial of Stand Watie." *Chronicles of Oklahoma* 12 (September 1934): 305–39.

— — —, ed. "Journey of a Party of Cherokee Emigrants." *Mississippi Valley Historical Review* 28 (September 1931): 232–45.

Goodpasture, Albert W. "Indian Wars and Warriors of the Old Southwest, 1730–1807." *Tennessee Historical Magazine* 4 (March, June, September, December 1918): 3–49, 106–45, 161–210, 252–89.

Hames, P. M. "Anglo-French Rivalry in the Cherokee Country, 1754–1757." *North Carolina Historical Review* 2 (July 1925): 303–22.

— — —. "Fort Loudoun in the Cherokee War, 1758–1761." *North Carolina Historical Review* 2 (October 1925): 442–58.

Hendrix, Janey B. "Redbird Smith and the Nighthawk Keetoowahs." *Journal of Cherokee Studies* 8 (spring 1983): 22–39.

Hoig, Stan. "Diana, Tiana or Talihina?" *Chronicles of Oklahoma* 44 (summer 1986): 53–59.

— — —. "The Genealogy of Jesse Chisholm." *Chronicles of Oklahoma* 47 (summer 1989): 194–205.

"The Journal of Elijah Hicks." *Chronicles of Oklahoma* 13 (March 1935): 68–99.

Keith, Harold. "Problems of a Cherokee Chief." *Chronicles of Oklahoma* 17 (September 1939): 296–308.

Kelly, James C. "Notable Persons in Cherokee History: Attakullakulla." *Journal of Cherokee Studies* 3 (winter 1978): 2–34.

— — —. "Oconostota." *Journal of Cherokee Studies* 3 (fall 1979): 221–38.

King, Duane H., and E. Raymond Evans. "The Death of John Walker, Jr." *Journal of Cherokee Studies* 1 (summer 1976): 4–16.

King, Duane H., and Danny E. Olinger. "Oconastota." *American Antiquity* 37 (April 1972): 222–28.

Lester, Charles. *Sam Houston and His Republic.* New York: Burgess, Stringer, 1846.

Lewis, Anna. "Camp Napoleon." *Chronicles of Oklahoma* 9 (December 1931): 359–64.

Littlefield, Daniel F. "The Treaties of 1866: Reconstruction or Re-Destruction?" In *Proceedings, War and Reconstruction in Indian Territory: A History Conference in Observance of the 130th Anniversary of the Fort Smith Council,* 97–109. Fort Smith, Ark.: National Park Service, Oklahoma Historical Society, Arkansas Historical Association, 1995.

Litton, Gaston L. "The Principal Chiefs of the Cherokee Nation." *Chronicles of Oklahoma* 15 (September 1937): 253–70.

Lowe, Marjorie J. "W. W. Keeler and Cherokee Removal." *Chronicles of Oklahoma* 74 (summer 1996): 116–29.

Lowery, George. "Notable Persons in Cherokee History: Sequoyah or George Gist." *Journal of Cherokee Studies* 2, no. 4 (fall 1877). Introduction and transcription by John Howard Payne.

McLoughlin, William G. "Jefferson and Cherokee Nationalism, 1806–1809." *William and Mary Quarterly* 32 (October 1975): 547–80.

———. "New Angles of Vision on the Cherokee Ghost Dance Movement." *American Indian Quarterly* 5 (1979): 317–45.

McLoughlin, William G., and Walter H. Conser Jr. "The Cherokees in Transition: A Statistical Analysis of the Federal Census of 1835." *Journal of American History* 44 (December 1977): 678–703.

Meserve, John Bartlett. "Chief Colonel Johnson Harris." *Chronicles of Oklahoma* 17 (March 1939): 17–21.

———. "Chief Dennis Wolfe Bushyhead." *Chronicles of Oklahoma* 14 (September 1936): 349–59.

———. "Chief Lewis Downing and Chief Charles Thompson (Oochalata)." *Chronicles of Oklahoma* 16 (September 1938): 315–25.

———. "Chief Thomas Mitchell Buffington and Chief William Charles Rogers." *Chronicles of Oklahoma* 17 (June 1939): 135–46.

——— "Chief William Potter Ross." *Chronicles of Oklahoma* 15 (March 1937): 21–29.

———. "The Mayes." *Chronicles of Oklahoma* 15 (March 1937): 56–65.

Mooney, James. "Cherokee Mound-Building." *The American Anthropologist* 2 (April 1889): 167–71.

Moulton, Gary E. "John Ross and the 1865 Fort Smith Council." In *Proceedings, War and Reconstruction in Indian Territory: A History Conference in Observance of the 130th Anniversary of the Fort Smith Council*, 92–95. Fort Smith, Ark.: National Park Service, Oklahoma Historical Society, Arkansas Historical Association, 1995.

Muckleroy, Anna. "The Indian Policy of the Republic of Texas." *Southwestern Historical Quarterly* 25 (April 1922): 229–60; 26 (July 1922): 1–29; 26 (October 1922): 128–48; 26 (January 1923): 184–206.

Peters, Richard. "The Case of the Cherokee Indians against the State of Georgia." *American Quarterly Review* (March 1832): 2–30.

Reagan, John H. "The Expulsion of the Cherokees from East Texas." *Quarterly of the Texas Historical Association* 1 (1897): 38–46.

Reid, William S., ed. "Extracts from the Diary of W. Y. Allen, 1838–39." *Southwestern Historical Quarterly* 17 (July 1913): 43–60.

Swanton, John R. "The Indians of the Southeastern United States." Bureau of American Ethnology *Bulletin 137*: Washington, GPO, 1946.

Thoburn, Joseph B. "The Cherokee Question." *Chronicles of Oklahoma* 2 (June 1924): 175–78.

Thornton, Russell. "Cherokee Population Losses during the Trail of Tears: A New Perspective and a New Estimate." *Ethnohistory* 31 (1984): 289–300.

"A Treaty between Virginia and the Catawbas and Cherokees." *Virginia Magazine of History and Biography* 13 (January 1906): 225–64.

"Treaty of Peace and Friendship, December 26, 1759." *London Magazine*, February 1760, 144–45.

"Treaty with the Cherokees at Lochabor, S.C., 1770." *Virginia Magazine of History and Biography* 9: (April 1902): 360–64.

Trickett, Dean. "The Civil War in the Indian Territory." *Chronicles of Oklahoma* 18 (September 1940): 266–80.

White, Kate. "John Chisholm, a Soldier of Fortune." *Chronicles of Oklahoma* 8 (June 1930): 233–39.

Williams, Samuel C. "The Father of Sequoyah: Nathaniel Gist." *Chronicles of Oklahoma* 15 (March 1937): 3–20.

———, ed. "Tatham's Characters among the North American Indians." *Tennessee Historical Magazine* 7 (October 1921): 154–79.

Winfrey, Dorman H. "Chief Bowles of the Texas Cherokees." *Chronicles of Oklahoma* 32 (1954): 29–41.

Winkler, Ernest William. "The Cherokee Indians in Texas." *Quarterly of the Texas State Historical Association* 7 (October 1903): 95–165.

Woldert, Albert. "The Last of the Cherokees in Texas, and the Life and Death of Chief Bowles." *Chronicles of Oklahoma* 1 (1921–23): 179–226.

Wright, Muriel, ed. "The Journal of John Lowery Brown of the Cherokee Nation En Route to California in 1850." *Chronicles of Oklahoma* 12 (June 1934): 177–213.

Collections

Gilcrease Institute, Tulsa, Oklahoma
    Col. George Chicken's Journal, 1725.
    Grant Foreman Papers.
    Hannah Worcester Hicks Diary.
    Howard, H. "A New Humorous Song of the Cherokee Chiefs. Inscribed to the Ladies of Great Britain."
Western History Collection, University of Oklahoma
    Cherokee Nation Papers.
    Paschal, George W., "A Report of the Trial of Stand Watie." M943-2-1-E, box 1, Cherokee Nation Papers.
Archives/Manuscripts, Oklahoma Historical Society
    Athey Collection.
    Cherokee Removal File, Section X.

1860 Census Slave Schedules, Arkansas plus the Indian Territory West
of Arkansas, M-653, Roll 54.
Grant Foreman Collection.
Journal of Daniel Sabin Butrick. Microfilm ABC 18.3.3., Roll 753.
Lt. Joseph Harris Journal, February–May 1834.
Moulton Collection.
Emmet Starr Collection.
Manuscript Collections, University of Arkansas
William Minor Quesenbury Diary, 1845–1861.
Special Collections, Northeastern State University
Cherokee Chiefs Vertical File.
Cherokee Nation Historical Map.
University of Central Oklahoma
American Periodicals 1741-1900. Microfilm Collection, Jean Hoornstra
and Trudy Heath, eds. Ann Arbor: University Microfilms
International, 1979.
Oklahoma Collection.
Western Americana: Frontier History of the Trans-Mississippi West.
Microfilm Collection. Woodbridge, Conn.: Research Publications,
1980.

Official Documents and Papers, Published

Cherokee Nation

*Communication of the Delegation of the Cherokee Nation to the President of the
United States . . . with the Correspondence between John Ross, Principal
Chief, and Certain Officers of the Rebellious States*. Washington: Gibson
Brothers, Printers, 1866.
Constitution and Laws of the Cherokee Nation. St. Louis: R. & T.A. Ennis,
Stationers, 1875.
Laws of the Cherokee Nation Adopted by the Council at Various Periods.
Tahlequah, C.N.: Cherokee Advocate Office, 1852.

State

Calendar of Virginia State Papers, OHS/LIB.
Colonial Records of North Carolina, OHS/LIB.
*Colonial Records of South Carolina, Journals of the Commissioners of the Indian
Trade, 1710–1718*. Edited by W. L. McDowell. Columbia: South
Carolina Archives Dept., 1955, OHS/LIB.

Colonial Records of South Carolina, Documents Relating to Indian Affairs, May 21, 1750–August 7, 1754. Edited by William McDowell Jr. Columbia: South Carolina Archives Dept., 1958, OHS/LIB.
North Carolina State Records, OHS/LIB.
South Carolina Public Records, OHS/LIB.

Federal

American State Papers, Indian Affairs, Congressional Series, Class II, UCO/LIB.
Commissioner of Indian Affairs 1839, 1845, 1852, 1853, 1854, 1856, 1857, 1858, 1860, 1865, 1866, OSL.
"Impeachment of William Blount," *Annals of Congress, 1789–1824.* 42 vols. Washington, D.C., 1834-56, UCO/LIB.
New American State Papers, 1789–1860. 13 vols. Wilmington, Del.: Scholarly Resources, 1972, UCO/LIB.
Report of Secretary of War, 1822, OSL.
Territorial Papers of the United States. Edited and compiled by Clarence Edwin Carter. 26 vols. Washington, D.C.: GPO, 1934–62.
Trail of Tears National Historic Trail: Comprehensive Management and Use Plan. Denver: U.S. National Park Service Center, 1992.
U.S. Register of Debates, UCO/LIB.
U.S. Statutes at Large, UCO/LIB.
U.S. Supreme Court Reports (Law Edition), U.S., UCO/LIB.
The War of the Rebellion: A Compilation of the Official Records of the Union and Confederate Armies. Washington: GPO, 1880-1901.

U.S. Congress, House of Representatives

Capture of Reputed Indian Refugees. 25th Cong., 3d sess. (1838-39), H. Doc. 109.
Cherokee Indians. 26th Cong., 1st sess. (1839-40), H. Doc. 188.
Cherokee Disturbances. 29th Cong., 1st sess. (1845), H. Doc. 185.
Final Report of the United States de Soto Expedition. 76th Cong., 1st sess. (1939), H. Doc. 71.
Indian Chiefs. Letter of Delegation to Commission in Indian Affairs. 26th Cong., 1st sess. (1839-40) H. Doc. 222.
Indian Removal to West of Mississippi from 1789. 25th Cong., 3d sess. (1838-39) H. Doc. 147.
Letters on Cherokee Treaty of 1846. 30th Cong., 2d sess. (1848-49) H. Doc. 43.
Memorial and Protest of the Cherokee Nation. 24th Cong., 1st sess. (1836-37) H. Doc. 286.
Memorial of the Cherokee Nation Remonstrating against the Instrument of Writing (Treaty) of December, 1835. 25th Cong., 2d sess. (1837-38) H. Doc. 99.

Memorial of the Delegation of the Cherokee Nation. 26th Cong., 1st sess. (1839-40) H. Doc. 129.
Report of Lt. Col. Hitchcock. 27th Cong., 3d sess. (1842-43) H. Doc. 219.

U.S. Congress, Senate

Agreement between Commission to Five Civilized Tribes and Cherokee Indians in Indian Territory. 56th Cong., 1st sess. (1899-1900) S. Doc. 296.
Documents in Relation to the Validity of the Cherokee Treaty of 1835. 25th Cong., 2d sess. (1837-38) S. Doc. 121.
Encroachment of Indians of United States on Territories of Mexico. 32d Cong., 2d sess. (1852-3) S. Ex. Doc. 14.
First Annual Report of the Dawes Commission. 53d Cong., 3d sess. (1894-95) S. Doc. 24.
Message of the President of the U.S. Regarding the Internal Feuds among the Cherokees. 29th Cong., 1st sess. (1845-46) S. Doc. 298.
The Report and Correspondence of the Board of Inquiry, to Prosecute an Examination into the Causes and Extent of the Discontents and Difficulties among the Cherokee Indians. 28th Cong., 2d sess. (1844-45) S. Doc. 140.
Report of C of IA in Relation to Claims against the Cherokees. 30th Cong., 2d sess. (1848-49) S. Doc. 28.
Report of Payment of Cherokee Freedmen under Decree of Court of Claims. 55th Cong., 3d sess. (1898-99) S. Doc. 101.

Government Documents, Unpublished

National Archives

Arkansas Superintendency, 1824–34 (RG 75) M-234.
Census Roll, 1835, of Cherokees East of Mississippi (RG 75) M-685.
Central Superintendency, 1851–80 (RG 75) M-234.
Cherokee Agency East, 1824-74 (RG 75) M-234.
Cherokee Agency West, 1824–36 (RG 75) M-234.
Cherokee Emigration, 1826–54 (RG 75) M-234.
Cherokee Old Settler Pay Roll, 1895 (RG 75) M-685.
Correspondence and Miscellaneous Records, Cherokee Indian Agency in Tennessee, 1801–35 (RG 75) M-208.
Correspondence of Office of Indian Affairs (Central Office) (RG 75) M-18.
Documents Relating to the Negotiations of Ratified and Unratified Indian Treaties with Various Indian Tribes, 1801–69 (RG 123) T-494.
Drennan Roll, Records of the BIA—Cherokee Old Settler Roll of 1851 (RG 75) M-685.
Eastern Cherokee Applications, 1906–9 (RG 75) M-685.

Final Rolls of Citizens and Freedmen of the Five Civilized Tribes (RG 75) M-1186.

First Cherokee Commission (original document) (RG 75).

Fiscal Records, Cherokee Agency, 1801–4 (RG 75) M-208.

Henderson Roll (RG 75) T-496.

Letters Received, AGO (RG 75) M-567.

Letters Received, Cherokee Agency, East, 1824–36 (RG 75) M-234.

Letters Received, Cherokee Agency, 1836–80 (RG 75) M-234.

Letters Received by Secretary of War, Unregistered (RG 107) M-222.

Letters Sent by Secretary of War Relating to Indian Affairs, 1880–24 (RG 75) M-271.

"Proceedings of a Council Held at Fort Gibson, Arkansas, in September 1834." T. B. Wheelock Journal, September 1834, RG 75.

Records of the Cherokee Indian Agency in Tennessee (RG 75) M-208.

Records of Joseph McMinn, Agent for Cherokee Removal, 1817–21 (RG 75) M-208.

Records of the Superintendent of Indian Trade (M 75) T-58.

Smithsonian Institution MS 3706, Bureau of American Ethnology.

Dissertations, Theses

Dickson, John Lois. "The Judicial History of the Cherokee Nation from 1721–1835." Ph.D. diss., University of Oklahoma, 1965.

Markman, Robert Paul. "The Arkansas Cherokees." Ph.D. diss., University of Oklahoma, 1972.

Lindsey, Virginia Lee. "History of the Western Cherokees." Master's thesis, University of Oklahoma, 1935.

Personal Document

Fields, George W. "Texas Cherokees, 1820–1839," legal brief supplied by Mrs. James Lowe, Houston, Tex., 1921.

Newspapers and Journals

American Magazine (Woodbridge, N.J.)

American Register or General Repository of History, Politics, and Science (Philadelphia)

Arkansas Democrat (Little Rock)

Arkansas Gazette

Arkansas Intelligencer (Van Buren)

Arkansas Times and Advocate (Little Rock)

Army-Navy Chronicles

Baltimore Sun
Baptist Missionary Magazine
British Magazine (London)
Cherokee Advocate (Tahlequah)
Cherokee Phoenix (New Echota, Ga.)
Christian Observer
Columbian Fountain (Washington)
Congressional Record
Courier des Natchitoches
The Court Magazine (London)
Daily Missouri Democrat (St. Louis)
Daily National Intelligencer (Washington)
Daily Oklahoman
The Daily Post
Edinburgh Weekly Magazine
Fort Gibson Post
Fort Smith Herald
Grub Street Journal (London)
Indian Chieftain (Vinita)
Journal of the American Geographical Society of New York
Lawrence Republican
London Journal
London Magazine
Maryland Gazette (Annapolis)
Missionary Herald
National Intelligencer and Washington Advertiser
New Orleans Picayune
New York Evening Post
New-York Journal and the General Advertiser (Kingston/Poughkeepsie)
New York Times
Niles' Register
Pennsylvania Gazette (Philadelphia)
Pennsylvania Mercury and Universal Advertiser
Purcell Register (Purcell, Oklahoma)
Scot's Magazine (Edinburg)
South Carolina Weekly Museum (Charleston)
Southwest Independent (Fayetteville)
Tahlequah Telephone
The Universal Magazine (London)
Van Buren Press
Virginia Magazine (Richmond)
Washington (Arkansas) *Telegraph*
Wichita Eagle

Index